MANAGEMENT ACCOUNTING TERMINOLOGY

管理会计术语选编 （英中对照版）

英国皇家特许管理会计师公会 (CIMA)
上海国家会计学院 (SNAI)　财政部会计资格评价中心 (NAACC)　主编

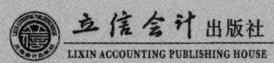 立信会计 出版社
LIXIN ACCOUNTING PUBLISHING HOUSE

图书在版编目(CIP)数据

　　管理会计术语选编:英中对照版/英国皇家特许管理会
计师公会(CIMA),上海国家会计学院(SNAI),财政部会计
资格评价中心(NAACC)主编.—上海:立信会计出版社,
2015.12

　　ISBN 978 - 7 - 5429 - 4900 - 4

　　Ⅰ.①管… Ⅱ.①英… ②上… ③财… Ⅲ.①管理会
计—名词术语—选编—英语、汉语 Ⅳ.①F234.3-61

　　中国版本图书馆 CIP 数据核字(2016)第 014775 号

策划编辑	窦瀚修	
责任编辑	赵志梅	
封面设计	南房间	

管理会计术语选编(英中对照版)
Guanli Kuaiji Shuyü Xuanbian

出版发行	立信会计出版社		
地　　址	上海市中山西路 2230 号	邮政编码	200235
电　　话	(021)64411389	传　　真	(021)64411325
网　　址	www.lixinaph.com	电子邮箱	lxaph@sh163.net
网上书店	www.shlx.net	电　　话	(021)64411071
经　　销	各地新华书店		

印　　刷	上海天地海设计印刷有限公司
开　　本	787 毫米×1 092 毫米　　1/16
印　　张	22.5
字　　数	512 千字
版　　次	2015 年 12 月第 1 版
印　　次	2015 年 12 月第 1 次
印　　数	1—3 100
书　　号	ISBN 978 - 7 - 5429 - 4900 - 4/F
定　　价	48.00 元

如有印订差错,请与本社联系调换

《管理会计术语选编（英中对照版）》 编委会

主　编（以姓氏拼音为序）

　　冯卫东　李扣庆　李　颖

编　者（以姓氏拼音为序）

　　韩　笑　胡　诚　季玉华　李守忠

　　刘凤委　刘正阳　佟成生　王珍霖

　　叶小杰　余　坚　张　迪　张瀚文

　　朱　丹　朱海林　Noel Tagoe　Shane Balzan

Preface

With the rising of globalization, technical innovation, mobile Internet and big data, we have entered the VUCA age (Volatile, Uncertain, Complex and Ambiguous). Over the past decade, global business environment has seen more changes than the previous centuries. Businesses are facing unprecedented challenges and opportunities. The quality decision-making has never been become more important or more difficult. Businesses have to make in-time responses to various risks so as to protect the value that they have created. All successful businesses have an efficient management accounting function, which is to "sourcing, analysis, communication and use of decision—relevant financial and non-financial information to generate and preserve value for organisations" (Quoted from the *Global Management Accounting Principles*, jointly issued by the Chartered Institute of Management Accountants (CIMA) and the American Institute of Certified Public Accountants AICPA in Oct. 2014), in order to optimize the decision-making process. Management accounting is the core of an organization, locating at the intersection of finance and management. It provides structured solutions for non-structured problems through simplifying complex issues.

Western countries and China share similar understanding of management accounting and China's application of it can date back into history. More planning and preparation brings winning; less planning and preparation leads failure; let alone no planning and preparation at all! Management accounting was widely applied, from the ancient Chinese imperial court to merchants. Today, China's economy is booming and businesses are proactively transforming their economic development mode so as to participate in global competition, which cries for the advancement of management accounting. Since the Third Plenary Session of the 18th Central Committee of CPC in 2014, reform has been comprehensively deepened. The Ministry of Finance issued the *Guidance on Comprehensively Improving the Building of Management Accounting System* and openly recruited a number of management accounting consulting experts. Practical research of management accounting has become a trend in academia and the business community has accelerated practices in this field. In addition, talent training has been significantly prioritized. All of these represent a new century of management accounting and formally mark the beginning year of it.

As the world's largest organization of management accountants, CIMA has a history of nearly 100 years and has always been committed to frontier research and talent cultivation of management accounting. In 2012, CIMA jointly launched the CGMA designation (Chartered Global Management Accountant) with AICPA. Since then, they have been working together to elevate the management accountant profession across the world. As early as 2006, CIMA formally entered China and it has supported and witnessed the development of China's management accounting. Over the past few years, management accounting has been "tacitly" growing in China. This "standalone" way of exploration has its implicit surprises; however, deficiencies of systemic and integral research render management accounting struggling of forging ahead. In order to accelerate the development of management accounting, it is inevitable to introduce and exchange international experience. It is also the way to establish the management accounting with Chinese characteristics.

CIMA, National Accountant Assessment & Certification Centre of MoF and Shanghai National Accounting Institute have jointly held several workshops and meetings. We have a common goal that is to lay a solid foundation for rapid development of China's management accounting and to strengthen communication and practice sharing between China and other countries. In Autumn 2014, the three parties set up a joint team of international cooperation and we take the old version of *CIMA Management*

Accounting Terminology as the basis to compile and localize the latest terms of management accounting in the west. As a result, it is now very easy for researchers, managers, educators and learners to look through and search for relevant terms and definitions of management accounting. This work lasted for a year; and during which time, teachers and researchers in the field were organized by the three parties to conduct compilation, translation, input and expert seminars. Thanks to their endeavor, it was finally launched in 2015 for the first time. In the compiling process, we found definitions of management accounting and its compiling standards are not unified, and we cannot accommodate each and every way. We have used the whole set of CIMA's 2015 management accounting textbooks as our blueprint to add the latest terms. We know this work is yet to be further improved and we hope to gain your support. Your comment and feedback are highly appreciated.

Now, this *Management Accounting Terminology* (English-Chinese version) has been successfully accomplished and we would like to extend our gratitude to those who have made great contribution to this work. We would also like to give our special thanks to Jiang Zhanhua, Meng Yan, Pan Fei, Peng Zhengyin, Sun Mao Zhu, Sun Zheng, Wang Huacheng、Whang Liyan and Wu Hui (in the alphabetical order of their surnames) for their insights, and thanks North Asia Management Accounting Leaders' think tank (CGMA100) President Professor Xu Ding Bo and members and to esnai. com for their professional support.

The editorial committee

前　言

随着全球化、技术革新、移动互联网、大数据的出现,我们已经进入了 VUCA 时代(volatile 动荡的、uncertain 不确定的、complex 复杂的、ambiguous 模糊的)。过去几十年,全球商业环境经历了比以往数百年都要多的变化,企业也在面临着前所未有的挑战和机遇,决策过程的专业化从未如此关键但又如此困难。企业必须对各类风险及时做出反应,以保护它们所创造的价值。成功的企业都有高效的管理会计,而管理会计正是"为组织创造价值和保值而收集、分析、传递和使用与决策相关的财务和非财务信息"(选自全球管理会计原则,英国皇家特许管理会计师公会(CIMA)和美国注册会计师协会(AICPA)2014 年 10 月联合发布),从而改善决策。管理会计位于一个组织的核心,处于财务与管理的交叉点上,通过将复杂问题简单化,为非结构化问题提供结构化的解决方案。

管理会计思想中西相通,在中国也早有应用,多算胜,少算不胜,而况于无算乎!上至庙堂下到货殖者,都能看到管理会计应用的影子。在中国经济蓬勃发展的今天,企业正在积极转变经济发展模式参与全球化竞争,而这恰恰更加需要推动管理会计的发展。2014年,中共十八届三中全会对财会深化改革作出总体部署,财政部发布了《关于全面推进管理会计体系建设的指导意见》,并公开选聘了一批管理会计咨询专家,学术界掀起了管理会计理论研究的热潮,企业界加快了管理会计的实践脚步,管理会计人才培养也备受重视。这代表着管理会计新纪元的到来,也正式宣布进入了中国管理会计的"元年"。

CIMA 作为全球最大的管理会计师专业组织,拥有近百年的历史,一直致力于管理会计的前沿研究和人才培养,并于 2012 年联合 AICPA 推出全球特许管理会计师(CGMA)专业称号,共同推动管理会计在全球范围的发展。CIMA 早在 2006 年就正式进入中国,支持和见证了中国管理会计的发展。过去数年间,管理会计在中国一直以"润物细无声"般的姿态自然生长着。然而,"单打独斗式"探索虽然暗藏惊喜,但由于缺乏系统化、整体化研究,管理会计在中国踟蹰前行。如何加速管理会计发展,国际经验的交流和引进无疑是发展中国特色管理会计的必经之路。

CIMA 在与财政部会计资格评价中心和上海国家会计学院的多次研讨和会谈中有了一个共同的想法,就是为迎来中国管理会计的大发展做一些扎扎实实的基础工作,为加强中外管理会计的交流和实践分享尽绵薄之力。2014 年秋,三方共同组建团队,在 CIMA《管理会计术语》老版本的基础上进行中外合作,将最新的西方管理会计术语选编入册,并进行汉化,让所有研究者、管理者、教育工作者和学习者可以轻松翻阅并查找相关的管理会计理论术语和定义。该项工作历时 1 年,三方组织了相关的教学和研究人员进入项目组,进行了选编、翻译、录入,召开了专家讨论会,终在 2015 年首次发布。由于管理会计术语的定义及汇编标准各家说法不一,无法兼顾,在术语的选编过程中,我们以 CIMA 2015年版本管理会计全套教材为蓝本对管理会计最新术语进行了扩充。书中的疏漏之处还望广大读者予以指正,提出宝贵意见和反馈。

在《管理会计术语选编(英中对照版)》付梓之际,我们向为此工程做出卓越贡献的业界同仁表示感谢,特别感谢蒋占华、孟焰、潘飞、彭正银、孙茂竹、孙铮、王化成、王立彦、吴辉(以姓氏拼音为序)提供专家意见,同时感谢北亚管理会计领袖智库(CGMA100)主席许定波教授及智库成员们以及"中国会计视野"网站提供的专业支持。

编 委 会

目　录

CHAPTER 1
Management Accounting

第一章
管 理 会 计

abnormal gain

Improvement on the accepted or normal level of loss associated with a production activity. It is isolated as a period entry rather than as an adjustment to product cost.

非正常收益

与生产活动有关、高于可接受或正常损失水平的部分。非正常收益被单独记入期间分录而非对产品成本的调整。

abnormal loss

Any loss in excess of the normal loss allowance. It is isolated as a period entry rather than as a component of product cost.

非正常损失

超出正常损失的任何损失。非正常损失被单独记入期间分录而非产品成本的组成部分。

absorbed overhead

Overhead attached to products or services by means of an absorption rate or rates.

under-or over-absorbed overhead: The difference between overhead incurred and overhead absorbed, using an estimated rate, in a given period.

If overhead absorbed is less than that incurred there is under-absorption, if overhead aborbed is more than that incurred there is over-absorption.

Over-and under-absorptions are treated as period cost adjustments. See Figure 1.1.

已分摊的间接费用

按一定分摊率分摊到产品和服务中的间接费用。

少分摊或多分摊的间接费用：在一定时期内，实际发生的间接费用与按照估计的分摊率分摊的间接费用之间的差额。

如果分摊的间接费用比实际发生的少就是少分摊的间接费用，如果分摊的间接费用比实际发生的多就是多分摊的间接费用。

多分摊和少分摊的间接费用按照期间成本调整处理，参见图表1.1。

FIGURE 1.1 COST ALLOCATION, APPORTIONMENT AND OVERHEAD ABSORPTION

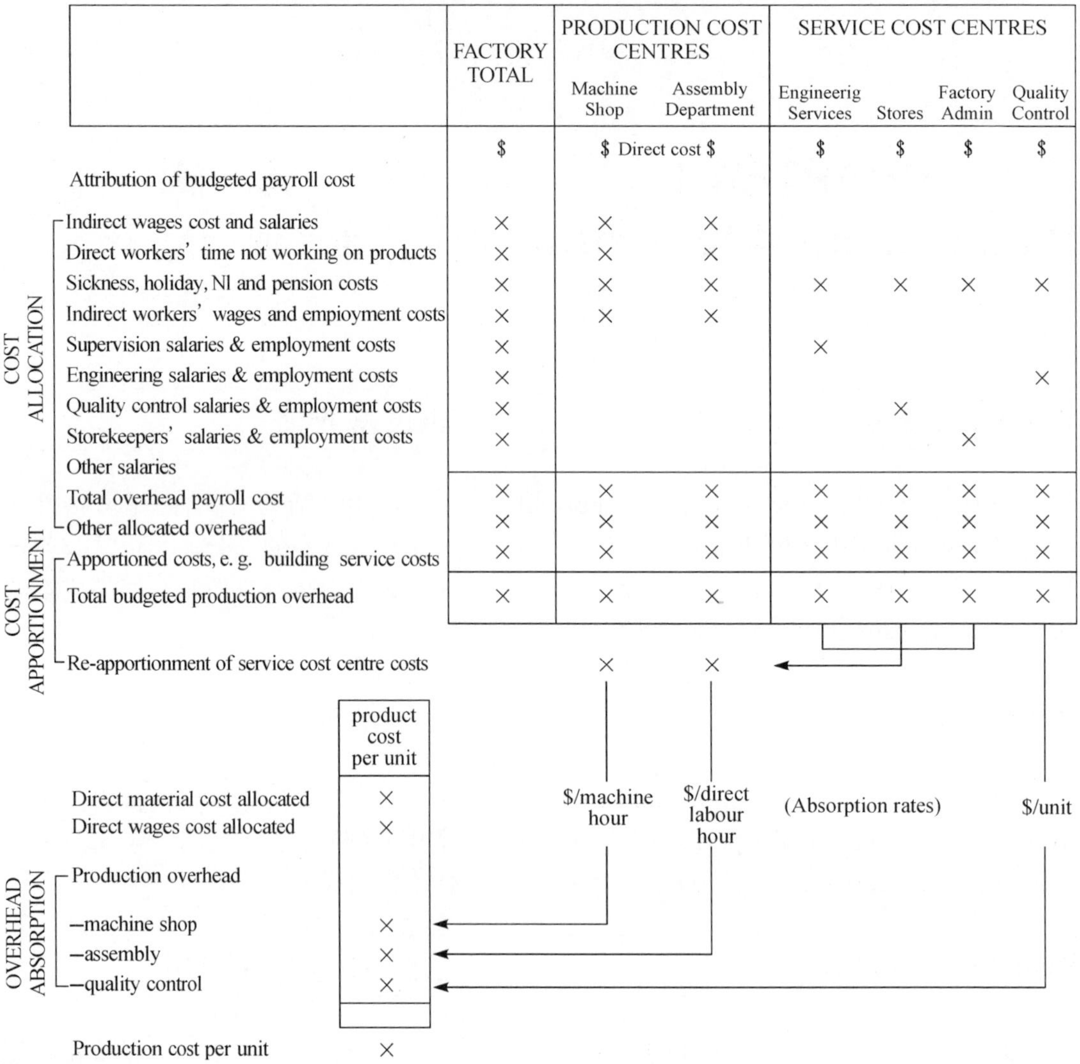

---

absorption rate

See "overhead absorption rate".

accounting manual

Collection of accounting instructions governing the responsibilities of persons，and the procedures，forms and records relating to

分摊率

参见"间接费用分摊率"。

会计手册

与编制和使用会计数据有关的人员责任、程序、表格和记录的会计指令管理集合。会计系统的组成部分包括

图表 1.1   成本的分配、分摊和间接费用的分摊

	合计	生产成本中心		服务成本中心			
		机械车间	装配车间	工程服务	存货	工厂行政	质量控制
	$	$	$	$	$	$	$
预算工资的分配							
间接工资成本和工资	×	×	×				
直接工人的非生产时间	×	×	×				
病假、节假日和养老金	×	×	×	×	×	×	×
间接人工工资和雇佣费	×	×	×				
监管人员工资和雇佣费	×			×			
工程人员工资和雇佣费	×						×
质量控制人员工资和雇佣费	×				×		
仓管人员工资和雇佣费	×					×	
其他工资							
间接工资费用合计	×	×	×	×	×	×	×
其他间接费用分配	×	×	×	×	×	×	×
分摊成本(如建筑服务成本)	×	×	×	×	×	×	×
生产阅检费用预算合计	×	×	×	×	×	×	×
服务成本中心成本再分摊							

成本分配 / 成本分摊

间接费用吸收

	每单位生产成本				
直接材料成本分配	×				
直接工资成本分配	×	$/机器工时	$/直接人工工时	(分摊率)	$/单位
生产间接费用					
——机械车间	×				
——装配	×				
——质量控制	×				
每单位生产成本	×				

the preparation and use of accounting data. There can be separate manuals for the constituent parts of the accounting system，such as a budget manual or cost accounting manual.

了独立的手册，如预算手册或成本会计手册。

accounting period

会计期间

Time period covered by the accounting statements of an entity. There may be

实体会计报表所涵盖的时间周期。不同的会计报表会对应不同的会

different time periods for different accounting statements，for example management accounts may be for four-or five-week periods to coincide with a thirteen-week financial accouting period.

计期间,例如管理类账户可能以 4 周或 5 周为一个会计周期,而财务会计周期为 13 周。

accounts, integrated

综合账簿

Set of accounting records that integrates both financial and cost accounts using a common input of data for all accounting purposes.

为了满足所有会计目标而通过录入的普通数据综合了财务和成本账户的一组会计记录。

accounts, interlocking

连锁账户

Set of accounting records where the cost and financial accounts are distinct，the two being kept continuously in agreement by the use of control accounts or reconciled by other means.

当成本账户和财务账户互相独立时,通过控制账户或其他方式进行调整使两类账户保持一致的一组会计记录。

activities, hierarchy of

作业层级

Classification of activities by level of organisation，for example unit，batch，product sustaining and facility sustaining.

例如,对组织不同层级作业的分类。根据部门、批次、产品维护以及设施维护等标准。

activity, batch level

批次级作业

Activity（such as setting-up machines） where volume varies directly with the number of batches of output but is independent of the number of units in a batch. See "activities，hierarchy of".

作业量随着产出批次的数量(例如安装机器设备)变化而变化、但独立于每批次数量的作业,参见"作业层级"。

activity, cost pool

作业成本池

Aggregation of all costs related to a

与特定作业相关的所有成本

specific activity.

集合。

activity, driver

作业动因

Transaction that causes an activity. For example，receipt of a sales order sets in train the order processing activity.

一项作业发生的原因。例如，收到一笔销售订单就引发了订单处理作业。

activity, driver analysis

作业动因分析

Identification and evaluation of the activity drivers used to trace the cost of activities to cost objects.

识别并评价作业动因，以便追踪成本对象的成本活动。

activity, facility sustaining

设备维护作业

Activity undertaken to support the organisation as a whole，and which cannot be logically linked to individual units of output.

Accounting is a facility sustaining activity. See "activities，hierarchy of".

为支持整个组织而进行的、无法归属于某个单独产出的部门作业。

会计活动就是一种设备维持作业，参见"作业层级"。

activity, product sustaining

产品维护作业

Activity undertaken to develop or sustain a product（or service）. Product sustaining costs are linked to the number of products or services，not to the number of units produced.

为开发或维护一种产品（或服务）而进行的作业。产品维护成本与产品或服务数量有关，与从事生产的部门数量无关。

activity-based budgeting

作业预算法

Method of budgeting based on an activity framework and utilising cost driver data in the budget setting and variance feedback processes.

以作业框架为基础的预算方法，该方法在编制预算和差异分析反馈时使用了作业成本动因数据。

activity-based costing（ABC）

Approach to the costing and monitoring of activities which involves tracing resource consumption and costing final outputs. Resources are assigned to activities，and activities to cost objects based on consumption estimates. The latter utilise cost drivers to attach activity costs to outputs. See Figure 1.2.

作业成本法

一种跟踪资源消耗和最终产出成本的核算和监控方法。根据估计的消耗将资源分配给各项作业,然后再将作业分配给成本对象。后者使用成本动因将作业成本与产出联系起来,参见图表1.2。

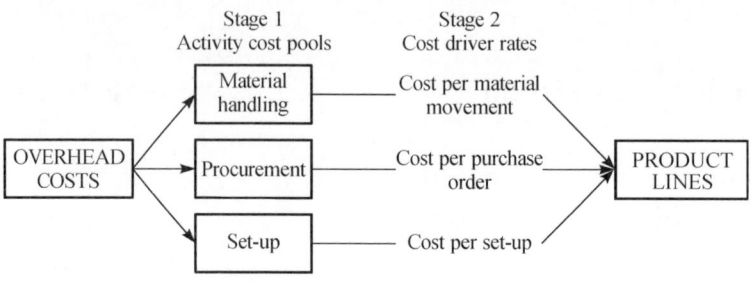

FIGURE 1. 2   The FRAMEWORK OF ACTIVITY-BASED COSTING

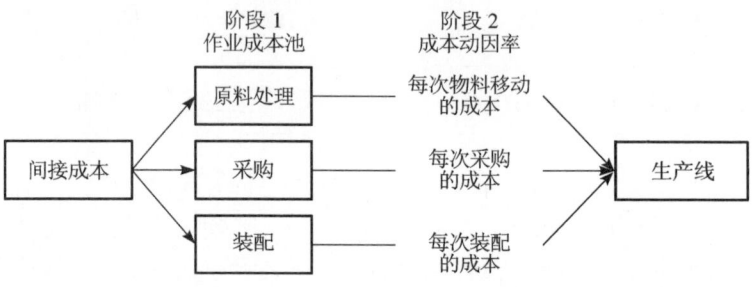

图表1.2   作业成本法的框架

activity-based costing, time -driven （time-driven ABC）

Approach to ABC based on the time required for each unit activity. The method avoids the use of interviews with operating managers in order to estimate percentage of time spent on different areas of work. It is claimed that ″time-driven ABC″ based on

时间驱动作业成本法

以每个单位作业所需时间为基础的作业成本法。该方法可以避免通过对营运经理进行访谈来估计每项不同工作所占的时间比例。以"每笔交易作业的时间"为基础的"时间驱动作业成本法"更易于实施和更新,并且能够

"time per transactional activity" is simpler to install and update and can highlight unused capacity.

揭示未能利用的产能。

activity-based management (ABM)

operational ABM：Actions，based on activity driver analysis，that increase efficiency，lower costs and/or improve asset utilisation.

strategic ABM：Actions，based on activity-based cost analysis，that aim to change the demand for activities so as to improve profitability.

作业管理

营运性作业管理是基于作业动因分析，以提高效率、降低成本和（或）提高资产利用率为目标的活动。

战略性作业管理是基于作业成本分析，旨在通过改变作业需求来提高盈利能力的活动。

allocate

To assign a whole item of cost，or of revenue，to a single cost unit，centre，account or time period. In the US，"allocate" does not have this precise meaning，it is used more generally to refer to the whole process of overhead apportionment，allocation and absorption. See Figure 1.1.

分配

把整个项目的成本或收入分配到单个的成本单位、成本中心、账户或者会计期间。在美国，"分配"一词没有准确的定义，它可以泛指间接费用分摊、分配和吸收的整个过程。参见图表1.1。

apportion

To spread indirect revenues or costs over two or more cost units，centres，accounts or time periods. This may also be referred to as "indirect allocation".

re-apportion：The re-spread of costs apportioned to service departments to production departments. See Figure 1.1.

分摊

在两个及以上的成本单元、中心、账户或时期之间分摊间接收入或成本。这也被称为"间接分配"。

再分摊是指将分摊给服务部门的成本再次分摊到生产部门。参见图表1.1。

apportionment basis

Physical or financial unit used to

分摊基础

将成本分摊到成本中心时作为分

apport costs to cost centres.

摊依据的实物或财务单位。

backward integration

后向整合

Backward integration refers to development concerned with the inputs into the organisation，e. g. rawmaterials，machinery and labour.

后向整合指的是原材料、机器设备以及劳动力等组织投入的发展情况。

balanced scorecard approach

平衡计分卡法

Approach to the provision of information to the management to assit strategic policy formulation and achievement. It emphasizes the need to provide the user with a set of information which addresses all relevant areas of performance in an objective and unbiased fashion. The information provided may include both financial and non-financial elements，and cover areas such as profitability，customer satisfaction，internal efficiency and innovation.

一种为管理层提供信息以帮助制定并实现战略政策的方法。该方法强调必须以客观公正的态度为使用者提供涉及绩效所有方面的一整套信息。所提供的信息包括了财务和非财务要素,涵盖了盈利能力、客户满意度、内部效率以及创新等领域。

batch

批次

Group of similar units which maintains its identity throughout one or more stages of production and is treated as a cost unit.

在一个或多个生产阶段都具有同一性的相似产品,被视作一个成本单位。

behavioral implications，accounting

会计行为的影响

Ways in which people affect，and are affected by，the creation，existence and use of accounting information. For example，see "budgeting，behavioural aspects and consequences".

人们与会计信息的创建、存在以及使用相互影响。例如,参见"预算的行为后果"。

bill of materials

Detailed specification, for each product, of the subassemblies, components and materials required, distinguishing items purchased externally from those manufactured in-house.

材料清单

对每个产品的组件、部件和所需材料的详细说明,将外购和内部生产的组件区分开来。

bottleneck

Facility that has lower capacity than prior or subsequent facilities and restricts output based on current capacity. See "theory of constraints, throughput".

瓶颈

设备生产能力低于上游或下游的生产水平,或者说当前产能限制了产量。参见"产量约束理论"。

breakeven chart

Chart that indicates approximate profit or loss at different levels of sales volume within a limited range. For examples of conventional breakeven charts under different cost structures, see Figures 1.3 and 1.4.

盈亏平衡图

反映了一定范围内不同销售量水平上的利润或亏损的图表。例如,不同成本结构下的常见盈亏平衡图,参见图表 1.3 和图表 1.4。

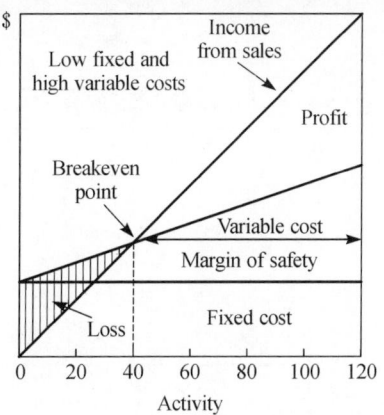

FIGURE 1.3　CONVENTIONAL BREAKEVEN CHART Ⅰ

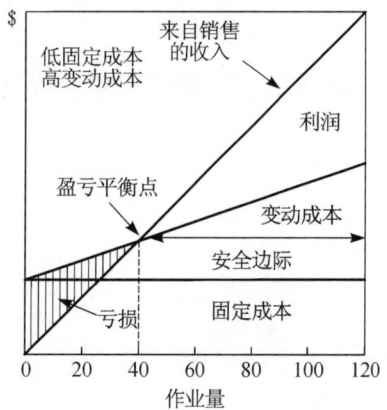

图表 1.3　传统盈亏平衡图 Ⅰ

FIGURE 1.4   CONVENTIONAL BREAKEVEN CHART Ⅱ

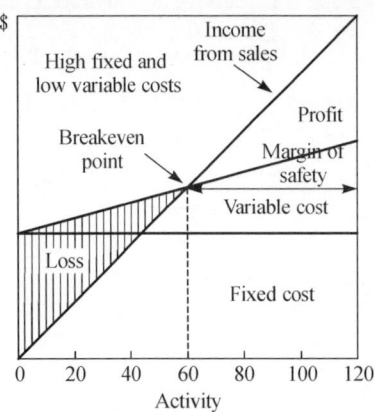

图表1.4   传统盈亏平衡图Ⅱ

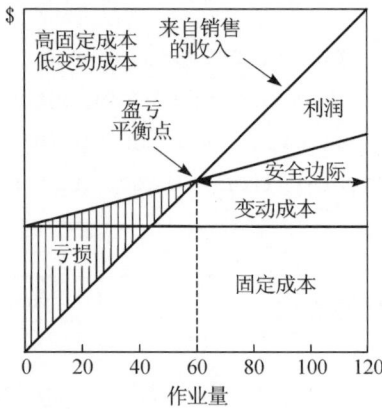

Figure 1.5 shows a contribution breakeven chart and Figure 1.6 a profit-volume chart.

图表1.5展示了一张边际贡献盈亏平衡图,图表1.6是一张利润销量图。

FIGURE 1.5   CONTRIBUTION BREAKEVEN CHART

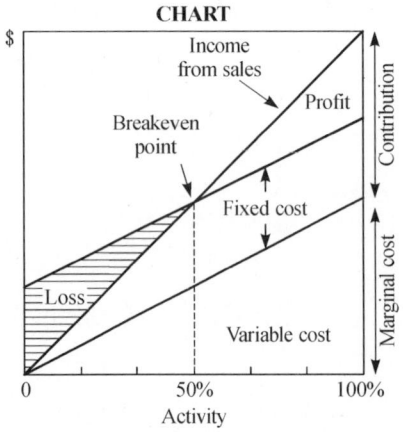

图表1.5   贡献盈亏平衡图

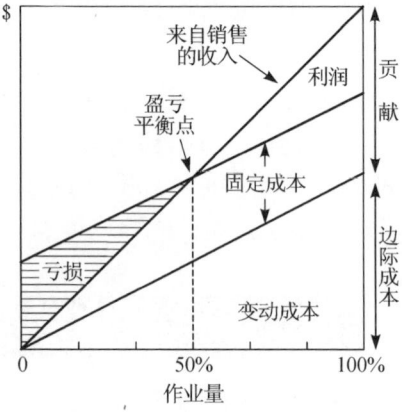

FIGURE 1.6   PROFIT-VOLUME CHART

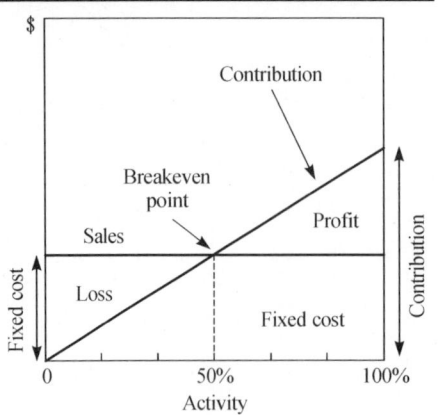

图表1.6   利润销量图

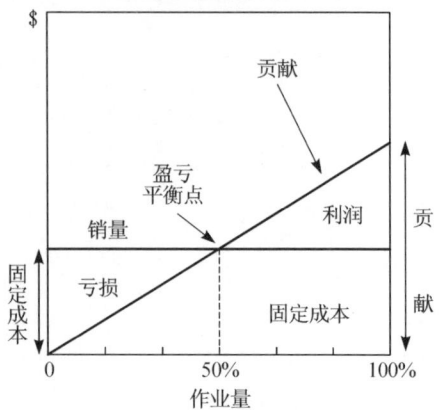

breakeven point

Level of activity at which there is neither profit nor loss. It can be ascertained by using a breakeven chart or by calculation. See Figures 1.3, 1.4, 1.5, 1.6 and example：

	$
Sales	10,000
Variable costs(e. g. direct materials, direct labour)	6,000
Contribution	4,000
Fixed cost	2,000
Profit	2,000
Number of units sold	1,000
Contribution per unit	$ 4

Contribution to sales ratio

$$\frac{\$\,4,000}{\$\,10,000} \times 100\% = 40\%$$

Number of units to be sold to breakeven

$$\frac{\text{Total fixed cost}}{\text{Contribution per unit}} = \frac{\$\,2,000}{\$\,4}$$

$$= \$\,500 \text{ units}$$

Sales value at breakeven point

$$\frac{\text{Total fixed cost}}{\text{Contribution to sales ratio}} = \frac{\$\,2,000}{40\%}$$

$$= \$\,5,000$$

Time to breakeven

$$\frac{\text{Total fixed cost} \times 365}{\text{Total contribution}} = \frac{\$\,2,000}{\$\,4,000} \times 365$$

$$= 6 \text{ mth}$$

（assuming that the period is one year, and that the date of sales is constant within that period）

budget

Quantitative expression of a plan for a defined period of time. It may include planned sales volumes and revenues; resource

盈亏平衡点

既无利润也不亏损的作业量水平。盈亏平衡点可以用盈亏平衡图或直接计算确定。参见图表1.3至图表1.6和举例：

	$
销售收入	10 000
变动成本(例如直接材料、直接人工)	6 000
边际贡献	4 000
固定成本	2 000
利润	2 000
产品销售数量	1 000
单位边际贡献	$ 4

边际贡献率

$$\frac{\$\,4\,000}{\$\,10\,000} \times 100\% = 40\%$$

盈亏平衡点的销售数量

$$\frac{\text{总固定成本}}{\text{单位边际贡献}} = \frac{\$\,2\,000}{\$\,4}$$

$$= 500 \text{ 件}$$

盈亏平衡点的销售额

$$\frac{\text{总固定成本}}{\text{销售贡献率}} = \frac{\$\,2\,000}{40\%}$$

$$= \$\,5\,000$$

盈亏平衡时间

$$\frac{\text{总固定成本} \times 365}{\text{总贡献}} = \frac{\$\,2\,000}{\$\,4\,000} \times 365$$

$$= 6 \text{ 个月}$$

（假设会计期间是1年，并且销售日期在会计期间内是固定不变的）

预算

针对一个确定的期间计划的定量表述，包括了计划销售量和销售收入；资源数量、成本和费用；资产、负债和

quantities, costs and expenses; assets, liabilities and cash flows.

现金流量。

budget, cash

现金预算

Detailed budget of estimated cash inflows and outflows incorporating both revenue and capital items.

包含了收入和资本项目的估计现金流入和流出的详细预算。

budget centre

预算中心

Section of an entity for which control may be exercised through prepared budgets. It is often a responsibility centre where the manager has authority over and responsibility for, defined costs and (possibly) revenues.

在实体中,通过编制预算来执行控制的部门。该部门通常也是责任中心,部门管理者有确定成本和收入的权利和责任。

budget cost allowance

预算成本折让

Calculated after an accounting period, the cost allowance reflects the actual level of output achieved. Variable costs are flexed in proportion to volume achieved and fixed costs are based on the annual budget.

预算成本折让是在一个会计期间结束后计算的,反映了取得产出量的实际水平。变动成本随实际产量的变动而呈比例的变动,固定成本基于年度预算确定。

budget, departmental/functional

部门预算/职能预算

Budget of income and/or expenditure applicable to a particular function frequently including sales budget, production cost budget (based on budget production, efficiency and utilisation), purchasing budget, human resources budget, marketing budget, and research and development budget.

适用于特定职能的收入或支出预算,一般包括销售预算、生产成本预算(基于预算生产、效率和利用率)、购买预算、人力资源预算、营销预算和研发预算。

budget, fixed

固定预算

Budget set prior to the control period and

在预算控制期之前就编好、不随

not subsequently changed in response to changes in activity, costs or revenues. It may serve as a benchmark in performance evaluation.

作业量、成本或收入的变化而变化的预算,可以作为业绩评价的标杆。

budget, flexible

See "budget flexing".

弹性预算

参见"预算调整"。

budget, flexing

Flexing variable costs from original budgeted levels to the allowances permitted for actual volume achieved while maintaining fixed costs at original budget levels.

(Variable cost allowance = Ratio of actual volume achieved to budget volume × Original budget variable cost)

预算调整

将变动成本从原来的预算水平调整到实现实际产量所要求的折让,同时将固定成本维持在原来的预算水平。

(变动成本折让 = 实际产量与预算产量之比×原始预算变动成本)

budget, lapsing

Withdrawal of unspent budget allowance due to the expiry of the budget period.

预算终止

预算期满收回未使用的预算额度。

budget, line item

Traditional form of budget layout showing, line by line, the costs of a cost centre analysed by their nature (for example salaries, occupancy, maintenance).

明细支出预算

根据成本中心的性质,逐项安排成本的传统预算方式(例如工资、租用成本、维护成本)。

budget, manual

Detailed set of guidelines and information about the budget process typically including a calendar of budgetary events, specimen budget forms, a statement of budgetary objectives and desired results, listing of budgetary activities and budget assumptions regarding, for example, inflation and interest

预算手册

与预算过程有关的一整套详细的指导方针和信息,包括了预算事项日程安排、预算表格样本、关于预算目标和期望结果的陈述、预算活动清单以及通货膨胀、利率等预算假设前提。

rates.

budget, master

Consolidates all subsidiary budgets and is normally comprised of the budgeted profit and loss account, balance sheet and cash flow statement.

总预算

整合了所有子预算,通常包含了预计损益表、预计资产负债表和预计现金流量表。

budget, operating

Budget of the revenues and expenses expected in a forthcoming accounting period.

经营预算

对未来会计期间预期收入和支出的预算。

budget padding

See "budget slack".

预算虚报

参见"预算松弛"。

budget period

Period for which a budget is prepared and used, which may then be subdivided into control periods.

预算期间

编制和使用预算的期间,可被细分为几个控制期间。

budget, principal factor

Principal budget factor limits the activities of an undertaking. Identification of the principal budget factor is often the starting point in the budget setting process. Often the principal budget factor will be sales demand but it could be production capacity or material supply.

主预算因素

限制活动开展的主预算因素。识别主预算因素通常是预算编制流程的起点。主预算因素往往是销售需求,但也可能是生产能力或材料供应。

budget purposes

Budgets may help in authorising expenditure, communicating objectives and

预算目的

预算可以帮助批准支出、沟通目标和计划、控制营运、协调作业、评估

plans，controlling operations，co-ordinating activities，evaluating performance，planning and rewarding performance. Often，reward systems involve comparison of actual with budgeted performance.

budget，rolling/continuous

Budget continuously updated by adding a further accounting period（month or quarter）when the earliest accounting period has expired. Its use is particularly beneficial where future costs and/or activities cannot be forecast accurately. See rolling forecast.

budget，setting processes

bottom-up budgeting：Budgeting process where all budget holders have the opportunity to participate in setting their own budgets.

imposed/top-down budgeting：Budgeting process where budget allowances are set without permitting ultimate budget holders the opportunity to participate in the process.

negotiated budget：Budget in which budget allowances are set largely on the basis of negotiations between budget holders and those to whom they report.

participate budgeting：See ＂bottom-up budgeting＂.

budget，slack

Intentional overestimation of expenses and/or underestimation of revenue during budget setting. Also known as budget padding.

绩效、计划和奖励绩效。奖励机制主要将实际绩效和预算绩效进行比较。

滚动预算/连续预算

用新会计期间的预算代替已到期会计期间的预算，逐月滚动或逐季滚动。这种方法特别有利于未来成本和活动不能准确预测的情形。参见"滚动预测"。

预算编制流程

自下而上式预算：所有预算承担者都有机会参与编制自身预算的预算编制流程。

权成式/自上而下式预算：不给予最终预算承担者参与机会的预算编制流程。

协商式预算：预算限额的设定在很大程度上是基于预算承担者与上级协商的预算编制流程。

参与式预算：参见"自下而上式预算"。

预算松弛

在编制预算时，故意高估费用和（或）低估收入，又称为预算虚报。

budget，virement

Authority to apply saving under one budget subhead to meet excesses on others.

budgetary control

Master budget，devolved to responsibility centres，allows continuous monitoring of actual results versus budget，either to secure by individual action the budget objectives or to provide a basis for budget revision. See "control，feedback" and "control，feedforward".

budgeting， behavioural aspects and consequences

budget constrained style：Excessive pressure to achieve budgets that can lead to job-related tension，recriminations，buck-passing and budget padding.

non-accounting style：Management style that largely ignores budgets and financial information.

profit conscious style：Management style that takes account of budgets together with other information and evaluates managerial performance in a flexible manner.

Target setting："Tight but achievable" levels are recommended to motivate optimum performance. Too loose a budget can lead to under-achievement as can too tight a budget-and this can also be de-motivating.

budgeting，beyond

Idea that companies need to move

预算调剂

用一个预算的节余来弥补其他预算的超支。

预算控制

下放到责任中心的总预算持续监控实际结果与预算的比较情况，由个别行动保障预算目标，或为预算修正提供基础。参见"反馈控制和前馈控制"。

预算的行为后果

预算限制型：实现预算的过度压力会导致工作压力、相互指责、推诿责任和预算虚报。

非会计型：很大程度上忽视预算和财务信息的管理风格。

利润意识型：考虑预算的同时也考虑其他信息，并且以灵活的方式评估管理绩效的管理风格。

目标设定：用来激励实现最佳绩效的"有难度但可实现"的水平。过于宽松的预算会导致低成就，而过于紧缩的预算会带来消极的影响。

超越预算

由于预算存在固有缺陷，公司需

beyond budgeting because of the inherent flaws in budgeting especially when used to set incentive contracts. It is argued that a range of techniques, such as rolling forecasts and market-related targets, can take the place of traditional budgets.

要具备超越预算的理念,尤其是在制定激励性合同时。有人主张用滚动预测和市场相关目标等一系列技术手段取代传统预算。

budgeting, incremental

增量预算

Method of budgeting based on the previous budget or actual results, adjusting for known changes and inflation, for example.

在以前预算或者实际结果的基础上,根据已知的变化和通货膨胀编制预算的方法。

budgeting, priority-based

优先预算

Method of budgeting whereby budget requests are accompanied by a statement outlining the changes expected if the prior period budget were increased or decreased by a certain amount or percentage. These changes are prioritised.

如果前期预算增加或减少一定金额或比例,预算请求会附有一份概括了预期变化的说明,这些变化将被优先处理。

budgeting, zero-based

零基预算

Method of budgeting that requires all costs to be specifically justified by the benefits expected.

要求所有成本都要根据预期收益来证明其合理性的预算方法。

building block model (Fitzgerald and Moon)

积木式模型(菲茨杰拉德和穆恩)

Fitzgerald and Moon adopted a framework for the design and analysis of performance management systems. The model was first devised as a solution to performance measurement problems in service industries. But it can be applied successfully to other manufacturing and retail businesses to evaluate business performance. See Figure 1.7.

菲茨杰拉德和穆恩采用了一种框架来设计和分析绩效管理系统。该模型最初的设计是为了解决服务性行业的绩效评估问题。但它也可以成功地应用于其他的制造和零售企业,评估经营绩效。参见图表 1.7。

FIGURE 1.7   Building Block Model

Dimensions
Profit
Competitiveness
Quality
Resource utilization
Flexibility
Innovation

Standards	Rewards
Ownership	Clarity
Achievability	Motivation
Equity	Controllabilitily

图表 1.7   积木式模型

维度
利润
竞争
质量
资源利用
灵活性
创新

标准	报酬
所有权	清晰度
成就感	动机
公平	可控性

burden

US equivalent of "overhead".

负担

在美国等同于"间接费用"。

by-product

Output of some value produced incidentally while manufacturing the main product. See "joint products".

副产品

在生产主要产品的同时产出的一些其他有价值的产品。参见"联产品"。

capital employed

Investment in an entity. In assessing managers it is usually calculated as total assets less current liabilities.

Equity capital employed: Shareholders' stake in the company. This is important when calculating return to shareholders.

已占用资本

对一个实体的投资。在评估时,等于总资产减去流动负债。

已占用/权益资本:股东在公司的股份,在计算股东投资回报时很重要。

capital expenditure control

Procedures for authorising and subsequently monitoring capital expenditure.

资本支出控制

授权并随后对资本支出进行监控的程序。

capital expenditure proposal/authorisation

Formal request for authority to incur capital expenditure usually supported by the case for expenditure in accordance with capital investment appraisal criteria. Levels of authority should be clearly defined with reporting of actual expenditure to the equivalent authority levels.

资本支出申请/授权

根据资本投资评价标准判定为合理的资本支出正式授权请求。授权级别应当明确界定为与实际支出报告相符的授权级别。

centre

Department，area or function to which costs and/or revenues are charged. See Figure 1.1

budget centre：Centre for which an individual budget is drawn up.

cost centre：Production or service location，function，activity or item of equipment for which costs are accumulated. See Figure 1.1.

investment centre：Profit centre with additional responsibilities for capital investment and possibly for financing, and whose performance is measured by its return on investment.

profit centre：Part of a business accountable for both costs and revenues.

responsibility centre：Departmental or organisational function whose performance is the direct responsibility of a specific manager.

revenue centre：Centre devoted to raising revenue with no responsibility for costs, for example a sales centre. Often used in not-for-profit organisations.

service cost centre：Cost centre providing services to other cost centres. When the output of an organisation is a service, rather than goods，an alternative name is normally used，for example support cost centre or util-

中心

成本和(或)收入所归属的部门、区域或职能。参见图表1.1。

预算中心：单独编制预算的中心。

成本中心：用来累积成本的产品或服务的定位、功能、活动或者设备项目。参见图表1.1。

投资中心：额外增加了资本投资和融资责任的利润中心，其绩效根据投资报酬率来衡量。

利润中心：既对成本又对收入负责的部门。

责任中心：绩效是特定管理者直接负责的部门或组织职能。

收入中心：致力于提高收入而不对成本负责的中心，例如销售中心。通常存在于非营利性组织中。

服务成本中心：为其他成本中心提供服务的成本中心。当一个组织的产品是一种服务而非商品时，通常会使用别的名称，例如支持成本中心或者公用成本中心。参见图表1.1。

ity cost centre. See Figure 1.1.

classification

Arrangement of items in logical groups by nature，purpose or responsibility. Classification systems allow financial information to be reported under subjective headings，by cost object or responsibility centre. See "code".

分类

按性质、目的或责任将项目进行分组。分类系统允许财务信息根据成本对象或责任中心以主观标题进行报告。参见"代码"。

code

Brief，accurate reference designed to assist classification of items by facilitating entry，collation and analysis. For example，in costing，the first three digits in the composite symbol 211.392 might indicate the nature of the expenditure（subjective classification），and the last three digits might indicate the cost centre or cost unit to be charged（objective classification）.

代码

为项目分类提供简洁且准确的参照，以便方便地登记、校对和分析。例如，在成本计算中，组合符号 211.392 的前三位数字表示支出的性质（主观分类），后三位数字表示成本中心或者计入的成本单位（客观分类）。

constraint

Activity，resource or policy that limits the ability to achieve an objective. See theory of constraints. In linear programming，constraints define the feasible region within which a solution must lie. See linear programming. See Figure 1.20.

约束条件

限制实现某一目标的活动、资源或政策。参见"约束理论"。在线性规划中，约束条件决定了可行区域，解决方案必须在此区间内。参见"线性规划"。参见图表1.20。

contribution

（sales value-variable cost of sales）
Contribution may be expressed as total contribution，contribution per unit or as a percentage of sales. See Figure 1.8.

边际贡献

（售价－变动销售成本）
边际贡献可以表达为边际贡献总额、单位边际贡献或者销售百分比。参见图表1.8。

FIGURE 1. 8   BUDGETED TRADING AND PROFIT AND LOSS ACCOUNTS, ABSORPTION COSTING AND MARGINAL COSTING

ABSORPTION COSTING	MARGINAL COSTING
Net turnover	**Net turnover**
Less：	Less：
Direct Materials	Direct Materials
Direct Labour	Direct Labour
Total Production	Variable Producion Overhead
Overhead	**Variable Cost of Sales**
Production Cost of Sales	Variable Selling and Distribution Overhead
Gross (or Factory) Profit	**Contribution**
Less：	Less *fixed costs*：
Selling Overhead	Production Overhead
Distribution Overhead	Selling Overhead
Administrative Expenses	Distribution Overhead
	Administrative Expenses
Non-production Overhead	
R & D Cost	R & D Cost **Total Fixed Cost**
Net Profit before Tax	**Net Profit before Tax**

* Note：In an "actual" absorption costing-based Trading and Profit and Loss Account，production overhead would normally be over-or under-absorbed，due to both cost and activity levels differing from those upon which the budget was based.

An over-absorption occurs when overhead costs absorbed by output exceed the actual costs incurred.

An under-absorption occurs when the actual costs incurred exceed the overhead costs absorbed by output.

图表 1.8   预算交易、利润和损失账户,吸收成本法和边际成本法

吸收成本法	边际成本法
净收入	**净收入**
减：	减：
直接材料	直接材料
直接人工	直接人工
总生产	变动间接生产成本
间接费用	变动间接销售和营销成本 **变动销售成本**
生产销售成本	**贡 献**
毛利润(工厂利润)	减固定成本：
减：	生产间接费用
销售间接费用	销售间接费用
营销间接费用	营销间接费用
管理费用	管理费用
研发成本	研发成本
非生产间接费用	**总固定成本**
税前净利润	**税前净利润**

* 注意:在"真正"的吸收成本法为基础的交易,利润和损失账户,生产间接费用通常会过度吸收或者不足吸收,因为成本和作业量都会与预算基础有差距。

在间接费用吸收得比实际发生的成本多时,发生了过度吸收。

在间接费用吸收得比实际发生的成本少时,发生了不足吸收。

control

In management accounting, control usually means ensuring that activities planned and undertaken lead to desired outcomes. See

控制

在管理会计中,控制通常意味着确保计划好的作业和项目取得期望的结果。参见"反馈控制"和"前馈控

"control，feedback" and "control，feedforward".

制"。

control，contingency

A back-up facility and a contingency plan to restore business operations as quickly as possible in the event that security or integrity controls fail.

应急控制

如果安全控制和整体控制失败，尽快恢复企业正常经营所需的备用设备和应急预案。

control，feedback

Measurement of differences between planned outputs and actual outputs achieved，and the modification of subsequent action and/or plans to achieve future required results.

Feedback control is an integral part of budgetary control and standard costing systems. See Figure 1.9.

反馈控制

对计划产出和实际产出的差异进行测量，以及为了取得未来所期望的结果对随后的行为和(或)计划进行修正。

反馈控制是预算控制和标准成本系统的有机组成部分。参见图表1.9。

FIGURE 1.9 A FEEDBACK CONTROL SYSTEM

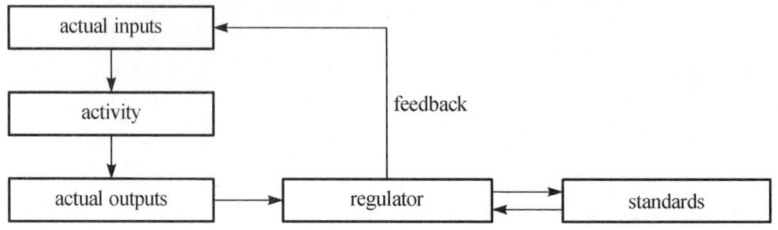

图表1.9 反馈控制体系

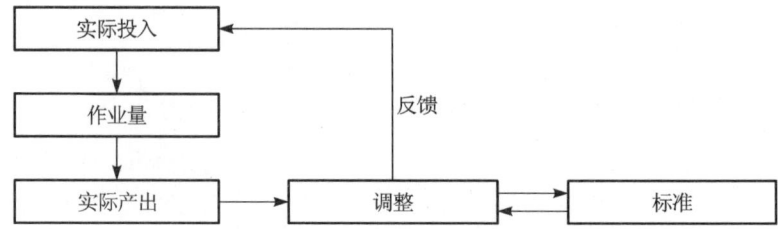

control, feedforward

Forecasting of differences between actual and planned outcomes, and the implementation of action, before the event, to avoid such differences. See Figure 1.10.

前馈控制

对实际产出和计划产出之间的差异进行预测,并在事前实施避免此类差异发生的行动。参见图表1.10。

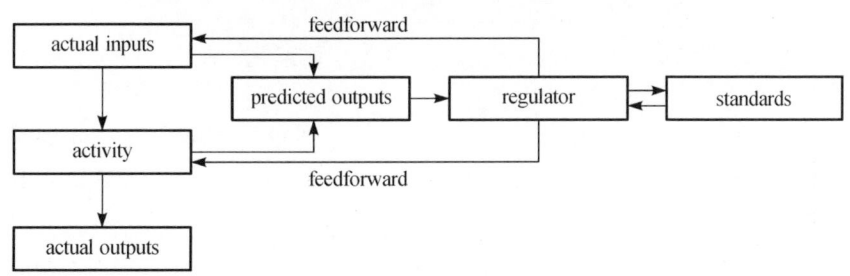

FIGURE 1.10　A FEEDFORWARD CONTROL SYSTEM

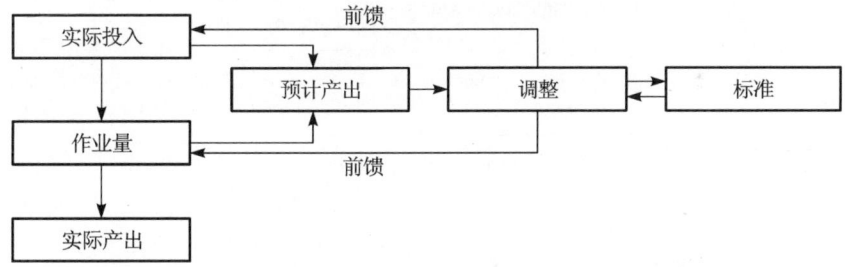

图表1.10　前馈控制系统

control (in the context of an asset)

Ability to obtain the future economic benefits relating to an asset and to restrict the access of others to these benefits.

控制(在资产背景下)

获取源自某项资产的未来经济收益,同时限制他人获得该收益的能力。

control, management

All of the processes used by managers to ensure that organisational goals are achieved and procedures adhered to, and that the or-

管理控制

管理者为了保证实现组织目标,组织能够对环境变化做出恰当反映而采取的所有程序。

ganisation responds appropriately to changes in its environment.

closed loop system：Control system that includes provision for corrective action，taken on either a feedforward or a feedback basis. See Figures 1.9 and 1.10.

open loop system：Control system that includes no provision for corrective action to be applied to the sequence of activities.

control, operational

Management of daily activities in accordance with strategic and tactical plans. See Figure 1.11.

闭环系统:包括纠正措施预案,具有前馈或者反馈基础的控制系统。参见图表1.9和图表1.10。

开环系统:不包括纠正措施预案,运用于作业顺序的控制系统。

营运控制

根据战略和战术计划对日常活动进行的管理。参见图表1.11。

FIGURE 1.11 POLICIES, STRATEGIES, TACTICS AND OPERATIONAL CONTROL

	Industry examples	Services examples
Policies	Produce technically superior products	Offer low cost services and cultivate customer brand awareness
Strategy	Spend 15% + of gross revenue on research and development	Local price setting to undercut competition Television advertising to increase brand awareness
Tactics	Recruit engineers from the best university technology courses	Price deals to boost volume Introduce cost reducing technologies
Operational control	Monitor customer feedback on product performance	Focus on absolute margin to encourage low price but a high volume Systematic use of brand awareness feedback

图表1.11 政策、战略、战术和经营控制

分类	行业举例	服务举例
政策	生产技术领先的产品	提供低成本的服务和培养客户的品牌知名度
战略	将毛收入的15%以上花在研究和开发上	地区性定价来削弱竞争 电视广告来提高品牌知名度
策略	从最好的大学技术课程中招聘工程师	用优惠价格来增加销售量 引进成本节约技术
经营控制	监控顾客对产品性能的反馈	关注绝对边际来鼓励薄利多销 应用品牌知名度的反馈机制

internal control, operational features

● Embedded within operations and not treated as a separate exercise.

● Able to respond to changing risks within and outside the company.

● Includes procedures for reporting control failings or weakness.

control, activities

These are policies and procedures that ensure that decisions and instructions of management are carried out.

control, application

These are controls to ensure that data are correctly input，processed and correctly maintained，and only distributed to authorized personnel.

control, environment

The control environment can be thought of as management's attitude，actions and awareness of the need for internal controls.

control, personnel

Recruitment，training and supervision needs to be in place to ensure the competency of those responsible for programming and data entry.

control, physical

Measures and procedures to protect

内部控制运行特征

● 内嵌于运营之中,不视为是一个独立的操作。

● 能够应对公司内外部不断变化的风险。

● 包括了报告控制缺陷或弱点的程序。

控制活动

确保管理层的决策和指令得到执行的政策和程序。

控制应用

确保数据被正确输入、处理和维护的控制,由获得授权的人员专门负责。

控制环境

控制环境指的是管理层对内部控制需求的态度、行动和意识。

人员控制

针对招聘、培训和监督等建立措施,确保有能力对规划和数据录入进行监管。

实物控制

防止实物资产被盗或未经授权进

physical assets against theft or unauthorized access and use.

行访问和使用的措施和流程。

controls, software

软件控制

Software control prevents making or installing unauthorized copies of software. Illegal software is more likely to fail, comes without warranties or support, can place systems at risk of viruses and the use of illegal software can result in significant financial penalties.

软件控制是指防止制作或安装未经授权的软件。非法软件更容易失效,没有保修或支持服务,让系统有感染病毒的风险,同时,使用非法软件可能导致巨额的经济处罚。

controls, security

安全控制

Controls designed to ensure the prevention of unauthorized access, modification or destruction of stored data.

旨在确保阻止对存储的数据进行未经授权的访问、修改或销毁的控制措施。

cost

成本

As a noun-The amount of cash or cash equivalent paid or the fair value of other consideration given to acquire an asset at the time of its acquisition or construction (IAS 16).

作为名词,成本是指在获得或建造一项资产时支付的现金或现金等价物,或者考虑了其他事项的公允价值(《国际会计准则 16 号——不动产、厂房和设备》)。

As a verb-To ascertain the cost of a specified thing or activity. The word cost can rarely stand alone and should be qualified as to its nature and limitations.

作为动词,成本是指确定一项特定物品或活动的成本。"成本"这个词几乎不能单独使用,应该根据其性质和局限性进行定义。

cost, account

成本账户

Record of expenditure associated with a cost object such as a job, batch, contract or process. Revenue may be credited to the account as, for example, when a process by-product has value.

与工作、批次、合同或程序等成本对象有关的支出记录。收入有可能贷记到该账户,例如,当加工的副产品有价值时。

cost accounting

Gathering of cost information and its attachment to cost objects，the establishment of budgets，standard costs and actual costs of operations，processes，activities or products；and the analysis of variances，profitability or the social use of funds. The use of the term costing is not recommended except with a qualifying adjective，for example：

- standard costing
- batch costing
- continuous operation costing
- contract costing
- job costing
- service /function costing
- specific order costing
- marginal costing

cost accounting - for cost objects

batch costing：Form of specific order costing where costs are attributed to batches of product（unit costs can be calculated by dividing by the number of products in the batch）. See Figure 1.12..

contract costing：Form of specific order costing where costs are attributed to contracts. See Figure 1.12.

job costing：Form of specific order costing where costs are attributed to individual jobs. See Figure 1.12.

operations costing：Form of costing where costs are attributed to individual operations within a manufacturing process.

process costing：Form of costing applicable to continuous processes where process

成本会计

成本信息和相对应成本对象的集合，确立了经营、加工、作业或产品的预算、标准成本和实际成本；对成本差异、盈利能力和资金的社会使用进行分析。一般不推荐使用"成本法"这个术语，除非有特定的定语，比如：

- 标准成本法
- 分批成本法
- 持续经营成本法
- 合同成本法
- 工作成本法
- 服务/职能成本法
- 特定订单成本法
- 边际成本法

成本会计-针对成本对象

分批成本法：特定订单成本计算的一种形式，成本被分配到各产品批次（单位成本可以通过除以该批次产品数量求得）。参见图表 1.12。

合同成本法：特定订单成本计算的一种形式，成本被分配到各个合同中。参见图表 1.12。

工作成本法：特定订单成本计算的一种形式，成本被分配到各项工作中。参见图表 1.12。

运营成本：成本计算的一种形式，成本被分配到生产过程中的各项操作中。

分步成本法：适用于连续过程的成本计算形式，工序成本被分配到产

costs are attributed to the number of units produced. This may involve estimating the number of equivalent units in stock at the start and end of the period under consideration. See Figure 1.12.

　　specific order costing：Basic cost accounting method applicable if work consists of separately identifiable batches，contracts or jobs. See Figure 1.12.

成品之中。可能涉及相应会计期间同种产品库存量的期初和期末估计。参见图表1.12。

　　特定订单成本法：当工作中包含了可辨识的批次、合同或订单时的基本成本计算方法。参见图表1.12。

FIGURE 1. 12　ELEMENTS OF A PRODUCT COSTING SYSTEM

Overall Control System；Budgetary Control				
Product costing system	Specific order		Continuous operations	
Costing method	Job costing	Batch costing　Contract costing	Continuous operation/ process costing	Service/ function costing
Treatment of fixed production overhead	Absorption or marginal			
Method of cost control	Standard or actual			

图表 1. 12　产品成本体系的要素

全面控制体系：预算控制				
产品成本计算体系	特定订单		持续经营	
成本法	工作成本法	分批 合同 成本法　成本法	持续 经营/ 分步 成本法	服务/ 职能 成本法
对固定生产间接 费用的处理	吸收或者变动/边际			
成本控制方法	标准或者实际			

cost accounting-methods

成本会计方法

　　absorption costing：Assigns direct costs and all or part of overhead to cost units using one or more overhead absorption rates. See Figure 1.1.
Sometimes referred to as full costing although this is a misnomer if all costs are not

　　吸收成本法：用一个或多个分摊率将直接成本和全部或部分的间接费用分配到成本单位。参见图表1.1。

　　有时也被称为完全成本法,但在并非所有成本都被分配到成本单位

attributed to cost units.

Direct costing: See variable costing.

full costing: See "absorption costing".

marginal costing: See "variable costing".

uniform costing: Used by several undertakings, usually in the same industry, of the same costing methods, principles and techniques.

variable costing: Assigns only variable costs to cost units while fixed costs are written off as period costs. See Figure 1.8. Also known as marginal costing and, especially in the US, as direct costing.

cost, allocation/apportionment

See "allocation" and "apportionment".

cost, avoidable

Specific cost of an activity or sector of a business that would be avoided if the activity or sector of a business that would be avoided if the activity or sector did not exist.

cost, behavior

Variability of input costs with activity undertaken. Cost may increase proportionately with increasing activity (the usual assumption for a variable cost), or it may not change with increased activity (a fixed cost). Some costs (semi-variable) may have both variable and fixed elements. Other behaviour is possible, cost may increase more or less than in direct proportion, and there may be step changes in cost, for example. To a large extent cost behavior will be dependent on the timescale assumed. See Figures 1.13 and 1.14.

时,这种表述并不恰当。

直接成本法:参见"变动成本法"。

完全成本法:参见"吸收成本法"。

边际成本法:参见"变动成本法"。

统一成本法:被几个采用相同成本方法、原则和技术的项目使用,这些项目通常是在同一个产业。

变动成本法:只把变动成本分配到成本单位,同时把固定成本看作是期间费用。参见图表1.8。也叫做边际成本法,在美国又被称为直接成本法。

成本分配/分摊

参见"分配"和"分摊"。

可避免的成本

源自企业的一项活动或一个部门的特定成本,如果该活动或部门不复存在时可以避免的成本。

成本习性

投入的成本与业务活动之间的变动关系。成本随着业务活动的增加而呈比例的增加(变动成本通常的假设前提),或成本不随业务活动的增加而变化(固定成本)。某些成本(半变动成本)则既包括变动成本又包括固定成本。同时也可能存在其他成本习性,成本或多或少地呈正比增长,例如成本可能呈现阶梯式的变化。在很大程度上,成本习性依赖于时间尺度的假设。参见图表1.13和图表1.14。

FIGURE 1.13　COST BEHAVIOUR

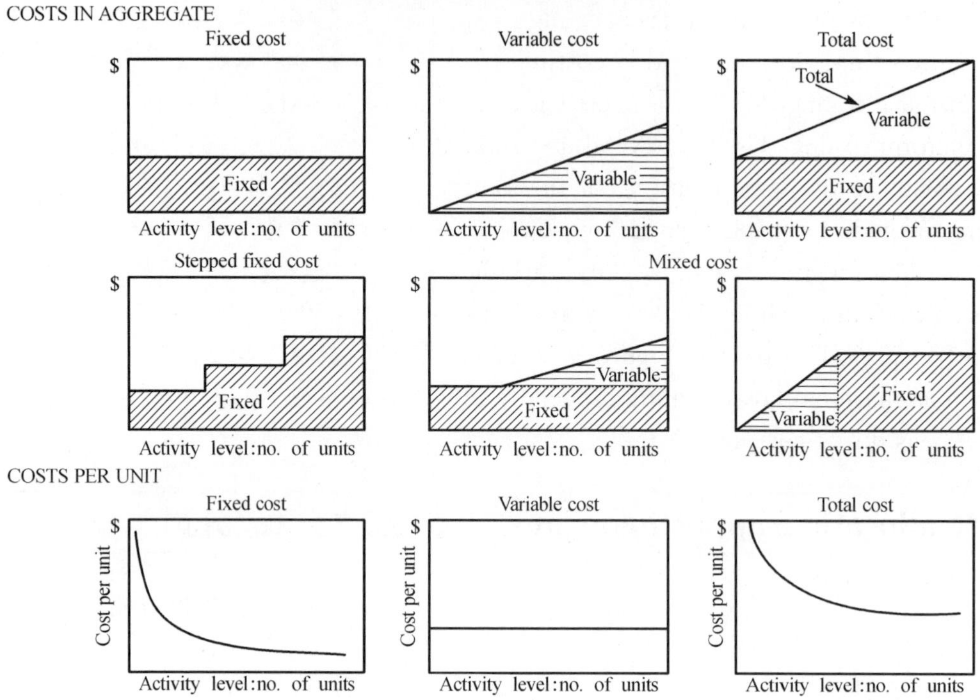

COSTS IN AGGREGATE

Fixed cost

$ | Fixed
Activity level：no. of units

Variable cost

$ | Variable
Activity level：no. of units

Total cost

$ | Total → Variable | Fixed
Activity level：no. of units

Stepped fixed cost

$ | Fixed
Activity level：no. of units

Mixed cost

$ | Variable | Fixed
Activity level：no. of units

$ | Variable | Fixed
Activity level：no. of units

COSTS PER UNIT

Fixed cost

$ | Cost per unit
Activity level：no. of units

Variable cost

$ | Cost per unit
Activity level：no. of units

Total cost

$ | Cost per unit
Activity level：no. of units

图表 1.13　成本习性

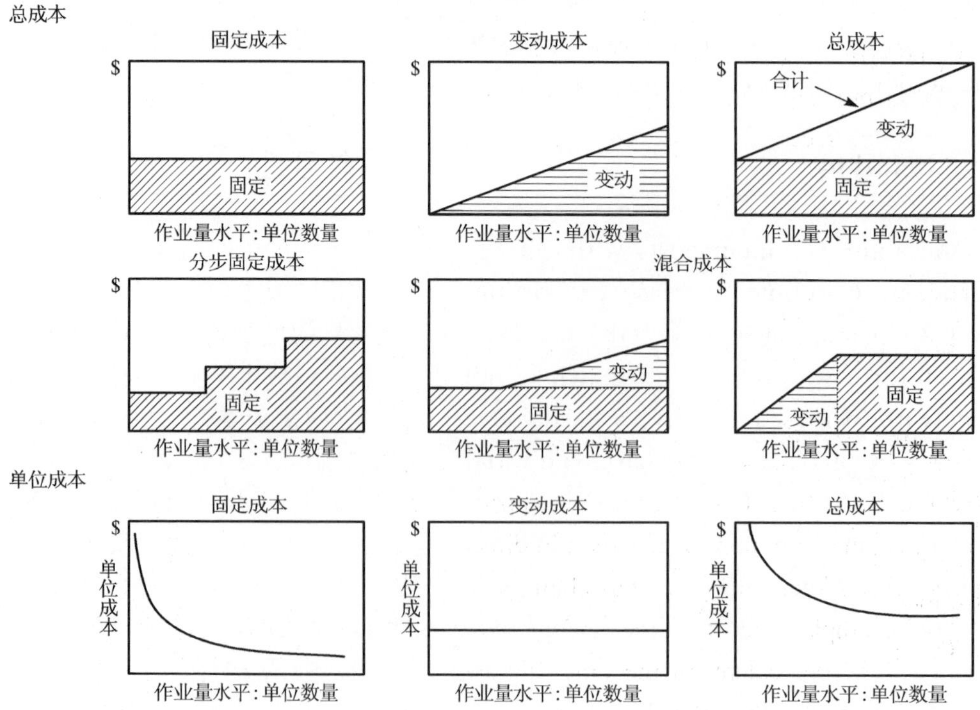

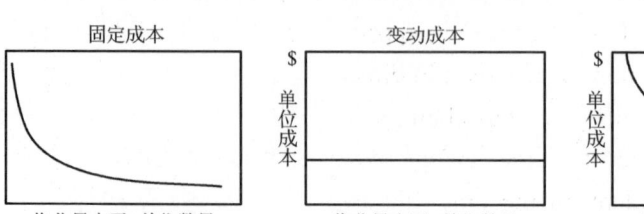

总成本

固定成本

$ | 固定
作业量水平：单位数量

变动成本

$ | 变动
作业量水平：单位数量

总成本

$ | 合计 → 变动 | 固定
作业量水平：单位数量

分步固定成本

$ | 固定
作业量水平：单位数量

混合成本

$ | 变动 | 固定
作业量水平：单位数量

$ | 变动 | 固定
作业量水平：单位数量

单位成本

固定成本

$ | 单位成本
作业量水平：单位数量

变动成本

$ | 单位成本
作业量水平：单位数量

总成本

$ | 单位成本
作业量水平：单位数量

FIGURE 1. 14   ASSESSMENT OF FIXED COST ELEMENT BY THE USE OF A SCATTERGRAPH

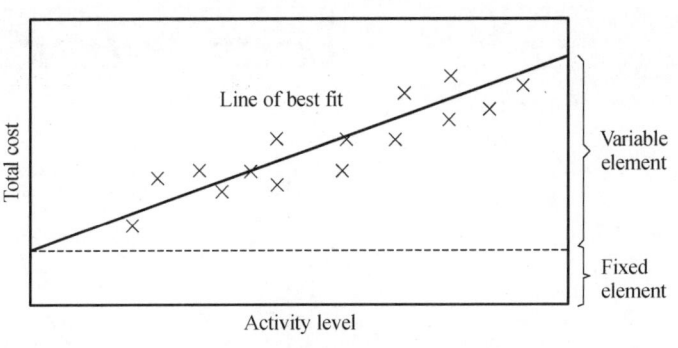

The use of a scatter graph gives no indication of the direction of the cause and effect relationship, nor does it accurately measure the strength of the relationship. Further, by being interpreted visually, its use is subject to considerable risk of error.

图表 1. 14   用散点图来评估固定成本要素

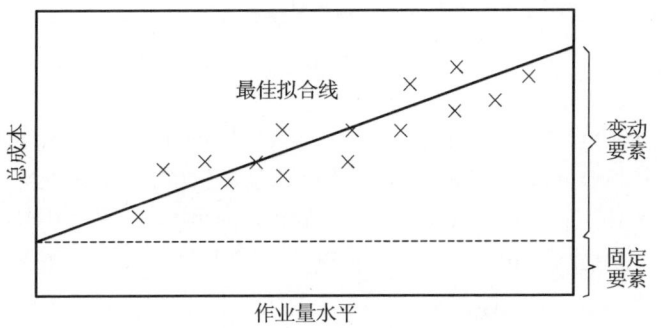

用散点图不能表现出走向的原因和关联效应，也不能精确计量关联的强度。另外，以可视化的表达，它的作用受制于一定风险和误差。

cost classification

Arrangement of elements of cost into logical groups with respect to their nature （fixed，variable，value adding），function （production，selling)or use in the business of the entity.

成本分类

按照性质（固定、可变、增加值）、功能（生产、销售）或在企业中的使用情况对成本要素进行的分类。

cost，committed

Cost arising from prior decisions，which cannot，in the short run，be changed. Committed cost incurrence often stems from strategic decisions concerning capacity with resulting expenditure on plant and facilities. Initial control of committeed costs at the decision point is

已承诺成本

源于先前决策、在短期内不能改变的成本。已承诺成本通常源自工厂和设备的产能和支出战略决策。在决策时点,通过投资评估技术对已承诺成本进行最初的控制。参见"承诺确认会计"。参见图表 1.15。

through investment appraisal techniques. See
"commitment accounting". See Figure 1.15.

FIGURE 1.15   COMPARISON, OVER THE LIFE OF A PROJECT, OF THE DIFFERENCES BETWEEN COST COMMITMENT AND COST INCURRENCE

图表 1.15   一个项目在生命周期内承诺成本和产生的成本之间差异的比较

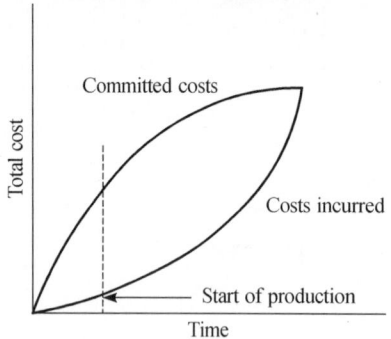

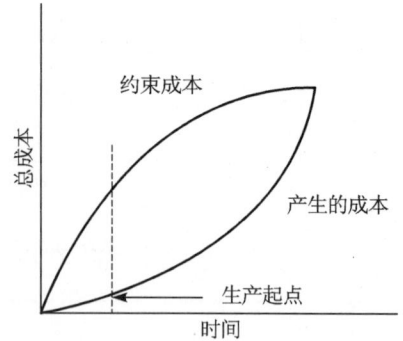

By the start of the production period, most of the costs which will be incurred have already been designed into the product and the selected production technology，and are，once production starts，only marginally susceptible to change.

在产品的生命周期开始阶段，大部分将会发生的成本都已经被设计到产品和选择的生产技术中去，一旦生产开始，成本只允许少量变动。

cost，common

共同成本

Cost relating to more than one product or service.

与多个产品或服务有关的成本。

cost，contract

合同成本

Aggregated costs of a single contract. This usually applies to major long-term contracts rather than short-term jobs.

单个合同的总成本，主要适用于大型长期合同而非短期工作。

cost control

成本控制

Process that ensures action is taken it costs exceed a pre-set allowance（see

为防止成本超出事前设定的限额（参见"反馈控制"），或当预测到成本

"control, feedback") or that action is taken if costs are forecast to exceed expected levels (see "control, feedforward").

会超过预期水平时所采取的措施(参见"前馈控制")。

cost, controllable

①Cost that can be controlled, typically by a cost, profit or investment centre manager.

可控成本

可以控制的成本,通常包括成本中心、利润中心以及投资中心管理者可控制的成本。

cost, conversion

Cost of converting material into finished product, typically including direct labour, direct expense and production overhead.

转换成本

将原材料转换为产成品的成本,通常包括直接人工、直接费用和生产间接费用。

cost, differential/incremental

Difference in total cost between alternatives. This is calculated to assist decision making.

差异成本/增量成本

不同方案造成的总成本差异,计算成本差异有助于决策。

cost, direct

Expenditure that can be attributed to a specific cost unit, for example material that forms part of the product. See Figure 1.1.

直接成本

可以直接归属于特定成本单位的支出,例如构成产品组成部分的材料。参见图 1.1。

cost, discretionary

Cost whose amount within a time period is determined by a decision taken by the appropriate budget holder. Marketing, research and training are generally regarded as discretionary costs. Also known as managed or policy costs.

酌量成本

一段时期内,受预算管理者决策影响的成本。营销、研发和培训支出通常被认为是酌量成本。也被称为是可管理成本或政策性成本。

cost driver

Factor influencing the level of cost.

成本动因

影响成本水平的因素。在作业成

Often used in the context of ABC to denote the factor which links activity resource consumption to product outputs, for example the number of purchase orders would be a cost driver for procurement cost.

本法中,通常用来表示生产活动资源消耗和生产产出之间的关系,例如订单数量就是采购成本的一个成本动因。

cost elements

成本要素

Constituent parts of costs according to the factors upon which expenditure is incurred, namely material, labour and expenses. See Figure 1.16.

成本的组成部分,支出发生的因素,即原材料、人工和费用。参见图表1.16。

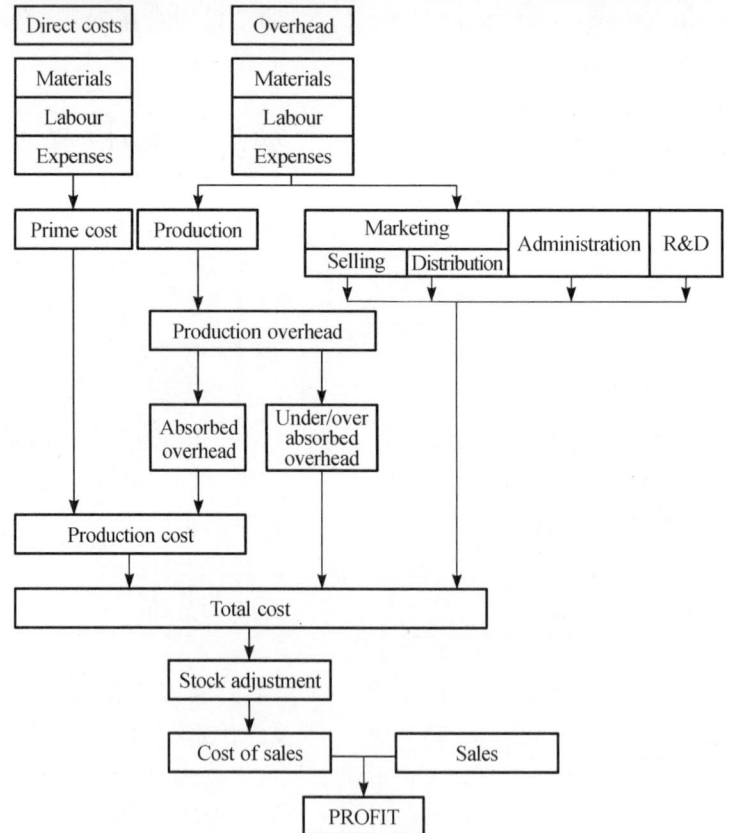

FIGURE 1.16 ELEMENTS OF AN ABSORPTION COSTING SYSTEM

Notes: 1. The above Chart is based on the absorption costing principle.

2. In the case of marginal costing, the amount of production overhead absorbed would relate to the variable element only.

3. The relative sizes of the boxes are no significance.

图表 1.16　吸收成本核算系统的要素

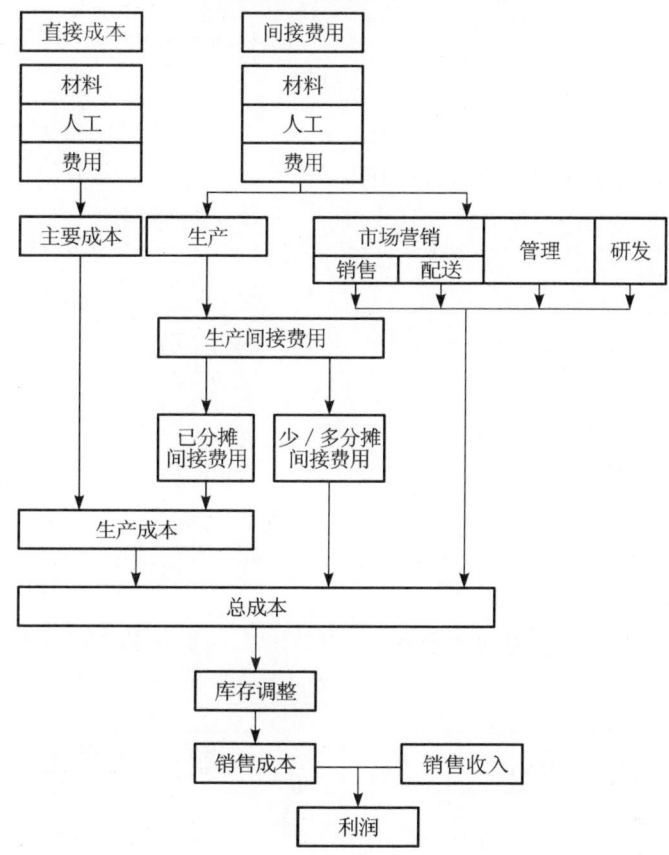

注:1. 上图是基于吸收成本原则。

　　2. 在边际成本中,吸收的生产间接费用的量只和可变要素有关。

　　3. 图中格子的相对大小没有任何意义。

cost, estimation

Determination of cost behaviour. This can be achieved by engineering methods, analysis of the accounts, use of statistics or by the pooling of expert views.

成本估计

成本习性的确定,可以借助工程方法、账户分析、统计应用或者汇集专家意见等来实现。

cost, fixed

Cost incurred for an accounting period, that, within certain output or turnover limits, tends to be unaffected by fluctuations in

固定成本

一个会计期间内发生的、在一定产出或营业额的限制内,金额不受活动(产出或营业额)变动影响的成本。

the levels of activity (output or turnover).

cost, holding

Cost of retaining an asset, generally stock. Holding cost includes the cost of financing the asset in addition to the cost of physical storage.

cost, joint

Cost of a process which results in more than one main product.

cost, leadership

Based upon a business organising itself to be the lowest-cost producer.

cost, long-term variable

All costs are variable in the long run. Full unit costs may be surrogates for long-term variable costs if calculated in a manner which utilises long-term cost drivers, for example activity-based costing.

cost management

Application of management accounting concepts, methods of data collection, analysis and presentation in order to provide the information needed to plan, monitor and control costs.

cost, marginal

Part of the cost of one unit of product or service that would be avoided if the unit were

持有成本

持有一项资产的成本,通常是指股票。持有成本包括融资资产成本以及实物存储成本。

联合成本

在生产多种主要产品的过程中发生的成本。

成本领先

企业基于成本最低来组织自己的业务活动。

长期变动成本

从长期来看,所有的成本都是变动的。如果在计算中采用长期成本驱动的方式,例如作业成本法,那么全部的单位成本都是长期变动成本。

成本管理

管理会计的概念以及数据收集、分析和列报方法的应用,旨在为计划、监控以及控制成本提供信息。

边际成本

增加一个单位的产品或服务而产生的成本,如果不生产产品或服务就

not produced, or that would increase if one extra unit were produced.

不会发生,或者是额外增加一个单位产出所增加的成本。

cost, notional

Cost used in product evaluation, decision making and performance measurement to reflect the use of resources that have no actual (observable) cost. For example, notional interest for internally generated funds or notional rent for use of space.

估计成本

适用于产品估价、决策和绩效衡量、以反映资源使用情况但并未实际发生(用于观察)的成本。例如,内部资金的估计利息或者场地使用的估计租金。

cost, object

For example a product, service, centre, activity, customer or distribution channel in relation to which costs are ascertained.

成本对象

承担成本的客体,例如产品、服务、中心、作业、客户或者分销渠道。

cost of quality

Different between the actual cost of producing, selling and supporting products or services and the equivalent costs if there were no failures during production or usage. The cost of quality can be analysed into:

cost of conformance: Cost of achieving specified quality standards.

cost of prevention: Costs incurred prior to or during production in order to prevent substandard or defective products or services from being produced.

cost of appraisal: Costs incurred in order to ensure that outputs produced meet required quality standards.

cost of non-conformance: Cost of failure to deliver the required standard of quality.

cost of internal failure: Costs arising from inadequate quality which are identified

质量成本

产品或服务在生产或使用的过程中如果没有失败的话,质量成本是产品或劳务在生产、销售和支持的实际成本与约当成本的差额。质量成本可以分解为:

合规成本:实现特定质量要求的成本。

预防成本:在生产之前或生产过程中,为防止出现不合格或者有缺陷的产品或服务而发生的成本。

检验成本:为保证产出符合质量标准发生的费用。

不合规成本:未能达到质量标准所产生的成本。

内部失败成本:所有权从供应商转移给购买者之前,质量缺陷引起的

before the transfer of ownership from supplier to purchaser.

cost of external failure：Cost arising from inadequate quality discovered after the transfer of ownership from supplier to purchaser.

Note：There is no universally accepted definition of quality，which may be assessed on a number of bases，such as conformance to specification，ability to satisfy wants，inclusion of attractive performance/aesthetic attributes，or offering value for money.

成本。

外部失败成本:所有权从供应商转移给购买者之后,质量缺陷引起的成本。

注:质量没有公认的定义,可以基于是否符合规格、具备满足需求的能力、包含吸引人的特性/审美属性或者物有所值来判定。

cost of sales

The cost of goods sold during an accounting period. For a retail business this will be the cost of goods available for sale（opening stock plus purchase）minus closing stock. For a manufacturing business it will include all direct and indirect production costs.

销售成本

在某一会计期间内,已售出商品的成本。对于零售业务来说,销售成本等于可供出售商品的成本(期初存货＋购入的商品)减去期末存货。对于制造业务来说,则包括了所有直接成本和间接生产成本。

cost, opportunity

The value of the benefit sacrificed when one course of action is chosen in preference to an alternative. The opportunity cost is represented by the foregone potential benefit from the best rejected course of action.

机会成本

在选择一个方案之后,放弃的另一个方案所能带来的收益价值。机会成本代表了被放弃方案的最佳潜在利益。

cost, overhead/indirect

Expenditure on labour，materials or services that cannot be economically identified with a specific saleable cost unit.

The synonymous term burden is in common use in the US and in subsidiaries of American companies.

间接成本

无法直接归于某一特定成本单位的人工、材料或服务成本。

它的同义术语"负担"广泛应用于美国和美国公司的子公司。

cost, period

Cost relating to a time period rather than to the output of products or services.

cost, pool

Grouping of costs relating to a particular activity in an activity-based costing system.

cost, post-purchase

Cost incurred after a capital expenditure decision has been implemented and facilities acquired. May include training, maintenance and the cost of upgrades.

cost, prime

Total cost of direct material, direct labour and direct expenses.

cost, product

Cost of a finished product built up from its cost elements.

cost, production

Prime cost plus absorbed production overhead.

cost, replacement

Costs of replacing an asset. This is important in relevant costing because if, for example, material that is in constant use is

期间成本

与一个时间段有关、与产品或服务无关的成本。

成本池

在作业成本法系统中,将与特定作业有关的成本进行的归集。

采购后成本

在做出资本支出决策和取得设备设施之后发生的成本,包括了培训、维护和升级的成本。

主要成本

包含了直接材料、直接人工和直接费用的总成本。

产品成本

由成本要素构成的产成品成本。

生产成本

主要成本与分摊的间接生产成本的和。

重置成本

重置一项资产的成本。在相关成本计算中,确定重置成本是非常重要的,例如,如果在产品和服务中经常使

needed for a product or service, the relevant cost of that material will be its replacement cost. Replacement cost has also been proposed as an alternate to historic cost accounting and it can, therefore, be an important concept with relevance to accounting for inflation or measuring performance where the value of assets is important.

用某种材料,那么这种材料的相关成本就是它的重置成本。重置成本也被建议用于替代历史成本,因此,当资产的价值非常高时,重置成本是一个与通货膨胀会计或绩效衡量同等重要的概念。

cost, semi-variable

Cost containing both fixed and variable components and thus partly affected by a change in the level of activity.

半变动成本

包含了固定成本和变动成本,因此,在一定程度上受到作业水平变动的影响。

cost, standard

Planned unit cost of a product, component or service. The standard cost may be determined on a number of bases (see standard). The main uses of standard costs are in performance measurement, control, stock valuation and in the establishment of selling prices. See "standard product specification".

标准成本

产品、组件或服务的计划单位成本。大量的基本因素共同决定了标准成本(参见"标准")。标准成本主要用于绩效衡量、控制、股票估值和建立销售价格。参见"标准产品规格"。

cost, sunk

Cost that has been irreversibly incurred or committed and cannot therefore be considered relevant to a decision. Sunk costs may also be termed irrecoverable costs.

沉没成本

已经发生或承诺支付的不可逆成本,因此与决策无关。沉没成本也被称为不可收回成本。

cost, table

Database containing costs associated with production of a product, broken down by function and/or components and sub-assemblies. It incorporates cost changes that would result

成本表

包含了产品生产成本的数据库,根据功能和(或)部件以及组件进行细分,包含了投入组合的可能变化所导致的成本变化。

from possible changes in the input mix.

cost, target

Product cost estimate derived by subtracting a desired profit margin from a competitive market price.

cost, unit

Unit of product or service in relation to which costs are ascertained. See Figure 1.17.

FIGURE 1.17   COST UNITS

Examples of cost units

Industry sector	Cost unit
Brewing	Barrel
Brick-making	1,000 bricks
Coal mining	Tonne/ton
Electricity	Kilowatt hour (KwH)
Engineering	Contract, job
Oil	Barrel, tonne, litre
Hotel/Catering	Room/meal
Professional services	Chargeable hour, job, contract
Education	Course, enrolled student, successful student
Hospitals	Patient day

Activity	Cost unit
Credit control	Account maintained
Materials storage/handling	
Requisition unit issued/received, material movement value issued/received	
Personnel administration	Personnel record
Selling	Customer call, value of sales, orders taken

cost, variable

①Cost that varies with a measure of activity.

目标成本

通过有竞争力的市场价格减去期望的利润来估算的产品成本。

成本单位

用于确定成本的单位产品或服务。参见图表1.17。

图表1.17　成本单位

成本单位示例

工业部门	成本单位
酿造	桶
制砖	1 000 块
煤矿开采	公吨/吨
电力	千瓦时（KwH）
工程	合同、工作量
石油	桶、公吨、升
酒店/餐饮	房间/餐
专业服务	收费小时、工作量、合同
教育	课程、在校生、毕业生
医疗	病人日

作业	成本单位
信贷控制	维护的账户数量
材料存储/处理	
发出/收到的申请单位，发出/收到的材料移动价值	
人事管理	人事档案
销售	顾客呼叫次数、销售额、签订的订单数

变动成本

随着作业量的变化而变化的成本。

cost-volume-profit analysis, CVP

Study of the effects on future profit of changes in fixed cost, variable cost, sales price, quantity and mix.

cost, weighted average

Method of unit cost determination, often applied to stocks, in which an average unit cost is calculated, when a new purchase quantity is received:

$$\frac{\text{Cost of opening stock} + \text{Cost of acquisitions}}{\text{Total number of units}}$$

See Figure 1.18.

本量利分析

研究固定成本、变动成本、销售价格以及销售数量及其组合的变动对未来利润影响的方法。

加权平均成本

一种确定单位成本的方法,经常应用于股票,购进存货后平均单位成本的计算如下:

$$\frac{\text{期初存货成本} + \text{采购成本}}{\text{总数量}}$$

参见图表1.18。

FIGURE 1.18   PRICING STOCK ISSUES

Date	Purchase quantity	Unit cost	Total cost	Issue quantity	Issue cost	Balance	
	Units	$	$	Units	$	Units	$
1 April	200	1.20	240	—	—	200	240
12 April	350	1.30	455	—	—	550	695
13 April	420	1.10	462	—	—	970	1,157
15 April	—		—	500	(a)	470	(b)

图表1.18   存货的定价

日期	采购量	单位成本	总成本	发出量	发出成本	余额	
	个	美元	美元	个	美元	个	美元
4月1日	200	1.20	240	—	—	200	240
4月12日	350	1.30	455	—	—	550	695
4月13日	420	1.10	462	—	—	970	1 157
4月15日	—		—	500	(a)	470	(b)

The valuation of the issues made on 15 April (a) and the valuation of the residual stock (b) are as follows:

Valuation of issues: Valuation of residual stock:

4月15日的发出价值(a)和剩余存货价值(b)的计算如下:

发出价值: 剩余存货价值:

FIFO：$(200 \times \$1.20) + (300 \times \$1.30)$
　　　$= \$630$　　　　　　　　　　$\$527$
LIFO：$(420 \times \$1.10) + (80 \times \$1.30)$
　　　$= \$566$　　　　　　　　　　$\$591$
Weighted average：$(500 \times \$1,157/970)$
　　　　　　　　$= \$596$　　　　　$\$561$

Note：The valuation of stock issues is independent of any policy with respect to the order in which physical stock should be issued, which would, where practicable, be FIFO.

先进先出法：$(200 \times \$1.20) + (300 \times \$1.30) = \$630$　　$\$527$
后进先出法：$(420 \times \$1.10) + (80 \times \$1.30) = \$566$　　$\$591$
加权平均法：$(500 \times \$1\ 157/970) = \$596$　　　　　$\$561$

注：发出存货的价值独立于存货的发出政策,在可行的情况下,也可以采用先进先出法。

cost-benefit analysis

Comparison between the costs of the resources used plus any other costs imposed by an activity (for example pollution, environmental damage) and the value of the financial and non-financial benefits derived.

成本效益分析

比较使用的资源成本以及作业的其他费用(例如,污染、环境破坏)与获得的财务和非财务收益的价值。

costing, backflush

Method of costing, associated with a JIT (just-in-time) production system, which applies cost to the output of a process. Costs do not mirror the flow of products through the production process, but are attached to output produced(finished goods stock and cost of sales), on the assumption that such backflushed costs are a realistic measure of the actual costs incurred. See just-in-time.

倒推成本法

一种与准时生产系统有关、将成本应用于产出过程的成本核算方法。假设倒推成本是实际发生成本的真实计量,成本并不反映生产过程中的产品流动,而是与产出(产成品库存和销售成本)有关。参见"适时生产"。

costing, life-cycle

Maintenance of physical asset cost records over entire asset lives, so that decisions concerning the acquisition use or disposal of assets can be made in a way that achieves the

生命周期成本法

在资产的整个生命周期中记录资产的维护成本,以便做出使用还是处置资产的决定,实现实体在最低成本水平上充分利用资产。这个概念可被

optimum asset usage at the lowest possible cost to the entity. The term may be applied to the profiling of cost over a product's life, including the pre-production stage (terotechnology), and to both company and industry life cycles. See Figure 1.19.

应用于包括预生产阶段(保养技术)在内的产品生命周期、公司和行业生命周期的成本分析。参见图表1.19。

FIGURE 1.19 LIFE CYCLE COSTS OF A PRODUCT OR SERVICE

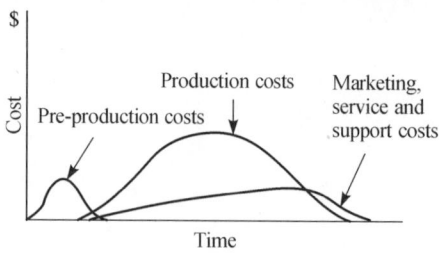

图表 1.19 产品或服务的生命周期成本

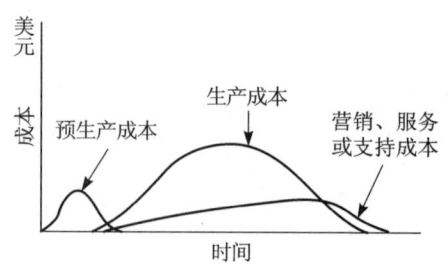

costing, standard

Control technique that reports variances by comparing actual costs to pre-set standards so facilitating action through management by exception.

标准成本法

通过比较预先确定的标准成本与实际成本,分析成本差异的一种控制技术,以便通过例外管理来促进纠正措施的开展。

direct product profitability, DPP

Used primarily within the retail sector, DPP involves the attribution of both the purchase price and other indirect costs(for example distribution, warehousing and retailing) to each product line. Thus a net profit, as opposed to a gross profit, can be identified for each product. The cost attribution process utilises a variety of measures (for example warehousing space and transport time) to reflect the resource consumption of individual products.

直接产品盈利能力

主要用于零售业,DPP 按照产品线对购买价格和其他间接成本(例如分销、仓储和零售)进行了归集。因此,能够确认每个产品的净利润,而不是总利润。这种成本归因过程利用了多种度量手段(例如仓储空间和运输时间),以反映单个产品的资源消耗。

environmental management accounting

Identification，collection，analysis and use of two types of information for internal decision making：physical information on the use，flows and rates of energy，water and materials（including wastes）；and monetary information on environment-related costs，earnings and savings(EMARIC).

equivalent units

Notional whole units representing uncompleted work. Used to apportion costs between work in progress and completed output，and in performance assessment.

feasible region

Area contained within all of the constraint lines shown on a graphical depiction of a linear programming problem. All feasible combinations of output are contained within or located on the boundaries of the feasible region. See Figure 1.20.

环境管理会计

识别、收集、分析和使用两种类型的信息来为内部决策服务：关于能源、水资源以及材料（包括废弃物）的使用、流动以及评估等物理信息；与环境相关的成本、收益和节约等货币信息（EMARIC）。

约当产量

代表未完成工作中已完成的部分占整个工作的比例。用于在完工产品和在产品之间分摊成本，还可用于绩效评价。

可行域

在一个线性规划问题中，满足所有约束线的区域叫做可行域。所有可行的产出组合都分布在可行域内或边界上。参见图表1.20。

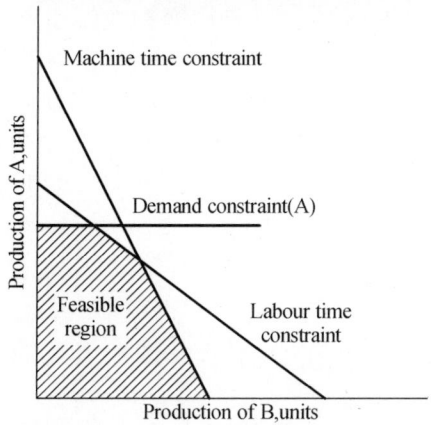

FIGURE 1.20 FEASIBLE REGION

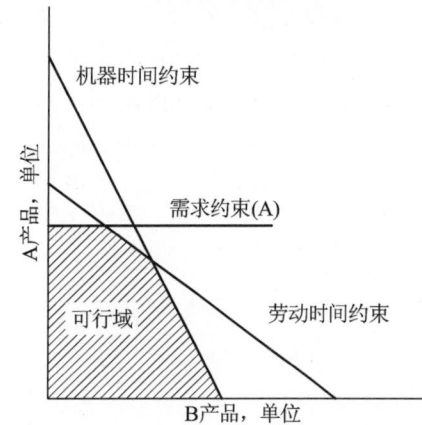

图表 1.20 可行域

financial performance measurement

Investors (both shareholders and lenders) will often appraise the financial performance of an organisation, to assess whether the organisation represents a good investment.

To appraise financial performance, it is necessary to first calculate ratios under the following headings: profitability ratios; lender ratios; investor ratios.

Fitzgerald and Moon

See "building block model".

first in, first out; FIFO

See "stock (inventory)valuation".

gross profit percentage

See "ratio gross profit to sales revenue".

high/low method

Method of estimating cost behaviour by comparing the total costs associated with two different levels of output. The difference in costs is assumed to be caused by variable costs increasing, allowing unit variable cost to be calculated. Following from this, since total cost is known, the fixed cost can be derived.

job

Customer order or task of relatively short duration.

财务绩效评价

投资者(包括股东和债权人)经常对组织的财务绩效进行评估,以确定该组织是否是一个好的投资对象。

为了评估财务绩效,需要先计算盈利比率、贷款比率和投资比率。

菲茨杰拉德和穆恩

参见"积木式模型"。

先进先出法

参见"库存(存货)估值"。

毛利率

参见"毛利与销售收入的比率"。

高低点法

通过比较两种不同产出水平下的总成本来估计成本习性的方法。假定成本的差异是由变动成本引起的,就可以计算出单位变动成本,因为总成本已知,所以固定成本也可以求出。

订单

客户订单或期限相对较短的任务。

job cost sheet

Detailed record of the amount, and cost, of the labour, material and overhead charged to a specific job.

joint products

Two or more products produced by the same process and separated in processing, each having a sufficiently high saleable value to merit recognition as a main product. See "by-product".

key performance indicators (KPIs)

Quantitative but not necessarily financial metrics that can indicate progress or lack of progress towards a strategic objective. For example, metrics may be devised for safety, quality, turnover of key staff. Key performance indicators were important to the idea of management by objectives and are integral to the scorecard ideas developed in the 1990s.

knowledge management

Systematic process of finding, selecting, organising, distilling and presenting information so as to improve comprehension of a specific area of interest. Specific activities help focus the organisation on acquiring, storing and utilising knowledge for such things as problem solving, dynamic learning, strategic planning and decision making.

分批成本单

归属于特定订单的劳动力、原材料以及间接费用的数量和成本的详细记录。

联产品

在同一生产过程中,生产出两个或两个以上的产品,每一种都有足够高的可售价值,都可以作为一个主要产品。参见"副产品"。

关键绩效指标

能够显示是否向战略目标迈进、不一定是财务指标的可量化指标。例如,可以根据安全、质量以及关键员工流动率等因素来设计指标。关键绩效指标是非常重要的目标管理概念,对20世纪90年代出现的记分卡来说是不可或缺的。

知识管理

发现、选择、组织、提炼以及呈现信息,并以此提升对某个特定利益领域的理解力的系统过程。特定的活动可以协助组织关注知识的获取、存储和利用,并解决问题、动态学习、战略规划和做出决策。

last in, first out; LIFO

See "stock (inventory) valuation".

learning curve

Mathematical expression of the commonly observed effect that, as complex and labour-intensive procedures are repeated, unit labour times tend to decrease. The equation(see Figure 1.21) usually relates the average time taken per unit/batch to the cumulative number of units/batches produced. An alternative, little used, formulation uses the same equation but relates the incremental (not average) time for the nth unit to the cumulative number of units/batches produced. See Figure 1.21.

后进先出法

参见"库存(存货)估值"。

学习曲线

用于反映当复杂和劳动密集型的过程不断重复,单位劳动时间趋于减少的常见观察效应的数学表达式。等式(参见图表 1.21)将每单位/批次的平均处理时间与生产的单位/批次积累数量联系起来。还有一个比较少用的方法是用同样的等式将第 n 个单元的增量(不是平均)时间和生产的单位/批次积累数量联系起来。参见图表 1.21。

FIGURE 1.21　LEARNING CURVE

Engines	Cumulative engines	Average hours per engine	Cumulative hours
1	1	2,000	2,000
1	2	1,600(2,000×0.8)	3,200
2	4	1,280(1,600×0.8)	5,120
4	8	1,024(1,280×0.8)	8,192

图表 1.21　学习曲线

发动机数量	累计发动机数量	每台发动机平均工时	累计工时
1	1	2 000	2 000
1	2	1 600(2 000×0.8)	3 200
2	4	1 280(1 600×0.8)	5 120
4	8	1 024(1 280×0.8)	8 192

Example：

A team of technicians has assembled the first of a new model of aircraft engine in a total of 2,000 hours. Assuming an 80% learning curve, determine：

1. How long it will take to manufacture the next engine

2. How long it will take to manufacture the next three engines

例子:

一个技术团队用了 2 000 小时组装了 1 台新的飞机发动机模型。假设 80% 的学习曲线,做出如下决定:

1. 生产后面 1 台发动机需要多少时间

2. 生产后面 3 台发动机需要多少时间

3. Having already produced two engines，the average time per engine required for the next six

1. The next engine will take（3,200－2,000）hours＝1,200 hours

2. The next three engines will take（5,120－2,000）hours＝3,120 hours

3. （8,192－3,200）÷6＝832 hours

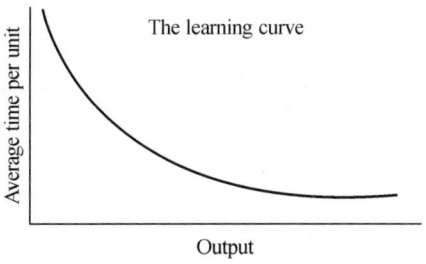

The learning curve can also be expressed mathematically as：

$$Y = ax^{\beta}$$

Where Y is the average time taken per unit/batch to produce a cumulative number of units/batches：

a is the time required to produce the first unit

x is the cumulative number of units to be produced

β is the coefficient of learning，which can be calculated as：

$$\frac{\text{logarithm of rate of learning}^*}{\text{logarithm of 2.0}}$$

＊ for an 80% learning curve，this would be log 0.8

lease or buy decision

If a new project requires the use of an asset，such as a machine，a business often has the choice of whether to buy the asset out-

3. 已生产2台发动机，则生产后面6台发动机平均每台需要多少时间

1. 后面1台发动机需要（3 200－2 000）小时＝1 200 小时

2. 后面3台发动机需要（5 120－2 000）小时＝3 120 小时

3. （8 192－3 200）÷6＝832 小时

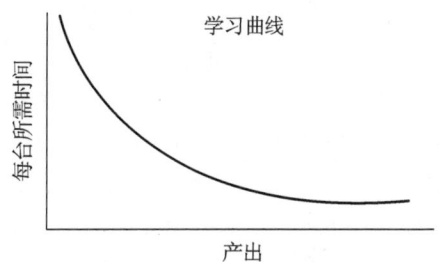

学习曲线同样可以用数学方程表示为：

$$Y = ax^{\beta}$$

Y 指每台的平均工时/生产一批的累计工时/生产数批的累计工时

a 指生产第1台所需时间

x 指生产的累计台数

β 指学习的协同效应，计算公式如下：

$$\frac{\text{学习比率的对数}^*}{\text{2.0 的对数}}$$

＊ 对于一个80%的学习曲线，就是 log 0.8

租赁或购买决策

如果一个新项目需要使用资产，比如1台机器，企业做出的购买还是租赁的决策。

right，or whether to lease it.

management accounting

Management accounting is the application of the principles of accounting and financial management to create，protect，preserve and increase value for the stakeholders of for-profit and not-for-profit enterprises in the public and private sectors.

Management accounting is an integral part of management. It requires the identification，generation，presentation，interpretation and use of relevant information to：

- Inform strategic decisions and formulate business strategy
- Plan long，medium and short-run operations
- Determine capital structure and fund that structure
- Design reward strategies for executives and shareholders
- Inform operational decisions

- Control operations and ensure the efficient use of resources
- Measure and report financial and non-financial performance to management and other stakeholders
- Safeguard tangible and intangible assets
- Implement corporate governance procedures，risk management and internal controls.

management by exception

Practice of concentrating on activities that

管理会计

管理会计是会计和财务管理原则的应用,旨在创建、保护、保存和增加公共和私营部门中的营利和非营利企业利益相关人的价值。

管理会计是管理活动不可或缺的组成部分。它需要识别、生成、陈述、解释和使用相关信息：

- 告知战略决策和制定商业策略

- 计划长期、中期和短期的运营活动
- 确定资本结构并按此结构进行筹资
- 针对高管和股东设计奖酬策略

- 对运营活动进行控制并确保资源的有效利用
- 计量并向管理层和其他利益相关者报告财务与非财务绩效
- 保护有形和无形资产

- 实施公司治理程序、风险管理和内部控制

例外管理

专注于需要关注的活动,忽视那

require attention and ignoring those which appear to be conforming to expectations.

Typically，standard cost variances or variances from budget are used to identify those activities that require attention.

management commentary

A narrative report that provides a context within which to interpret the financial position，financial performance and cash flows of an entity. Management are able to explain their objectives and strategies for achieving those objectives. Users routinely use the type of information provided in management commentary to help them evaluate an entity's prospects and its general risks，as well as the success of management's strategies for achieving the entity's stated objectives. For many entities，management commentary is already an important element of their communication with the capital markets，supplementing as well as complementing the financial statements.

manufacturing resource planning (MRP II)

Expansion of matrial requirements planning（MRP）to give a broader approach than MRP to the planning and scheduling of resources embracing areas such as finance，logistics，engineering and marketing.

margin

Difference between the selling price and cost of sales expressed either as a percentage of sales or as an absolute amount. See "mark-up".

些符合预期的活动。

通常,根据标准成本差异或者预算差异来定义需要关注的活动。

管理评述

一种阐述实体的财务状况、财务业绩以及现金流状况的叙述性报告。管理层可以解释财务目标以及为实现财务目标所采取的策略。使用者可以利用管理评论提供的信息来评估实体的发展前景、总体风险以及管理层为实现实体目标而实施的战略是否成功。对许多企业来说,管理评论已经成为其与资本市场沟通的重要手段,并成为了财务报表的有益补充。

制造资源计划

对原材料需求计划（MRP）的扩充,形成了以一种比 MRP 更为宽泛的途径来规划和安排财务、物流、工程以及营销等多个领域的资源。

边际

以销售百分比或绝对数表示的销售价格与销售成本的差额。参见"加成"。

marginal revenue

Additional revenue generated from the sale of one additional unit of output.

边际收入

额外销售 1 个单位产品所带来的增加收入。

materiality

An item in the financial statements is material if its omission or a misstatement of its value would be likely to influence a user of the financial statements.

重要性

如果遗漏或误报财务报表中的某个项目就可能会影响财务报表使用人,那么这个项目就具有重要性。

maximax criterion

Criterion used to make a choice between alternative strategies. This favours the strategy that might lead to the highest possible profit,irrespective of the probability of that profit actually being achieved and the outcome if it is not successful.

最大最大准则

用来从替代策略中做选择的准则。它偏爱可能取得最高利润的策略,不考虑利润实现的可能性和失败所造成的结果。

maximin criterion

Criterion used to make a choice between alternative strategies. This favours the strategy that generates the highest profit if the worst outcome occurs.

最大最小准则

用来从替代策略中做选择的准则。它偏爱当最差的结果出现时能取得最高利润的策略。

minimax regret criterion

Criterion used to make a choice between alternative strategies. This is the difference between the best and worst possible payoff for each option. This criterion favours the strategy that minimises the maximum regret.

最小最大后悔准则

用来从替代策略中做选择的准则。它与每个选项的最好和最差的可能回报不同。这个准则偏爱那些可以最小化最大后悔值的策略。

noise

Random fluctuations that can be mistaken for important information. Noise can confuse or divert attention from relevant information; efficiency in a system is enhanced as the ratio of information to noise increases.

non-financial performance measures

Measure of performance based on non-financial information that may originate in and be used by operating departments to monitor and control their activities without any accounting input.

Non-financial performance measures may give a more timely indication of the levels of performance achieved than financial measures do, and may be less susceptible to distortion by factors such as uncontrollable variations in the effect of market forces on operations.

Non-financial measures are now integrated with financial measures in systems such as the balanced scorecard. Examples of non-financial performance measures:

Area assessed	Performance measure
Service quality	Number of complaints
	Proportion of repeat bookings
	Customer waiting time
	On-time deliveries
Production performance	Set-up times
	Number of suppliers
	Day's inventory in hand
	Output per employee
	Material yield percentage
	Schedule adherence
	Proportion of output requiring rework
	Manufacturing lead times

噪声

可能被误认为重要信息的随机波动。噪声会混淆或者转移对相关信息的注意力；当信息噪声比增加时，系统的效率会提高。

非财务绩效指标

基于非财务信息的非财务绩效指标源自同时又应用于业务部门，旨在不需要任何会计信息的情况下，监督和控制业务部门的活动。

相较于财务指标，非财务绩效指标能够更加及时地提供关于业绩水平的信息，而且非财务指标较少受到诸如市场力量左右经营活动等不可控因素的影响，不太容易失真。

现在，平衡计分卡等系统已经实现了非财务指标与财务指标的结合。非财务指标如下所示：

评估范围	绩效指标
服务质量	投诉数量
	重复预定比例
	顾客等待时间
	及时交付
生产绩效	安装时间
	供应商数量
	库存周转期
	每位员工的产量
	材料产出比率
	进度执行比率
	产品返工比例
	制造提前期

Marketing	Trend in market share	营销有效性	市场份额趋势
effectiveness	Sales volume growth		销售规模增长
	Customer visits per salesperson		每位销售人员客户访问量
	Client contact hours per salesperson		每位销售人员联系客户时数
	Sales volume forecast v. actual		销售预测与实际比较
	Number of customers		顾客数量
	Customer survey		客户调查
	Response information		反馈信息
Personnel	Number of complaints received	员工	收到的投诉数量
	Staff turnover		员工流动率
	Days lost through absenteeism		旷工缺勤天数
	Days lost through accidents/sickness		事假/病假缺勤天数
	Training time per employee		每位雇员的训练时间

The values expected may vary significantly between industries/sectors.

不同行业或领域的期望价值可能有很大的差异。

normal loss

正常损耗

Expected loss，allowed for in the budget，and normally calculated as a percentage of the good output from a process during a period of time. Normal losses are generally either valued at zero or at their disposal values.

列入预算的预期损耗，通常按照一定时期内合格产品的百分比计算。一般情况下，正常损耗为零或者是产品的残值。

operational gearing

经营杠杆

Relationship of fixed cost to total cost of an operating unit. The greater the proportion of total costs that are fixed（high operation gearing）. the greater is the advantage to the organisation of increasing sales volume. Conversely, should sales volumes drop, a highly geared organisation would find the high proportion of fixed costs to be a major problem，possibly causing a rapid swing from profitability into loss. Gearing may also be referred to as leverage. See "ratio，gearing/leverage".

某个业务部门的固定成本和总成本的关系。总成本中固定成本的比例越大(高经营杠杆)，组织增加销量就能获得更多的利润。相反，当销量下降时，拥有高杠杆的组织会发现高固定成本比例就成为了一个棘手的问题，可能会导致有盈利的组织迅速亏损。参见"比率/杠杆"。

overhead absorption rate

间接费用分摊率

A means of attributing overhead to a

基于直接人工小时数、直接劳动

product or service, based for example on direct labour hours, direct labour cost or machine hours.

direct labour cost percentage rate: Overhead absorption rate based on direct labour cost.

direct labour hour rate: Overhead absorption rate based on direct labour hours.

machine hour rate: Overhead absorption rate based on machine hours.

See Figure 1.1.

payroll analysis

Analysis of labour costs for accounting purposes identifying, for example: gross pay by department, operation or product; and/or gross pay analysed into direct pay or lost time.

performance measurement

Process of assessing the proficiency with which a reporting entity succeeds, by the economic acquisition of resources and their efficient and effective deployment, in achieving its objectives. Performance measures may be based on non-financial as well as on financial information. See "non-financial performance measures".

performance measurement mix

Performance measurement mix includes such aspects: link to strategy, problems, benchmarking, communication, divisional performance and models.

成本或机器工时,将间接费用归集到某个产品或服务的方法。

直接人工成本百分率:根据直接人工成本计算间接费用的分摊率。

直接人工小时率:根据直接人工小时数计算间接费用的分摊率。

机器工时率:根据机器工时计算间接费用的分摊率。

参见图表1.1。

工资分析

出于会计目的对人工成本进行的分析,例如,按部门、操作或产品计算工资总额,和(或)把工资总额分解为直接支付或浪费的时间。

绩效评价

通过评价经济资源获取以及经济资源是否得到充分有效地分配,来评估报告实体成功程度的过程。绩效评价以财务信息或非财务信息为基础。参见"非财务绩效衡量指标"。

绩效评价组合

绩效评价组合包括以下几个方面:与战略的联系、问题、标杆管理、交流、部门绩效和模型。

performance pyramid

The performance pyramid was developed as a model to understand and define the links between objectives and performance measures at different levels in the organisation.

profit margin

sales − cost of sales

This can be expressed either as a value or as a percentage of sales value. The profit margin may be calculated at different stages, hence the terms gross and net profit margin.

The level of profit reported is also influenced by the extent of the application of accounting conventions, and by the method of product costing used, for example marginal or absorption costing.

profit sharing

Allocation of a proportion of company profit to stakeholders, for example employees, by an issue of shares or other means.

profit-volume/contribution graph

Graph showing the effect on contribution and on overall profit of changes in sales volume or value. See Figure 1.6.

profitability index

$$\frac{\text{Present value of cash inflows}}{\text{Initial investment}}$$

Used in investment appraisal. Repre-

绩效金字塔

作为一个模型,绩效金字塔可用于理解和定义组织不同级别的目标和绩效评价之间的联系。

边际利润

销售额－销售成本

边际利润可以用具体金额或者占销售价值百分比来表示。可以在不同的阶段计算边际利润(具体术语是边际利润总额和边际利润净额)。

列报的利润水平会受到会计惯例的应用以及产品成本计算方法(例如边际成本法或完全成本法)的影响。

利润分享

以发行股票或其他方式向利益相关者(例如员工)分配公司的部分利润。

量利图/贡献图

用于显示销量或销售价格变动对于贡献和利润总额影响的图表。参见图表1.6。

获利指数

$$\frac{\text{现金流量现值}}{\text{初始投资额}}$$

该公式用于投资评估,代表了1

sents the net present value of each $1 invested in a project.

| 美元项目初始投资所对应的净现值。

project costing

See "contract costing" (cost accounting for cost objects).

项目成本核算

参见"合同成本核算"(关于成本项目的成本会计)。

qualitative factors

Factors that are relevant to a decision but are not expressed numerically.

定性因素

与决策有关但无法量化的因素。

quantitative factors

Factors that are relevant to a decision and are expressed numerically.

定量因素

与决策有关且可以量化的因素。

ratio, accounting rate of return

$$\frac{\text{Average annual profit from an investment}}{\text{Average investment}} \times 100\%$$

Sometimes used in investment appraisal, derived in the same way as return on investment. Unlike net present value and internal rate of return, the ratio is based on profits not cash flows. Exclusive use of this ratio is not recommended.

会计收益率

$$\frac{\text{年平均投资收益}}{\text{平均投资额}} \times 100\%$$

有时用于投资评估,与投资报酬率的计算方法相同。与净现值和内部收益率不同的是,该比率的计算基础是收益而不是现金流。不推荐单独使用该比率。

ratio analysis

When external stakeholders, such as potential investors and lenders, try to assess the performance of an entity, the most readily available source of information is the published accounts of the entity.

In trying to interpret the ratios calculated from the published accounts Figures, it is

比率分析

当潜在投资者和借款人等外部利益相关者试图评估一个实体的业绩时,最容易获得的信息来源是实体已发布的会计报表。

在解释根据会计报表中的数字计算的比率时,重要的是理解报表中数

important to understand the limitations of the published Figures.

字的局限性。

ratio, asset cover

资产担保比率

$$\frac{\text{Net tangible assets before deducting overdraft and other borrowings}}{\text{Total borrowings including overdraft}}$$

Indicates the safety of lenders' money. Net tangible assets are usually calculated after deducting trade payables(hence, net).

$$\frac{\text{扣除透支和其他借款之前的有形资产净额}}{\text{包括透支的借款总额}}$$

表明借款人资金的安全性。通常情况下,有形资产净额是扣除了贸易应付款的(因此是净额)。

ratio, asset value per share

每股资产价值

$$\frac{\text{Total assets} - \text{liabilities}}{\text{Number of issued equity shares}}$$

Shows the value of net assets per share and may aid investment and disinvestment decisions. Note that this ratio is equivalent to net worth per share.

$$\frac{\text{总资产} - \text{负债}}{\text{发行在外的普通股数量}}$$

表明了每股净资产的价值,可帮助做出投资和收回投资的决策。注意这个比率相当于每股资产净值。

ratio, bad debts

坏账率

$$\frac{\text{Bad debts}}{\text{Revenue on credit}} \times 100\%$$

Numerator and denominator should relate to the same period, bad debts should be calculated as an average Figure for the relevant time period.

$$\frac{\text{坏账金额}}{\text{信贷收入}} \times 100\%$$

分子和分母应该是同一时期的数字,坏账金额应以相关时期的平均值来计算。

$$\frac{\text{Bad debts}}{\text{Total receivables at a point in time}} \times 100\%$$

Indicates the significance of bad debts as a proportion of debtors.

$$\frac{\text{坏账金额}}{\text{某一时点应收账款总额}} \times 100\%$$

表明应收账款中坏账比例的严重程度。

ratio, capacity

产能比率

Capacity is usually measured in standard units, typically standard labour or machie hours in manufacturing, and, correspondingly, standard hours in professional practices

产能通常是以标准单位来衡量的,在制造业中,标准单位是标准人工或机器工时,而会计师或咨询顾问等专业服务则是标准小时。经常使用的

such as accountants and consultants. The more commonly used capacity levels are：

full capacity：Output achievable if sales orders，supplies，workforce，for example，were all available.

practical capacity：Full capacity less an allowance for known，unavoidable volume losses.

budgeted capacity：Standard hours planned for the budget period，taking account of，for example，budgeted sales，workforce and expected efficiency.

normal capacity：Measure of the long-run average level of capacity that may be expected. This is often used in setting the budgeted fixed overhead absorption rate（giving it stability over time，although budgeted fixed overhead volume variances may be produced as a consequence）.

On the following given data，the related ratios are set out below：

Full capacity standard hours　　100

Practical capacity standard hours 95

Budgeted capacity（budgeted input hours，90 at 90% efficiency）　　81

Actual input hours　　85

Standard hours produced　　68

idle capacity ratio：

$$\frac{\text{Practical capacity} - \text{budgeted capacity}}{\text{Practial capacity}} \times 100\%$$

$$= \frac{95-81}{95} \times 100\% = 15\%$$

Indicates the budgeted shortfall in capacity as a proportion of practical capacity.

production volume ratio：

$$\frac{\text{standard hours produced} \times 100}{\text{Budgeted capacity}} = \frac{68}{81} \times 100\% = 84\%$$

Shows the actual output as a proportion of budgeted output.

产能水平有：

满负荷产能：当销售订单、物料以及劳动力等全部都可以获得时的最大产出。

实际产能：满负荷产能减去不可避免的已知产能损耗。

预算产能：考虑了销售预算、劳动力以及预期效率，针对预算期制定的标准工时。

正常产能：可预期的长期产能平均水平。通常在确定预算固定间接费用分摊率时使用（虽然预算固定间接费用会产生差异，但我们假定一段时间内它是固定不变的）。

基于给出的数据，相关比率如下：

满负荷产能标准时间　100 h

实际产能标准时间　　95 h

预算产能标准时间（预算投入时间，90%有效）　　81 h

实际投入时间　　85 h

标准生产时间　　68 h

闲置生产能力比率：

$$\frac{\text{实际生产能力} - \text{预算生产能力}}{\text{实际生产能力}} \times 100\%$$

$$= \frac{95-81}{95} \times 100\% = 15\%$$

表明预算产能的不足是实际产能的一部分。

产量比率：

$$\frac{\text{标准生产时间}}{\text{预算生产能力}} \times 100\% = \frac{68}{81} \times 100\% = 84\%$$

表示实际产出占预算产出的比例。

production efficiency ratio：

$$\frac{\text{Standard hours produced}}{\text{Actual hours}} \times 100\% = \frac{68}{85} \times 100\% = 80\%$$

Measures the relationship between output produced and productive time taken，which may be measured in either direct labour or machine hours，as appropriate.

生产效率比：

$$\frac{\text{标准生产时间}}{\text{实际时间}} \times 100\% = \frac{68}{85} \times 100\% = 80\%$$

衡量产出和生产时间关系时,生产时间可以用直接劳动时间或者机器小时来确定,这样比较恰当。

ratio，capital/asset turnover

$$\frac{\text{Revenue for the year}}{\text{Average capital employed in year}}$$

Expresses the number of times that capital is covered by sales in a year or the revenue generated by each $1 of catital emplopyed. Capital employedis usually calculated as either：

(a) total net assets (fixed assets + current assets- current liabilities) or

(b) captial employed(equity + long-term debt)

The two methods are equivalent.

资本/资产周转率

$$\frac{\text{年收入}}{\text{年均占用资本}}$$

表示1年中资本运用的次数或者1美元的资本可以获得的收入。占用的资本通常有以下两种计算方法：

(a) 净资产总额(固定资产 + 流动资产 - 流动负债)

(b) 长期资本(股权 + 长期负债)

两者的计算结果是相等的。

ratio，contribution per unit of limiting factor

$$\frac{\text{Product/service contribution}}{\text{Product/service usage of units of limiting factor}}$$

Used in short-term decision making to measure the contribution to fixed overhead and profit generated by the use of each unit of limiting factor. This is used to rank alternative uses of the limiting factor.

单位限定因素的贡献比率

$$\frac{\text{产量/服务贡献}}{\text{产量/服务的限制因素使用量}}$$

在短期决策中,用于衡量使用每个单位限定因素所产生的固定费用和利润,可以对可供选择的限制因素进行排序。

ratio，contribution to sales

$$\frac{\text{Revenue} - \text{all variable costs}}{\text{Revenue}} \times 100\%$$

Of particular use in product profit planning and as a means of ranking alternative products. Also important in breakeven

销售贡献比率

$$\frac{\text{收入} - \text{所有变动成本}}{\text{收入}} \times 100\%$$

特别应用于产品利润规划,以及作为一种工具对两种产品进行排序。对于假设的固定产品组合收支平衡问

problems that assume a constant product mix.

Note, although contribution to sales ratio can be used to rank products, it cannot be used to solve limiting factor problems (unless the limiting factor is sales revenue).

题,该比率同样具有重要的作用。

注:虽然销售贡献比率可以对产品进行排序,但是不能够解决限定因素问题(除非限定因素就是销售收入)。

ratio, creditor days

See "ratio, payables days".

应付账款天数

参见"应付账款天数"。

ratio, debt

$$\text{Debt ratio} = \frac{\text{total long term debt}}{\text{total assets}}$$

This can provide very useful information for creditors as it measures the availability of assets in the business in relation to the total debt.

负债比率

$$\text{负债比率} = \frac{\text{长期负债总额}}{\text{资产总额}}$$

这个比率给债权人提供了有用的信息,可以衡量相对于总负债而言,资产的可用性。

ratio, debtor days

See "ratio, receivables days".

应收账款天数

参见"应收账款天数"。

ratio, dividend cover

$$\frac{\text{Earning per share}}{\text{Dividend per share}}$$

Indicates the number of times the profits attributable to the equity shareholders cover the net dividends payable for the period.

股利保障倍数

$$\frac{\text{每股收益}}{\text{每股股利}}$$

表明归属于普通股股东的利润对于应付股利的保障程度。

ratio, fixed asset turnover

$$\frac{\text{Revenue for the year}}{\text{Average net book value of fixed assets}}$$

Indicated the revenue generated by each $1 of fixed assets, or the number of times fixed assets are turned over in the year.

固定资产周转率

$$\frac{\text{本年度收入}}{\text{固定资产平均账面净值}}$$

表示 1 美元固定资产产生的收入,或者 1 年内固定资产周转的次数。

ratio, gearing/leverage

Relates to financial gearing, which is the relationship between an entity's borrowings, which includes both prior charge capital, for example preference shares, and long-term debt, and its share-holders' funds (ordinary share capital plus reserves). Gearing calculations can be made in a number of ways, and may be based on capital values or on earning/interest relationships. Overdrafts and interest paid thereon may also be included.

$$\frac{\text{Profit before interest and tax}}{\text{Profit before tax}}$$

Shows the effect of interest on the operating profit (income gearing). See also "ratio, interest cover".

$$\frac{\text{Total long-term debt}}{\text{Shareholder' funds} + \text{long-term debt}}$$

Shows the proportion of long-term financing which is being supplied by debt (balance sheet gearing).

$$\frac{\text{Total long-term debt}}{\text{Total assets}}$$

A measure of the capacity to redeem debt obligations by the sale of assets.

$$\frac{\frac{\text{Operating}}{\text{cashflows}} - \frac{\text{taxation}}{\text{paid}} - \text{returns on} \frac{\text{ivestment and}}{\text{servicing of finance}}}{\text{Repayments of debt due within one year}}$$

Measure ability to redeem debt. An entity with a high propotion of prior charge capital to shareholders' funds is high geared, and is low geared if the reverse situation applies.

ratio, gross profit to sales revenue (gross profit margin)

$$\frac{\text{Sales} - \text{cost of sales}}{\text{Sales for the period}} \times 100\%$$

Used to gain an insight into the

杠杆率

与财务杠杆有关，反映的是实体的债务资本（包括具有优先索取权的资本，如优先股和长期借款）与权益资本（普通股股本和留存利润）之间的关系。可以基于资本价值或者利润与利息关系等多种方式来计算杠杆率。计算时，应包括透支和支付的利息。

$$\frac{\text{息税前利润}}{\text{税前利润}}$$

与"利息保障倍数"一样，该公式表明了利息对经营利润（利润杠杆）的影响。

$$\frac{\text{长期负债总额}}{\text{权益资本} + \text{长期负债}}$$

该公式表明了长期融资中债务的比例（资产负债杠杆）。

$$\frac{\text{长期债务总额}}{\text{资产总额}}$$

该公式是对通过出售资产偿还借款的能力的衡量。

$$\frac{\frac{\text{经营现}}{\text{金流}} - \frac{\text{支付的}}{\text{税款}} - \frac{\text{投资和金融}}{\text{服务收益}}}{1 \text{年内到期的债务}}$$

该公式衡量了偿还借款的能力。如果实体拥有的具有优先索取权的资本高于股东权益资本，则属于高杠杆，反之则是低杠杆。

毛利率

$$\frac{\text{销售收入} - \text{销售成本}}{\text{当期销售收入}} \times 100\%$$

被用于深入了解生产成本、采购

relationship between production/purchasing costs and sales revenues.

成本和销售收入之间的关系。

ratio, interest cover

$$\frac{\text{Profit before interest and tax}}{\text{Interest payable}}$$

Used by lenders to determine vulnerability of interest payments to a drop in profit.

利息保障倍数

$$\frac{\text{息税前利润}}{\text{应付利息}}$$

债权人用来判断当利润下降时利息支付的安全性。

ratio, inventory days

number of days' inventory：

$$\frac{\text{Stock value}}{\text{Average daily cost of sales in period}}$$

Number of days' inventory at the forecast or recent usage rate. Can be applied to finished goods，raw material and work in progress by using appropriate numerators and denominators.

number of weeks' inventory：

The efiiciency of inventory utilisation is indicated by：

$$\frac{\text{Finished goods stock}}{\text{Average weekly despatches}}$$

$$\frac{\text{Raw material stock}}{\text{Average weekly raw material usage}}$$

$$\frac{\text{Work in progress}}{\text{Average weekly production}}$$

These ratios are normally calculated using appropriate values although，in certain circumstances，quantities may be used.

存货周转天数

存货周转天数：

$$\frac{\text{存货价值}}{\text{日平均销售成本}}$$

预期或在近期使用水平上的存货周转天数。通过使用恰当的分子和分母,该指标可以应用于产成品、原材料和在产品。

存货周转周数：

存货使用效率可以通过以下比率表示：

$$\frac{\text{产成品}}{\text{周平均发货量}}$$

$$\frac{\text{原材料}}{\text{周平均原材料使用量}}$$

$$\frac{\text{在产品}}{\text{周平均生产量}}$$

这三个比率通常使用价值量来计算,但在特定条件下可能会使用实物量来计算。

ratio，length of order book

$$\frac{\text{Sales value of orders outstanding}}{\text{Sales value of production per day/week/month}}$$

The sales value of production may be based on planned，current or available capacity production.

订单周期

$$\frac{\text{未完成订单销售价值}}{\text{每日/每周/每月产品销售价值}}$$

产品销售价值的基础可以是计划、当前或可用的生产能力。

ratio(s), liquidity

Relate to working capital and indicate the ability to meet liabilities from assets available. The most commonly used are：

acid test/quick ratio：

$$\frac{\text{Current assets} - \text{stock at end of period}}{\text{Current liabilities at end of period}}$$

Indicates the ability to pay creditors in the short term.

current ratio：

$$\frac{\text{Current assets at end of period}}{\text{Current liabilities at end of period}}$$

An overall measure of liquidity.

ratio, margin of safety

$$\frac{\text{Forecast revenue} - \text{breakeven revenue}}{\text{Forecast revenue}} \times 100\%$$

Indicates the percentage by which forecast revenue exceeds or falls short of that required to break even.

ratio, net profit to sales revenue (net profit margin %)

$$\frac{\text{Net profit before interest and tax}}{\text{Revenue}} \times 100\%$$

A key profitability ratio. If the numeratoris not multiplied by 100 it shows the profit generated by each $1 of sales.

ratio, payables days

$$\frac{\text{Average trade payables}}{\text{Average daily purchases on credit terms}}$$

Indicates the average time taken，in calendar days，to pay for supplies received on credit. Adjustment is needed if the ratio is materially distorted by value added or other

流动比率

与营运资本有关,表明通过流动资产偿付债务的能力。最常用的比率有：

酸性测试/速动比率：

$$\frac{\text{流动资产} - \text{期末存货}}{\text{期末流动负债}}$$

该公式反映短期偿债能力。

流动比率：

$$\frac{\text{期末流动资产}}{\text{期末流动负债}}$$

该比率是对流动性的综合衡量。

安全边际比率

$$\frac{\text{预期收入} - \text{盈亏平衡收入}}{\text{预期收入}} \times 100\%$$

该比率表示预期收入超过或低于盈亏平衡收入的百分比。

销售净利率

$$\frac{\text{息税前净利润}}{\text{收入}} \times 100\%$$

关键的盈利能力比率。如果分子不乘以 100%,则该指标表示每 1 元销售额产生的利润。

应付账款天数

$$\frac{\text{平均应付账款}}{\text{日平均赊购额}}$$

表示支付赊购商品应付款的平均时间。如果该指标因增加值或其他税收因素而被严重扭曲,则应进行调整。

taxes.

ratio, price/earnings (P/E ratio)

$$\frac{\text{Market price per share}}{\text{Earning per share}}$$

Shows the number of years it would take to recoup an equity investment form its share of the attributable profit. The P/E ratio values the shares of the company as a multiple of current or attributable profit. The P/E ratio values the shares of the company as a multiple of current or prospective earnings. The P/E ratio is the most common way of reporting the relationship between earnings and share prices, although its inverse, the earnings yield, is probably intuitively easier to grasp. A low P/E ratio implies a high earnings yield. A low P/E ratio might indicate that the market perceives earnings to be "low quality".

ratio, profit per employee

$$\frac{\text{Profit for the year before interest and tax}}{\text{Average number of employees}}$$

Indication of the effectiveness of the employment of staff. When there are full-and part-time employees, full-time equivalents should be used. See "sales per employee".

ratio pyramid

The analysis of a primary ratio into mathematically linked secondary ratios. For example：

primary ratio

Ratio $a = b \times c$. Ratios b and c can be

市盈率

$$\frac{\text{每股市价}}{\text{每股收益}}$$

表明了从可分配利润中回收股权投资所需要的时间。可以用市盈率乘以目前或未来的收益来计算公司的价值。市盈率是最常见的报告收益和股票价格之间关系的比率,尽管市盈率的倒数——收益率,可能在直观上更容易把握。低市盈率意味着高盈余收益率。低市盈率可能表明市场认为收益是"低质量的"。

每员工利润率

$$\frac{\text{息税前本年利润}}{\text{平均员工人数}}$$

表明员工聘用有效性的指标。当同时存在全职和兼职员工时,应使用全职员工当量来衡量。参见"每员工销售额"。

比率金字塔

对初级指标进行分析,将其与二级指标建立起数学关系。例如:

初级比率

比率 $a = b \times c$。如有需要,比率

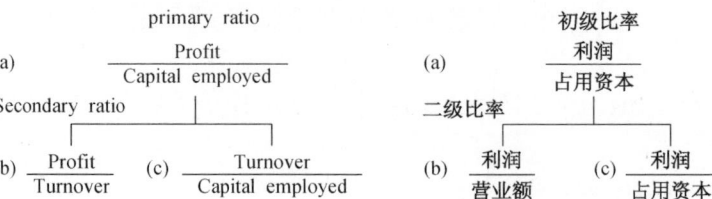

analysed by further ratios if desired. The pyramid continues with further analysis of the secondary ratios. See Figures 1.22，1.23 and Figure 1.24.

b 和比率c 可以进一步分解为其他比率进行分析。金字塔可以通过对二级比率进行分析来进一步地分拆。参见图表 1.22,图表 1.23 和图表 1.24。

FIGURE 1.22   RATIO PYRAMID FOR A MANUFACTURER

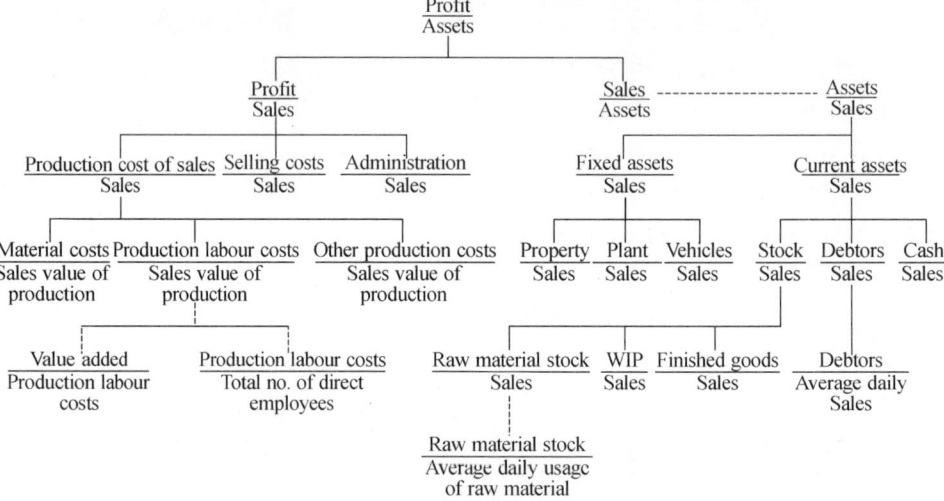

图表 1.22   一个制造商的比率金字塔

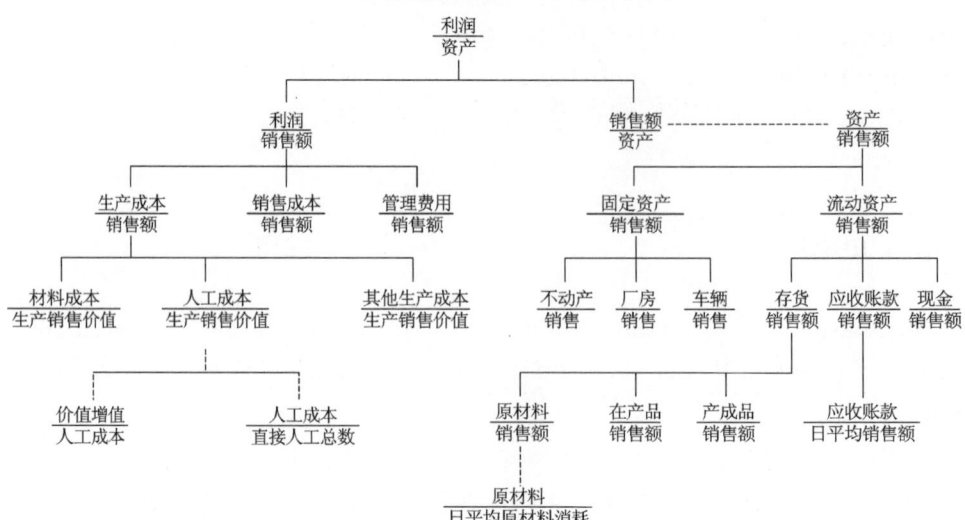

FIGURE 1. 23   RATIO PYRAMID FOR A RETAILER

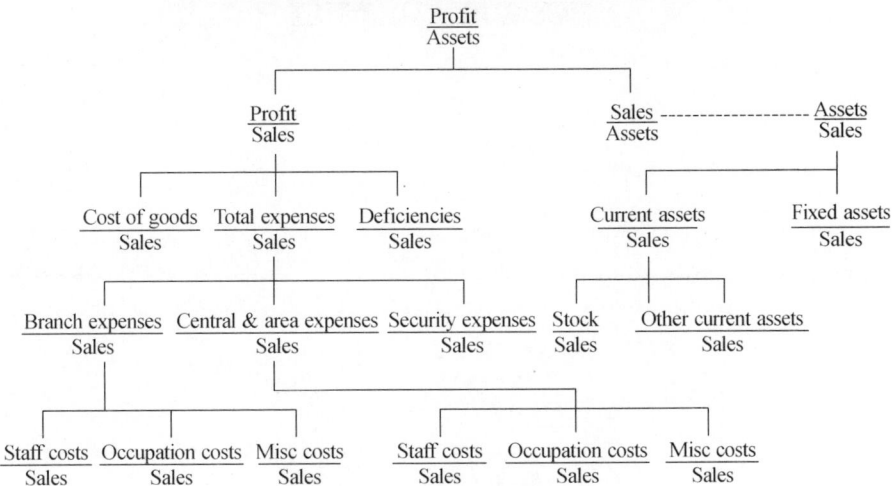

图表 1. 23   一个零售商的比率金字塔

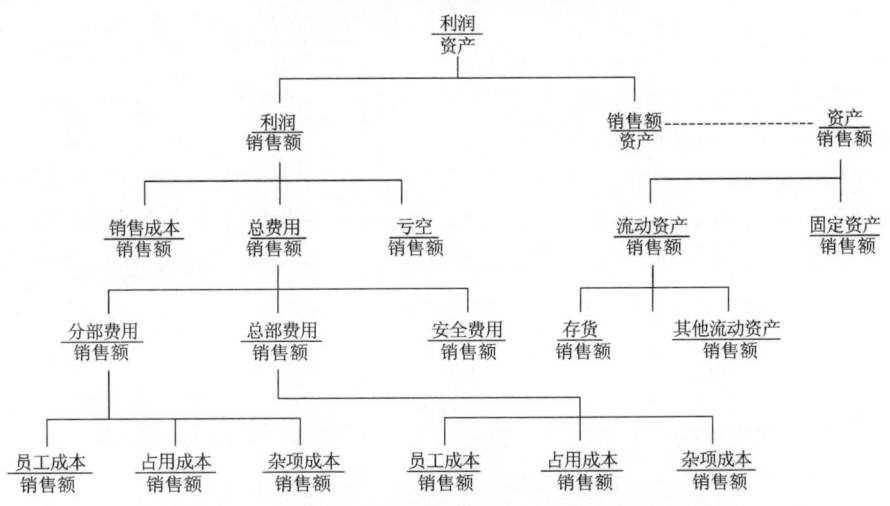

FIGURE 1. 24   RATIO PYRAMID FOR SERVICES

图表 1.24　服务比率金字塔

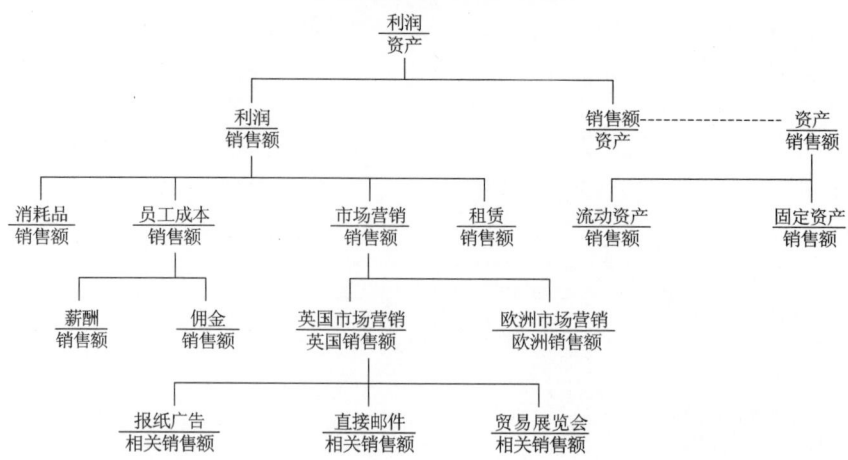

ratio, receivables days

$$\frac{\text{Average trade receivalbles}}{\text{Average daily revenue on credit terms}}$$

Indicates the average time taken，in calendar days，to receive payment from credit customers. Adjustment is needed if the ratio is materially distorted by value added or other taxes.

应收账款周转天数

$$\frac{\text{平均应收账款}}{\text{日平均赊销额}}$$

表明收回赊销产品款项所需要的平均时间。如果该指标因附加值或其他税收因素而被严重扭曲,则应进行调整。

ratio, sales per employee

$$\frac{\text{Revenue for the year}}{\text{Average number of employees}}$$

Indicator of labour productivity. See "profit per employee".

每位员工销售额

$$\frac{\text{年度销售额}}{\text{平均员工人数}}$$

员工生产率指标。参见"每员工利润率"。

ratio, stock turnover

See "ratio，inventory days".

存货周转率

参见"存货周转天数"。

realizable value

See "net realizable value".

可变现价值

参见"可变现净值"。

reciprocal cost allocation

Method of reallocating（strictly apportioning）service centre costs in a number of iterations until all service costs have been recharged to user centres. Can also be formulated as a set of equations and solved by matrix algebra. See "re-apportion（apportioning）".

recognition

The process of incorporating in the balance sheet or income statement an item that meets the definition of an element of financial statements and satisfies the following criteria：

（a）it is probable that any future economic benefit associated with the item will flow to or from the entity；and

（b）the item has a cost or value that can be reliably measured（IASB framework）.

rejects/defects

Units of output which fail a set quality standard and are subsequently rectified，sold as substandard or disposed of as scrap.

relevant costs/revenues

Costs and revenues appropriate to a specific management decision. These are represented by future cash flows whose magnitude will vary depending upon the outcome of the management decision made. If stock is used，the relevant cost in the determination of the

交互成本分配法

一种多次重复分配（严格分配）服务中心成本、直至所有服务成本都被使用中心承担的成本分配办法。也可以利用一组方程式，通过矩阵代数来解决成本交叉分配的问题。参见"再分配"。

确认

对满足财务报表要素定义并满足下列条件的资产负债表或损益表项目进行合并的过程：

（a）与该项目有关的未来经济利益很可能将会流入或流出企业；

（b）该项目的成本或价值能够可靠地计量（国际会计准则理事会框架）。

不良品/残次品

没有达到质量标准的产品，改良后作为次品出售或按废料处理。

相关成本/收入

与一项特定管理决策有关的成本与收入，未来现金流的大小取决于管理决策结果。如果涉及股票，那么决定交易盈利性的相关成本是股票的替代成本，不是已经成为沉没成本的初始购买价格。

profitability of the transaction, would be the cost of replacing the stock, not its original purchase price, which is a sunk cost.

Abandonment analysis, based on relevant cost and revenues, is the process of determining whether or not it is more profitable to discontinue a product or service than to continue it.

基于相关成本和收入的放弃分析是指确定终止提供一项产品或服务是否比继续提供更为有利的过程。

relevant range

相关范围

Actitvity levels within which assumptions about cost behaviour in breakeven analysis remain valid.

假定成本习性在盈亏分析时仍然有效的活动水平。

replacement price

重置价格

Price at which identical goods or capital equipment could be purchased at the date of valuation.

在估值日,相同商品或者资本设备的购买价格。

residual income

剩余收益

Profit minus a charge for capital employed in the period. The calculation is exactly the same as that for economic value added.

利润减去相关期间的资本成本。本指标的计算过程和经济增加值相同。

However, in the latter case, accounting profit is often adjusted before the calculation of economic value added. See "economic value added".

然而,在后面的案例中,在计算经济附加值之前,通常要对会计利润进行调整。参见"经济附加值"。

retained earnings

留存收益

A company can only use internal sources of finance to fund new projects if it has enough cash in hand.

企业如果拥有充足的现金,那么企业就只能使用内部资金来对新项目进行投资。

The level of retained earnings reflects

留存收益的水平反映了公司多年

the amount of profit accumulated over the company's life. It is not the same as cash.

的累积利润,不等同于现金。

return on capital employed （ROCE）

投资资本回报率

$$\frac{\text{Profit before interest and tax}}{\text{Average capital employed}} \times 100\%$$

$$\frac{\text{息税前利润}}{\text{平均投入资本额}} \times 100\%$$

Indicates the productivity of capital employed. The denominator is normally calculated as the average of the capital employed at the beginning and the end of the year. Problems of seasonality，new capital introduced or other factors may necessitate taking the average of a number of periods within the year. The ROCE is known as the primary ratio in a ratio pyramid. See "capital employed".

表示投入资本的生产率。分母通常使用期初期末投入资本的平均值。考虑到季节性问题,新投入资本或其他因素可能会需要取 1 年内某些期间的平均值。投入资本回报率是比例金字塔中的初级比率。参见"占用资本"。

return on equity

净资产收益率

$$\frac{\text{Profit after interest and tax}}{\text{Ordinary share capital} + \text{reserves}}$$

$$\frac{\text{息税后利润}}{\text{普通股股本} + \text{留存收益}}$$

Form of return on capital employed which measures the return to the owners on their investment in an entity.

投入资本回报率的一种形式,衡量了权益所有者对一个实体投资的回报。

return on investment （ROI）

投资报酬率

$$\frac{\text{Profit before interest and tax}}{\text{Average capital employed}}$$

$$\frac{\text{息税前利润}}{\text{平均投入资本额}}$$

Often used to assess managers' performance. Managers are responsible for all assets （normally defined as non-current assets plus net current assets）. See "ratio，capital turnover".

经常被用于评估管理者绩效。管理者需对全部资产(通常指非流动资产加上净流动资产)负责。参见"资本周转率"。

return on sales

销售利润率

See "profit margin".

参见"利润率"。

scrap

Discarded material having some value.

废料

有一些价值的废弃材料。

shadow price

Increase in value which would be created by having available one additional unit of a limiting rescurce at its original cost. This represents the opportunity cost of not having the use of the one extra unit. This information is routinely produced when mathematical programming（especially linear programming）is used to model activity.

影子价格

按照原始成本投入有限资源增加一个额外单位所带来的价值增量。这反映不增加一个额外单位的机会成本。通常,建模活动中使用数学规划（尤其是线性规划）会产生此信息。

Standard

Benchmark measurement of resource usage or revenue or profit generation，set in defined conditions. Standard can be set on a number of bases：

（a）On an ex ante estimate of expected performance；

（b）On an ex post estimate of attainable performance；

（c）On a prior period level of performance by the same organisation；

（d）On the level of performance achieved by comparable organisations；or

（e）On the level of performance required to meet organisational objectives.

Standards may also be set at attainable levels that assume efficient levels of operation，but that include allowance for normal loss，waste and machine down time，or at ideal levels that make no allowance for the above losses，and are only attainable under

标准

在确定的条件下,用于衡量资源使用量、收入或产生的利润的基准。可以在一系列基础上制定标准:

（a）基于对预期绩效的事前估计;

（b）基于对可实现绩效的事后估计;

（c）基于同一组织之前时期的绩效水平;

（d）基于可比组织实现的绩效水平;

（e）基于能够实现组织目标的必要绩效水平。

标准可以基于假定有效操作之上的可实现水平来制定,但是要包括正常损失、浪费和停工时间;抑或是不包括上述损失,在最优条件下所能达到的理想水平。使用不同的标准会对不同层次的员工激励产生重大的影响。

the most favourable conditions. The effect of different levels on staff motivation will be an important influence on the type of standards that are used. See "standard，ex ante"，and "ex post".

参见"事前标准"和"事后标准"。

standard cost card/standard product specification

标准成本卡/标准产品说明书

Document or digital record detailing for each individual product，the standard inputs required for production as well as the standard selling price. Inputs are normally divided into labour，material and overhead categories，and both price and quantity information is shown for each.

详细记录每一个产品、生产产品所必需的标准投入以及标准售价的文档或电子记录。投入通常分为人工、材料和期间费用，分别显示价格和数量信息。

standard direct labour cost

标准直接人工成本

Planned cost of direct labour.

（standard direct labour time for one unit of product×standard labour rate）

There are separate calculations for different processes and/or grades of labour.

直接人工计划成本。

（每单位产品标准直接人工时间×标准人工单位费率）

对于不同的过程或等级的人工有不同的计算方式。

standard，ex ante

事前标准

Before the event. An ex ante budget or standard is set before a period of activity commences.

事件发生之前制定的标准。事前预算或标准建立于活动开始之前。

standard，ex post

事后标准

After the event. An ex post budget，or standard，is set after the end of period of activity，when it can represent the optimum achievable level of performance in the conditions which were experienced. Thus the budget can be flexed，and standards can

事件发生之后制定的标准。事后预算或标准建立于活动结束之后，代表了过去条件下可实现的最佳绩效水平。因此，预算可以被改变，标准可以反映技术和价格水平等变化无法预期的因素。可在复杂的成本与收入模型

reflect factors such as unanticipated changes in technology and in price levels. This approach may be used in conjunction with sophisticated cost and revenue modelling to determine how far both the plan and the achieved results differed from the performance that would have been expected in the circumstances which were experienced.

中使用该方法,以确定在已经过去的条件下,计划和实际绩效结果的偏离程度。

standard hour or minute

标准小时或分钟

Amount of work achievable, at a standard efficiency levels, in an hour or minute.

在标准效率水平上,1小时或1分钟内完成的工作量。

standard performance – labour

标准绩效-人工

Level of efficiency which appropriately trained, motivated and resourced employees can achieve in the long-run.

经过适当培训、具有工作积极性且配备了充足资源的员工在长期能够达到的效率水平。

stock (inventory) valuation

存货估价

average cost: Used to price issues of goods or materials at the weighted average cost of all units held.

first-in, first-out(FIFO): Used to price issues of goods or materials based on the cost of the oldest units held, irrespective of the sequence in which the actual issue of units held takes place. Closing stock is, therefore, valued at the cost of the oldest purchases.

last-in, first-out(LIFO): Used to price issues of goods or materials based on the cost of the most recently received units. Cost of sales in the income statement is, therefore, valued at the cost of the most recent purchases. LIFO is permitted under US GAAP but is not permitted by IAS 2(or SSAP 9 in the UK).

平均成本法:根据所有持有存货的加权平均成本来确定商品或原材料的价格问题。

先进先出法:基于最早持有的存货的成本来确定商品或原材料的价格问题,与实际发出的存货的顺序无关。因此,期末存货以最早购买的存货的成本来计量。

后进先出法:基于最近持有的存货的成本来确定商品或原材料的价格问题。因此,利润表上的销售成本以最近购买的成本进行计量。美国公认会计原则允许使用后进先出,但是《国际会计准则第2号——存货》和英国《标准会计实务公告第9号》不允许

standard cost: All units held as stock are valued at a standard cost so that units issued and closing stock are valued at a standard cost so that units issued and closing stock are valued at standard cost, with any variance between actual costs incurred and standard cost reported in the income statement in the period in which it is incurred. All the above methods value stock to be valued at the lower of cost and net realisable value. See "fair value less costs to sell".

strategic business unit

Section, usually a division, within a larger organisation that has a significant degree of autonomy, typically being responsible for developing and marketing its own products and services.

super variable costing

See "throughput accounting".

tableau de bord

Performance measurement approach, similar to the balance scorecard, but developed and commonly used in France. A tableau de bord is a dashboard, such as that found in a car or aircraft. The tableau, in strategic management, sets out the various performance indicators in related groups.

theory of constraints (TOC)

Procedure based on identifying

使用。

标准成本法：所有存货，包括已出库和期末的存货都以标准成本计量，并且在利润表上报告当期实际成本和标准成本的差异。以上所有方法都以成本与可变现净值孰低来计量存货价值。参见"扣除销售成本原的公允价值"。

战略业务单元

指在大型组织内具有相当大自主权的分部或分支机构，这些分部负责自身产品与服务的开发和营销。

超级变动成本法

参见"有效产出会计"。

仪表盘

一种绩效衡量方法，与平衡计分卡相似，源于并在法国广泛使用。仪表盘是一种类似于汽车、飞机中的仪表板。在战略管理中，仪表盘会在相关组别内列示多个绩效指标。

约束理论

识别瓶颈资源（约束条件），将瓶

bottlenecks （constraints）, maximising their use, subordinating other facilities to the demands of the bottleneck facilities, alleviating bottlenecks and re-evaluating the whole system.

（Goldratt created this concept）.

颈资源的使用程度发挥到最大化,使其他设备服从于瓶颈设备的需求,从而缓解瓶颈并重新评估整个系统的过程。

（高德拉特创造了这一概念）。

throughput

有效产出

Term defined, in work by Goldratt, as sales minus material and component costs. Similar to contribution except material is considered the only variable cost. Goldratt argues that labour costs should be treated as fixed. In Goldratt's analysis operating expense is all non-material costs and inventory cost is defined as the cost of assets employed.

高德拉特将其定义为销售减去原材料和要素成本。与边际贡献相类似,原材料是唯一的变动成本。高德拉特认为人工成本是固定的。在他的分析中,经营费用是非原材料成本,存货成本被定义为属于投入资产的成本。

throughput accounting （TA）

有效产出会计

Variable cost accounting presentation based on the definition of throughput （sales minus material and component costs）. Sometimes referred to as super variable costing because only material costs are treated as variable.

建立在"有效产出"定义（销售收入减去原材料和要素成本）上的变动成本会计。有时,在只有原材料成本被当成是变动成本的情况下也被称为"超级变动成本法"。

throughput per bottleneck minute

每瓶颈分钟有效产出

Method of ranking products that share the same （bottleneck） facility. Very similar to the use of contribution per unit of limiting factor.

对使用同一（瓶颈）设备的产品进行排序的方法。与每单位限制因素的贡献非常类似。

throughput ratios

有效产出率

Several ratios were defined by Galloway and Waldron based on the definition of

加洛韦和沃尔德伦基于有效产出的定义界定了几个比率。有效产出会

throughput. The TA(throughput accounting) ratio is:

$$\frac{\text{Throughput per bottleneck minute}}{\text{Factory cost per bottleneck minute}}$$

Note: Galloway and Waldron define factory cost in the same way that Goldratt defines operating expense. See "throughput".

If the TA ratio greater than I the product in question is "profitable" because, if all capacity were devoted to that product, the throughout generated would exceed the total factory cost. If there was a bottleneck products could be ranked by a variant of the TA ratio (although the ranking is the same as that derived by the use of throughput per bottleneck minute). Other performance ratios suggested include:

$$\frac{\text{Throuput}}{\text{Labour cost}} \text{ and } \frac{\text{Throughput}}{\text{Matreial cost}}$$

计比率是:

$$\frac{\text{每瓶颈分钟的有效产出}}{\text{每瓶颈分钟的工厂成本}}$$

注:加洛韦和沃尔德伦对于工厂成本的定义与高德拉特对于经营费用的定义是相同的。参见"有效产出"。

如果有效产出会计比率大于1,则此产品是"盈利的",因为如果将所有产能投入到此产品,产生的有效产出将大于工厂总成本。如果存在瓶颈,则产品可以根据有效产出会计比率来排序(尽管和每瓶颈分钟有效产出的排序结果是一样的)。其他绩效比率包括:

$$\frac{\text{有效产出}}{\text{人工成本}} \text{和} \frac{\text{有效产出}}{\text{原材料成本}}$$

transfer price

Price at which goods or services are transferred between different units in the same company. May be set on a number of bases, such as marginal cost, full cost, market price or negotiation. For the transfer of goods between units in different countries, tax implications mean that the respective governments have to accept the method used. They are likely to insist on arm's-length transfer prices.

转移价格

商品或服务在同一公司的不同部门之间流转时的价格,可在多个基础上设定,如原材料成本、总成本、市场价或者协商价等。当商品在不同的国家之间流转时会涉及税收问题,不同国家政府需要商定解决办法,一般会采用公平交易转移价格。

uniform accounting

System by which different entities in the same industry adopt common concepts, principles and assumption in order to generate

统一会计核算

同一行业的不同企业采用相同的概念、原则和假定,从而使得生成的会计信息可以进行企业间比较,或者是

accounting information that facilitates inter-entity comparison or a system of classifying financial accounts in a similar manner within defined business sectors of a national economy to ensure comparability.

在国民经济所定义的业务部门内以相似的方式区分财务账户从而确保可比性。

value added

附加值

Traditionally the difference between sales revenue and the cost of materials and bought-out services. Alternatively，it might be calculated as the sum of profit，interest and all conversion costs. Recently，more commonly used in the context of economic value added. See "economic value added".

传统意义上指的是销售收入减去原材料和外包服务成本后得出的价值。也可以计算利润、利息以及所有转换成本之和。近年来,主要以"经济附加值"的概念出现。参见"经济增加值"。

value analysis

价值分析

Systematic interdisciplinary examination of factors affecting the cost of a product or service，in order to devise means of achieving the specified purpose most economically at the required standard of quality and reliability.

对于影响产品或服务成本的因素进行系统性的跨领域检查,旨在设计以最经济的方式、按照既定的质量标准和可靠性实现特定目标的方法。

value driver

价值驱动因素

Activity or organisational focus which enhances the perceived value of a product or service in the perception of the consumer，and which therefore creates value for the producer. Advanced technology, reliability or reputation for customer care may be value drivers.

站在消费者的角度,提升产品或服务的感知价值的行为或组织重点活动,从而为生产者创造价值。价值驱动因素包括先进技术和客户服务的可靠性与声誉。

value engineering

价值工程

① Redesign of an activity，product or

对于一项作业、产品或服务的再

service so that value to the customer is enhanced while costs are reduced (or, at least, increase by less than the resulting price increase).

设计,从而实现在降低成本(或者至少是成本增加的程度小于价格的增加)的同时提升对消费者的价值。

Variance

Difference between a planned, budgeted or standard cost and the actual cost incurred. The same comparisons may be made for revenues.

差异

计划成本、预算成本或标准成本与实际成本之间的差额。也可以对销售额进行同样的比较。

variance, administrative cost

Measurement of the extent of any over- or underspend on administrative costs.

(budgeted cost of administration – actual cost)

管理费用差异

衡量超支或少支管理费用的程度。

(预算管理费用 – 实际费用)

variance analysis

Evaluation of performance by means of variances, whose timely reporting should maximise the opportunity for managerial action. See Figure 1.35.

差异分析

通过差异对绩效进行评估,及时报告可以最大化管理行为的机会。参见图表1.35。

variance, budget

Difference, for each cost or revenue element in a budget, between the budgeted amount and the actual cost or revenue. Where flexible budgeting is employed, it is the difference between the flexed budget and the actual value.

预算差异

在预算中,各个成本或收入因素的预算数和实际值的差额。当使用弹性预算时,预算差异指的是弹性预算和实际值之间的差额。

variance, direct labour efficiency

Standard labour cost of any change from the standard level of labour efficiency.

[(actual production in standard hours – actual hours worked) × standard direct labour rate per hour]

直接人工效率差异

不同标准人工效率水平导致标准人工成本的变化。

[(实际产量的标准生产时间 – 实际生产时间) × 每小时标准直接人工费用]

See Figure 1.29.

参见图表1.29。

variance, direct labour idle time

This variance, occurs when the hours paid exceed the hours worked and there is an extra cost caused by this idle time. Its computation increases the accurancy of the labour efficiency variance.

［(hours paid − hours worked) × standard direct labour rate per hour］

variance, direct labour mix

Subdivision of the direct labour effiency variance. If grades of labour can be substituted the mix variance measures the cost of any variation from the standard mix of grades.

［(actual hours for grade − hours for grade based on total labour hours split in standard proportions) × (weighted average cost per hour − standard cost per hour)］

Alternatively, the caculation can be made without reference to the relative cost of the various labour inputs.

［(hours for grade based on total labour hours split in standard proportions − actual labour hours for grade) × standard cost per hour］

When the individual grade variances are summed the same total mix variance is calculated. The first method is recommended because the individual grade variances are meaningful, whereas in the second method they are not.

variance, direct labour rate

Indicates the actual cost of any change from

直接人工闲置时间差异

支付报酬的工作时数超过实际工作时数的差异，由闲置时间所引起的额外成本。通过计算该指标，可以提高人工效率差异的准确性。

［(支付报酬的工时数 − 实际工时数) × 每小时标准直接人工费用］

直接人工组合差异

对于直接人工效率差异的进一步细分。如果可以对人工进行分级，就可以用分级后的人工代替分级的标准组合。

［(某级别的实际工作时间 − 基于总时间按标准比例分配的某级别工作时间) × (每小时加权平均成本 − 每小时标准成本)］

或者，计算时也可以不参照不同人工投入的相关成本。

［(基于总时间按标准比例分配的某级别工作时间 − 某级别的实际工作时间) × 每小时标准成本］

每个级别的差异之和即为组合差异总额。建议使用第一种方法，因为该方法中每个级别的差异具有意义，但在第二种方法中则无法体现。

直接人工工资率差异

说明了标准人工费用与实际人工

the standard labour rate of remuneration.

〔(actual hours paid × standard direct labour rate per hour) − (actual hours paid × actual direct labour rate per hour)〕

See Figure 1.29.

variance, direct labour total

Indicates the diffrence between the standard direct labour cost of the output which has been produced and the actual direct labour cost incurred.

〔(standard hours produced × standard direct labour rate per hour) − (actual hours paid × actual direct labour rate per hour)〕

See Figure 1.29.

variance, direct labour yield

Subdivision of the direct labour efficiency variance. Measures the effect on cost of any difference between the actual usage of labour and that justified by the output produced. It is recommended that the variance be calculated in total and not for individual labour grade inputs.

〔(standard labour hours allowed for actual output − actual labour hours input) × standard weighted average cost per direct labour hour〕

It may also be calculated in the following way:

〔(standard labour hours required for good output − actual labour hours worked in standard proportions) × standard cost per labour hours〕

variance, direct material mix

Subdivision of the material usage variance. If different materials can be substituted the mix

费用之间的差额。

〔(实际支付报酬的小时数 × 每小时标准直接人工费用) − (实际支付报酬的小时数 × 每小时实际直接人工成本费用)〕

参见图表1.29。

直接人工总差异

说明了生产产出的标准直接人工成本和实际产生成本之间的差额。

〔(标准生产时数 × 每小时标准直接人工费用) − (实际支付报酬的小时数 × 每小时实际直接人工费用)〕

参见图表1.29。

直接人工生产率差异

对直接人工效率差异的进一步细分,衡量了实际人工使用量和根据产出调整的标准人工使用量差异所产生成本的影响。建议计算总差异,而不是对各个级别的人工投入进行分别计算。

〔(实际产出标准人工时数 − 实际投入人工时数) × 每小时标准直接人工加权平均成本〕

也可以按如下方法计算:

〔(生产产品所需的标准人工时数 − 基于标准比例的实际人工时数) × 每小时标准人工成本〕

直接材料组合差异

对于原材料耗用量差异的进一步细分。用不同的原材料来代替组合差

variance measures the cost of any variation from the standard mix of materials.

［(actual quantity of material - quantity of material based on total material quantity split in standard proportions) × (weighted average cost per kg，litre，other - standard cost per kg，litre，other)］

Alternatively，the calculation can be made without reference to the relative cost of the various material inputs.

［(quantity of material based on total material quantity split in standard proportions - actual quantity of material) × standard cost per kg，litre，other］

When the individual material variances are summed the same total mix variance is calculated. The first method is recommended because the individual material variance are meaningful，whereas in the second method they are not. See Figure 1.32.

variance，direct material price

Difference between the actual price paid for purchased materials and their standard cost.

［(actual quantity of material purchased × standard price) - actual cost of material purchased］

The material price variance may also be calculated at the time of material withdrawal from stores. In this case，the stock accounts are maintained at actual cost，price variances being extracted at the time of material usage rather than of purchase.

［(actual material used × standard cost) - actual cost of material used］

The latter method is not usually recommended because one of the advantages of a standard costing system is the valuation of all stock at standard costs. See Figure 1.29.

异,衡量原材料标准组合变化所产生的成本。

［(原材料实际数量 - 基于标准比例分配的原材料数量) × 每单位(千克、升或其他)加权平均成本 - 每单位(千克、升或其他)标准成本)］

或者,计算时也可以不参照不同材料投入的相关成本。

［(基于标准比例分配的原材料数量 - 原材料实际数量) × 每单位(千克、升或其他)标准成本］

每种原材料单独差异的合计数与总组合差异的计算结果相同。建议使用第一种方法,因为该方法中每种原材料单独的差异具有意义,但在第二种方法中则无法体现。参见图表1.32。

直接材料价格差异

购买原材料实际支付的价格和标准成本之间的差额。

［(原材料实际购买数量 × 标准价格) - 原材料实际购买成本］

原材料价格差异也可以在原材料从库存中取出时计算。在这种情况下,存货科目中记录的是原材料实际价格,而价格差异是在原材料使用时而不是购买时计算。

［(原材料实际耗用量 × 标准成本) - 原材料的实际成本］

不推荐使用后一种方法,原因是标准成本系统的一大优势是根据标准成本对所有存货进行计量。参见图表1.29。

variance, direct material total

Measurement of the difference between the standard material cost of the output produced and the actual material cost incurred.

（standard material cost of output produced-actual cost of material purchased）

Where the quantities of material purchased amd used are different，the total variance should be calculated as the sum of the usage and price variances.

variance, direct material usage

Measures efficiency in the use of material，by comparing standard material usage for actual production with actual material used，the difference is valued at standard cost.

〔（actual production × standard material per unit − actual material usage）× standard cost per kg，litre，other〕

The direct material usage variance may be divided into mix and yield variances if several materials are mixed in standard proportions. See Figure 1.29.

variance, direct material yield

Subdivision of the material usage variance. Measures the effct on cost of any difference between the actual usage of material and that justified by the output produced. It is recommended that the variance be calculated in total and not for individual material inputs.

〔（standard material quantity allowed for actual output − actual material quantity input）× standard weighted average cost per kg, litre, other〕

直接材料总差异

衡量生产产出的标准原材料成本和实际原材料成本之间的差额。

（实际产出的标准原材料成本－实际购买原材料成本）

当原材料购买和耗用的数量不同时，总差异应为耗用量和价格差异的乘积。

直接材料耗用量差异

通过比较实际生产中标准原材料耗用和实际原材料耗用量来衡量效率，以标准成本来衡量差异。

〔（实际产出×每单位标准原材料－实际原材料耗用量）×每单位（千克、升或其他）标准成本〕

如果多种原材料是以标准比例进行组合，那么直接原材料耗用量差异可以分为组合及产出差异。参见图表1.29。

直接材料产出差异

对原材料耗用量差异的细分。衡量了实际原材料耗用量和根据产出调整原材料标准耗用量差额所产生成本的影响。建议计算总差异而不是对单个原材料投入进行分别计算。

〔（实际产出标准原材料投入数量－实际投入原材料数量）×每单位（千克、升或其他）标准加权平均成本〕

It may also be calculated in the following way：

［(standard material quantity required for actual output － actual material quantities used in standard proportions)×standard cost per kg, litre, other］

See Figure 1.32.

也可以按如下方法计算：

［(实际产出标准原材料投入数量－基于标准比例的实际原材料耗用数量)×每单位(千克、升或其他)标准成本］

参见图表 1.32。

variance, fixed production overhead capacity

固定制造费用产能差异

Little used subdivision of the fixed production overhead volume variance.

对固定制造费用量差异的细分，很少使用。

variance, fixed production overhead efficiency

固定制造费用效率差异

Little used subdivision of the fixed production overhead volume variance.

对固定制造费用量差异的细分，很少使用。

variance, fixed production overhead expenditure

固定制造费用支出差异

The difference between the fixed production overhead which should have been incurred in the period, and that which was incurred.

本期应该发生的和本期实际发生的固定制造费用之间的差值。

(budgeted fixed production overhead － actual fixed production overhead)

(预算固定制造费用－实际固定制造费用)

variance, fixed production overhead total

固定制造费用总差异

The difference between the fixed production overhead absorbed by actual production and the actual fixed production overhead incurred.

实际生产分配的固定制造费用和实际发生的固定制造费用之间的差额。

［(actual production in standard hours × fixed production overhead absorption rate per hour) － actual fixed production overhead］

This variance can be divided into fixed production overhead expenditure and fixed production overhead volume variances.

［(标准时间内的实际产出×每小时固定制造费用分配率)－实际发生的固定制造费用］

此差异可以分为固定制造费用支出差异和固定制造费用量差异。

variance, fixed production over-head volume

A measure of the over-or under-absorption of overhead cost caused by actual production volume differing from that budgeted.

〔(actual production in standard hours × fixed production overhead absorption rate per hour) − budgeted fixed production overhead.〕

See Figure 1.29.

variance, joint

A variance which is caused by both the prices and quantities of inputs differing from the specifications in the original standard. See Figure 1.25.

variance, market share

A subdivision of the sales volume contribution or margin variance, applicable when the actual market size of a product or product group is known. It indicates the change in contribution or margin caused by a change in market share.

〔(actual sales volume − sales volume based on budgeted share of actual market) × standard contribution or margin per unit〕

See Figure 1.34.

variance, market size

A subdivision of the sales volume contribution or margin variance, applicable when the actual market size of a product or product group is known. It indicates the change in contribution or margin caused by a change in the size of the market.

固定制造费用产量差异

用于衡量因实际生产量与预算生产量不同而导致的过多或过少分摊的制造费用。

〔(实际产出标准时间×每小时固定制造费用分配率)−预算固定制造费用〕

参见图表1.29。

联合差异

由投入的价格和数量都与原始标准不同而产生的差异。参见图表1.25。

市场份额差异

对销量贡献或利润差异的细分,适用于当产品或产品组合的实际市场份额已知的时候,说明了由市场份额变化引起的贡献或利润的变化。

〔(实际销量−基于实际市场预计占有率的销量)×每单位标准贡献或利润〕

参见图表1.34。

市场规模差异

对销量贡献或利润差异的细分,适用于当产品或产品组合的实际市场规模已知的时候,说明了由市场规模变化带来的贡献或利润的变化。

[(sales volume based on budgeted share of actual market − budgeted sales volume) × standard contribution or margin per unit]

See Figure 1.34.

[(基于实际市场预计占有率的销量 − 预计销量)×每单位标准贡献或利润]

参见图表1.34。

variance, marketing cost

市场营销成本差异

Where marketing cost contains both fixed and variable components，separate variances should be calculated.

营销成本包含固定和变动部分，差异应分别计算。

(budgeted marketing cost − actual marketing cost)

(预算营销成本 − 实际营销成本)

variance, operational

运营差异

Classification of variance in which non-standard performance is defined as being that which differs from an ex post standard.

对被界定为非事后分析标准的非标准绩效的分类。

Operational variances can relate to any element of the standard product specification. See Figure 1.35.

运营差异可以与任何标准产品指标要素相关。参见图1.35。

variance, planning

计划差异

Classification of variances caused by ex ante budget allowances being changed to an ex post basis. Also known as a revision variance. See Figure 1.35.

对由于事前预算限额变更为事后标准所引起的差异进行分类。又称"修正差异"。参见图1.35。

variance, sales mix contribution/profit margin

销量组合贡献/利润率差异

Subdivision of the sales volume contribution/profit margin variance. The change in the contribution/profit margin caused by a change in the mix of the products or services sold.

对销量贡献/利润率差异的细分，由出售的产品或服务组合变化带来的贡献/利润率的变化。

[(actual sales units − sales units based on total sales in budget proportions) × (standard contribution/profit margin per unit − budget weighted average contribution/profit margin per unit)]

[(实际销售数量 − 基于总销售预算比例计算的销售数量)×(每单位标准贡献/利润 − 每单位预算加权平均贡献/利润)]

This method of computation highlights the contribution/profit margin effect，by product，of sales deviating from budget proportions. A favourable variance denotes either selling proportionately more of a relatively high contribution/profit margin product or proportionately less of a relatively low contribution/profitmargin product.

It can also be calculated as：

［（actual sales units－sales units based on total sales in budget proportions）×standard contribution/ profit margin per unit］

When summed up for all products this method gives the same result as the first method. The first method is recommended because the results for individual products are meaningful，whereas in the second method they are not. See Figure 1.33.

variance, sales price

Change in revenue caused by the actual selling price differing from that budgeted.

［actual sales revenue－（actual sales volume× standard selling price per unit）］

See Figure 1.29.

variance，sales quantity contribution/profit

Subdivision of the sales volume contribution/profit variance. It is relevant if there are multiple products and the actual sales mix differs from the budgeted sales mix. In these situations this variance，together with the sales mix contribution/profit variance，will comprise the sales volume contribution/profit variance（for all products）. It can be calculated in either of the following ways：

这一方法突出了当销售偏离预算时对产品贡献/利润率的影响。顺差意味着在组合中，售出的较低贡献或利润产品的比例更少。

另一种计算方法是：

［（实际销售数量－基于总销售预算比例计算的销售数量）×每单位标准贡献/利润率］

这一方法在计算总数时与第一种方法结果相同。建议使用第一种方法，因为单个产品的计算结果是有意义的，而在第二种方法中无法体现。参见图表1.33。

销售价格差异

实际销售价格与预算销售价格不同造成的收入差异。

［实际销售收入－（实际销售量×每单位标准售价）］

参见图表1.29。

销量规模贡献/利润差异

对销量贡献/利润差异的一个细分。这涉及多个产品且实际销售组合与预算销售组合不同的情况。在这种情况下，此差异与销量组合贡献/利润差异一同构成了销量贡献/利润差异（对于所有产品）。可以以下任一方法计算：

〔(actual total sales volume – budgeted total sales volume) × budgeted weighted average contribution/profit per unit〕

or

〔(actual total sales volume in budgeted mix – budgeted sales volume) × budgeted contribution/profit per unit〕

If the second method is used the sum of the variance for all products will be the same as the result obtained using the first formula.

See Figure 1.33.

variance, sales volume contribution/profit

Measure of the effect on contribution/profit of not achieving the budgeted volume of sales.

〔(actual sales volume – budgeted sales volume) × standard contribution/profit per unit〕

See Figure 1.29.

variance, sales volume revenue

Change in sales revenue caused by sales volume differing form that budgeted.

〔(actual sales volume – budget sales) × standard selling price per unit〕

This variance is logical but little used because it cannot be combined with contribution/profit variances in reconciling budget with actual contribution/profit. In principle, if several products are considered, the sales mix revenue variance and total sales volume revenue variance can be calculated. See "variance, sales mix contribution" and "variance, sales quantity contribution/profit" for the method of derivation – subsititute "selling price" for "contribution" in the appropriate formula.

〔(实际总销量－预算总销量)×每单位预算加权平均贡献/利润〕

或者

〔(预算组合下实际总销量－预算销量)×每单位预算贡献/利润〕

如果使用第二种方法,则所有产品差异之和与使用第一种方法计算结果相同。

参见图表1.33。

销量贡献/利润差异

衡量无法完成预算销量对贡献/利润的影响。

〔(实际销量－预算销量)×每单位标准贡献/利润〕

参见图表1.29。

销量收入差异

由实际与预算销售量差异引起的销售收入的变化。

〔(实际销量－预算销量)×每单位标准售价〕

这一差异合乎逻辑但是很少使用,因为它无法结合贡献/利润差异,对预算和实际的贡献/利润进行分析。原则上,如果涉及多个产品,就可以计算销售组合收入差异与销售总量收入差异。参见"销售组合贡献/利润差异"和"销售数量贡献/利润差异",在适当的公式里用"贡献"代替"销售价格"。

variance, total profit

Difference between the actual profit and the profit in the budget. The total profit variance is the sum of all the subsidiary variances.

（actual profit － budgeted profit）

variance, variable production overhead efficiency

Standard variablr overhead cost of any change from the standard level of efficiency.

〔（actual production in standard hours-actual hours worked）×standard variable overhead rate per hour〕

This is directly analogous to the calculation of direct labour efficiency variance and implicitly assumes that variable overhead is recovered on a direct labour hour base. However, the formula can equally be used if variable overhead is recovered on a machine or process hour base. See Figure 1.29.

variance, variable production overhead expenditure

Indicates the actual cost of any change from the standard rate per hour.

〔（standard variable rate per hour － actual variable rate per hour）×actual hours worked〕

Hours refer to either labour or machine hours depending on the recovery base chosen for variable production overhead. See Figure 1.28.

variance, variable production overhead total

Measures the difference between variable overhead that should be used for actual output and variable production overhead actually used.

总利润差异

实际利润与预算利润的差额。总利润差异是一系列子差异的总和。

（实际利润－预算利润）

变动制造费用效率差异

由于标准效率水平变化带来的标准变动间接费用成本变化。

〔（实际产出的标准时间－实际工作时间）×每小时标准变动制造费用）〕

这与"直接人工效率差异"类似，且隐含了假定变动创造费用以直接人工时数为计算基础。也可用于以机器时数或程序时数为基础的计算。参见图表1.29。

变动制造费用支出差异

说明了由每小时标准费用的变化带来的实际成本变化。

〔（每小时标准变动费率－每小时实际变动费率）×实际工作时间〕

小时数可以指人工时数或机器时数，可根据变动制造费用的计算基础来确定。参见图表1.28。

变动制造费用总差异

衡量应该用于实际产出的变动制造费用与真正使用的变动制造费用之间的差异。

〔(actual production in standard hours × standard variable production overhead absorption rate per hour) − actual cost incurred〕

The variable production overhead efficiency and rate variances are subdivisions of this variance.

〔(实际产出标准工时 × 每小时标准变动制造费用分配率)−实际产生成本〕

变动制造费用效率差异与费率差异是此差异的细分。

Waste

Discarded material having no value.

废弃物

被丢弃的没有价值的原材料。

FIGURE 1. 25　JOINT VARIANCES

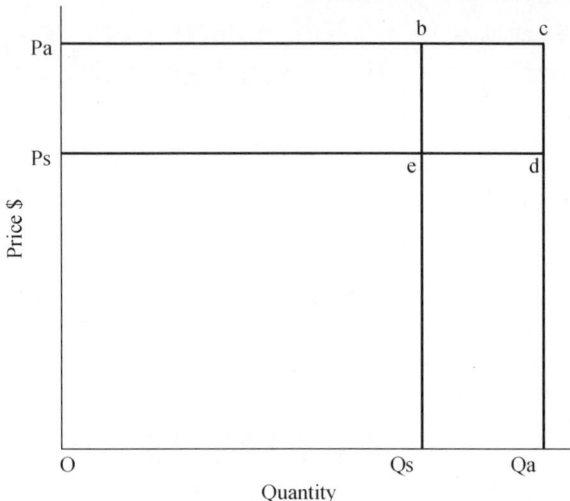

Ps is the standard material price
Pa is the actual material price paid
Qs is the standard quantity of material
Qa is the actual quantity of materia used

The area of the box bcde represents the joint variance, whose cause lies in both the quantity and the price exceeding the standard allowances. A standard costing system normally incorporates the joinit variance into the material price variance computation

图表 1. 25　联合差异

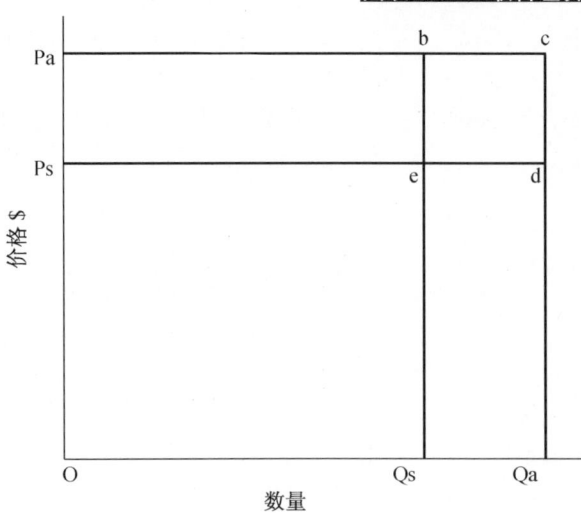

Ps 是标准原材料价格
Pa 是实际支付的原材料价格
Qs 是标准原材料数量
Qa 是实际使用的原材料数量

区域 bcde 代表了联合差异，由数量和价格超过标准限额部分共同引起。一个标准成本系统通常将联合差异吸收进原材料价格差异计算中。

FIGURE 1. 26 CHART OF VARIANCES (MARGINAL COSTING PRINCIPLES)

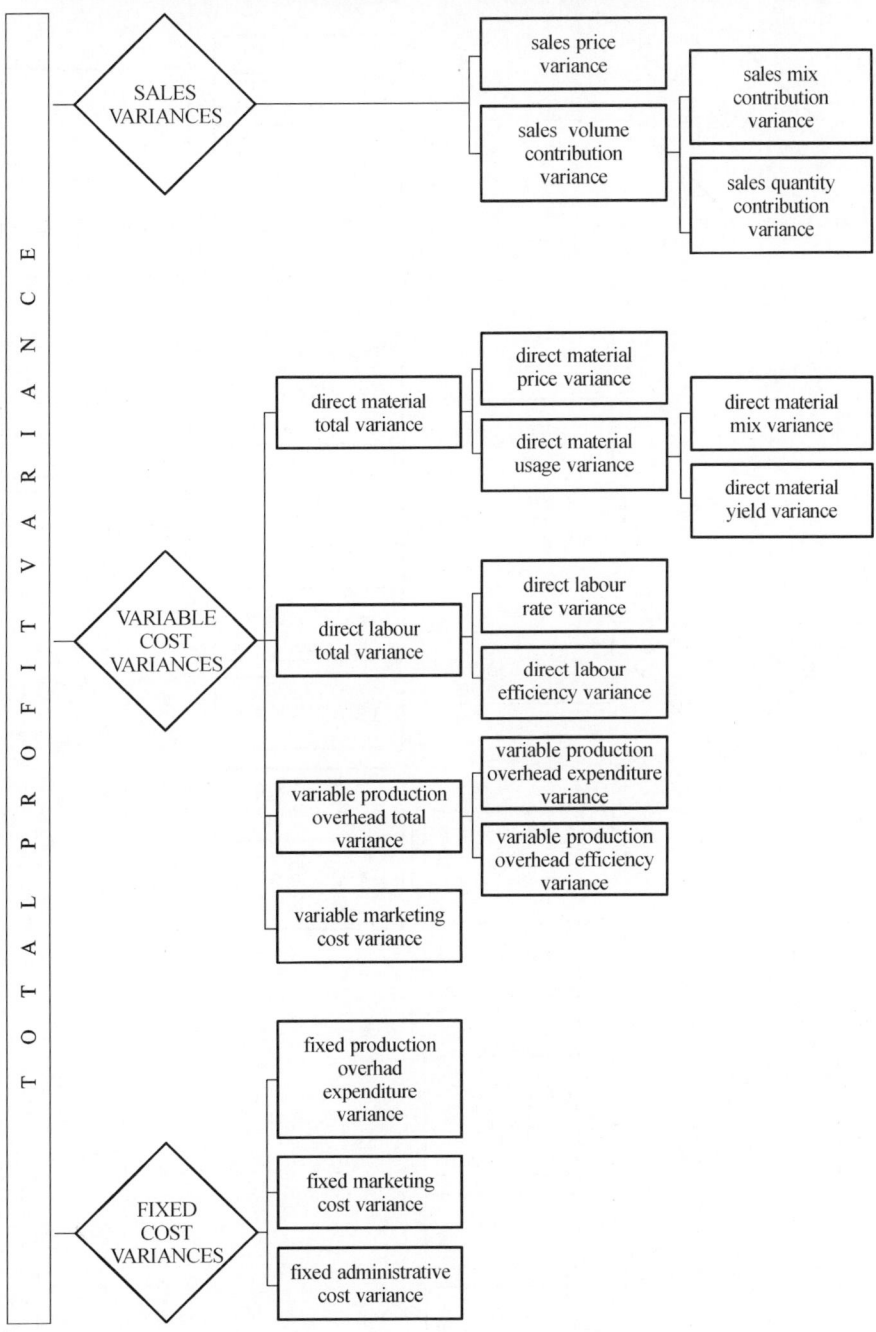

图表 1.26　差异图(边际成本法)

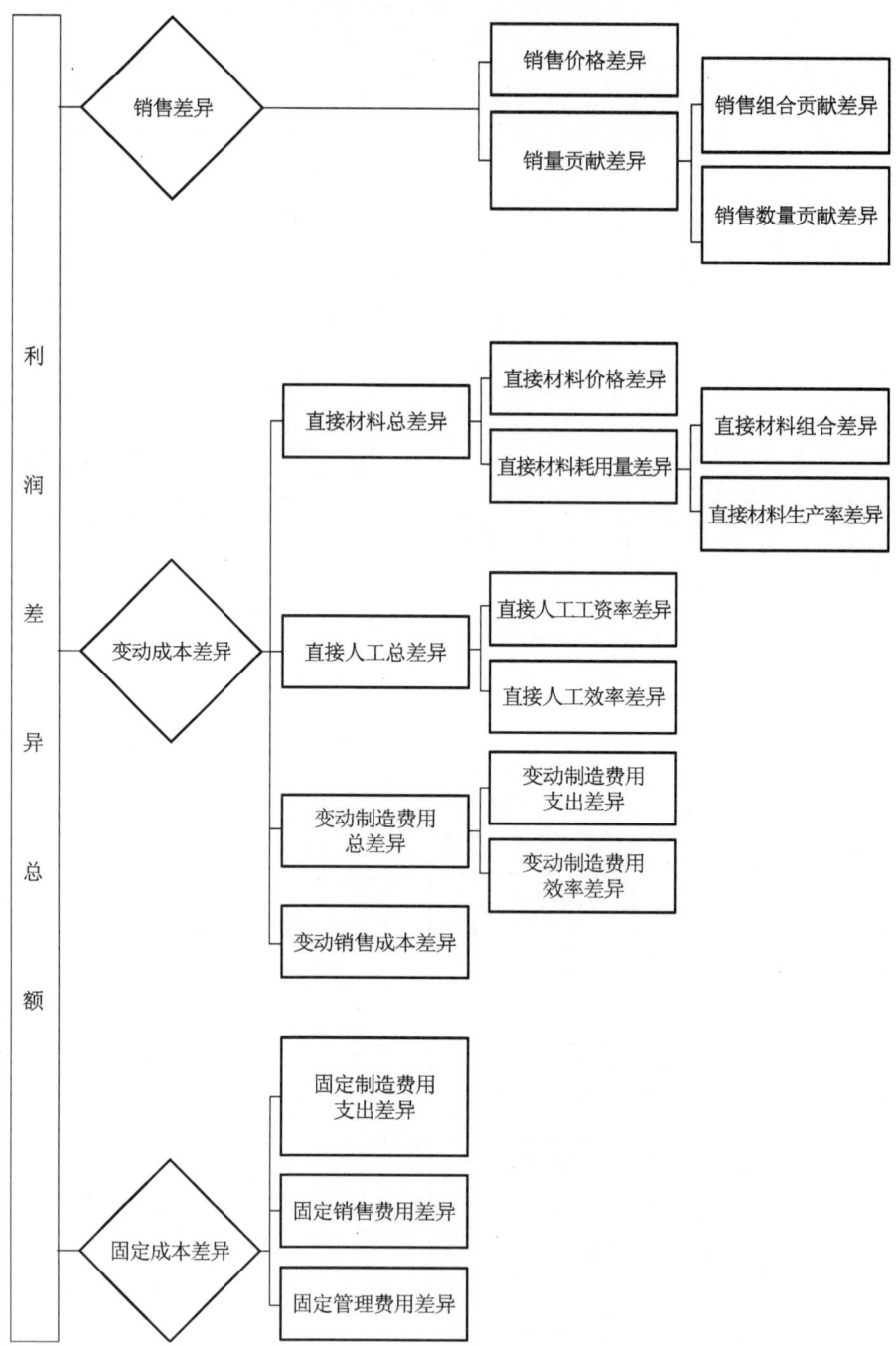

FIGURE 1. 27   CHART OF VARIANCES (ABSORPTION COSTING PRINCIPLES)

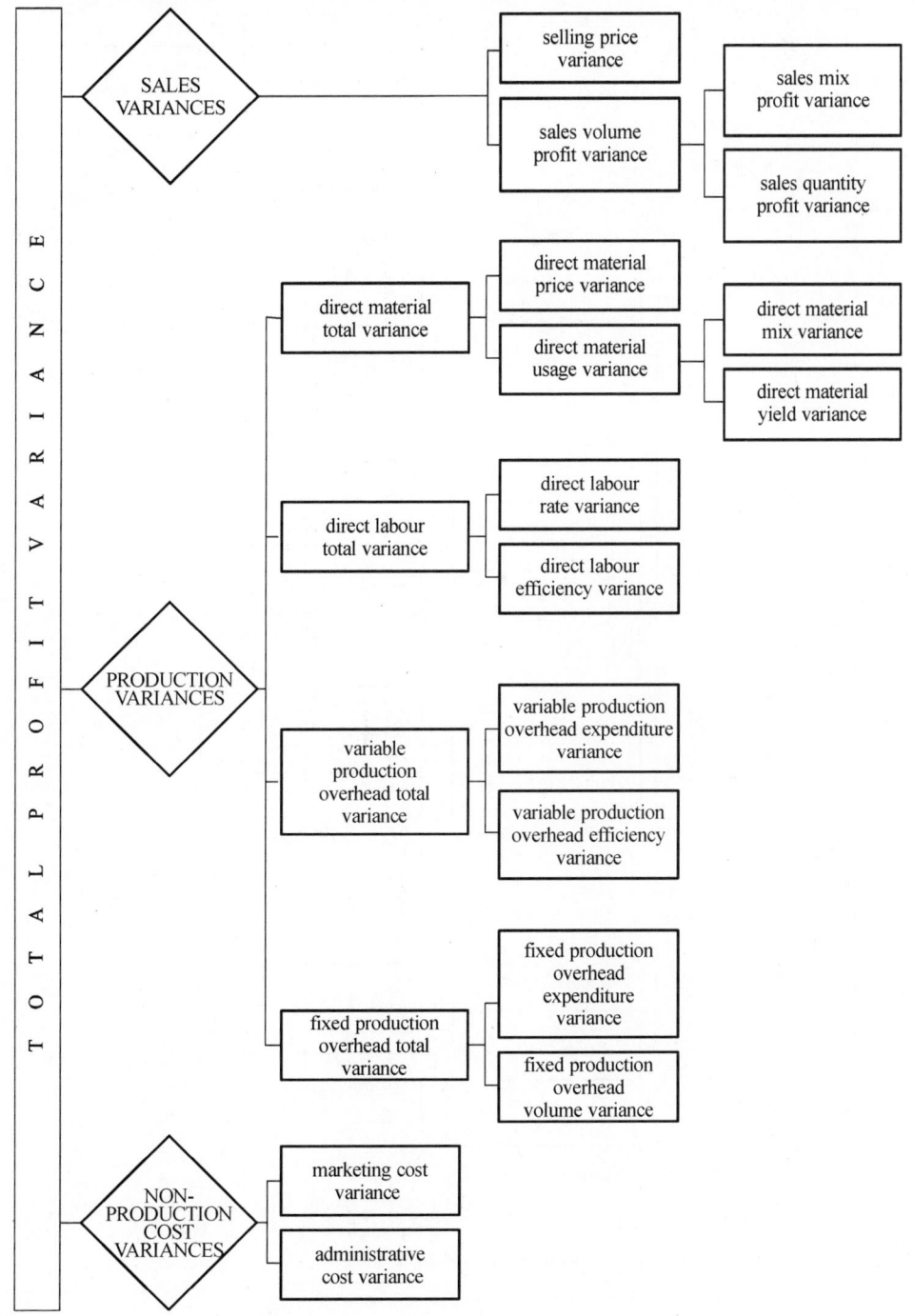

图表 1.27　差异图(吸收成本法)

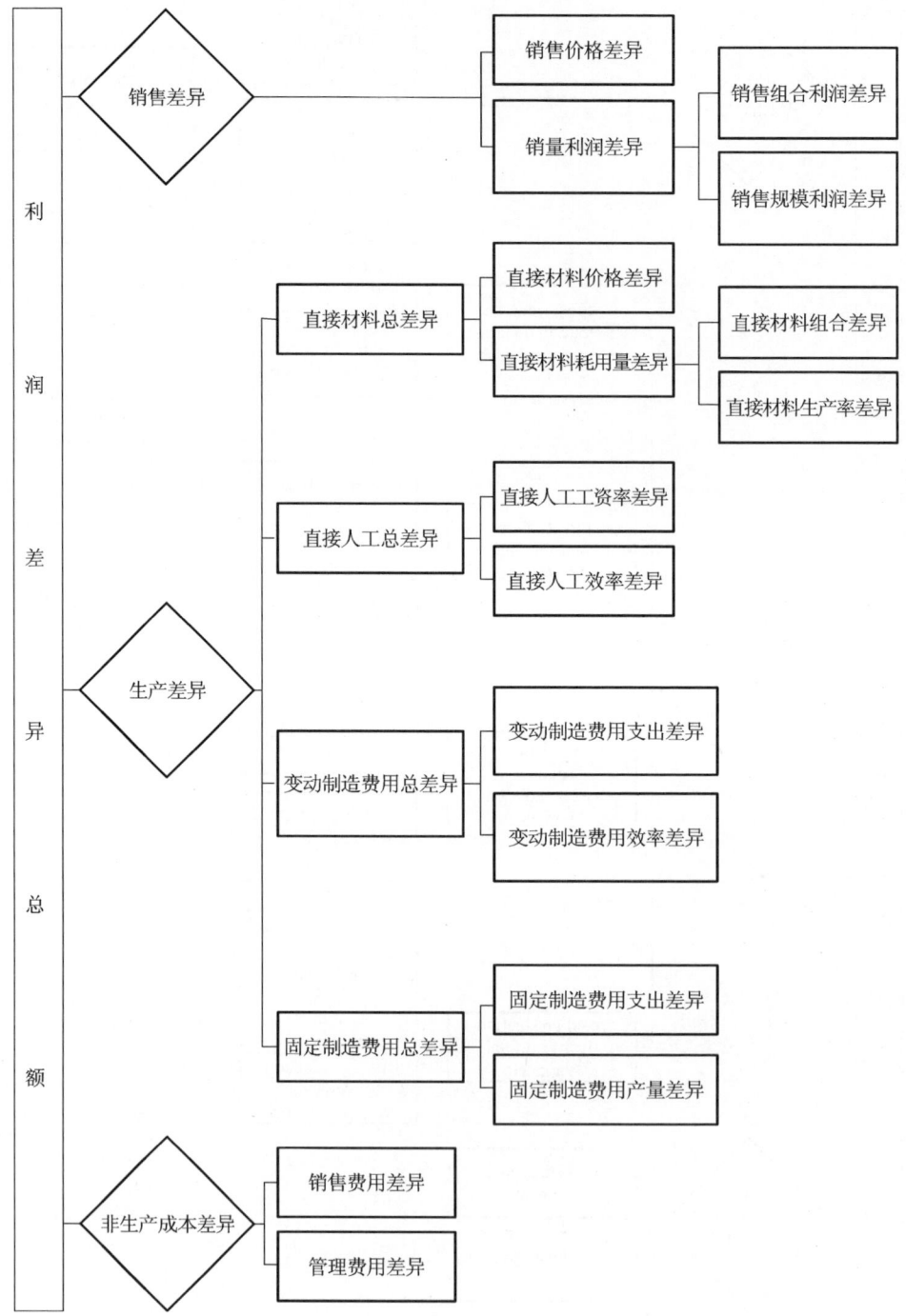

FIGURE 1. 28   OPERATING STATEMENT WITH FLEXED BUDGET

Period...............................

	Standard per unit	Fixed Budget*	Flexed Budget	Actual	Flexible Budget Variance
No. of units made and sold	1	1,000	1,100	1,100	
	$	$	$	$	$
Sales	70.00	70,000	77,000	82,500	5,500
Direct material: 1 kg@ $15	15.00	15,000	16,500	17,000	(500)
Direct labour: 1 hr@ $10	10.00	10,000	11,000	11,250	(250)
Variable production overhead: 1 hr @ $2.50	2.50	2,500	2,750	3,050	(300)
Total variable costs	27.50	27,500	30,250	31,300	
Contribution	42.50	42,500	46,750	51,200	
Fixed production overhead: 1 hr @ $5	5.00	5,000	5,000	5,300	(300)
Gross profit	37.50	37,500	41,750	45,900	
Fixed marketing cost		12,500	12,500	12,950	(450)
Fixed administrative cost		13,000	13,000	13,550	(550)
		25,500	25,500	26,500	
Operating profit		12,000	16,250	19,400	3,150

$4,250
$3,150

Sales volume contribution variance   Price, usage and expenditure variances

Fixed budget profit – actual profit =

$7,400
Total profit variance

图表 1. 28   弹性预算下的经营报表

期间...............................

	标准每单位	固定预算*	弹性预算	实际值	弹性预算差异
制造并出售产品的数量	1	1 000	1 100	1 100	
	$	$	$	$	$
销售收入	70.00	70 000	77 000	82 500	5 500
直接材料:15美元/千克	15.00	15 000	16 500	17 000	(500)
直接人工:10美元/小时	10.00	10 000	11 000	11 250	(250)
变动制造费用:2.5美元/小时	2.50	2 500	2 750	3 050	(300)
总变动成本	27.50	27 500	30 250	31 300	
贡献	42.50	42 500	46 750	51 200	
固定制造费用:5美元/小时	5.00	5 000	5 000	5 300	(300)
毛利润	37.50	37 500	41 750	45 900	
固定销售售用		12 500	12 500	12 950	(450)
固定管理费用		13 000	13 000	13 550	(550)
		25 500	25 500	26 500	
经营利润		12 000	16 250	19 400	3 150

$4 250
$3 150

销售量贡献差异   价格、使用量、支出差异

固定预算利润 – 实际利润 =

$7 400
总利润差异

FIGURE 1.29 STANDARD COSTING VARIANCES (MARGINAL COSTING BASIS)

These calculations are based on Figure 1.27 and note that 1,200 kg of materials were purchased and used; 1,250 labour hours were worked

Sales volume contribution

(actual sales volume − budgeted sales volume) × standard contribution per unit

$(1,100 − 1,000) × \$42.5$ = 4,250

Sales price

actual sales revenue − (actual sales volume × standard selling price per unit)

$82,500 − (1,100 × \$70)$ = 5,500

Direct material price

(Actual quantity of material purchased × standard price) − actual cost of material purchased

$(1,200 × \$15) − \$17,000$ = 1,000

Direct material usage

(Actual production × standard material cost per unit) − (actual material used × standard material cost per unit)

$(1,100 × \$15) − (1,200 × \$15)$ = (1,500)

Direct labour rate

(Actual hours paid × standard direct labour rate per hour) − (actual hours paid × actual direct labour rate per hour)

$(1,250 × \$10) − \$11,250$ = 1,250

Direct labour efficiency

(Actual production in standard hours − actual hours worked) × standard direct labour rate per hour

$(1,100 × 1 − 1,250) × \$10$ = (1,500)

Variable production overhead expenditure

(standard variable rate per hour − actual variable rate per hour) × actual hours worked

$(\$2.50 − 3,050/1,250) × 1,250$ = 75

Variable production overhead efficiency

(actual production in standard hours − actual hours worked) × standard variable overhead rate per hour

$(1,100 × 1 − 1,250) × \$2.50$ = (375)

Fixed production overhead expenditure

Budgeted fixed production overhead − actual fixed production overhead

$\$5,000 − \$5,300$ = (300)

ADDITIONAL VARIANCES FOR STANDARD ABSORPTION COSTING

Sales volume profit

(actual sales volume − budgeted sales volume) × standard profit per unit

$(1,100 − 1,000) × \$37.50$ = 3,750

Fixed production overhead volume

(Actual production in standard hours × standard fixed production overhead absorption rate per hour) − budgeted fixed production overhead

$(1,100 × 1 × \$5) − \$5,000$ = 500

图表 1.29 标准成本差异(基于边际成本)

下列计算基于图表1.27,并且请注意原材料购买和耗用数量是1 200千克;实际工作时间是1 250小时

销量贡献

(实际销售量 − 计划销售量) × 每单位标准贡献

$(1\,100 − 1\,000) × \$42.5$ = 4 250

销售价格

实际销售收入 − (实际销售量 × 每单位标准销售价格)

（续表）

82 500 − (1 100 × $ 70)	=	5 500

直接材料价格

（实际原材料购买数量×标准价格）−实际原材料购买成本

(1 200 × $ 15) − $ 17 000	=	1 000

直接材料耗用

（实际产出量×每单位产出标准原材料成本）−（实际原材料使用×每单位标准原材料成本）

(1 100 × $ 15) − (1 200 × $ 15)	=	(1 500)

直接人工工资率

（实际支付时数×每小时标准直接人工费用）−（实际支付时数×每小时实际直接人工成本费用）

(1 250 × $ 10) − ($ 11 250)	=	1 250

直接人工效率

（实际产出标准时间−实际工作时间）×每小时标准直接人工费用

(1 100 × 1 − 1 250) × $ 10	=	(1 500)

变动制造费用支出

（每小时标准变动费用−每小时实际变动费用）×实际工作时间

($ 2.50 − 3 050/1 250) × 1 250	=	75

变动制造费用效率

（实际产出标准时间−实际工作时间）×每小时标准变动制造费用

(1 100 × 1 − 1 250) × $ 2.50	=	(375)

固定制造费用支出

预算固定制造费用−实际固定制造费用

$ 5 000 − $ 5 300	=	(300)

标准吸收成本法下额外差异

销售量利润

（实际销售量−计划销售量）×每单位销售量标准利润

(1 100 − 1 000) × $ 37.50	=	3 750

固定制造费用量

（实际产出标准时间×每单位时间标准固定制造费用）−计划固定制造费用

(1 100 × 1 × $ 5) − $ 5 000	=	500

FIGURE 1.30 OPERATING STATEMENT-STANDARD MARGINAL COSTING

Period..............................

	$	$	$	$
Budgeted sales				70,000
Budgeted variable cost of sales				27,500
Budgeted contribution				42,500
Sales volume contribution variance				4,250
Budgeted contribution from actual sales				46,750
Variances		(F)	(A)	
Sales price		5,500	—	
Direct material usage		—	(1,500)	
Direct material price		1,000	—	
Direct labour efficiency		—	(1,500)	
Direct labour rate		1,250	—	
Variable overhead efficiency		—	(375)	
Variable overhead expenditure		75	—	
		7,825	3,375	4,450

CONTINUED

	$	$	$
Actual contribution			51 200
Fixed costs			

	Budget	Expenditure Variance	
Production	5,000	(300)	
Marketing	12,500	(450)	
Administration	13,000	(550)	
	30,500	(1,300)	31,800
Actual profit			19,400

图表 1. 30　经营报表——标准边际成本法

期间.............................

	$	$	$	$
计划销售额				70 000
计划销售额变动成本				27 500
计划贡献				42 500
销量贡献差异				4 250
基于实际销售额的预算贡献				46 750
差异		(F)	(A)	
销售价格		5 500	—	
直接材料耗用量		—	(1 500)	
直接材料价格		1 000	—	
直接人工效率		—	(1 500)	
直接人工工资率		1 250	—	
变动制造费用效率		—	(375)	
变动制造费用支出		75	—	
		7 825	3 375	4 450
实际贡献				51 200
固定成本				

	预算	支出差异	
	$	$	
生产	5 000	(300)	
销售	12 500	(450)	
管理	13 000	(550)	
	30 500	(1 300)	31 800
实际利润			19 400

FIGURE 1. 31　OPERATING STATEMENT—STANDARD ABSORPTION COSTING

Period...........

	$	$	$
Budgeted sales			70,000
Budgeted cost of sales			32,500
			37,500
Budgeted marketing cost		12,500	
Budgeted administration csot		13,000	25,500

CONTINUED

	$	$	$
Budgeted profit			12,000
Sales volume profit variance			3,750
Budgeted profit from actual sales			15,750
Variances	(F)	(A)	
Sales price	5,500	—	
Marketing cost	—	(450)	
Direct material usage	—	(1,500)	
Direct material price	1,000	—	
Direct labour efficiency	—	(1,500)	
Direct labour rate	1,250	—	
Variable overhead efficinecy	—	(375)	
Variable overhead expenditure	75	—	
Fixed overhead volume	500	—	
Fixed overhead expenditure	—	(300)	
Fixed administrative cost	—	(550)	
	8,325	(4,675)	3,650
Actual profit			19,400

图表 1.31 经营报表——标准吸收成本法

期间...........

	$	$	$
计划销售额			70 000
计划销售额的成本			32 500
			37 500
计划销售成本		12 500	
计划管理成本		13 000	25 500
计划利润			12 000
销量利润差异			3 750
实际销售额下预算利润			15 750
差异	(F)	(A)	
销售价格	5 500	—	
营销成本	—	(450)	
直接材料耗用量	—	(1 500)	
直接材料价格	1 000	—	
直接人工效率	—	(1 500)	
直接人工工资率	1 250	—	
变动制造费用效率	—	(375)	
变动制造费用支出	75	—	
固定制造费用产量	500	—	
固定制造费用支出	—	(300)	
固定管理成本	—	(550)	
	8 325	(4 675)	3 650
实际利润			19 400

FIGURE 1.32 WORKED EXAMPLE OF DIRECT MATERIALS YIELD AND MIX VARIANCES

1. Initial date: Materials Y and Z are mixed in the proportions 60% and 40% respectively and a standard loss of 4.5% is set. Standard and actual costs for a period show:

	Standard			Actual		
	Quantity in mix kg	Unit cost $/kg	Total cost $	Quantity in mix kg	Unit cost $/kg	Total cost $
Material Y	30,000	3.20	96,000	24,000	3.40	81,600
Material Z	20,000	2.40	48,000	21,000	2.00	42,000
Input	50,000		144,000	45,000		123,600
4.5% loss	2,250					
Output	47,750			42,000		

2. The results of the calculations and the relationships between the variances are as follows:

Direct material total variance	$3,060

Direct material price variance	$3,600		Direct material usage variance	($540)

Direct material mix variance	$2,400		Direct material yield variance	($2,940)

Direct material price variances $

(Actual quantity of material purchased × standard price) − actual cost of material purchased

Y$(24,000 × \$3.20) − 81,600$ = (4,800)

Z$(21,000 × \$2.40) − 42,000$ = 8,400

3,600

Direct material usage variances

(actual production × standard material per unit − actual material)

× standard cost per kg, litre, other

Y$(((42,000 × 0.6)/0.955) − 24,000) × \$3.20$ = 7,640

Z$(((42,000 × 0.4)/0.955) − 21,000) × \$2.40$ = (8,180)

(540)

Direct material mix variance

(actual quantity of material − quantity of material based on total material
quantity split in standard proportions) × (weighted average cost per kg, litre, other
− standard cost per kg, liter, other)

Y$(24,000 − 27,000) × (\$2.88 − \$3.20)$ = 960

Z$(21,000 − 18,000) × (\$2.88 − \$2.40)$ = 1,440

2 400

Direct material yield variance

(standard material quantity allowed for actual output − actual material
quantity in put) × standard weighted average cost per kg, liter other

$(42,000/0.955 − 45,000) × \$2.88$ = (2,940)

Unlike mix and price variances, the yield variances for each individual
material in a mix are of no managerial interest.

Note: The material mix variance may also be calculated without reference to the relative costs of the
inputs in the mix − although the individual material mix variances then have no meaning:

(quantity of material based on total material quantity split in standard
proportions − actual quantity of material) × standard cost per kg, liter, other

Y$(27,000 − 24,000) × \$3.20$ = 9,600

Z$(18,000 − 14,000) × \$2.40$ = (7,200)

2,400

图表 1.32　例:直接原材料生产率与组合差异

1. 初始数据:原材料 Y 和 Z 分别以 60% 和 40% 的比例组合,标准损耗率为 4.5%。标准成本和实际成本如下:

	标准			实际		
	组合数量	单位成本	总成本	组合数量	单位成本	总成本
	千克	$/千克	$	千克	$/千克	$
原材料 Y	30 000	3.20	96 000	24 000	3.40	81 600
原材料 Z	20 000	2.40	48 000	21 000	2.00	42 000
投入	50 000		144 000	45 000		123 600
4.5%损失	2 250					
产出	47 750			42 000		

2. 计算结果及差异之间的关系如下:

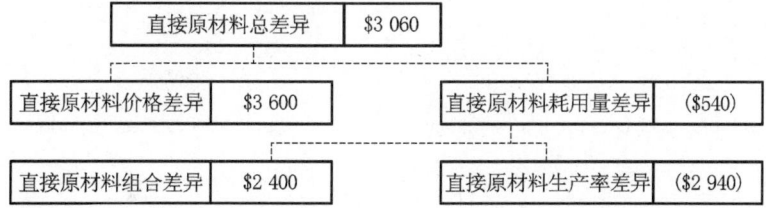

直接原材料价格差异　　　　　　　　　　　　　　　　　　　　　　　　　　　　　　　$
(实际购买原材料数量×标准价格)－实际购买原材料成本
Y(24 000×$3.20)－81 600　　　　　　　　　　　　　　　　　　　　　　　　= 　(4 800)
Z(21 000×$2.40)－42 000　　　　　　　　　　　　　　　　　　　　　　　　= 　 8 400
　　　　　　　　　　　　　　　　　　　　　　　　　　　　　　　　　　　　　 3 600

直接原材料耗用量差异
(实际产量×每单位标准原材料－实际原材料耗用量)×每单位(千克,升,其他)标准成本
Y{[(42 000×0.6)/0.955]－24 000}×$3.20　　　　　　　　　　　　　　　　= 　 7 640
Z{[(42 000×0.4)/0.955]－21 000}×$2.40　　　　　　　　　　　　　　　　= 　(8 180)
　　　　　　　　　　　　　　　　　　　　　　　　　　　　　　　　　　　　 (540)

直接原材料组合差异
(原材料实际数量－基于标准比例分配的原材料数量)×[每单位(千克,升,其他)加权平均成本－每单位(千克,升,其他)标准成本]
Y (24 000－27 000)×($2.88－$3.20)　　　　　　　　　　　　　　　　　　= 　 960
Z (21 000－18 000)×($2.88－$2.40)　　　　　　　　　　　　　　　　　　= 　1 440
　　　　　　　　　　　　　　　　　　　　　　　　　　　　　　　　　　　　 2 400

直接原材料生产率差异
(实际产出的标准原材料数量－实际原材料投入量)×标准每单位(千克,升,其他)加权平均成本
(42 000/0.955－45 000)×$2.88　　　　　　　　　　　　　　　　　　　　　= 　(2 940)
与组合及价格差异不同的是,组合情况下每种原材料的生产率差异不受管理关注。
注:原材料组合差异可以在不考虑组合情况投入的相关成本的基础上进行计算——尽管每种原材料的组合差异因此失去意义:
Y (27 000－24 000)×$3.20　　　　　　　　　　　　　　　　　　　　　　　= 　 9 600
Z (18 000－21 000)×$2.40　　　　　　　　　　　　　　　　　　　　　　　= 　(7 200)
　　　　　　　　　　　　　　　　　　　　　　　　　　　　　　　　　　　　 2 400

FIGURE 1.33　WORKED EXAMPLE OF SALES PROFIT VARIANCES

Budgeted sales data

Product F 3,000 units with standard profit of $2.00 per unit

Product G 4,000units with standard profit of $2.50 per unit

Product H 3,000units with standard profit of $3.00 per unit

Weighted average standard profit is $2.50 per unit

Actual sales data

Product F 3,000 units

Product G 3,000 units

Product H 6,000 units

Sales volume profit variance $

(actual sales volume − budgeted sales volume) × standard contribution/profit per unit

Product F $(3,000 - 3,000) \times \$2.00$	=	—
Product G $(3,000 - 4,000) \times \$2.50$	=	(2,500)
Product H $(6,000 - 3,000) \times \$3.00$	=	9,000
		6 500

Sales quantity profit variance

(actual total sales volume − budgeted total sales volume) × budgeted weighted average contribution/profit per unit

$(12,000 - 10,000) \times \$2.50$	=	5,000

Sales mix profit variance
(actual sales units − sales units based on total sales in budget proportions) × (standard profit per unit − budget weighted average profit per unit)

Product F $(3,000 - 3,600) \times (\$2.00 - \$2.50)$	=	300
Product G $(3,000 - 4,800) \times (\$2.50 - \$2.50)$	=	—
Product H $(6,000 - 3,600) \times (\$3.00 - \$2.50)$	=	1,200
		1,500

The sales mix profit variance can also be calculated as follows (but individual variances have no meaning)
(actual sales units − sales units based on total sales in budget proportions)
X standard profit per unit

Product F $(3,000 - 3,600) \times \$2.00$	=	(1,200)
Product G $(3,000 - 4,800) \times \$2.50$	=	(4,500)
Product H $(6,000 - 3,600) \times \$3.00$	=	7,200
		1,500

Sales volume profit variance	$6,500

Sales quantity profit variance	$5,000		Sales mix profit variance	$1,500

Note 1: Where unit quantities are not available or relevant, units would be replaced by sales, and profit per unit replaced by profit to sales ratios.

Note 2: If a marginal costing system was in operation, the following variances would be calculated with respect to sales:

    i   Sales volume contribution variance

    ii   Sales quantity contribution variance

    iii   Sales mix contribution variance

These variances would be calculated in an identical manner to the sales profit variances, although based on standard unit contribution, rather than standard unit profit.

图表 1.33　范例:销量利润差异

预算销售数据

产品 F, 3 000 单位,每单位标准利润 $2.00

产品 G, 4 000 单位,每单位标准利润 $2.50

产品 H, 3 000 单位,每单位标准利润 $3.00

加权平均每单位标准利润 $2.50

实际销售数据

产品 F, 3 000 单位

产品 G, 3 000 单位

产品 H, 6 000 单位

销量利润差异		$
(实际销售量 - 预算销售量)×每单位标准贡献/利润		
产品 F (3 000 - 3 000)× $2.00	=	—
产品 G (3 000 - 4 000)× $2.50	=	(2 500)
产品 H (6 000 - 3 000)× $3.00	=	9 000
		6 500

销量规模利润差异		
(实际总销售量 - 预算总销售量)×预算每单位加权平均贡献/利润		
(12 000 - 10 000)× $2.50	=	5 000

销量组合利润差异		
(实际销售量 - 基于预算比例的销售量)×(每单位标准利润 - 预算每单位加权平均利润)		
产品 F (3 000 - 3 600)×($2.00 - $2.50)	=	300
产品 G (3 000 - 4 800)×($2.50 - $2.50)	=	—
产品 H (6 000 - 3 600)×($3.00 - $2.50)	=	1 200
		1 500

销量组合利润差异也可以用如下方法计算(但单个差异无意义)		
(实际销售量 - 基于预算比例的销售量)×每单位标准利润		
产品 F (3 000 - 3 600)× $2.00	=	(1 200)
产品 G (3 000 - 4 800)× $2.50	=	(4 500)
产品 H (6 000 - 3 600)× $3.00	=	7 200
		1 500

销量利润差异	$6 500

销量规模利润差异	$5 000		销量组合利润差异	$1 500

注1:当销量不可得或者无关时,销量可以用销售额来代替,每单位利润则用销售利润率来代替。

注2:如果使用的是边际成本系统,则下列差异应根据销售量来计算:

　　i 销量贡献差异

　　ii 销量规模贡献差异

　　iii 销量组合贡献差异

虽然这些差异基于每单位标准贡献,而不是每单位标准利润,但是计算与销量利润差异计算的方法完全相同。

FIGURE 1. 34   WORKED EXAMPLE OF MARKET VARIANCES

These calculations are based on Figure 1.27

Budget:	1,000 units representing 20% of the market of 5,000 units	
Actual:	1,100 units in a market of 6,500 units	
Standard contribution:	$ 42.50 per unit	
		$
Actual contribution	1,100@ $ 42.50	46,750
Budget contribution	1,000@ $ 42.50	42,500
Sales volume contribution variance		4,250
Market size variance	$(6,500-5,000)\times 20\% \times $ 42.50$	12,750
Market share variance	$(1,100-(6,500\times 20\%))\times $ 42.50$	(8,500)
Sales volume contribution variance		4,250

图表 1. 34   范例：市场差异

以下计算基于图表1.27

计划：	1 000 单位,代表了市场规模 5 000 单位的 20%	
实际：	1 100 单位,市场规模 6 500 单位	
标准贡献：	每单位 42.50 美元	
		$
实际贡献	1 100× $ 42.50	46 750
计划贡献	1 000× $ 42.50	42 750
销量贡献差异		4 250
市场规模差异	$(6 500-5 000)\times 20\% \times $ 42.50$	12 750
市场份额差异	$[1 100-(6 500\times 20\%)]\times $ 42.50$	(8 500)
销量贡献差异		4 250

FIGURE 1. 35   WORKED EXAMPLE OF PLANNING AND OPERATIONAL VARIANCES

Before the start of the period
● the standard purchase price of material was set at $ 2.00 per kg
During the period
● the standard quantity of material for the output in the period: 20,000 kg
● the actual material prchased and used: 21,000 kg
● the actual purchase price paid: $ 2.80, due to an unforeseen occurrence which led to a material shortage
At the period end a price of $ 3.00 was agreed to have been an efficient buying price in the period.
The standard costing system shows an adverse direct material total variance of $ 18,800 made up of:
    material usage variance($ 2,000)
    material price variance($ 16,800)
Management wishes to distinguish between controllable and uncontrollable effects on performance.
 Variance calculations
Planning price variance
    Standard material quantity×(ex post efficient standard
purchase price per kg − budgeted standard purchase price per kg)
    20,000×($ 3.00 − $ 2.00)   (20,000)
Operational usage variance
    (Actual production×ex post efficient standard material cost/unit)

CONTINUED

– (actual material used × *ex post* efficient standard material cost per unit)

(20,000 × $3.00) – (21,000 × $3.00)   ($3,000)

Operational price variance

　Actual material purchase quantity × (ex post efficient standard

purchase price per kg – actual purchase price per kg)

21,000 × ($3.00 – $2.80) $4,200

Operating statement

	$	$
MATERIAL		
Standard cost of output(20,000 kg × $2)		40,000
Planning price variance(20,000 kg × $1)		(20,000)
Revised standard cost of output		60,000
Operational usage variance(1,000 kg × $3)		(3,000)
Operational price variance (21,000 kg × $0.20)	4,200	1,200
Actual cost of material used		58,800

● The planning price variance indicates that the original standard purchase price was not achievable.

● The operational usage variance indicates the standard cost (*ex post*) of the excess usage of material which took place in the period.

● The operational price variance indicates the cost saving which has been achieved by purchasing material at a price lower than the *ex post* standard.

图表 1.35　范例：计划与营运差异

开始之前：

● 原材料标准购买价格被定为每千克　$2.00

营运期间：

● 产出的标准原材料使用：20 000 千克

● 实际原材料购买与使用：21 000 千克

● 实际支付购买价格：每千克　$2.80，未预见的原因引起了原材料短缺

在期末时，认定期间有效购买价格为 $3.00

标准成本系统显示不利的 $18 800 的直接原材料总差异来源于：

原材料耗用量差异（$2 000）

原材料价格差异（$16 800）

管理层希望能够区分其中可控和不可控影响

差异的计算：

计划价格差异

标准原材料数量 × (事后每千克有效标准购买价格 – 每千克预算标准购买价格)

20 000 × ($3.00 – $2.00)   (20 000)

营运中耗用量差异

(实际生产量 × 事后每单位有效标准原材料成本) – (实际原材料使用量 × 事后每单位有效标准原材料成本)

(20 000 × $3.00) – (21 000 × $3.00)   ($3 000)

营运中价格差异

实际原材料购买量 × (事后每千克有效标准购买价格 – 实际每千克购买价格)

21 000 × ($3.00 – $2.80) $4 200

营运报表： $ $

（续表）

原材料		
产出的标准成本(20 000 千克× $ 2)		40 000
计划价格差异(20 000 千克× $ 1)		(20 000)
修正产出的标准成本		60 000
营运中耗用量差异(1 000 千克× $ 3)		(3 000)
营运中价格差异(21 000 千克× $ 0.20)	4 200	1 200
实际使用原材料成本		58 800

● 计划价格差异说明原定的标准购买价格无法达到。

● 营运中耗用量差异说明原材料超额使用的标准成本(事后)。

● 营运中的价格差异说明了通过以一个比标准成本更低的价格购买原材料节约的成本。

FIGURE 1.36 PERFORMANCE MEASUREMENT RATIOS*

Asset cover and liquidity ratios indicate ability to repay borrowings

Asset cover

$$\frac{\text{Net tangible assets}}{\text{Total borrowings}}$$
$$\frac{3,119 - 356 - 288 + 1,948}{1,660 + 1,138} = 1.58$$

Note: that intangible assets and goodwill are excluded from the numerator

Current ratio

$$\frac{\text{Current assets}}{\text{Current liabilities}}$$
$$\frac{1,948}{1,137} = 1.71$$

Sometimes 2 : 1 is considered "safe" but this depends on the industry

Acid test ratio

$$\frac{\text{Current assets} - \text{inventory}}{\text{Current liabilities}}$$
$$\frac{1,948 - 636}{1,137} = 1.15$$

Sometimes 1 : 1 is considered "safe" but this depends on the industry

Gearing ratios indicate the safety of debt holders' funds and ability to service debt

Balance sheet gearing

$$\frac{\text{Long-term debt}}{\text{Shareholders' funds} + \text{long-term debt}}$$
$$\frac{1,660}{2,270 + 1,660} = 0.42$$

Note: "short-term" borrowings might be added to the numerator if these are judged to be "really" long-term liabilities

Interest cover

$$\frac{\text{Profit before finance costs and tax}}{\text{Finance costs}}$$
$$\frac{403 + 85}{85} = 5.74$$

Indicates ability to service(rather than repay)the debt
Note: the reference to finance costs rather than interest is consistent with IAS presentation

Asset utilisation ratios indicate the efficiency with which assets are employed

(Note that, ideally, the numerators in these ratios would be average figures over the appropriate period. Only end of period information is available.)

Inventory days (Often calculated as the inverse: inventory turnover)

$$\frac{\text{Inventory value}}{\text{Daily cost of sales}}$$
$$\frac{636}{3,649/365} = 65 \text{ days}$$

ideally the numerator would be average inventory over the period and there would be separate calculations with appropriate denominators for raw material inventory and finished goods inventory but this information is not available.

Receivables days

$$\frac{\text{Average trade receivables}}{\text{Daily revenue on credit}}$$
$$\frac{917}{4,347/365} = 77 \text{ day}$$

If payment terms are strictly 30 days then this ratio ought to be close to 30 days, if payment terms are net 30 days then close to 45 days might be expected

CONTINUED

Payables days	$\dfrac{\text{Average trade payables}}{\text{Daily purchase on credit}}$ $\dfrac{477}{2,220/365}=78.4\text{ days}$	Ideally purchases would be entered in the denominator but the most appropriate figure available is raw materials and consumables used

Profitability ratios indicate the profitability of sales

Net profit margin %	$\dfrac{\text{Profit from operation}}{\text{Revenue}}\times100\%$ $\dfrac{285}{4,347}\times100\%=6.6\%$	Note: that profit should be related to the sales that have generated the profit. If sales relate to operations then so should profit
Gross profit margin %	$\dfrac{\text{Gross profit}\times100}{\text{Revenue}}$ $\dfrac{698}{4,347}\times100\%=16.1\%$	Useful for comparison to other entities. Gross profit % will usually be lower in retailing and wholesaling than in manufacture

Return on capital employed relates profitability to assets employed

Return on capital employed (ROCE)	$\dfrac{\text{Profit before finance costs and tax}}{\text{Capital employed}}$ $\dfrac{403+85}{2,270+1,660}=12.4\%$	Often calculated to evaluate senior management performance. They have responsibility for all the capital employed (equity and debt) There is a strong argument for including all interest bearing debt in the denominator (including short-term borrowings) but these are often omitted
Return on investment (ROI)	$\dfrac{\text{Profit before finance costs and tax}}{\text{Investment}}$ $\dfrac{403+85}{3,119+1,948-1,137}=12.4\%$	An alternative calculation based on the use of funds (rather than there source). Again there is a strong argument that interest bearing debt, even thoguth a "current" liability, should not be deducted in the denominator
Return on equity	$\dfrac{\text{Profit after finance cost}}{\text{Total equity}}$ $\dfrac{403}{2,270}=17.8\%$	The return to equity holders matches their return to teir investment. Note the importance of matching numerator and denominator. This ratio may also be calculated with profit stated after deduction of tax

＊ These calculations are based on Figures 3.2 and 3.6. See Chapter 3.

图表 1.36 资产保全与流动比率表示偿债能力

资产保障率和流动比率表明偿还借款的能力 资产保障率	$\dfrac{\text{有形资产金额}}{\text{总借款}}$ $\dfrac{3\ 119-356-288+1\ 948}{1\ 660+1\ 137}=1.58$	注:无形资产与商誉需从分子中剔除
流动比率	$\dfrac{\text{流动资产}}{\text{流动负债}}$ $\dfrac{1\ 948}{1\ 137}=1.71$	有时 2:1 被认为是"安全的",但和所处行业有关
酸性测试比率(速动比率)	$\dfrac{\text{流动资产}-\text{存货}}{\text{流动负债}}$ $\dfrac{1\ 948-636}{1\ 137}=1.15$	有时 1:1 被认为是"安全的",但和所处行业有关
杠杆比率表明债权人资金的安全性以及偿债能力 资产负债表杠杆率	$\dfrac{\text{长期负债}}{\text{股东资金}+\text{长期负债}}$ $\dfrac{1\ 660}{2\ 270+1\ 660}=0.42$	注:如果属于"真实的"长期借款,则短期借款和1年内到期的长期借款也包括在内

(续表)

利息保障率	$\dfrac{未扣除财务费用和税款的利润}{财务费用}$	表示还本付息(而不是偿还债务)的能力
	$\dfrac{403+85}{85}=5.74$	注:根据 IAS 的表述,财务费用不仅仅只是利息

资产利用率表明资产使用的效率

(注:理想状态下,以下比率的分母应为期间平均数。通常只有期末数可得)

存货周转天数(通常会计算其倒数:存货周转率)	$\dfrac{存货价值}{日销售成本}$ $\dfrac{636}{3\,649/365}=65$ 天	理想状态下分子应该是期间存货平均数,而且应分别计算原材料与产成品对应的日销售成本,但通常很难得到相应数据
应收账款周转天数	$\dfrac{平均应收账款}{日平均赊销额}$ $\dfrac{917}{4\,347/365}=77$ 天	如果付款条件严格限定为30天,那么该比率应该接近30天。如果付款条件是净30天,则应采用45天
应付账款周转天数	$\dfrac{平均应付账款}{日平均赊购额}$ $\dfrac{477}{2\,220/365}=78.4$ 天	理想状态下分母应该是购买款,但是通常最适合的数据是原材料和消耗品

盈利比率表明销售的盈利

销售净利率(%)	$\dfrac{营业利润}{总收入}\times100\%$ $\dfrac{285}{4\,347}\times100\%=6.6\%$	注:利润必须与营业收入相对应
毛利率(%)	$\dfrac{毛利润}{总收入}\times100\%$ $\dfrac{698}{4\,347}\times100\%=16.1\%$	适用于同业比较。零售、批发行业的毛利率通常会比制造业的要低

已占用资本回报率将盈利能力与占用资产联系起来

已占用资本回报率(ROCE)	$\dfrac{扣除融资成本和税之前的利润}{已占用资本}$ $\dfrac{403+85}{2\,270+1\,660}=12.4\%$	经常用于评估高级管理层业绩,其应对所有投入资本负责(权益与借债)。对于是否将所有付息借款(包括短期借款)包括在分母内具有很大争议,但通常被省略
投资回报率(ROI)	$\dfrac{扣除融资成本和税之前的利润}{投资}$ $\dfrac{403+85}{3\,119+1\,948-1\,137}=12.4\%$	基于资金使用情况(而非资金来源)的一个替代计算。同理,有看法认为一些短期付息的借款不应该从分母中减除
净资产收益率(ROE)	$\dfrac{扣除融资本后的利润}{总权益}$ $\dfrac{403}{2\,270}=17.8\%$	股东权益的回报和股东投资的回报相匹配。注意匹配分子分母的重要性。此比率也可以用税后利润来计算

＊以上计算基于图表3.2和图表3.6。见第3章。

CHAPTER 2
Strateic and Organisational Management

第二章
战略与公司管理

Ansoff's product/market matrix

A commonly used model for analyzing the possible strategic directions that an organisation can follow. Hence useful in areas of strategic choice. See Figure 2.1.

安索夫产品/市场矩阵

一种常用的分析模型,用于分析组织可以追随的、可能的战略方向,因此,它也可用于战略选择。参见图表2.1。

FIGURE 2.1 Ansoff's produt/Market Matrix

products / Markets	existing	new
exsisting	Market penetration	Product development
new	Market development	diversification

图表 2.1 安索夫产品/市场矩阵

产品 / 市场	已有的	新的
已有的	市场渗透	产品开发
新的	市场发展	多样化

Anthony's triangle

The different levels of management within an organisation will take different types of decision and will require different information to take those decisions. See Figure 2.2.

安东尼三角理论

在一个组织中,不同的管理层级需要做出不同类型的决策,而制定决策所需的信息也不同。参见图表2.2。

FIGURE 2.2 Anthny's Triangle

图表 2.2 安东尼三角理论

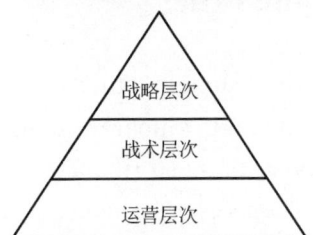

assurance map

A common qualitative way of assessing the significance of risk is to produce a "risk map" or sometimes called an "assurance map".

风险识别图

通常,评估风险大小的一种定性方法就是绘制"风险识别图",有时也称为"风险鉴别图"。

balanced scorecard approach

Approach to the provision of information to the management to assist strategic policy formulation and achievement. It emphasises the need to provide the user with a set of information which addresses all relevant areas of performance in an objective and unbiased fashion. The information provided may include both financial and non-financial elements, and cover areas such as profitability, customer satisfaction, internal efficiency and innovation.

平衡计分卡法

一种为管理层提供信息以帮助他们制定并实现战略政策的方法。该方法强调必须为用户提供客观公正的、全面的绩效相关信息。所提供的信息可能包括财务信息和非财务信息,其内容涵盖盈利性、客户满意度、内部效率和创新等方面。

barrier to entry

Any impediment to the free entry of new competitors into a market.

准入障碍

限制新竞争对手自由进入市场的任何障碍。

barrier to exit

Any impediment to the exit of existing competitors from a market.

退出障碍

限制现有竞争对手退出市场的任何障碍。

benchmarking

Establishment, through data gathering, of targets and comparators, that permit relative levels of performance and (particularly areas of underperformance) to be identified.

标杆管理

通过收集数据来设定目标和比较基准,以便确定绩效的相对水平(尤其是绩效表现不佳的领域)。

Adoption of identified best practices should improve performance.

internal benchmarking：Comparing one operating unit or function with another within the same industry.

functional benchmarking：Comparing internal functions with those of the best external practitioners，regardless of their industry（also known as operational benchmarking or generic benchmarking）.

competitive benchmarking：In which information is gathered about direct competitors through techniques such as reverse engineering.

strategic benchmarking：Type of competitive benchmarking aimed at strategic action and organisational change.

识别并采纳最佳实践，借以改善绩效。

内部标杆管理：对同一行业内的两个营运部门或职能部门进行比较。

职能性标杆管理：将内部职能部门与具有最佳表现的外部机构的相同职能部门进行比较，而不论该外部机构属于哪个具体行业（也称为操作性标杆管理或一般标杆管理）。

竞争性标杆管理：通过逆向工程等技术来收集直接竞争对手的相关信息。

战略性标杆管理：一种竞争性标杆管理，旨在制定战略行动和酝酿组织变革。

big data

Big data is a term for collection of data which is so large that it becomes difficult to store and process using traditional databases and data processing applications. Big data often also includes more than simply financial information and can involve other organisational external data which is often unstructured.

大数据

大数据是一个描述数据集合的术语，这个数据集合非常大，使用传统的数据库和数据处理应用程序难以进行贮存和处理。大数据往往不限于简单的财务信息，它还可以包括组织的其他外部数据，这些数据通常是非结构化的。

Boston Consulting Group matrix

A representation of an entity's product or service offerings which shows the value of each product's sales expressed in relation to the growth rate of the market served and the market share held. The objective of the matrix is to assist in the allocation of funds to products. Products can be classified as star,

波士顿矩阵

反映实体产品或服务的情况，通过所服务市场的增长率和所占市场份额来体现各产品的销售价值。矩阵的目的在于协助组织针对产品进行资金分配。根据在矩阵中所处的位置，产品可分类为：明星产品、现金牛产品、问题产品以及瘦狗产品。参见图表

cash cow, problem child or dog, according to their position on the matrix. See Figure 2.3.

2.3。

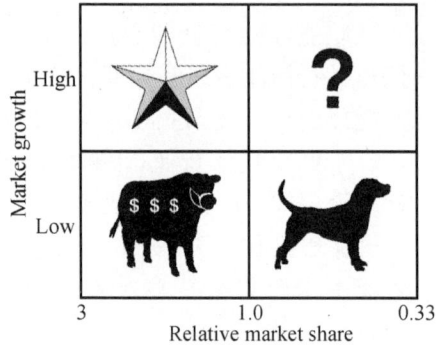

FIGURE 2.3   Boston Consulting Group Matrix

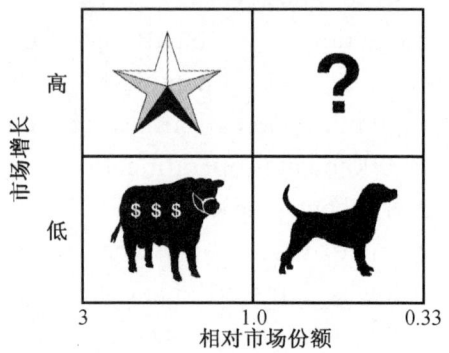

图表2.3   波士顿咨询集团矩阵

brainstorming

A method of generating ideas. There are different approaches but a popular one is for a number of people drawn from all levels of management and expertise to meet and propose answers to initial single question posed by the session leader.

头脑风暴

一种激发创意的方法。具有多种不同形式,但最常见的一种形式是从各级管理人员中抽一些人员出来,与专家一起面对面,就活动领导者最初提出的单个问题提供解答建议。

brand strategy

brand strategy, line extensions:An existing brand is applied to new variants/products within the same product category.

brand strategy, brand extensions:An existing brand is applied to products in a new product category.

brand strategy, multibrands: Having many different brand in the same product category.

brand strategy, new brands:New brands are created for new products and/or markets, usually because existing brands

品牌战略

线性延伸战略:现有品牌被应用到同一产品类别中的新产品上。

品牌延伸战略:现有品牌被应用到新产品类别中的产品上。

多品牌战略:在同一产品类别里,存在许多不同的品牌。

新品牌战略:为新产品和(或)新市场创建新品牌,这通常是因为组织认为现有品牌不适合。

are not deemed suitable.

brand strategy, cobrands: Two brands are combined in an offer so the brand reinforce each other.

品牌组合战略：两个品牌以组合形式出现在一个产品或服务中，并相得益彰。

business process re-engineering

打造业务流程

Selection of areas of business activity in which repeatable and repeated sets of activities are undertaken, and the development of improved understanding of how they operate and of the scope for radical redesign with a view to creating and delivering better customer value.

选择涉及可重复或重复性活动的业务活动领域，更好地了解这些领域的运作方式以及需彻底进行重新设计的范围，以便为客户创造和提供更高的价值。

cash cow

现金牛

Product characterised by a high market share but low market growth, whose function is seen as generating cash for use elsewhere within the entity.

具备较高市场份额、较低市场增长率的产品。它能为企业提供现金，供其他业务使用。

Change

变革

Organisation must continually assess their position within the environment and their performance compared to competitors, and be prepared to change their strategic direction in order to survive.

企业必须持续评估在外界环境中自身位置和相对于竞争者的业绩，并且为了生存准备改变自身的战略方向。

Change Agents

变革推动者

Many organisations seek to identify and reward change agents to encourage and facilitate change. They can play a major role in helping deal with resistance to change. Usually change agents are figures who are familiar and non-threatening to other people.

许多组织都在寻求识别和奖励变革推动者，以鼓励和推动变革。变革推动者在帮助组织应对变革阻力方面发挥了重要作用。通常，变革推动者都是一些为他人所熟悉而无害的人。

Change, Ethics

Most ethical issues focus on how one stakeholder group is benefited at the expense of another, so within any change process there will be a number of potential ethical dilemmas that need managing.

Change, Group and team formation

A group is simply a collection of individuals. The group the change leader selects may well come from various parts of the organisation, such as finance, human resources and sales. A team is more than a group. It is a set of individuals who must work together in order to accomplish shared objectives.

Change, Resistance to

Resistance to change is the action taken by individuals and groups when they perceive that a change that is occurring is a threat to them.

Change, Triggers

External triggers: Environmental pressure for change can be divided into two groups (general environemental factors that can be identified using the familiar PEST frameword and task factors that can be assessed using Porter's five forces model).

Internal triggers: The reasons for change within the organisation could span any functional area of operation or level of control from strategic to operational.

变革道德规范

大多数道德问题集中在一个利益相关者群体是如何以其他利益相关者群体的利益为代价而受益的,所以,在任何一个变革过程中,组织都会碰到一些需要处理的潜在道德困境。

变革群体和团队的形成

一个群体仅仅是个体的集合。变革领导者所选择的群体可能来自于组织的各个部分,如财务、人力资源和销售。而团队要比群体广泛得多,它是指一群个体为了实现共同的目标而必须在一起努力工作。

变革阻力

变革的阻力是指个人和群体认为正在发生的变革对他们构成威胁而采取的行动。

变革诱因

外部诱因:变革的环境压力可分为两组(可以使用大家所熟悉的 PEST 框架来鉴别一般性环境因素,也可以使用波特的竞争五力模型来评估任务型因素)。

内部诱因:组织内部的变革原因,可能跨越从战略到运营的任何职能领域或控制层级。

change，Types

Change can be classified by the extent (or scope) of the change required，and the speed with which the change is to be achieved.

competences

A group of abilities，resources or skills that enable the organisation to act effectively.

competence syndication

A situation where the different parties benefit from each other's competencies.

competitive advantage

Situation where an organisation exerts more competitive force on its competitors than they exert on it. See "Porter's five forces".

competitive forces

See "Porter's five forces".

competitive analysis

Identification and quantification of the relative strengths and weaknesses (compared with competitors or potential competitors)，which could be of significance in the development of a successful competitive strategy. A set of activities which examines

变革的种类

变革可以按所需的变革程度（或范围）以及变革的实现速度来进行分类。

竞争力

让组织能够有效运转的能力、资源或技能的组合。

能力聚合

不同各方能从彼此的竞争力中受益的情况。

竞争优势

组织相对其竞争者能发挥更大的竞争力。参见"波特竞争五力分析模型"。

竞争力

参见"波特竞争五力分析模型"。

竞争对手分析

通过对比竞争对手或潜在竞争对手，识别和量化自身的相对优势和劣势，这对于制定切实可行的竞争战略可能具有重大意义。它是指一组活动，用于检验在某个给定的战略领域内竞争企业的相对位置。

the comparative position of competing enterprises within a given strategic sector.

computer assisted audit techniques (CAATs)

计算机辅助审计技术

Methods of using a computer to carry out an audit of a computer system. There are two main categories of CAAT：audit software，such as audit interrogation software，Test data.

一种用计算机来执行计算机系统审计的方法，主要包括两类：一类是审计软件（例如，审计询问软件）；另一类是测试数据。

conglomerate diversification

复合多元化

See "Unrelated diversification".

参见"非相关多元化"。

contingency plan

应急计划

A plan，formulated in advance，to be implemented upon the occurrence of certain specific future events.

提前制订的一项计划或方案，在未来发生特定事件时予以执行。

continuous improvement

持续改善

Derived from the Japanese term kaizen. A simple idea but when taken seriously over a period can lead to significant improvements. See "kaizen".

源自日本术语 kaizen（改善式经营原则）。一个简单的概念，但若在某段时间内认真执行，便会带来重大改善。参见"改善式经营原则"。

corporate appraisal

企业评估

Critical assessment of the strengths and weaknesses，opportunities and threats（SWOT analysis）in relation to the internal and environmental factors affecting an entity in order to establish its condition prior to the preparation of the long-term plan.

对影响实体的、与内部因素和外部环境因素有关的优势与劣势、机会与威胁（SWOT 分析）进行批判性评估，以便在制订长期计划之前确定实体的状况。

corporate level strategy

It raises the question of which businesses and markets should an organisation be in. This may involve consideration of acquisition and diversification and will see an organisation being in more than one business.

critical success factor

An element of organisational activity which is central to its future success. Critical success factors may change over time, and may include items such as product quality, employee attitudes, manufacturing flexibility and brand awareness.

customer acquisition

Methods of acquiring customers can be split between traditional off-line techniques (e.g. advertising, direct mail, sponsorship, etc) and rapidly-evolving on-line techniques (e-marketing).

culture

A set of values, guiding beliefs, understandings and ways of thinking that are shared by the members of an organisation and is taught to new members as correct.

cultural web

The cultural web was devised by Gerry Johnson as part of his work to attempt to explain why firms often failed to adjust to environmental

公司层级的战略

公司层级战略提出了企业应该选择什么样的业务和市场的问题。这可能需要考虑收购和多元化,企业将从事多种业务。

关键成功因素

对未来成败至关重要的组织活动要素。关键成功因素会随着时间的变化而变化,可能包括产品质量、员工态度、制造灵活性和品牌意识等方面。

获取客户

获取客户的方法可以分为传统的离线技术(如广告、直接邮件投送、赞助等)以及发展迅速的在线技术(电子营销)。

文化

组织成员所共有的一套价值观、引导信念、认知以及思考方式,新员工应该学习这些内容并将其视为正确行为标准。

文化网络

文化网络是由格里·约翰逊提出的,试图解释为什么企业往往没能根据自身需要快速地适应环境变化。文

change as quickly as they needed to. The cultural web includes: the organisational paradigm and values, stories and myths, symbols, power structure, organisational structure, control systems, routines and rituals.

化网络包括:组织模式和价值观,故事与神话、符号象征、权力结构、组织结构、控制系统、惯例和传统。

customer extension

Customer extension has the objective of increasing the lifetime value of a customer and typically involves the following: ①"resell" similar products to previous sales. ②"cross sell" closely related products. ③"up sell" more expensive products. ④For example, having bought a book from Amazon you could be contacted with offers of other books, DVDs or DVD players. ⑤Reactivate customers who have not bought anything for some time.

客户延伸

客户延伸以提高客户的终身价值为目标,通常包括以下内容:①"再销售"与以往销售类似的产品给客户。②"交叉销售"密切相关的产品。③"向上销售"更为昂贵的产品。④例如,如果客户已从亚马逊购买了1本书,商家可以向客户提供关联书籍、DVD或DVD播放器。⑤"激活"那些已有一段时间没有购买任何东西的客户。

customer lifetime value (CLV)

The present value of the future cash flows attributed to the customer relationship.

客户终身价值

客户关系能够带来的未来现金流量的现值。也称为客户生命周期价值。

customer profitability analysis

Analysis if the revenue streams and service costs associated with specific customers or customer groups.

客户盈利分析

与特定客户或客户群有关的收入流和服务成本的分析。

customer relationship management (CRM)

A culture, possibly supported by appropriate information systems, where emphasis is placed on the interfaces between the entity and its customers. Knowledge is shared, within the

客户关系管理

一种强调实体与客户之间沟通互动的文化,其可能需要适当的信息系统作为支持。实体内部将分享知识,以确保客户获得始终如一的优质

entity, to ensure that the customer receives a consistently high service level.

服务。

data encryption

A technique of disguising information to preserve its confidentiality.

数据加密

一种将信息加以伪装以保持其机密性的技术。

data mining

The analysis of data to unearth unsuspected of unknown relationships, patterns and associations. Data mining is also the process of analysing data from different perspectives and summarising it into useful information—information that can be used to increase revenue, cut costs, or both.

数据挖掘

对数据进行分析以发掘未知的关系、模式和联系。数据挖掘也是从不同角度对数据进行分析,将其总结为有用信息,用于增加收入、减少成本或两个目的兼而有之。

data warehousing

Data warehousing is also defined as "the concept of integrating data from disparate internal and external sources centrally within the organisation such that the database thus establish can be used for flexible reporting and analysis".

数据仓储

数据仓储还可被定义为"将内部和外部不同来源的数据集中整合到组织中,以此建立信息库,灵活用于报告和分析工作"。

decision support systems(DSS)

A computer based system which enables managers to confront ill-structured problems by direct interaction with data and problem-solving program.

决策支持系统

一个以计算机为基础的系统,让管理者能够与数据和问题解决方案直接互动,以应对结构不良问题。

decision tree

Pictorial method of showing a sequence of interrelated decisions and their expected

决策树

以图片形式列示一系列关联决策及其预期结果的方法。决策树可同时

outcomes. Decision trees can incorporate both the probabilities of, and values of, expected outcomes, and are used in decision making. See Figure 2.4.

包含预期结果的可能性和价值,用于决策制定过程。参见图2.4。

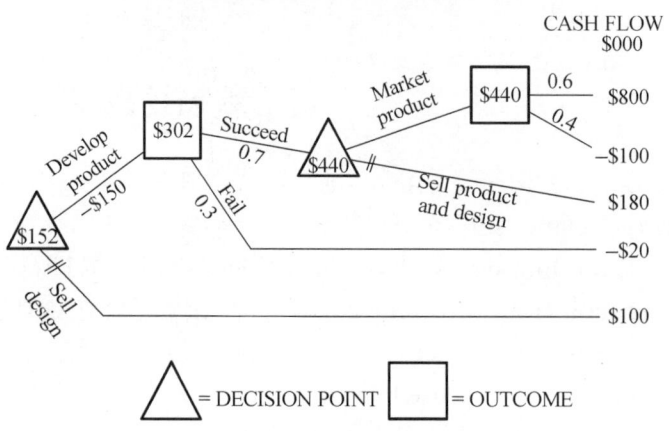

FIGURE 2.4   DECISION TREE

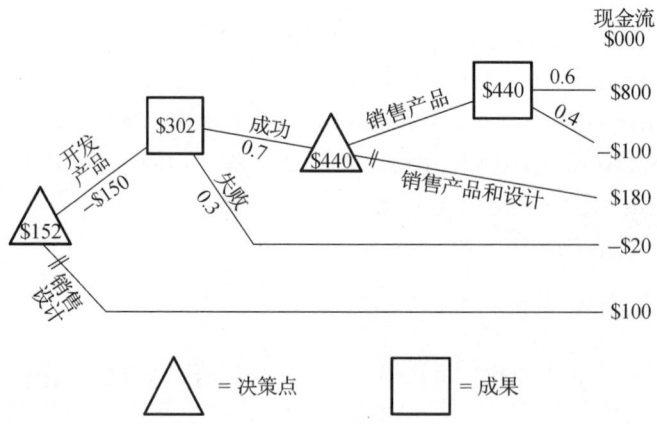

图表2.4   决策树

The decision tree shows the cash flows associated with the activities of (i) developing a product and (ii) selling the design. Problems are solved using decision trees by working from right to left. The decision tree on the left shows that the optimum course of action is to develop the product, generating a cash flow of $152 000, which is better than

从决策树可以看出,现金流与以下活动有关:(i)开发产品;(ii)销售设计。利用决策树,从右向左逐步推进,问题就可以得到解决。决策树左侧表明,最佳行动为开发产品,这将产生152 000美元的现金流,优于另一可选方案——销售设计,后者产生的现金流为100 000美元。

the alternative of selling the design which generates \$ 100 000.

Delphi technique

A technique to avoid the group pressures to conformity that are inherent in the think tank method. It does this by individually, systematically and sequentially interrogating a panel of experts.

differentiation

Differentiation strategy is based upon the idea of persuading customers that a product is superior to that offered by the competition. Differentiation can be based on product features or creating/altering consumer perception. Differentiation can also be based upon process as well as product. It is usually used to justify a higher price.

disaster recovery

Disaster recovery planning takes place in order to recover information systems from business critical events after they have happened. It involves: making a risk assessment; developing a contingency plan to address those risks.

E-business

The transformation of key business processed through the use of internet technologies.

德尔菲技术

一种避免群体一致性压力的技术，这种一致性压力是智囊团方法所固有的。它通过独立、系统、依次地询问一组专家的意见来避免这种压力。

差异化

差异化策略是基于这样一种理念：说服顾客，让其明白自身的产品优于竞争对手提供的产品。差异化可以通过产品的特点或建立（改变）消费者的认知来加以实现，也可以通过流程和产品。这种策略通常为提高产品价格提供合理理由。

灾后恢复

灾后恢复规划是在重大业务事件发生之后，重新恢复组织的信息系统。它涉及：做出风险评价、制定一项应急计划以应对这些风险。

电子商务

转向使用互联网技术来处理关键业务。

E-business, barriers

Barriers to e-business can be seen in both the organisation itself and in its suppliers and customers. It includes: technophobia, security, set-up costs, running costs, limited opportunities to exploit e-business, limited IT resources in-house and customers.

E-business, benefits

Most companies employ e-business to achieve the following: cost reduction, increased revenue, better information for control, increased visibility, enhanced customer service, improved marketing, market penetration, the combination of the above should be to enhance the company's competitive advantage, new business partnerships, enable employees to work from anywhere, increasing organisational flexibility, improve segmenting of the organisation's market, as well as better analysis of customers for improved target marketing.

E-business, categories

The categories of e-business functions are B2B (business to business), B2C (business to consumer), C2B (consumer to business) and C2C (consumer to consumer).

E-business, stages

The stages of e-business can be described as: Web presence, E-commerce, Integrated e-commerce, E-business.

电子商务的壁垒

电子商务的壁垒存在于组织本身以及组织的供应商和客户中。这些壁垒包括:技术恐惧、安全问题、启动成本、运行成本、开发电子商务的机会有限、组织内部及客户的 IT 资源有限。

电子商务的好处

大多数公司利用电子商务来实现以下目标:缩减成本、提高收入、获取更好的控制信息、提高可视性、提升客户服务水平、提高市场营销水平、市场渗透,同时实现上述几点应该能够强化公司的竞争优势,加强新的商业合作伙伴关系,让员工能够在任何地方开展工作,提高组织的灵活性,改进组织的市场细分以及更好地分析客户来提升目标营销。

电子商务的分类

电子商务功能可分为:B2B(企业对企业)、B2C(企业对个人)、C2B(个人对企业)以及 C2C(个人对个人)。

电子商务的阶段

电子商务可以描述为以下阶段:网络呈现阶段;电子交易阶段;整合的电子交易阶段;电子商务阶段。

E-commerce

E-commerce is described as "all electronically mediated information exchanges between an organisation and its external stakeholders".

economic order quantity(EOQ)

Most economic stock replenishment order size, which minimises the sum of stock ordering costs and stockholding costs. EOQ is used in an "optimising" stock control system.

EOQ may be calculated as：

$$\sqrt{\frac{2C_oD}{C_h}}$$

Where，

D is demand for a time period

C_o is the cost of placing one order

C_h is the cost of holding one item for that time period

economy

Acquisition of resources of appropriate quantity and quality at minimum cost. See Figure 2.5.

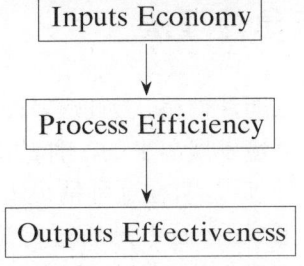

FIGURE 2.5　ECONOMY, EFFECIVENESS AND EFFICIENCY

Inputs Economy → Process Efficiency → Outputs Effectiveness

电子交易

电子交易是指"企业与其外部利益相关者之间以电子为媒介进行的所有信息交换"。

经济订货批量

最经济的库存补货订单量,可最大限度地降低库存订货成本和库存保管成本。EOQ 用于"优化"库存控制系统。

EOQ 的计算公式为：

$$\sqrt{\frac{2C_oD}{C_h}}$$

其中：

D 代表一段时间内的需求

C_o 代表单位订货成本

C_h 代表该段时间内单位库存的保管成本

经济

以最低成本购买合适数量和质量的资源。参见图表2.5。

图表 2.5　经济、效率、效果

投入经济 → 过程效率 → 产出效果

effectiveness

Utilisation of resources such that the output of the activity achieves the desired result. See Figure 2.5.

efficiency

Achievement of either maximum useful output from the resources devoted to an activity or the required output from the minimum resource input. See Figure 2.5.

eight-step process of change leadership

Step 1. establish a sense of urgency；

Step 2. creating the guiding coalition；

Step 3. developing a change vision；d

Step 4. communicating the vision；

Step 5. empowering broad-based action；

Step 6. generating short-term wins；

Step 7. never letting up；

Step 8. incorporating changes into the culture.

electronic word of mouth（eWoM）

The process of advertising through social media sites，such as Twitter and Facebook.

emergent approach

Mintzberg argued that in a changing environment，an emergent approach to strategy development occurs，whereby strategy tends to evolve rather than result from a logical，formal process. An emergent approach is

效果

有效利用资源，使活动产出达到预期结果。参见图表2.5。

效率

利用投入活动中的资源实现有用产出的最大化或者利用最少的资源投入获得所需的产出。具体参见图2.5。

变革领导力的八步骤流程

第一步，建立紧迫感；

第二步，创建领导团队；

第三步，制定变革愿景；

第四步，传达愿景；

第五步，采取广泛的行动；

第六步，产生短期利益；

第七步，不要松懈；

第八步，将变革融入文化。

电子口碑营销

通过社交媒体网站，如推特和脸谱进行广告营销的过程。

应急处理法

明茨伯格认为这是针对不断变化的环境发展出来的一种战略制定的应急处理方法，在这种情形下，战略是逐步形成的，而不是通过有逻辑的正式过程形成的。应急处理方法是不断改

evolving, continuous and incremental.

进的,是连续的、渐进的过程。

enterprise resource planning(ERP)

企业资源计划

Software system designed to support and automate the business processes of medium and large enterprises. ERP systems are accounting oriented information systems which aid in identifying and planning the enterprise wide resources needed to resource, make, account for and deliver cutomer orders.

一种用于支持和实现大中型企业业务流程自动运行的软件系统。企业资源计划系统是以会计为导向的信息系统,有助于识别和规划在获取、下达、核算和交付客户订单时企业范围内所需的资源。

Initially developed from MRPII systems, ERP tends to incorporate a number of software developments such as the use of relational databases, object-oriented programming and open system portability.

企业资源计划系统最初从 MRP II 系统发展而来,倾向于融合多个不同的软件开发成果,例如使用关系数据库、面向对象编程和开放系统的可移植性。

environmental impact assessment

环境影响评估

Study which considers potential environmental effects during the planning phase before an investment is made or an operation started.

在做出投资或者启动运营之前的规划阶段,研究潜在的环境影响。

E-souring

电子寻源

Electronic methods of finding new suppliers and establishing contracts.

以电子化方式寻求新供应商并签订合同。

Evaluating strategies

战略评估

Strategies need to have "strategic fit" with their environment if they are to be effective. This "fit" will be with both their internal and external environments.

战略如想发挥作用,就需要与其环境实现"战略性的契合"。这种"契合"既包含双方的内部环境也包含外部环境。

evolution

演进

Another way that evolution can be

演进可以通过另一种方式加以解

explained is by conceiving of the organisation as a learning system.

释,即把组织设想为一个学习系统。

exit strategies

退出战略

The most important fact that any investing institution will want to know is how and when they will get their money back. The exit strategy is an important part of the agreement to advance money in the first place.

Debt finance will normally have a specified repayment date, so the debt providers will have a clear exit route.

投资机构想要知道的最重要的事情就是他们何时以及将以何种方式收回自己投入的资金。退出战略是协议的重要组成部分,应把资金放在首位。

债务融资通常有指定的还款日期,债权方也有明确的退出途径。

expert systems

专家系统

A computerized system that performs the role of an expert or carries out a task that requires expertise.

一个计算机系统,可以扮演专家角色或执行需要专业知识的任务。

extranet

外联网

A private, secure extension of the enterprise via the corporate intranet. It allows the organisation to share part of its business information or operations with suppliers, customers, and other business partners using the internet.

外联网是企业运用内联网实现一种私密且安全的扩展,从而使企业能够与其供应商、客户以及其他业务合作伙伴有选择地共享业务信息或经营。

firewalls

防火墙

A firewall will consist of a combination of hardware and software located between the company's intranet(private network)and the public network(Internet). A set of control procedures will be established to allow public access to some parts of the organisation's computer system(outside the

防火墙是由硬件和软件组成的,是公司内网和外网之间的屏障。企业建立一套控制程序,允许公众访问企业计算机系统的某些部分(即在防火墙之外),同时限制他们访问其他部分(即在防火墙以内)。

firewall）whilst restricting access to other parts（inside the firewall）.

flexible manufacturing system（FMS）

Integrated，computer-controlled production system which is capable of producing any of a range of parts，and of switching quickly and economically between them.

Focus

This strategy is aimed at a segment of the market rather than the whole market. A particular group of consumers are identified with similar needs，possibly based upon age，sex，lifestyle，income or geography and then the company will either differentiate or cost focus in that area.

Force field analysis

Lewin argued that managers should consider any change situation in terms of：the factors encouraging and facilitating the change（the driving forces）；the factors that hinder change（the restraining forces）.

forecast

A prediction of future events and their quantification for planning purposes.

foresight

For organisations，foresight means not only predicting the future but developing an understanding of all the potential changes，

柔性制造系统

由计算机控制的一体化生产系统，能够生产任何类别的部件，并且能够以快速、经济的方式进行生产转换。

集中战略

这一战略瞄准细分市场，而不是整个市场。可基于消费者年龄、性别、生活方式、收入或所处地域等因素，识别出具有相似需求的独特群体，然后公司针对这个群体，采用差异化战略或成本集中战略。

力场分析

勒温认为管理者应该考虑以下方面的任何变化情况：鼓励和促进变革的因素（驱动力）；阻碍变革的因素（抑制力）。

预测

对未来事件进行预测并加以量化，以便进行规划。

远见

对组织而言，远见不仅意味着预测未来，也意味着需要理解所有潜在变化，如果管理得当，这些潜在变化可

which if managed properly could produce many new opportunities.

能会带来许多新机遇。

franchising

特许经营

The purchase of the right to exploit a business brand in return for a capital sum and a share of profits or turnover.

以资本投入和分享一部分利润或营业额的形式来换取某个商业品牌的使用权利。

freewheeling opportunism

随心所欲的机会主义

Freewheeling opportunists do not like planning. They prefer to see and take opportunities as they arise.

随心所欲的机会主义者不喜欢进行规划。他们更愿意在机会出现时发现并把握它们。

functional strategy

职能战略

This is concerned with how the component parts of the organisation in terms of resources, people and processed are pulled together to form a strategic architecture which will effectively deliver the overall strategic direction.

职能战略事关如何借助资源、人力和流程等将组织的各个部分整合到一起,形成一个战略架构以有效地决定总体战略方向。

game theory

博弈论

Game theory is concerned with the inter-relationships between the competitive moves of a set of competitors and, as such, can be a useful tool to analyze and understand different scenarios.

博弈论关注的是一组竞争对手的竞争性举动的相互作用关系,这是分析和理解不同情景的有用工具。

gap analysis

差距分析

A comparison between an entity's desired future performance level (most commonly expressed in terms of profit or ROCE) and the expected performance of projects

实体所期望的未来绩效水平(通常以利润或已占用资本回报率表示)与计划项目和进行中项目的预期表现之间的比较。对差异进行分类有助于

both planned and underway. Differences are classified in a way which aids the understanding of performance, and which facilitates improvement.

更好地了解业绩并推动改进。

generic strategies

See "three generic strategies".

一般性战略

参见"三大基本战略"。

goal congruence

In a cntrol system, the state which leads the individuals or groups to take actions which are in their self-interest and also in the best interest of the entity. Goal incongruence exists when the interests of individuals or of groups associated with an entity are not in harmony.

目标一致性

在控制系统内，一种能驱动个人或团队采取符合自身利益和实体最佳利益的行动的状态。当个人或团队的利益与相关实体的利益不一致时，就会出现目标不一致。

Groupware

Generic term for software that helps work groups to collaborate on projects.

群件

群件是一个通用软件术语，它能帮助工作组开展项目合作。

hacking

The gaining of unauthorized access to a computer system. It might be a deliberate attempt to gain access to an organisation's system and files, to obtain information or to alter data (perhaps fraudulently).

黑客行为

黑客行为是指未经授权就访问计算机系统的行为。它可能是有意为之的行为，试图进入企业的系统和文件，获取信息或篡改数据（也许是以欺诈的方式）。

horizontal diversification

Horizontal diversification refers to development into activities that are competitive with, or directly complementary to, a company's present activities.

横向多元化

横向多元化是指开发与公司现有活动相互竞争的或直接互补的活动。

horizontal integration

Results when two entities in the same line of business combine. For example，recent bank and building society mergers are a good example of this type of integration.

横向一体化

位于同一业务线的两个实体进行合并就能实现横向一体化。例如近来银行和房屋信贷互助会的合并就是横向一体化的很好例子。

Incrementalism

Lindblom believed that strategy-making involving small-scale extensions of past practices would be more successful as it was likely to be more acceptable since consultation，compromise and accommodation were built into the process.

渐进主义

林德布洛姆认为,如果战略制定包含以往实践的小范围延伸,将更可能取得成功,这是因为战略制定过程包括磋商、妥协与调解,更容易被接受。

information management strategy（IM strategy）

Information management strategy relates to the roles of those involved in the system and their relationship with the system itself. It aims to put management into IT.

信息管理战略

信息管理战略涉及系统人员的角色以及他们与系统相互关系的本身。它旨在将管理融入信息技术。

information systems strategy（IS strategy）

IS strategy（Information systems strategy）is concerned with aligning IS development with business needs and with seeking strategic advantage from IT.

信息系统战略

信息系统战略是把信息系统战略的制定与业务需求以及从信息技术中寻求战略优势结合起来。

information technology strategy（IT strategy）

Information technology strategy is described as activity-based，supply-orientated

信息技术战略

信息技术战略是以活动为基础的、以供给为导向的、聚焦于技术的战

and technology-focused. It focuses on the selection, use and management of the technology itself.

略。它着重于技术本身的选择、使用和管理。

information strategy, need for

对信息战略的需求

Many organisations have historically viewed their IT and information systems as a necessary resource, but one that was not strategically significant. Now days, this attitude has changed as businesses have realized the value of having an IT strategy that fits into the overall corporate strategy.

许多企业历来认为信息技术和信息系统是它们的必要资源,但其战略意义不大。如今,这种态度发生了转变,企业已经认识到符合企业整体战略的信息技术战略是具有价值的。

information value

信息价值

The net value of information in decision-making situations could be calculated as:

The difference in the values of outcomes in a decision with and without the information, minus the cost of obtaining the information.

信息在决策制定中的净现值可以通过以下方式计算:

在具备以及不具备这个信息的情况下,决策结果的价值差异,再减去信息获取成本。

intellectual capital

智力资本

Knowledge which can be used to create value. Intellectual capital includes:

human resources: The collective skills, experience and knowledge of employees;

intellectual assets: Knowledge which is defined and confined such as drawing, computer program or collection of data;

intellectual property: Intellectual assets which can be legally protected such as patents and copyrights.

可用来创造价值的知识。智力资本包括:

人力资源:员工的集体技能、经验和知识;

知识资产:经定义以及被限定的知识,例如图纸、计算机程序或数据集合;

知识产权:受到法律保护的知识资产,例如专利、版权。

International growth strategies

国际增长战略

When deciding whether to expand

在决定是否向海外扩张时,企业

abroad，a business has several possible strategies that it can adopt：exporting strategy，overseas manufacture，multinational，transnational.

可以采取一些可能的策略：出口战略、海外生产、多国经营、跨国经营。

international operations

Increasingly in the modern business environment，entities are expanding across national boundaries into many different countries.

Although there are risks associated with such strategies，the strategic and financial benefits to an entity can be enormous.

国际运营

在现代商业环境中，越来越多的实体跨出国门，在许多国家开展经营。

企业跨国经营战略虽然存在一定的风险，但它可实现巨大的战略和财务收益。

ISO 9000

Quality system standard which requires complying organisations to operate in accordance with a structure of written policies and procedures that are designed to ensure the consistent delivery of a product or service to meet customer requirements.

ISO 9000 质量认证体系

一种质量体系标准，它要求组织按照所确立的书面政策和流程框架来开展运营，这些政策和流程旨在确保组织始终如一地交付产品或服务，满足客户需求。

Intranet

Intranet are internal internets. They exist inside the organisation only，using website and browser technology to display information.

内联网

内联网是内部网络。它们只存在于组织内部，利用网站和浏览器技术来显示信息。

joint development Methods

Joint development methods include：joint venture，strategic alliances，franchising，licenses，outsourcing.

联合发展方法

联合发展法包括：合资、战略联盟、特许经营、许可证、外包。

just-in-time(JIT)

System whose objective is to produce or

适时生产系统

适时生产系统的目标是及时生产

to procure products or components as they are required by a customer or for use, rather than for stock.

just-in-time system: Pull system, which responds to demand, in contrast to a push system, in which stocks act as buffers between the different elements of the system such as purchasing, production and sales.

just-in-time production: Production system which is driven by demand for finished products, whereby each component on a production line is produces only when needed for the next stage.

just-in-time purchasing: Purchasing system in which material purchases are contracted so that the receipt and usage of material, to the maximum extent possible, coincide.

Kanter, power skill of change agents

Kanter identified seven power skills that change agents require to enable them to overcome apathy or resistance to change, and enable them to introduce new ideas:

(a) ability to work independently, without the power and sanction of the senior management hierarchy behind them, providing visible support

(b) ability to collaborate effectively

(c) ability to develop relationships based on trust, with high ethical standards

(d) self-confidence, tempered with humility

(e) being respectful of the process of change, as well as the substance of the change

(f) ability to work across different business functions and units

或获取客户所需的或需要使用的产品或部件，而无需事先库存。

准时生产系统："拉动"系统是针对需求做出回应，相比之下，"推动"系统是将库存作为采购、生产以及销售等多个不同系统要素之间的缓冲。

准时生产：由产成品需求驱动的生产系统，在此系统下，生产线仅在下一生产阶段需要时才生产部件。

准时采购：该系统按照合同约定采购材料，以最大可能地实现材料采购和使用的同步。

坎特（人名），变革促进者的能力

坎特确定了变革促进者需要的七项能力，这些能力能够帮助他们克服冷漠情绪或对变革的抵抗，并提出新的想法：

（a）在没有高级管理层授权和批准的情况下，独立开展工作、提供实际支持的能力

（b）有效合作的能力

（c）基于信任而建立关系的能力，遵循高道德标准

（d）自信、谦逊

（e）尊重变革过程和变革内容

（f）跨业务职能部门和单元的工作能力

（g）a willingness to stake personal rewards on results，and gain satisfaction from success.

（g）基于结果获取个人回报的意愿以及获得成功的满足感

kaizen

持续改善

Japanese term for continuous improvement in all aspects of an entity's performance at every level. See "continuous improvement".

日本术语,是指在各个层级上对实体的绩效进行全方位的持续改善。参见"持续改善"。

lead time

生产时间

Time interval between the start of an activity or process and its completion，for example the time between ordering goods and their receipt，or between starting production of a product and its completion. The latter is also known as process time.

某一活动或过程从开始到完成的时间间隔,举例而言,从订货到收货的时间、从产品开始生产到完成生产的时间,后者也称为"加工时间"。

learning organisation

学习型组织

An organisation skilled at creating, acquiring and transferring knowledge and at modifying its behavior to reflect new knowledge and insights.

学习型组织善于形成、获取和传递知识,同时也善于修正自身行为以反映新知识和新见解。

Lewin，three stage model

勒温,三阶段模型

The three-stage model of change was proposed by Lewin in the 1950's. He argued that，in order for change to occur successfully，organisations need to progress through three stages. This process includes unfreezing habits or standard operating procedures，changing to new patterns and refreezing to ensure lasting effects.

20世纪50年代,勒温提出了三阶段变革模型。他认为,为了成功实现变革,组织需要历经三个阶段。这个过程包括"解冻"习惯或标准作业程序、向新模式转变以及"再次冻结"以确保持久的影响。

Licensing

The right to exploit an invention or resource in return for a share of proceeds. Licensing differs from a franchise because there will be little central support.

limiting factor or key factor

Anything which limits the activity of an entity. An entity seeks to optimise the benefit it obtains from the limiting factor. Examples are a shortage of supply of a resource or a restriction on sales demand at a particular price. See "bottleneck".

logical access controls

Security over access is often based on a logical access system. See Figure 2.6.

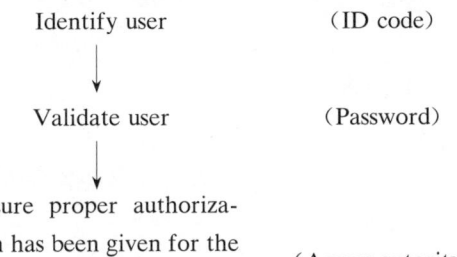

FIGURE 2.6   logical Access Control Chart

Passwords and user names are a way of identifying who is authorized to access the system, and granting access to the system, or to specific programs or files, only if an authorized password is entered. There may be several levels of password, with particularly

授权许可

以收益份额的形式换取使用一项发明或资源的权利。授权许可与特许经营不同，因为它很少获得中央支持。

限制因素或关键因素

限制实体活动的任何因素。实体寻求从限制因素中获取最大化利益。例如，资源的供应短缺或者特定价格对销售需求的限制。参见"瓶颈"。

逻辑访问控制

访问的安全保障往往是基于逻辑访问系统，参见图表2.6。

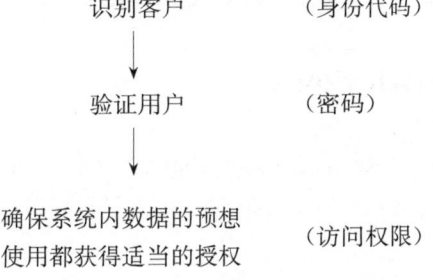

图表2.6   逻辑访问控制图

只有当输入经过授权的密码后，密码和用户名能够识别哪些人得到授权可以访问系统，并准许他们访问相应系统或特定的程序或文件。有时候可能需要几个层次的密码，这是因为特别敏感的应用程序需用多个密码加

sensitive applications protected by multiple passwords.

以保护。

long term planning-advantages and disadvantages

长期计划-优点与缺点

Advantages of adopting a long-term planning approach include：forces managers to look ahead；improved control；identifies key risks；encourages creativity.

采用长期规划方法的优点包括：迫使经理着眼于未来；改进控制；识别关键风险；鼓励创新。

Disadvantages of formal，long-term planning include：setting corporate objectives；short-term pressures；difficulties in forecasting accurately；bounded rationality；rigidity；cost；management distrust.

正式的长期规划的缺点包括：制定企业目标；短期压力；难以准确预报；有限的理性；刚性；费用；管理的信任缺失。

management information systems (MIS)

管理信息系统

A management information system is defined as "a system to convert data from internal and external sources into information，and to communicate that information in an appropriate form to managers at all level and in all areas of the business to enable them to make timely and effective decisions".

管理信息系统是指从内部和外部来源获取数据并转化为信息，而后以适当的形式将信息传递给企业各个业务领域以及各个层级的管理者，以便他们能够做出及时、有效的决策。

mark-down

减价

Reduction in the selling price of damaged or slow-selling goods.

下调受损商品或滞销商品的售价。

mark-up

涨价

Addition to the cost of goods or services which results in a selling price.

商品或服务成本的增加导致销售价格的上涨。

market development

市场开发

Aims to increase sales by taking the

把现有产品引入新市场（或新的

present product to new markets (or new segments).

market share

An entity's sales of a product or service in a specified market expressed as a proportion of total sales by all entities offering that product or service to the market. A planning tool and a performance assessment ratio.

marketing, relationship

The concept of relationship marketing has been defined as the technique of maintaining and exploiting the firm's customer base as a means of developing new business opportunities.

Mashups

The term "mashup" originated in music where artists would combine parts from different songs to create a new track. The web equivalent is where developers can now mix, match, reuse, and morph web content, data, and services.

material requirement planning(MRP)

System that converts a production schedule into a listing of the materials and components required to meet that schedule, so that adequate stock levels are maintained and items are available when needed.

McKinsey 7S model

Like the cultural web, McKinsey's model

细分市场),以期增加销售额。

市场份额

在特定市场中,实体产品或服务的销售情况,以在提供这一产品或服务的所有实体的销售总额中所占的比例来表示。市场份额是一种规划工具和绩效评估比率。

关系营销

关系营销概念是指一种技术,其通过维护和利用公司的客户群体来探寻新的商业契机。

混搭

"混搭"术语起源于音乐,是指艺术家从不同歌曲中取材并将其加以糅合以创作一支新的歌曲。就网络而言,混搭是指开发人员可以对网页内容、数据和服务加以混合、搭配、再利用和改变。

物料需求计划

此系统将生产计划转化为生产计划所需物料和部件的清单,以便维持充足的库存水平,以备不时之需。

麦肯锡 7S 模型

就像文化网络一样,麦肯锡模型

looks at corporate culture and the various components that it is made up of. McKinsey saw culture as seven interconnected elements，each beginning with the letter S—strategy，structure，styles，staff，skills，systems，shared values.

着眼于企业文化及其各个组成部分。麦肯锡认为文化是由七个相互关联的因素组成的，每个因素都以字母 S 开头——战略、结构、风格、员工、技能、系统和共同价值。

Mendelow's power/interest matrix

Mendelow's matrix is a mode which can be used to prioritise stakeholders and decide how to deal with each of them.

孟德尔洛的权力/利益矩阵

孟德尔洛矩阵是一种模式，可用于利益相关者优先顺序排序，并以此决定如何应对每一类利益相关者。

mission

Fundamental objective(s) of an entity expressed in general terms.

使命

使用通用术语表达的实体基本目标。

mission statement

Published statement，apparently of the entity's fundamental objective(s). This may or may not summarise the true mission of the entity.

使命宣言

使命宣言是针对实体基本目标发表的声明，它可能概括了实体的真正使命，也可能没有。

national competitive advantage (Porter's diamond)

Theory and model，proposed by M. Porter，for identifying why entities may achieve a competitive advantage over their rivals by virtue of being based or domiciled in a particular country. Often known as Porter's diamond，due to the shape of the diagrammatic representation of the model.

国家竞争优势(波特"钻石"理论)

迈克尔·波特提出的一种理论和模型，据此可辨别实体为何能因其所在国家而获得相对于对手更胜一筹的竞争优势。由于此模型的图示呈"钻石"形状，因此通常称为波特"钻石"理论。

network analysis

Quantitive technique used in project control. The events and activities making up the whole project are represented in the form of a diagram.

critical events：Any event which lies on the critical path

critical path：Longest path or paths through a network.

event：Start or completion of an activity. In a network an event is represented by a small circle （a node）, and an activity by an arrow.

Project evaluation and review technique （PERT）：Specification of all activities, events, probabilities and constraints relating to a project from which a network is drawn, providing a model of the way the project should proceed.

slack/float time：Time available for an activity over and above that required for its completion.

objective, hierarchy of

Arrangement of the objectives of an entity into a number of different levels, with the higher levels being more general and the lower more specific. These levels may be mission, goals, targets or, alternatively; strategic objectives, tactical objectives or operational objectives.

operations plans

Fully detailed specifications by which

网络分析

项目控制中应用到的一种定量分析方法。构成整个项目的事件和活动均以图表形式列示。

关键事件：位于关键路径上的任何事件。

关键路径：是指网络中的最长路径。

事件：活动的启动或完成。在一个网络中，事件以小圆圈（节点）表示，而活动以箭头表示。

项目评审技术：指明与项目相关的所有活动、事件、可能性和限制，并据此绘制出一张网络图，提供项目应该如何推进的路径模型。

富裕/浮动时间：某项活动可用的，超出其完成规定时间的那部分时间。

目标层级

将某一实体的目标分成若干不同级别，级别越高，目标越笼统；级别越低，目标越具体。这些级别可以是使命、目的、目标或是战略目标、战术目标或运营目标。

运行计划

详尽的规范，个人应遵照这个规

individuals are expected to carry out the pre-determined cycles of operations to meet sectoral objectives.

范来完成预定的运行周期,实现部门目标。

outsourcing

Use of external suppliers as a source of finished products, components or services. This is also known as contract manufacturing or subcontracting.

外包

利用外部供应商来提供产成品、部件或服务,又称为"合同制造"或"分包"。

Pareto (80/20) distribution

Frequency distribution with a small proportion (for example, 20%) of the items accounting for a large proportion (for example, 80%) of the value/resources. Common occurrences are sales, when 80% of turnover may arise from 20% of customers; inventory, when 20% of the items comprise 80% of the value. See Figure 2.4.

帕累托(80/20)分布

一种频率分布,是指小部分(如20%)物品创造了大部分(如80%)价值(或占用了大部分资源)。常见于销售,80%的营业额来自于20%的客户;在存货中,20%的物品包含了80%的价值。参见图表2.7。

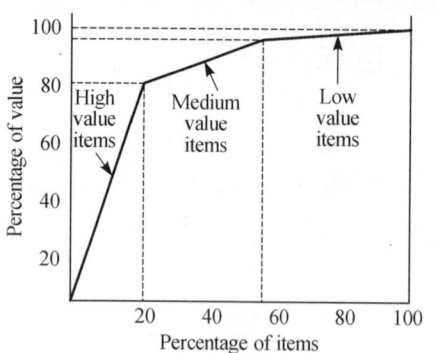

FIGURE 2.7 PARETO(80/20) DISTRIBUTION: INVENTORY

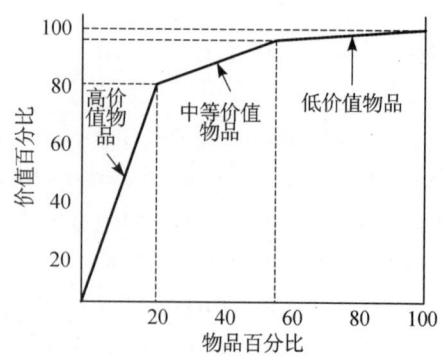

图表2.7 帕累托(80/20)分布:存货

PEST analysis

PEST analyses the general macro-envi-

PEST 分析

"PEST"是分析一般的宏观环境,

ronment，identifying key drivers of change and hence source of risk. P stands for political，E stands for economic，S stands for social，T stands for technological.

planning

　　Establishment of objectives，and the formulation，evaluation and selection of the policies，strategies，tactics and action required to achieve them. Planning comprises long-term/strategic planning and short-term/operational planning. The latter is usually for a period of up to one year.

　　capital funding planning：Process of selecting suitable funds to finance long-term assets and working capital.

　　capital resource planning：Process of evaluating and selecting long－term assets to meet strategies.

　　financial planning：Planning the acquisition of funds to finance planned activities.

　　futuristic planning：Planning for that period which extends beyond the planning horizon in the form of future expected conditions which may exist in respect of the entity, products/services and environment but which cannot usefully be expressed in quantified terms. An example would be working out the actions needed in a future with no motor cars.

　　strategic planning：Formulation，evaluation and selection of strategies for the purpose of preparing a long-term plan of action to attain objectives. Also known as corporate planning and long-range planning.

找出变革的关键驱动因素和风险源。P代表政治,E代表经济,S代表社会,T代表技术。

规划

　　设定目标,并为实现目标而制定、评估和选择政策、战略、战术和行动。规划包括长期/战略规划和短期/营运规划,后者涉及的时间通常在1年以内。

　　资本筹集规划:选择合适的资金为长期资产和营运资本提供资金支持的过程。

　　资本资源规划:评估和选择满足战略需要的长期资产的过程。

　　融资规划:规划如何获取资金为计划活动提供资金支持。

　　远景规划:规划工作着眼于当前规划期以外,预计企业、产品/服务以及环境未来可能出现的状况,但通常无法以量化方式加以表述。举例而言,可以设想未来在没有汽车的状况下需采取的行动。

　　战略规划:制定、评估和选择战略来编制长期行动计划以实现目标,亦称为"公司规划"和"长期规划"。

Factical planning：Planning the utilisation of resources to achieve specific objectives in the most effective and efficient way.

战术规划：以最行之有效的方式利用资源来实现特定目标的规划。

planning horizon

规划远景

Furthest time ahead for which plans can be quantified. It need not be the planning period. See "futuristic planning(planning)".

计划可实现量化的最长未来期限,不一定是规划期间。参见"远景规划(规划)"。

planning period

规划期间

Period for which a plan is prepared and used. It differs according to the product or process life cycle. For example, forestry requires a period of many years whereas fashion garments require only a few months.

编制及运用计划所针对的期间,不同于产品或流程的生命周期。例如,森林需要若干年才能形成,而时装仅需数月就可制成。

policy

政策

Undated, long-lasting and often unquantified statement of guidance regarding the way in which an organisation will seek to behave in relation to its stakeholders.

一份无期限的、持久的且通常无法量化的指导方针声明,其指明组织寻求何种行为方式来应对利益相关者。

Porter, generic strategies

波特,基本战略

See "three generic strategies".

参见"三大基本战略"。

Porter's five Competitive forces

波特竞争五力分析

External influences upon the extent of actual and potential competition within any industry which in aggregate determine the ability of firms within that industry to earn a profit. See Figure 2.8.

在任一行业内,影响实际和潜在竞争程度的外在影响力,这些影响力将共同决定公司在该行业内的盈利能力。参见图表2.8。

FIGURE 2.8　PORTER'S FIVE FORCES

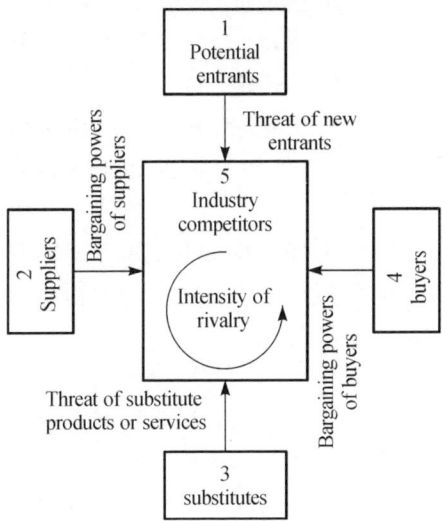

图表 2.8　波特竞争五力分析

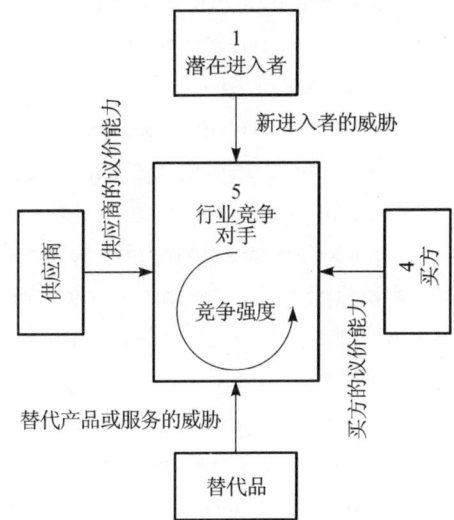

position audit

Part of the planning process which examines the current state of the entity in respect of: resources of tangible and intangible assets and finance; products, brands and markets; operating systems such as production and distribution; internal organisation; current results; and returns to stockholders.

地位审查

规划流程的一部分,它审查实体在以下方面的现状:有形和无形资产及融资的来源;产品、品牌和市场;生产、分销等营运系统;内部组织;当前业绩;利益相关者的回报。

pricing

Determination of a selling price for the product or service produced. A number of methodologies may be used including:

competive pricing: Setting a price by reference to the prices of competitive products.

cost plus pricing: Determination of price by adding a mark-up, which may incorporate a desired return on investment, to a measure

定价

确定所生产产品或所提供服务的售价。可采用的定价方法包括:

竞争性定价:通过参考竞争产品的价格进行定价。

成本加成定价:在产品/服务成本的基础上,加上一定的涨幅来确定价格,价格涨幅可能包含预期的投资

of the cost of the product/service.

dual pricing：Form of transfer pricing in which the two parties to a common transaction use different prices.

historical pricing：Basing current prices on prior period prices，perhaps uplifted by a factor such as inflation.

market-based pricing：Setting a price based on the value of the product in the perception of the customer. Also known as perceived value pricing.

penetration pricing：Setting a low selling price in order to gain market share.

predatory pricing：Setting a low selling price in order to damage competitors. May involve dumping, i. e. selling a product in a foreign market at below cost, or below the domestic market price(subject to, for example，adjustments for taxation differences，transportation costs，specification differences).

premium pricing：Achievement of a price above the commodity level，due to a measure of product or service differentiation.

price skimming：Setting a high price in order to maximise short-term profitability, often on the introduction of a novel product.

range pricing：Pricing of individual products such that their prices fit logically within a range of connected products offered by one supplier，and differentiated by a factor such as weight of pack or number of product attributes offered.

selective pricing：Setting different prices for the same product or service in different markets. Can be broken down as follows：

—category pricing：Cosmetically modifying a product such that the variations allow

回报。

双重定价：一种转移定价形式，在此模式下，同一交易的不同交易方采用不同的价格。

历史定价：基于过往价格确定当前价格，可能会根据通胀等因素做出上调。

市场导向定价：基于顾客对产品的价值认知进行定价，亦称作"认知价值定价"。

渗透定价：为获取市场份额而设定一个较低的售价。

掠夺性定价：为打击竞争对手而设定一个较低的售价，可能涉及倾销行为。倾销是指以低于成本或国内市场价格的价格在境外市场销售产品（可能基于税收差异、运输成本、规格差异做出调整）。

溢价定价：基于衡量产品或服务差异，设定一个高于商品水平的价格。

撇脂定价：设定一个较高价格，以期短期内尽可能地获取最大盈利，通常发生在新产品上市之初。

范围定价：对单个产品定价，使其价格在逻辑上与某一供应商供应的一系列关联产品相吻合，同时又因包装重量或产品属性数量等不同而有所差异。

选择性定价：针对不同市场，同一产品或服务设定不同价格，具体可分为：

——类别定价：美化产品外观，以令产品可按多个价格类别进行销售，

it to sell in a number of price categories, as where a range of "brands" are based on a common product.

—customer group pricing: Modifying the price of a product or service so that different groups of consumers pay different prices.

—reak pricing: Setting a price which varies according to level of demand.

—service level pricing: Setting a price based on the particular level of service chosen from a range.

—time material pricing: A form of cost-plus pricing in which price is determined by reference to the cost of the labour and material inputs to the product/service.

如同各种"品牌"都是基于同一产品一样。

——客户群定价:针对不同的客户群,更改产品或服务的价格,实行不同价格。

——高峰定价:因需求量不同而设定不同的价格。

——服务水平定价:根据所选择的特定服务水平进行定价。

——工时材料定价:成本加成定价的一种方式,此定价法参考产品/服务的劳动力和材料投入成本来确定价格。

probability

Likelihood of an event or a state of nature occurring, being measured in a range from 0(no possibility) to 1(certainty).

概率

某一事件或某种状态发生的可能性,以 0(不可能发生)至 1(肯定发生)之间的数值来衡量。

product bundling

Form of discounting in which a group of related products is sold at a price which is lower than that obtainable by the consumer were the products to be purchased separately.

产品捆绑销售

一种折扣销售形式,将一组相关产品以低于消费者单独购买组合中的产品的价格进行销售。

product life cycle

Period which begins with the initial product specification and ends with the withdrawal from the market of both the product and its support. It is characterised by defined stages including growth, development, introduction, maturity, decline and abandonment.

产品生命周期

产品生命周期是指从初步确定产品规格到从市场上撤回产品及其支持服务所涵盖的期间,其特点是分为成长期、发展期、引入期、成熟期、衰退期和退出期几个阶段。

programming

dynamic programming：Operational research technique used to solve multi-stage problems in which the decisions at one stage are the accepted assumptions applicable to the next stage.

linear programming：Series of linear equations used to construct a mathematical model. The objective is to obtain an optimal solution to a complex operational problem，which may involve the production of a number of products in an environment in which there are many constrains.

non-linear programming：Process in which the equations expressing the interactions of variables are not all linear but may，for example，be in proportion to the square of a variable.

projection

Expected future trend pattern obtained by extrapolation. It is principally concerned with quantitative factors，whereas a forecast includes judgements. See Figure 2.9.

规划

动态规划：一种解决多阶段问题的经营研究技术，在此方法中，前一阶段做出的决策用作经认可的、适用于下一阶段的假设。

线性规划：利用一系列线性方程式构建一个数学模型，其目标是获得复杂经营问题的最佳解决方案，譬如，在存在多种限制因素的环境中生产多种产品。

非线性规划：在非线性规划中，表达变量之间相互关系的方程式不全是线性方程式，而可能是其他方程式，譬如，可能与变量的平方呈一定的比例关系。

推测

通过推断得出的预期未来趋势模式，主要与定量因素有关，但预测也包含判断。参见图表2.9。

FIGURE 2.9 PROJECTION

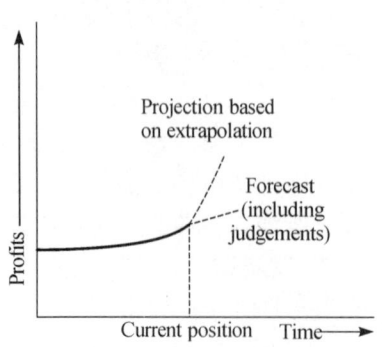

图表2.9 推测

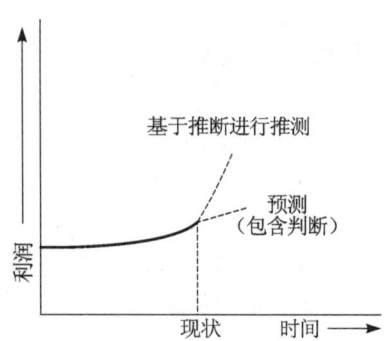

push and pull supply chain models

Driven by e-commerce's capabilities to empower clients，many companies are moving from the traditional "push" business model，where manufacturers，suppliers，distributors and marketers have most of the power，to a customer-driven "pull" model. This new business model is less product-centric and more directly focused on the individual consumer.

推拉供应链模式

受电子商务能力的推动，赋予客户更大的权利，很多企业都从传统的"推动"商业模式（在这种模式下，制造商、供应商、经销商和营销人员具有大部分权利）向客户驱动的"拉动"模式转变。这种新的商业模式很少以产品为中心，而是更多地直接关注个体消费者。

quality assurance

Ensuring products or service consistently meet quality specifications.

质量保证

确保产品或服务始终符合质量规范。

rational model

The rational model is a logical，step-by-step approach. It requires the organisation to analyse its circumstances，generate possible strategies，select the best one and then implement them.

理性模式

理性模式是一个合乎逻辑的、循序渐进的方法。它要求组织分析其所处环境，制定可行的战略，选择最优战略，而后加以实施。

related diversification

Concentric diversification：growth into similar industries；growth forward into the customer marketplace.

相关多元化

同心多元化：在相似行业中寻求增长；进军客户市场寻求增长。

re-order level

Level of stock at which a replenishment order should be placed. Traditional optimising systems use a variation on the following computation，which builds in a measure of

补充订货库存量

补充订货时的库存量。传统"优化"系统在下列计算式中使用一个变量，该计算式建立了安全库存量衡量指标，并最大限度地降低库存短缺的

safety stock and minimises the likelihood of a stock-out.

（maximum usage×maximum lead time）

可能性。

（最大使用量×最长前置时间）

reverse engineering

逆向工程

Decomposition and analysis of competitors' products in order to determine how they are made，costs of production and the way in which future development may proceed.

分解并分析竞争对手的产品，以确定该产品的制造工艺、生产成本以及未来可能的发展方向。

risk

风险

Condition in which there exists a quantifiable dispersion in the possible outcomes from any activity. Risk can be classified in a number of ways.

任何一个活动可能产生的结果之间存在可量化偏离的情形。风险可按多种方式进行分类。

Risk adjusted Weighted Average Cost of Copital

风险调整的加权平均资本成本

When using a proxy cost of capital，care must be taken to ensure that it reflects the business risk and the capital structure of the entity being valued. If necessary，a risk adjusted cost of capital could be used.

在运用资本代理成本时，必须注意确保其能够反映出被估值实体的商业风险和资本结构。如果必要，还可以应用经风险调整的资本成本。

risk appetite

风险偏好

The amount of risk an organisation is willing to accept in pursuit of value.

风险偏好是指一个组织在追求价值的过程中愿意接受的风险程度。

risk assessment

风险评估

Risk assessment is composed of the analysis and evaluation of risk through the process of identification，description and estimation.

风险评估由风险分析和评估组成，涉及风险的识别、描述和估计过程。

risk attitude

The overall approach to risk, in terms of the board being risk averse or risk seeking.

risk, business/operational

Relating to activities carried out within an entity, arising from structure, systems, people, products or processes.

risk capacity

The amount of risk that the organisation can bear.

risk, business

The business risk is the risk businesses face due to the nature of their operations and products.

risk, country

Associated with undertaking transactions with, or holding assets in, a particular country. Sources of risk might be political, economic or regulatory instability affecting overseas taxation, repatriation of profits, nationalisation or currency instability.

risk, culture

A risk that products, services and business practices that are acceptable in one country will be unacceptable in another. Failure to understand a national or local

风险态度

对待风险的整体思路,表现为董事会是规避风险还是寻求风险。

经营/营运风险

与实体开展的活动相关,源于实体结构、系统、人员、产品或流程。

风险容量

组织能够承受的风险量。

商业风险

商业风险是指公司因其经营和产品性质所面临的风险。

国家风险

与在特定国家开展交易或持有资产有关的风险。风险来源可能包括政治因素、经济因素、利润及国有化方面的监管不稳定或货币不稳定。

文化风险

企业产品、服务和商业行为在一个国家得到接受,而在另一个国家不被接受的风险。未能理解国家或当地文化可能意味着企业无法在该国或该

culture could mean that a company will fail to succeed in establishing its business.

地区顺利建立其业务。

risk, financial

The increased volatility of dividend payments to shareholders as gearing increases.

财务风险

随着资产负债率的增长,支付给股东的股利也面临着更大的不确定性。

risk, economic

Any change in the economy, home or abroad, which can affect the value of a transaction before a commitment is made i. e. payment or receipt.

经济风险

经济风险是指国内或国外经济形势的任何变化,这些变化能够在承诺实际履行(付款或收款)之前,影响到交易的价值。

risk, employee malfeasance

Malfeasance means doing wrong or committing an offence. Organisations might be exposed to risks of actions by employees that result in an offence or crime (other than fraud). This, like fraud risk, is a type of operational business risk.

员工渎职风险

渎职是指做错事或者违法。组织可能会因员工的违法或犯罪行为(而不是舞弊)而面临风险。和舞弊风险一样,这种风险属于运营层面的商业风险。

risk, environmental

Occurring due to changes in political, economics, socio-cultural, technological, environment and legal factors.

环境风险

因政治、经济、社会文化、技术、环境和法律方面的变化而产生的风险。

risk, financial

Relating to the financial operation of an entity and includes:

credit risk: possibility that a loss may occur from the failure of another party to perform according to the terms of a contract.

财务风险

与实体的财务运作有关的风险,包括以下方面:

信用风险:因另一方未能根据合同条款履行义务而造成损失的可能性。

currency risk：Risk that the value of a financial instrument will fluctuate due to changes in foreign exchange rates(IAS 32).

interest rate risk：Risk that interest rate changes will affect the financial well-being of an entity.

liquidity risk：Risk that an entity will encounter difficulty in realising assets or otherwise raising funds to meet commitments associated with financial instruments this is also known as funding risk.

货币风险：因外汇汇率变动而导致金融工具价值随之波动的风险(国际会计准则第 32 号)。

利率风险：因利率变动而影响到实体财务稳健性的风险。

流动性风险：实体难以变现资产或筹集资金以履行金融工具相关承诺的风险,亦称"融资风险"。

risk, gross

总体风险

An assessment of risk before the application of any controls, transfer or management responses.

总体风险是指在应用任何控制、进行任何转移或做出任何管理回应之前,对风险进行评估。

risk, legal/litigation

法律/诉讼风险

Legal/litigation risk arises from the possibility of legal action being taken against an organisation.

法律风险或诉讼风险来自于针对组织采取法律行动的可能性。

risk, political

政治风险

Risk due to political instability.

政治不稳定造成的风险。

risk, product reputation

产品声誉风险

Risk of change in product's reputation or image.

对产品的声誉或印象发生改变的风险。

risk, product

产品风险

Risk of failure of new product launches/loss of interest in existing products.

新产品发布失败或对现有产品丧失兴趣的风险。

risk management

Process of understanding and managing the risks that the entity is inevitably subject to in attempting to achieve its corporate objectives. For management purposes, risks are usually divided into categories such as operational financial; legal compliance; information and personnel. One example of an integrated solution to risk management is enterprise risk management. See "risk management, enterprise".

风险管理

风险管理是指认识并管理实体无法避免的风险,努力实现公司目标的过程。从管理角度而言,风险通常可分为营运财务目标;法律合规目标;信息和人员目标。企业风险管理就是一种综合的风险管理解决方案。参见"企业风险管理"。

risk management, enterprise(ERM)

Process effected by an entity's board of directors, management and other personnel, applied in strategy setting and across the enterprise, designed to identify potential events that may affect the entity, and manage risk to be within its risk appetite, to provide reasonable assurance regarding the achievement of entity objectives (Enterprise Risk Management-Integrated Framework COSO, 2004).

企业风险管理

企业风险管理过程受到实体董事会、管理层和其他人员的影响,应用在战略制定中并在整个企业范围内加以贯彻,旨在识别可能影响实体的潜在事件,将风险控制在风险偏好范围以内,为实体实现自身目标提供合理保证(COSO 企业风险管理——整体框架,2004 年)。

risk mapping

A common qualitative way of assessing the significance of risk is to produce a risk map.

绘制风险地图

一种常见的,用于评价风险重要性并绘制风险地图的定性方法。

risk, market/systematic

Risk that cannot be diversified away, also known as systematic risk, which is measured by beta.

Non-systematic or unsystematic risk

市场/系统性风险

无法分散的一类风险,亦称"系统性风险",通过贝塔系数进行衡量。

非系统性风险是指针对单项投资

applies to a single investment or class of investments, and can be reduced or eliminated by diversification.

See "market risk premium" and "beta factor".

或一类投资的,可通过分散投资来减少或消除的风险。

参见"市场风险溢价"和"贝塔因子"。

risk, reputation

声誉风险

Damage to entity's reputation as a result of failure to manage other risks.

因未能管理其他风险而令实体的声誉受损。

risk response

风险应对

See "risk treatment".

参见"风险处理"。

reporting, risk

风险报告

Risk reporting is concerned with regular reports to the board and to stakeholders setting out the organisation's policies in relation to risk and enabling the effective monitoring of those policies.

风险报告是指定期向董事会和股东提供风险相关报告,董事会和股东据此制定组织的风险政策并对这些政策实施有效的监控。

risk, residual

剩余风险

Residual risk is the risk a business faces after its controls have been considered.

剩余风险是在企业考虑控制之后,依然面临的风险。

risk, technology

技术风险

The risk that technology changes will occur that either present new opportunities to businesses, or on the down-side make their existing processes obsolete or inefficient.

技术风险是指技术变化的出现要么给企业带来新机遇,要么让企业现有流程过时或低效的风险。

risk treatment

风险处理

The process of selecting and

风险处理是选择和采取措施来修

implementing measures to modify the risk.

正风险的过程。

risk, two-way

Risk is two-way, and actual outcomes might be either better or worse than expected.

双向风险

风险是双向的,实际结果可能会比预期更好或更坏。

risk, uncontrollable

Uncontrollable risks could be risks that are caused by the external environment that the company operates in.

不可控风险

不可控风险是由公司经营所处的外部环境造成的风险。

risk, unsystematic

Unsystematic risk is the risk of the company's cash flows being affected by specific factors like strikes, R & D successes, systems failures, etc..

非系统风险

非系统风险是指因具体因素(如罢工、研发成功、系统故障等)影响到公司现金流量的风险。

risk, upside

See "two-way risk".

上行风险

参见"双向风险"。

rolling forcast

Continuously updated forecast whereby each time actual results are reported a further forecast period is added and intermediate period forecasts are updated. See "budget, rolling/continuous".

滚动预测

持续更新的预测,在每次报告实际业绩之后,新增进一步的预测期并更新中期预测。参见"滚动/持续预算"。

SFA model

For a strategy to be accepted, it must meet all three of these criteria—suitability, feasibility, acceptability.

SFA 模型

战略要想被接受,它就必须满足所有三个标准——适用性、可行性、可接受性。

Scenario planning

Managers need a picture or scenario of where the world may be in a few year' time.

情景规划

管理者需要一个画面或情景,以了解几年后世界可能是什么样的。

sell off

The sale of part of an entity to a third party, usually in return for cash. A sell-off may disrupt the rest of the organisation if key staff or products from within the organisation are part of the business unit sold off.

廉价出售

为换取现金将实体的一部分卖给第三方,如果廉价出售部分包括关键员工或产品,那么组织的剩余部分可能受到影响。

sensitivity analysis

Modelling and risk assessment procedure in which changes are made to significant variables in order to determine the effect of these changes on the planned outcome. Particular attention is thereafter paid to variables identified as being of special significance.

敏感度分析

一个建模及风险评估程序,对重要变量进行修改以确定这些变动对预计结果的影响。此后,对发现的具有重大意义的变量给予特别注意。

six markets model

The six markets model advocates that an organisation has six key markets, not just the traditional customer market. Marketing activity should be extended to build and manage relationships in all these areas—customer markets, referral markets, supplier markets, recruitment markets, influence markets, internal markets.

六大市场模型

六大市场模型提出,一个组织面对着六大重要市场,而不只是传统的客户市场。营销活动应该有所扩大,以建立和管理这些领域的所有关系——客户市场、口碑推荐市场、供应商市场、招聘市场、影响力市场、国内市场。

six Sigma

Methodology, developed by Motorola and others, based on Total Quality

六西格玛

摩托罗拉及其他公司在全面质量管理的基础上开发出的一种方法,可

Management, to achieve very low defect rates. The "sigma" refers to the Greek letter used to denote standard deviation, so six sigma means that the error rate lies beyond six standard deviations from the mean.

To achieve six sigma, an organisation must therefore produce not more than 3.4 defects per million products. See "total quality management".

实现极低的缺陷率。"西格玛"是希腊字母,用于指代标准偏差,因此,六西格玛是指错误率比偏离平均值的六个标准偏差还小。

为实现六西格玛,组织所生产产品的缺陷率不得超过百万分之 3.4。参见"全面质量管理"。

slack variables

宽松变量

Amount of each resource which will be unused if a specific linear programming solution is implemented.

在执行具体的线性规划解决方案时,未使用的各个资源量。

SMART

"SMART"原则

Objectives should be SMART: specific, measurable, attainable, relevant, timed.

目标应该符合"SMART"原则:特殊性、可衡量、可实现、相关性、时限性。

social media marketing

社交媒体营销

The process of advertising through social media sites, such as Twitter and Facebook.

这是指通过社交媒体网站,如推特和脸谱进行广告宣传的过程。

software as a Service(SaaS)

软件即服务

With SaaS customers only pay for software when they need it. The service is provided on-demand via a web browser and is highly attractive to smaller users who cannot justify buying a full version of the software.

客户需要使用 SaaS 时,只需支付软件费用。SaaS 通过网络浏览器按需提供服务,这对那些无法购买完整版软件的小型用户而言具有很大吸引力。

stakeholders

利益相关者

Those persons and organisation that have

在实体战略中拥有利益的人士和

an interest in the strategy of an organisation. Stakeholders normally include shareholders, customers, staff and the local community. Braithwaite and Drahos to consider the full range of 'actors' who may have an influence on the way an organisation conducts its business—organisations of states, states, organisations formed by firms, corporations, nongovernmental organisations, mass publics, knowledge based communities.

实体。利益相关者通常包括股东、客户、员工和当地社区。布雷斯韦特和德拉贺斯全方位考虑了可能对企业开展业务产生影响的参与者——国家机构、国家、公司组建的机构、公司、非政府组织、大众舆论、知识型社区。

stakeholders, analysis

See "Mendelow's power/interest matrix".

利益相关者分析

参见"孟德尔洛的权力/利益矩阵"。

stakeholders, alliances

Organizations do not exist in isolation and can be affected by a wide variety of stakeholders. Some of these stakeholders can become important allies, helping the organisationto achieve its goals.

利益相关者联盟

企业并不是孤立存在的,会受各种各样利益相关者的影响。一些利益相关者可以成为重要的盟友,帮助组织实现其目标。

stakeholders, power

Typically, stakeholder power can come from a number of sources: positional power, resource power, system power, expert power, personal power.

利益相关者权力

通常情况下,利益相关者的权力可以来自多个方面:地位权力、资源权力、系统权力、专家权力、个人权力。

stock, buffer

Stock of materials, or of work-in-progress, maintained in order to protect user department from the effect of possible interruptions to supply.

缓冲库存

物料或在制品库存,保障使用部门不会受到可能发生的供货中断的影响。

stock control

Systematic regulation of stock levels. Called inventory control in the US.

库存控制

系统地监管库存量,美国称作"存货控制"。

stock free

Stock on hand or on order which has not been scheduled for use.

(physical — stock-stock — ordered-stock scheduled for use)

可用库存

尚未计划使用的现有库存或已预定库存。

(实际库存-已预定库存－计划使用的库存)

stock level, maximum

Stock level, set for control purposes, which actual stockholding should never exceed.

[(reorder level + EOQ) − (minimum rate of usage × minimum lead time)]

最大库存量

出于控制目的而设定的库存量,实际库存持有量永远不能超过这个设定库存量。

[(补充订货库存量 + 经济订单批量) − (最低使用率 × 最短前置时间)]

stock level, minimum

Stock level, set for control purposes, below which stockholding should not fall without being highlighted.

[reorder level − (average rate of usage × average lead time)]

最小库存量

出于控制目的而设定的库存量,如果不明确指明,库存持有量不应低于此库存量。

[补充订货库存量 − (平均使用率 × 平均前置时间)]

stock, safety

Quantity of stocks of raw materials, work-in-progress and finished goods which are carried in excess of the expected usage during the lead time of an activity. The safety stock refuces the probability of operations having to be suspended.

安全库存

原材料、在制品和产成品的库存数量超出某一活动前置时间内的预期使用量。安全库存可降低营运中断的发生可能性。

strategic plan

Statement of long-term goals along with a definition of the strategies and policies which will ensure achievement of these goals.

strategy

Course of action，including the specification of resources required，to achieve a specific objective. See Figure 2.11.

strategic alliance

A cooperative business activity，formed by two or more separate organisations for strategic purposes，that allocates ownership，operational responsibilities，financial risks，and rewards to each member，while preserving their separate identity.

strategy，approaches

The traditional approach starts by looking at stakeholders and their objectives. The emphasis is then on formulating plans to achieve these objectives.

strategy，levels

Strategy can be broken down into three different levels：corporate strategy，business strategy，functional strategy.

strategy，non-market

A firm maintains relationships with its

战略计划

有关长期目标的声明，其中包括战略和政策说明，以确保这些目标得以实现。

战略

行动方案，包括实现特定目标所需资源的详细说明。参见图 2.11。

战略联盟

两个或多个独立的组织出于战略目的而共同从事一项商业合作活动，并将所有权、经营职责、财务风险以及报酬分配给各个成员，但同时保留成员各自独立的身份。

战略途径

传统的战略途径首先需要了解利益相关者和他们的目标，而后将重点放在制订计划以实现这些目标上。

战略层级

战略可以分为三个不同的层次：公司战略、业务战略、职能战略。

非市场性战略

一家公司不仅要维护与客户、供

customers, suppliers and competitors, but also with governments, regulator, non-government organisations, the media and society at large. Non-market matters, such as reputation, the ability to work with NGOs, the capability to foresee relevant government actions and even to shape policy—these are the factors that can make a difference.

应商和竞争对手的关系,还要维护与政府、监管机构、非政府组织、媒体以及整个社会的联系。非市场化事项,如声誉、与非政府组织合作的能力、预见政府相关行动的能力乃至影响政策的能力,都是影响因素。

strategy map/mapping

Diagram that describes how an entity creates value by linking the strategic objecitves of an organisation in explicit cause and effect relationships within the four quadrants of the balanced scorecard.

战略图/绘制战略图

一张示意图,它通过利用平衡计分卡四个象限中的明确因果关系将战略目标联系起来以说明实体如何创造价值。

stretch targets

Stretch targets are where the organisation sets goals for its employees that are possible, but very difficult for them to meet.

挑战目标

挑战目标是组织为员工设定的可能、但却很难达到的目标。

sub optimization

Sub-optimisation refers to actions taken to improve the divisional situation at the expense of the company as a whole.

次优化

次优化是指以牺牲企业整体利益为代价,来改善个别部门情况所采取的行动。

supply chain management(SCM), downstream

The downstream SCM would involve transactions between the firm and itscustomers (equivalent to sell-side commerce).

下游供应链管理

下游供应链管理涉及公司与客户之间的交易(相当于卖方交易)。

supply chain management, general

This typically involves distribution of the

一般供应链管理

一般供应链管理通常包括从供应

product from the supplier to the manufacturer to the wholesaler to the retailer and to the final consumer.

商到制造商、批发商、零售商再到最终消费者这一过程中的产品销售。

supply chain management，push and pull

See "push and pull supply chain models".

推拉式供应链管理

参见"推拉式供应链模式"。

supply chain management，upstream

The upstream SCM would involve transactions between the firm and its suppliers (equivalent to buy-side commerce). The key activities of upstream SCM are procurement and upstream logistics.

上游供应链管理

上游供应链管理涉及公司与供应商之间的交易（相当于买方交易），其主要活动是采购和上游物流。

sustainability

Sustainability is the use of resources in such a way that they do not compromise the needs of future generations. Business sustainability is about ensuring that organisations implement strategies that contribute to long-term success.

可持续发展

可持续发展是指以一种不损害子孙后代利益的方式来使用资源。企业的可持续发展就是要确保组织实施有助于其长期成功的战略。

suitability

Suitability is concerned with whether the strategy addresses the circumstances in which an organisation is operating—its strategic position.

适用性

适用性关注的是战略是否致力于应对企业运行所处的环境——其战略地位。

SWOT analysis

SWOT analysis，or corporate appraisal，evaluates the strategic position of an entity within its environment. Factors identified are listed as strengths，weaknesses，opportu-

SWOT 分析

SWOT 分析或公司评价，评估实体在所处环境中的战略地位，确定的因素为优势、劣势、机会或威胁。

nities or threats.

synergy

Two or more entities coming together to produce a result not independently obtainable. For example，a merged entity will only need one marketing department，so there may be savings generated compared to two separate entities.

tactical plan/tactics

Short-term plan for achieving an entity's objectives. See Figure 2.10.

协同效应

协同效应是指两个或两个以上的实体联合起来,共同取得一个成果,这个成果是实体无法单独实现的。例如,合并之后,实体只需要一个市场部门,与独立的两个实体需要两个市场部门相比,可以形成节约。

战术计划/战术

实现实体目标的短期计划。参见图表2.10。

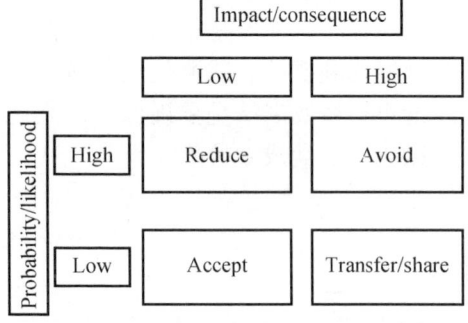

FIGURE 2.10　TARA

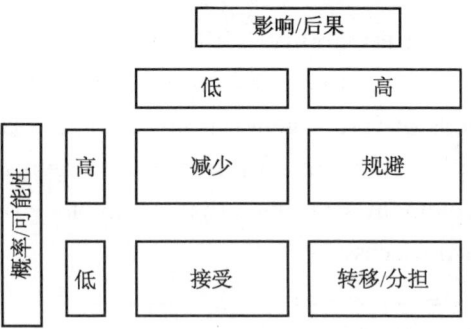

图表2.10　风险应对方法

TARA

Transference，avoidance，reduction \ mitigation，acceptance.

team building

Tasks that are designed to develop team members and their ability to work together.

风险应对方法

转移、规避、减少\缓解、接受。

团队建设

为了发展团队成员和他们的协作配合能力而设计的任务。

Theory E & Theory O

Theory E strategies—these are based on measures where shareholder value is the main concern. Change usually involves incentives，layoffs，downsizing and restructuring. Theory O strategies—these are ＂softer＂ approaches to change，often involving cultural adjustment or enhancing employee capabilities through individual and organisational learing.

think tank

A think tank comprises a group of experts who are encouraged，in a relatively unstructured atmosphere，to speculate about future developments in particular areas and to identify possible courses of action.

three generic strategies

Strategies of differentiation，focus and cost leadership outlined by Porter as offering possible means of outperforming competitors within an industry，and of coping with the five competitive forces. See Porter's five forces. See Figure 2.11.

E 理论和 O 理论

E 理论策略——基于以股东价值为主的措施。变革通常涉及激励、解雇、精简裁员以及重组。O 理论策略——以"更为柔和"的方法来应对变革，往往涉及文化调整、通过个人和组织学习来提高员工的能力。

智囊团

智囊团是由一组专家组成的。组织鼓励这些专家在一个非结构化的氛围中，推测特定领域未来的发展，并确定可以采取的行动。

三大基本战略

波特提出的差异化战略、集中化战略和成本领先战略，这三大战略为组织超越业内竞争对手以及应对五大竞争力提供了可能途径。参见"波特竞争五力分析模型"。参见图表 2.11。

FIGURE 2.11 PORTER'S THREE GENERIC STRATEGIES

	Competitive advantage	
	Low cost	Differentiation
Broad target	1 Cost leadership	2 Differentiation
Narrow target	3A Cost focus	3B Differentiation focus

(Competitive scope)

图表 2.11　波特三大基本战略

	竞争优势	
	低成本	差异化
广泛目标	1 成本领先	2 差异化
有限目标	3A 成本集中化	3B 差异集中化

（竞争范围）

three stage model of change

See "Lewin, three stage model".

thriving on chaos

One of Tom Peters's ideas relates to "excellent" companies that have succeeded by seeking to create a climate of continual and radical change.

through the computer

This approach actually interrogates the computer files and computer controls and relies much more on the processes that the computer uses.

The auditor follows the audit trail through the internal computer operations and attempts to verify that the processing controls are functioning correctly. The computer controls are directly testedand the accuracy of computer-based processing of input data is verified.

To audit through the computer requires more expertise and a longer set-up time; however, the results can be of very good quality.

This approach utilizes different computer-assisted audit techniques (CAATs) such as test data and audit software.

total quality management(TQM)

Integrated and comprehensive system of planning and controlling all business functions so that products or services are

变革的三阶段模型

参见"勒温的三阶段模型"。

乱中取胜

汤姆·彼得斯提出的一个理念,它指出"优秀"的公司通过寻求建立一种持续且激进的变革氛围而获得成功。

使用计算机

这种做法实际上是询问计算机文件和计算机控制,并更多地依赖于计算机使用的流程。

审计人员通过内部计算机操作来追踪审计痕迹,并尝试验证计算机处理控制是否正常发挥了功能。审计人员直接测试计算机控制,并验证计算机处理输入数据的正确性。

通过计算机进行审计,这需要具备更多的专业知识,花费更长的设置时间;然而,得到的结果可能具备相当高的质量。

这种方法利用不同的计算机辅助审计技术(CAATs),如测试数据和审计软件。

全面质量管理

规划和控制所有业务职能的综合及全面系统,目的是确保所生产的产品或所提供的服务符合甚至超出客户

produced which meet or exceed customer expectations.

TQM is a philosophy of business behaviour, embracing principles such as employee involvement continuous improvement at all levels and customer focus, as well as being a collection of related techniques aimed at improving quality such as full documentation of activities, clear goal-setting and performance measurement form the customer perspective.

期望。

全面质量管理是一种商业行为理念,其秉持员工参与、全面持续改善、客户至上等原则,同时也整合了一系列旨在改善质量的相关技术,例如完整的活动记录、明确设定目标、从客户角度来衡量绩效。

unrelated diversification

非相关多元化

Unrelated diversification: completely new areas with which the business shares no common ground; more risk from going into unknown markets and products.

非相关多元化:企业从未涉足的全新领域;进军未知市场和产品会带来更多的风险。

value chain

价值链

Sequence of business activities by which, in the perspective of the end-user, value is added to the products or services produced by an entity.

一系列业务活动,从终端用户的角度来看,价值不断添加到实体所生产的产品或所提供的服务中。

value creation

价值创造

Value created by an organisation over time manifests itself in increases, decreases or transformations of the capitals caused by the organisation's business activities and outputs.

随着时间的推移,一个组织所创造的价值证明自身通过组织的业务活动和产出实现了资产的增加、减少或转换。

value system

价值体系

Series of connected value chains belonging to the entity, its suppliers, rivals and customers.

由实体、供应商、竞争对手和客户构成的相互连接的一系列价值链条。

value-added activity

Activity necessary to engage customer perceived value in the good or service being provided. The procurement of high quality resource inputs would be a value-adding activity while activity required to correct errors would be non-value-added in nature.

value-chain analysis

Use of the value-chain model to identify the value adding activities of an entity.

vision statement

See "mission statement".

virtual organisation

This occurs where an organisation outsources many of its functions to other organisations and simply exists as a network of contracts with few, if any, functions being kept in-house.

viruses

A virus is a piece of software that seeks to infest a computer system, hiding and automatically spreading to other systems if given the opportunity. Most computer viruses have three functions—avoiding detection, reproducing themselves and causing damage. Viruses might be introduced into a computer system directly, or by disk or e-mail attachment.

增值活动

为提升客户对所提供商品或服务的认知价值而采取的必要活动。获取优质资源投入属于增值活动,为纠正错误采取的行动本质上则不属于增值活动。

价值链分析

利用价值链模型识别实体的增值活动。

愿景声明

参见"使命宣言"。

虚拟组织

虚拟组织是指组织将其大部分职能外包给其他组织,仅保留极少的内部职能(如果有的话),它仅仅以合约网络的形式存在。

病毒

病毒是一种软件,旨在侵扰计算机系统,隐藏于其中,并在机会成熟的情况下自动传播到其他系统。大多数计算机病毒具有三个功能——避免被检测到、自我复制并造成破坏。病毒可能被直接导入计算机系统中,或者通过磁盘或电子邮件附件传播。

V's model of big data

Big data can be described using the "3Vs": volume，variety，velocity.

world-class manufacturing

Position of international manufacturing excellence，achieved by developing a culture based on factors such as continuous improvement，problem prevention，zero defect tolerance，customer-driven JIT-based production and total quality management.

大数据的"V"模型

大数据可以用"3V"来描述：大量、多样、快速。

世界级制造

通过持续改善、问题预防、零缺陷容忍、客户驱动的准时生产和全面质量管理等因素来形成一种文化，进而推动组织取得卓越的世界级制造地位。

CHAPTER 3
Governance and Compliance

第三章
治 理 与 合 规

account

账户

Structured record of transactions in monetary terms kept as part of an accouting system. This may be a simple list, or entries on a debit and credit basis, maintained either manually or as a computer record. See Figure 3.1 for an illustration of the relationship of accounts.

作为会计系统的一部分,以货币形式对相关交易加以结构化记录。这可能是一个简单的列报、或以借方和贷方为基础的分录、手写或计算机保存的记录。参见图表3.1,它展示了账户之间的关系。

cash account：Record of receipts and payments of cash, cheques or other forms of money transfer.

现金账户:现金收款和付款、支票或者其他形式的资金转移的记录。

nominal account：Record of revenues and expenditures, liabilities and assets classified by their nature, for example sales, rent, rates, electricity, wages and share capital. These are sometimes referred to as impersonal accounts.

名义账户:按收入、支出、资产和负债的性质分类加以记录,例如销售、租金、利息、电费、工资和股本。有时也被称为非记名账户。

personal account：Record of amounts receivable from or payable to a person or an entity. A collection of these accounts is known as a sales/debtor ledger, or a purchases/creditors ledger. In the US the terms receivables ledger and payables ledger are used and are consistent with IAS 1.

记名账户:应向个人或者实体收取的款项或应支付给个人或者实体的款项的记录。这些账户的集合被称为销货/应收账款分类账或者购货/应付账款分类账。美国使用的是应收账款分类账和应付账款分类账,与《国际会计准则第1号》保持一致。

FIGURE 3. 1 RELATIONSHIP OF ACCOUNTS

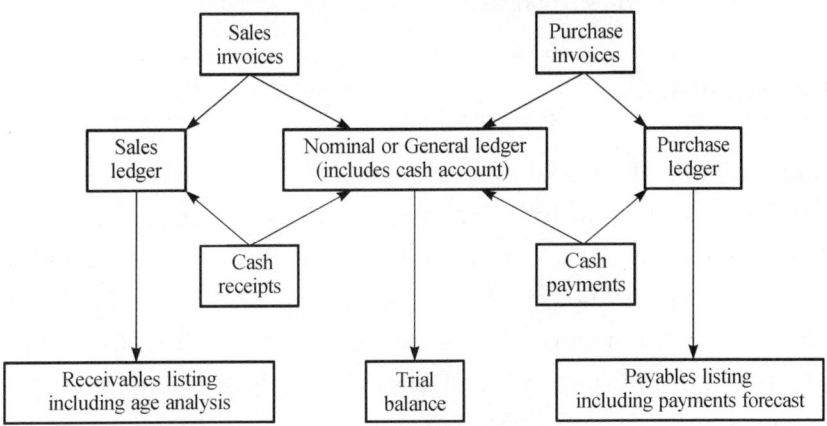

图表 3.1 账户之间的关系

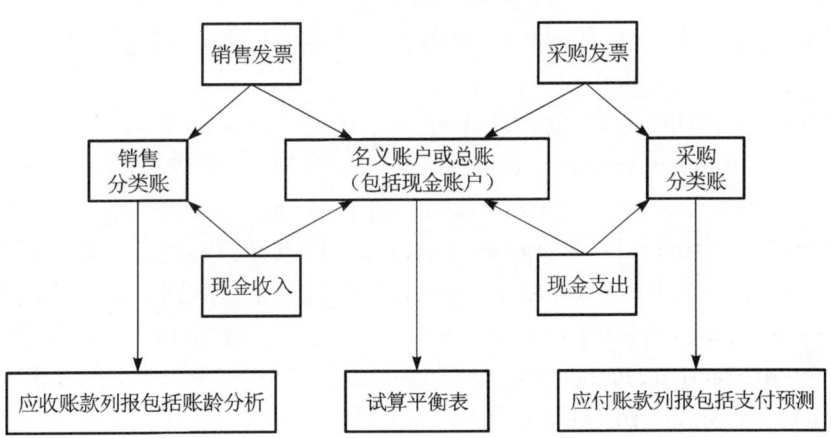

accounting policies	会计政策

Specific principles，bases，conventions，rules and practices applied by an entity in preparing and presenting its financial statements(IAS 8).

实体在编制和呈报财务报表时所采用的具体原则、基础、惯例、规则和实务(《国际会计准则第 8 号》)

accounting reference period	会计期间

Period for which an entity prepares its financial statements，This period is normally，though not necessarily，twelve months.

实体编制财务报告所覆盖的期间。虽然没有强制规定，但此期间一般为 12 个月。这一术语也应用于税

Also used for taxation where it represents the period upon which adjusted profits, for corporation/income tax purposes, is based.

收中,代表为计算公司所得税而调节利润所基于的期间。

accounting standards

会计准则

See Internationnal Financial Reporting Standards(IFRSs), which includes International Accouting Standards(IASs). In the UK there are Statements of Standard Accouting Practice (SSAPs) and Financial Reporting Standards(FRSs). All international and UK Accouting Standards are listed in Appendices 1 and 2.

参见《国际财务报告准则》(IFRSs),其中包括《国际会计准则》(IASs)。在英国,则为《标准会计实务公告》(SSAPs)及《财务报告准则》(FRSs)。所有国际及英国会计准则列于附录1和附录2中。

Accounting Standards Board(ASB)

会计准则委员会

Uk standard-setting body established to develop, issue and withdraw accounting standards. Its aims are to establish and improve standards of financial accounting and reporting, for the benefit of users, preparers and auditors of financial information(ASB). It will work with and influence the International Accounting Standards Board(IASB)in addressing UK accounting issues.

英国准则制定机构,其建立是为了制定、发布和撤销会计准则。它的目标是为了财务报告使用者、编制者和审计师的利益而建立和完善财务会计和报告准则。在解决英国会计问题上,它将和国际会计准则理事会(IASB)协同合作、相互影响。

accruals basis of accounting

权责发生制

Effects of transactions and other events are recognised in financial statements when they occur and not when cash and cash equivalents are received or paid (IASB Framework).

交易和其他事项发生时,就将其影响在财务报表中进行确认,而不是等到收到或支付现金及现金等价物时(IASB框架)。

Acquisition

收购

The term "merger" is usually used to

"合并"一词通常用于描述两个或

describe the joining together of two or more entities. Strictly, if one entity acquires a majority shareholding in another, the second is said to have been acquired (or "taken over") by the first. See "merger".

更多实体的结合。严格地说,如果一个实体获得了另一个实体的大部分股权,那么,后者就被前者收购(或"接管")了。参见"合并"。

acquisition date

收购日

Date on which the acquirer effectively obtains control of the acquire(IFRS 3).

收购方实际取得被收购方控制权的日期(《国际财务报告准则第 3 号》)。

actuarial assumptions

精算假设

An entity's unbiased best estimates of the demographic and financial variables that will determine the ultimate cost of providing post-employment benefits(IAS 19).

实体对人口和财务变量无偏的最佳估计,这项估计将决定企业提供离职后福利的最终成本(《国际会计准则第 19 号》)。

administrative expenses

管理费用

Cost of management, secretarial, accounting and other services which cannot be related to the separate production, marketing or research and development functions. These expenses are reported in the income statement.

管理、文秘、会计及其他服务的成本,与独立的生产、销售或者研发等职能不相关。这些费用在利润表中列报。

agency theory

代理人理论

Hypothesis that attempts to explain elements of organisational behavior through an understanding of the relationships between principals (such as shareholders) and agents (such as entity managers and accountants). A conflict may exist between the actions undertaken by agents in furtherance of their own self-interest, and those required to promote the interests of the principals. Within

一项假设,它试图通过理解委托人(如股东)和代理人(如管理层和会计师)之间的关系,来解释组织行为的要素。代理人为了促进自身利益而采取的行为,与他们按要求促进委托人利益所采取的行为之间存在冲突。在实体的等级制度中,当部门经理为了部门自身利益而破坏其他部门或者实体整体利益时,同样的目标不一致情

the hierarchy of entities, the same goal in-congruence may arise when divisional managers promote their own self-interest over those of other divisions and of the entity generally.

况就会产生。

amortisation

Systematic allocation of the depreciable amount of an Intangible asset over its useful life (IAS 38).

摊销

资产在其使用寿命期内对摊销额进行系统分配(《国际会计准则第 38 号》),通常适用于无形资产或商誉。

amortised cost(for a financial asset or liability)

Amount at which the financial asset or lia-bility is measured, at initial recognition minus principal repayments, plus or minus cumulative amortisation using the effective interest in the item(refer to IAS 39).

摊余成本(针对于金融资产或者金融负债)

金融资产或金融负债的计量金额,等于它的初始确认金额扣除已偿还的本金,再加上或减去以实际利率计算的累计摊销额(参照《国际会计准则第 39 号》)。

annual report and accounts

Package of information including a man-agement report, an auditor's report and a set of financial statements with supportive notes. In the case of companies these are drawn up for a period which is called the ac-counting reference period, the last day of which is known as the reporting date.

年报和账户

包含了管理层报告、审计报告和财务报表及其附注的信息汇总包。对公司而言,该信息汇总是针对某个会计参照期间编制的,该期间的最后一天即为报告日。

anti-dilution

Increase in earnings per share, or a reduc-tion in loss per share, resulting from the assump-tion that convertible instruments are converted or options or warrants are exercised(refer to IAS 33). Also see "dilution".

反稀释

假设由于可转换票据的转换、期权或者认购权证的行使所造成的每股收益的增加或者每股亏损的减少(参照《国际会计准则第 33 号》)。参见"股权稀释"。

appropriation account

Record of how the surplus / deficit of a period has been allocated to distributions to owners and retentions by the entity.

asset

Resource controlled by the entity as a result of past events and from which future economic benefits are expected to flow to the entity (IFRS Framework).

associate

An entity, including an unincorporated entity such as a partnership, over which the investor has significant influence and that is neither a subsidiary nor an interest in a joint venture (refer to IAS 28).

audit

Systematic examnination of the activities and status of an entity, based primarily on investigation and analysis of its systems, controls and records.

audit, competence

This will typically involve: analysis of what competences the organisation has, as well as how well resources are being deployed to create them. Categorization of competences as core or threshold. This will be done by looking at historic data, industry norms and benchnmarking exercises(which will usu-

盈亏分配账户

反映期间盈余或者亏损有多少分配给所有者以及有多少留存在实体的账户。

资产

由于过去事项形成而由实体控制的、预期会给实体带来未来经济利益流入的资源(《国际财务报告准则概念框架》)。

联营企业

投资者对其拥有重大影响,但又不是投资者的子公司或合营企业的实体,包括非公司实体,如合伙企业(参照《国际会计准则》第28号)。

审计

主要针对一个实体的系统、控制和记录进行调查和分析,并在此基础上对实体的活动和状态进行系统的检查。

能力审计

这项审计主要涉及:分析组织具有的能力以及如何部署资源来形成这些能力。把能力分为核心能力或入门能力。这项工作(通常由专家团队)通过查看历史数据、行业规范以及标杆运用来完成。

ally be undertaken by specialist teams).

audit, compliance

Audit of specific activities in order to determine whether performance is in conformity with a predetermined contractual, regulatory or statutory requirement.

audit, cost

Vertification of cost records and accounts, and a check on adherence to prescribed cost accounting procedures and their continuing relevance.

audit, environmental

Systematic documented, periodic and objective evaluation of how well an entity, its management and equipment are performing with the aim of helping to safeguard the environment by facilitating managemant control of environmental practices and assessing compliance with entity policies and external regulations.

audit, internal

Independent appraisal function established within an organisation to examine and evaluate its activities as a service to the organisation. The objective of internal auditing is to assit members of the organisation in the effective discharge of their responsibilities. To this end, internal auditing furnishes them with analyses, appraisals, recommendations, counsel and information concerning the activities reviewed

合规审计

对具体的活动进行审计,以确定其表现是否符合预先确定的合同、监管或法定要求。

成本审计

对成本记录和账户进行核查,并对成本会计程序规定的遵守情况和它们的持续相关性进行检查。

环境审计

对实体、其管理层和仪器设备表现如何进行系统的、有书面记录的、定期的和客观的评价,其目的在于帮助保护有利环境的实践操作,评估它们是否遵循了实体政策与外部法规。

内部审计

在组织内部建立的独立评估部门,向组织提供活动调查和评估方面的服务。内部审计的目的是协助组织成员有效履行职责,并为此向他们提供分析、评估、建议、咨询和受审查活动的有关信息(内部审计师协会-英国)。

（Institute of Internal Auditors – UK）.

audit, interrogation software

Audit software consists of computer programs used by auditors to interrogate the files of a client. Normally the client's data files are input into the audit software program on the auditor's computer，and the auditor can then test those files.

audits, marketing

A particular form of position audit which focuses on the products of the firm and the relationship it has with customers.

audit, management

Objective and independent appraisal of the effectiveness of managers and the corporate structure in the achievement of entity objectives and policies. Its aim is to identify existing and potential management weaknesses and to recommend ways to rectify them.

audit, operational

A management audit is sometimes called an operational audit. A management audit is defined by CIMA as "an objective and independent appraisal of the effectiveness of managers and corporate structure in the achievement of the entities objectives and policies".

audit, Quality

A systematic investigation to establish

审计查询软件

审计软件由审计师用于查询客户文件的计算机程序组成。通常情况下，客户端的数据文件被导入审计师电脑上的审计软件程序中，然后审计师可以测试这些文件。

销售审计

销售审计是一种特殊形式的地位审计，重点关注公司产品以及公司与客户的关系。

管理审计

对实现实体目标和落实实体政策过程中，管理层和企业结构的有效性进行客观和独立的评估，其目的是识别已经存在的或者潜在的管理缺陷并提出改正建议。

经营审计

管理审计有时也称为经营审计。CIMA 对管理审计的定义是"对实现实体'目标'和落实实体'政策'过程中，管理层和企业结构的有效性进行客观和独立的评估"。

质量审计

质量审计是一个系统的调查，以

whether quality objectives are being met.

确定是否符合质量目标。

audit, transaction

A transaction audit involves the checking of a sample of transactions against documentary evidence.

交易审计

交易审计涉及交易样本的检验，并与文件证据进行对照。

audit, post-completion

Objective，independent assessment of the success of a capital project in relation to plan. Covers the whole life of the project and provides feedback to managers to aid the implementation and control of future projects.

完工后审计

参照计划，就资本项目的成功与否提出客观独立的评估意见。这项工作涵盖了项目的整个生命周期，向管理层提供反馈意见，帮助他们开展未来项目的实施与控制。

audit, processes

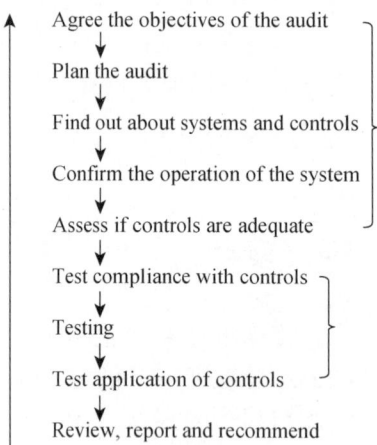

FIGURE 3.2　Audit Process Curt

audit processes

审计流程

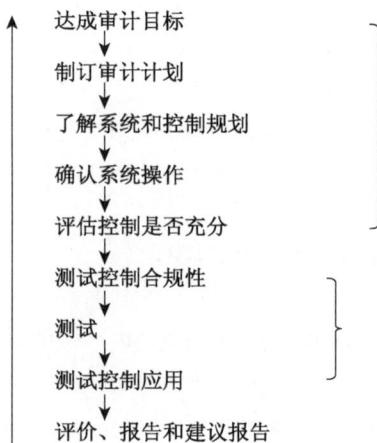

图表3.2　审计流程图

审计流程

audit, Quality

A systematic investigation to establish whether quality objectives are being met.

质量审计

质量审计是一个系统的调查，以确定是否符合质量目标。

audit，report

Formal document in which an auditor expresses an opinion as to whether the financial statements of an entity show a true and fair view of its position at a given date and the results of its operations for the accounting period ended on that date have been properly prepared in accordance with the relevant statutory requirements，accounting standards，or any report by an auditor in accordance with the terms of appointment.

审计报告

审计师就实体的财务报表是否真实公允地反映了实体给定日期的财务状况以及截止于该日的会计期间的经营成果，其编制是否恰当地遵循了相关法规要求、会计准则而发表意见的正式文件，或按委托条款由审计师出具的相关报告。

audit，resource

The resource audit identifies the resources that are available to an organisation and seeks to start the process of identifying competencies.

资源审计

资源审计用于确认一个组织可用的资源，并旨在启动能力识别过程。

audit，risk based

A risk based audit refers to a systems audit in which the auditors use their judgment to decide on the level of risk that exists in different areas of the system，and to plan their audit tests so that more effort is directed towards the most risky areas.

风险导向审计

风险导向审计是针对系统的审计，审计人员根据自己的判断确定系统不同领域的风险水平，并规划相应的审计测试以便将更多的精力放在最具风险的区域。

audit，social

The social audit would look at the company's contribution to society and the community. The contributions made could be through：donations，sponsorship，employment practices，education，health and safety，ethical investments，etc..

社会审计

社会审计是查看公司对社会和社区做出的贡献。这种贡献可以通过捐赠、赞助、雇佣员工、教育、安全健康、道德投资等途径来实现。

audit, statutory external

Periodic examination of the books of accounts and records of an entity carried out by an independent third party (the auditor) to ensure that they have been properly maintained, are accurate and comply with established concepts, principles, accounting standards, legal requirements and give a true and fair view of the financial state of the entity.

法定外部审计

由独立第三方(审计师)开展的定期审计,检查实体的账簿和账目,确保它们得到妥善维护,记录内容准确,符合既定的概念、原则、会计准则和法律要求,能够真实公允地反映实体的财务状况。

audit, systems-based auditing

A systems-based audit is an audit of internal controls within an organisation. It is often associated with the audit of accounting systems, such as the sales ledger system, purchase ledger system, receipts and payments, fixed asset records, stock records.

以系统为基础的审计

以系统为基础的审计是组织内部控制的审计,通常与会计账务系统的审计联系在一起,例如销售分类账系统、采购分类账系统、收入与支出、固定资产记录、库存记录等。

audit, trail

An audit trail consists of a record or series of records that allows the processing of a transaction or an amendment by a computer or clerical to be identified accurately.

审计线索

审计线索是由一项或一系列记录组成的,通过这些记录,审计师可以准确地辨认计算机或文档记录的交易处理过程或修改过程的痕迹。

audit, types

Types of audit work include compliance audit, transactions audit, risk-based audit, quality audit, post-completion audit, value for money audit, social and environment audit, management audit, systems-based audit.

审计种类

审计工作的种类包括合规审计、交易审计、风险导向审计、质量审计、完工后审计、效益审计、社会和环境审计、管理审计、以系统为基础的审计。

audit，value for money

Investigation into whether proper arrangements have been made for securing economy，efficiency and effectiveness in the use of resources.

效益审计

调查实体是否做出了适当的安排以保证资源得到经济、高效和有效的使用。

Auditing Practices Board（APB）

A body formed by an agreement between the six members of the Consultative Committee of Accountancy Bodies(CCAB)，to be responsible for developing and issuing professional standards for auditors in the UK and the Republic of Ireland.

From 2005，the APB will no longer issue its own standards but require the adoption of International Standards of Auditing（ISAs）issued by the International Auditing and Assurance Standards Board(IAASB). See "Consultative Committee of Accountancy Bodies".

审计实践委员会

由会计团体咨询委员会（CCAB）的 6 名成员达成协议组建的机构，负责为英国和爱尔兰共和国的审计师制定并发布职业准则。

自 2005 年以后，该委员会不再发布自己的准则，但要求采用国际审计与鉴证准则理事会（IAASB）发布的《国际审计准则》(ISAs)。

available-for-sale financial assets

Non-derivative financial asset that is designated as being available for sale and not classified as loans and receivables，held-to-maturity investments，or financial assets held at fair value(IAS 39).

可供出售金融资产

被指定为可供出售的，不属于以下三类金融资产的非衍生金融资产：贷款和应收款项；持有至到期的投资；按公允价值计量的金融资产（《国际会计准则第 39 号》）。

bad debt

Debt or trade receivable which is，or is considered to be，uncollectable and is，therefore，written off either as a charge to the income statement or against an existing doubtful debt provision. See "doubtful debts provision".

坏账

无法或者认为无法收回的债权或应收账款，因此将其注销，作为利润表的一项费用或冲销已提取的坏账准备。参见"坏账准备"。

balance sheet

Statement of the financial position of an entity at a given date disclosing the assets, liabilities and equity(such as shareholders' contributions and reserves) prepared to give a true and fair view of the entity at that date. See Figure 3.3.

资产负债表

实体在给定日期的财务状况报表,披露其资产、负债和所有者权益(如股本和资本公积),以真实且公允地反映实体的财务状况。参见表图3.3。

FIGURE3. 3   GROUP BALANCE SHEET

AT 31 DECEMBER 2005

	$ million	$ million
Assets		
Non-current assets		
Property, plant and equipment	1,503	
Investment properties	94	
Goodwill	356	
Other intangible assets	288	
Investments in associates and joint ventures	810	
Available-for-sale investments	68	3,119
Current assets		
Inventories	636	
Trade and other receivables	917	
Other current assets	291	
Cash and cash equivalents	104	1,948
Total assets		5,067
Equity and liabilities		
Equity attributable to equity holders of the parent		
Share capital	1,150	
Other reserves	452	
Translation reserve	(12)	
Retained earnings	434	2,024
Minority interest		246
Total equity		2,270
Non-current liabilities		
Long-term borrowings	1,030	
Deferred tax	320	
Long-term provisions	310	
Total non-current liabilities		1,660
Current liabilities		
Trade and other payables	477	
Short-term borrowings	283	

	$ million	$ million
		CONTINUED
Current portion of long-term borrowings	82	
Current tax payable	125	
Short-term provisions	170	
Total current liabilities		1,137
Total liabilities		2,797
Total equity and liabilities		5,067

图表 3.3 集团资产负债表

截止到 2005 年 12 月 31 日

	单位:百万美元	单位:百万美元
资产		
非流动资产		
不动产,厂房和设备	1 503	
投资性房地产	94	
商誉	356	
其他无形资产	288	
对联营企业和合营企业的投资	810	
可供出售投资	68	3 119
流动资产		
存货	636	
应收账款和其他应收款项	917	
其他流动资产	291	
现金和现金等价物	104	1 948
资产合计		5 067
所有者权益和负债		
归属于母公司的权益		
股本	1 150	
其他公积金	452	
汇兑准备	(12)	
留存收益	434	2 024
少数股东权益		246
权益合计		2 270
非流动负债		
长期借款	1 030	
递延税项	320	
长期减值准备	310	
非流动负债合计		1 660
流动负债		
应付账款和其他应付款项	477	
短期借款	283	
长期借款的本期应偿还部分	82	
应交税费	125	
短期减值准备	170	
流动负债合计		1 137
负债合计		2 797
所有者权益和负债合计		5 067

bookkeeping

Recording of monetary transactions, appropriately classified, in the financial records of an entry. See "double-entry bookkeeping".

簿记

在实体的财务记录中,对货币交易加以合理的分类和记录。参见"复式记账法"。

business combination

Bringing together of separate entities or businesses into one reporting entity(IFRS 3). In all business combinations, one entity (the acquirer)will obtain control of another entity (the acquire)and an acquirer should be identified for all such combinations. (This means all business combinations involving an acquirer and an acquire should be accounted for by applying the purchase (acquisition) method. The uniting of interests' (merger) method is now abolished.)Refer to IFRS 3.

企业合并

将单独的实体或企业合并为一个报告主体(《国际财务报告准则第3号》)。在所有的企业合并中,一个实体(收购方)将获得另一实体(被收购方)的控制权,所有的此类合并都需确认一个收购方。[这意味着涉及收购方和被收购方的所有企业合并都应采用购买(收购)法进行会计处理。权益结合法(合并法)现已取消]参考《国际财务报告准则第3号》。

business segment

Distinguishable component of an entity that is engaged in providing an individual product or service (or group of products or services) and that is subject to risks and returns that are different from those of other segments (IFRS 8). See geographic segment.

业务分部

一个实体中可加以区分的组成部分,其提供单项产品或服务(或一组相关产品或服务),并且面临着不同于其他业务分部的风险和收益(《国际财务报告准则第8号》)。参见"地区分部"。

capital expenditure

Costs incurred in acquiring, producing or enhancing non-current assets (both tangible and intangible). See "revenue expenditure".

资本性支出

在获取、生产和改良非流动资产(包括有形和无形资产)过程中所发生的成本。参见"收益性支出"。

capital gain/loss

Extent by which the net realised value of a capital asset exceeds (or in the case of a capital loss is less than) the cost of acquisition plus additional improvements, less depreciation charges where applicable. It can also arise from the exchange of such an asset for another of a different type. The term can have other interpretations for tax purposes.

capital maintenance

Principle that profit is only recorded after capital has been maintained intact. There are two bases on which capital can be defined, financial and physical.

capital redemption reserve

Account required to prevent a reduction in capital, where an entity purchase or redeems its own shares out of distributable profits.

capital surplus

Assets remaining in an entity after all costs and liabilities have been discharhed. It is distributed amongst the shareholders in accordance with the rights as determined at the time of the issue of shares.

Carroll, Corporate social Responsibility Model

Carroll divised a four-part model of CSR: economic responsibility, legal

资本利得/损失

资本利得是一项资本资产的可变现净值高于(如是资本损失,则低于)以下金额的部分,资本资产的购买成本加上额外改良成本,再扣除折旧费用(适用的情况下)。资本利得/损失也可能源于资本资产与另一种不同类型资产的交换。这个术语在税务方面有另外的解释。

资本保全

即只有在资本保持完好的情况下才能记录利润的原则。可从财物或实物的角度定义资本。

资本偿还准备金

为了防止实体利用可分配利润购买或赎回自身股票,导致资本减少而设置的账户。

资本盈余

实体清偿所有成本和负债后还剩余的资产,按照股票发行时决定的权利比例在股东之间进行分配。

卡罗尔,企业社会责任模型

卡罗尔设计了一个由四个部分组成的企业社会责任模型:经济责任、法

responsibility, ethical responsibility, philanthropic responsibility.

Carroll, CSR strategies

Carroll suggests four possible strategies that the organisation can adopt with regard to corporate social responsibility: reaction (The corporation denies any responsibility for social issues, arguing that it is not to blame or required to act); defence (The corporation admits responsibility but fights it, doing the very least that seems to be required. Typically this is only done as an attempt to defend the organisation's current position); accommodation (The corporation accepts responsibility and does what is demanded of it by relevant groups); proaction (The corporation seeks to go beyond industry norms and anticipates future expectations by doing more than is currently expected. The organisation attempts to improve society).

律责任、道德责任、慈善责任。

卡罗尔的企业社会责任策略:卡罗尔为组织履行其企业社会责任提出了四种可能的策略建议:反应性策略(公司拒绝对社会问题承担任何责任,并认为这样做无可厚非或不是必须按要求采取的行动);防御性策略(公司承认责任,但却有所抵触,只履行所要求的最基本责任。通常,只有在试图保护组织的现有地位时,才会这样做);适应性策略(公司承认责任,并履行相关团体要求公司履行的责任);主动性策略(公司试图超越行业规范,履行的责任超过当前社会期望,并以此来预测未来的社会期望。组织试图改善社会)。

carrying amount/book value

账面价值

Amount at which an asset is recognised in the balance sheet after deducting any accumulated depreciation (or amortisation) and accumulated impairment losses thereon (IAS 36).

资产在资产负债表中确认的,扣除累计折旧(或摊销)以及累计减值损失后的价值(《国际会计准则第36号》)。

cash

现金

Cash on hand and demand deposits (IAS 7).

库存现金和活期存款(《国际会计准则第7号》)。

cash equivalents

现金等价物

Short-term, highly liquid investments that are readily convertible to known

现金等价物是指实体持有的期限短、流动性强、易于转换为已知金额的

amounts of cash and which are subject to insignificant risk of changes in value(IAS 7).

现金、价值变动风险很小的投资。
(《国际会计准则第 7 号》)。

cash flow statement

Summarises the inflows and outflows of cash (and cash equivalents)for a period，classified under the following headings：operating activities，investing activities and financing activities (refer to IAS 7). See Figure 3.4.

现金流量表

现金流量表对实体一段期间内的现金(及现金等价物)的流入和流出情况进行汇总,分列为以下三类:经营活动现金流量、投资活动现金流量、筹资活动现金流量(《国际会计准则第 7 号》)。参见图表3.4。

FIGURE 3.4   GROUP CASH FLOW STATEMENT FOR THE YEAR ENDED 31 DECEMBER 2005(indirect method)(REFER TO IAS 7)

	$ million	$ million
Cash flows from operating activities profit before tax	403	
Adjustment for		
Depreciation	80	
Finance costs	85	
Finance income	(56)	
Share of profits of associates and joint ventures	(147)	
	365	
Increase in inventories	(49)	
Decrease in trade and other receivables	63	
Increase in trader and other payables	41	
Cash generated from operations	420	
Finance costs paid	(30)	
Income tax paid	(137)	
Net cash from operating activities		253
Cash flows from investing activities		
Purchase of property，plant and equipment	(273)	
Proceeds from sale of property and equipment	110	
Finance income received	16	
Dividends received from investments	92	
Net cash used in investing activities		(55)
Cash flows from financing activities		
Proceeds from issue of share capital	125	
Repayments of long-term borrowings	(75)	
Equity dividends paid(see note below)	(70)	
Net cash used in financing activities		(20)

CONTINUED

	$ million
Net increase in cash and cash equivalents	178
Cash and cash equivalents at 1 January 2005	(74)
Cash and cash equivalents at 31 December 2005	104

Note: Alternatively, equity dividens paid may be shown as cash flow from operating activities.

图表 3.4　集团现金流量表

间接法(参考 IAS 7)　　　　　　　　　2005 年 12 月 31 日

	单位:百万美元	单位:百万美元
经营活动产生的现金流量	403	
税前利润		
调整项目		
折旧	80	
财务费用	85	
利息收入	(56)	
来自联营企业和合营企业的收益	(147)	
	365	
存货增加	−49	
经营性应收项目的减少	63	
经营性应付项目的增加	41	
经营活动产生的现金流量	420	
已付财务费用	(30)	
已交所得税	(137)	
来自经营活动的净现金流量		253
投资活动产生的现金流量		
购买物业、厂房和设备	(273)	
销售物业、设备所得款项	110	
利息收入	16	
收到的投资收益	92	
投资活动的净现金流量		(55)
筹资活动产生的现金流量		
发行股份收到的款项	125	
偿还长期借款支付的现金	(75)	
分配给股东的股利(见注释)	(70)	
筹资活动的净现金流量		(20)
现金及现金等价物净增加额		178
2005 年 1 月 1 日的现金及现金等价物		(74)
2005 年 12 月 31 日的现金及现金等价物		104

注释:另外,向股东支付的股利也可列示在经营活动现金流量中。

cash generating unit

现金产出单元

Smallest identifiable group of assets that

能够产生现金流入的可辨认的最小

generates cash inflows that are largely independent of the cash inflows from other assets or groups of assets (IAS 36).

资产组,该资产组产生的现金流入在很大程度上独立于其他资产或资产组产生的现金流入(《国际会计准则第 36 号》)。

chart of accounts

会计科目表

Comprehensive and systematically arranged list of the named and numbered accounts applicable to an entity. See Figure 3.5.

对实体适用的会计科目进行命名和编号,并全面且系统地罗列出来。参见图表 3.5。

FIGURE 3.5 EXTRACT FROM CHAPT OF ACCOUNTS

Code	Account descriptor
1	Assets
2	Liabilities
3	Equity
4	Expenses
5	Revenue
11	Non-current assets
12	Current assets
111	Land
112	Buildings
113	Plant
114	Motor vehicles

图 3.5 摘自会计科目表

编号	会计要素
1	资产
2	负债
3	权益
4	费用
5	收入
11	非流动资产
12	流动资产
111	土地
112	建筑物
113	厂房
114	运输设备

closing rate

收盘汇率

Spot exchange rate (a rate for immediate delivery) at the balance sheet date (IAS 21).

资产负债表日的即期汇率(立即交割的汇率)(《国际会计准则第 21 号》)。

code of ethics

道德准则

Set of standards governing the conduct of members of a certain profession, by specifying expected standards for competence, professional behaviour and integrity.

All members of the International Federation Accountants (IFAC) are expected to model their ethical codes on the IFAC code. There is therefore a specific ethical code for

一套规范某个特定职业成员行为的标准,具体阐述了能力、职业行为和诚信方面的期望标准。

国际会计师联合会(IFAC)的所有会员都要遵守 IFAC 的道德准则;而英国皇家特许管理会计师公会(CIMA)的会员需遵守一套特定的道德

CIMA members.

准则。

commitment accounting

承诺会计

Method of accounting which recognises expenditure as soon as it is contracted.

合同一经签订即确认费用的会计处理方法。

committee, audit

审计委员会

Formally constituted committee of an entity's main board of directors whose responsibilities include: monitoring the integrity of any formal announcements on financial performance including financial statements; reviewing internal financial controls, internal control and risk managements systems; monitoring the effectiveness of the internal audit function; making recommendations in respect of the appointment or removal of the external auditor; reviewing and monitoring auditor independence and the effectiveness of the audit process.

由实体主要董事组成的正式委员会,其职责如下:监督包括财务报表在内的任何正式公布的财务业绩的完整性;审查内部财务控制、内部控制及风险管理系统;监督内部审计职能的有效性;就外部审计师的任免提出建议;审查和监督审计师的独立性以及审计程序的有效性。

committee, nominations

提名委员会

Formally constituted committee of an entity's main board of directors. The committee's main functions are to establish the criteria for board membership, identify suitable candidates and make recommendations for appointment to the Board.

由实体主要董事组成的正式委员会,其主要职能是建立董事会成员的任职标准、物色合适人选并提供任命建议。

committee, remuneration

薪酬委员会

Formally constituted committee of an entity's main board of directors whose primary function is to consider the performance and remuneration of the executive directors.

由实体主要董事组成的正式委员会,其主要职能是审议执行董事的绩效表现及薪酬。薪酬事务包括绩效相关支付、退休金权利、酬劳支付及股票

Remuneration issues will include performance-related payments, pension rights, compensation payments and share option schemes.

期权计划。

competition authorities

Competition authorities monitor take-overs and mergers on behalf of national governments. The role of the competition authorities varies from country to country but as a general rule their aims are: to strengthen competition, to prevent or reduce anti-competitive activities, to consider the public interest. If the competition authorities find that a proposed merger or takeover is ant-competitive, they have the power to block the takeover completely.

竞争主管机构

竞争主管机构代表国家政府对收购和兼并活动进行监督。不同国家，其竞争主管机构的职能也有所不同，但它们的共同目标是：加强竞争、防止或减少反竞争行为、考虑公众利益。如果竞争主管部门发现拟议的兼并或收购活动是反竞争的，它们有权彻底阻止收购的进行。

compliance risk

Risk of non-compliance with the law resulting in fines/penalties, etc.

合规风险

违反法规将导致罚款或处罚的风险。

compliance tests

Observe the functioning of the quality control staff to ensure they are checking output.

合规测试

观察质量控制人员的工作开展情况，确保他们对产品进行检查。

component of an entity

Operations and cash flows that can be clearly distinguished operationally, and for financial reporting purposes, from the rest of the entity (IFRS 5).

实体组成部分

出于财务报告的目的，能从经营角度将其经营和现金流与实体其他部分的经营和现金流明确区分开来（《国际财务报告准则第5号》）。

compound instrument

Financial instrument that, from the

复合工具

从发行人的角度来看，既包含负

issuer's perspective, contains both a liability and an equity element (IAS 32).

债要素又包含权益要素的金融工具(《国际会计准则第 32 号》)。

consignment inventory

寄售存货

Inventory held by one party (the dealer) but legally owned by another (the manufacturer) on terms that may give the dealer the right to sell the inventory in the normal course of business or, at the dealer's option, return it unsold to the manufacturer.

由一方(经销商)持有但所有权归属于另一方(生产商)的存货,寄售条款可能授权经销商在正常经营活动中销售这些存货,或由经销商选择是否将未售出的存货退给生产商。

consolidated financial statements

合并财务报表

Financial statements of a group presented as those of a single economic entity (IAS 27).

将集团的财务报表视作单个经济实体的财务报表予以列报(《国际会计准则第 27 号》)。

construction contract

建造合同

Specially negotiated for the construction of an asset or a combination of assets that are closely inter-related or inter-dependent in terms of their design, technology and function or their ultimate purpose or use (IFRS 15).

为了建造一项资产或者在设计、技术、功能以及最终目的或用途上密切关联或相互依赖的一组资产而专门签订的合同(《国际会计准则第 15 号》)。

constructive obligation

推定义务

Obligation that derives from an entity's actions where:

由实体行动而引发的义务:

(a) by an established pattern of past practice, published policies or a sufficiently specific current statement, the entity has indicated to other parties that it will accept certain responsibilities; and

(a) 由于以往的习惯做法、公开发布的政策或相当明确的现有声明,实体向其他方表明它将承担特定的责任;

(b) as a result, the entity has created a valid expectation on the part of those other

(b) 因此,这些责任也使受影响的各方形成了实体将履行责任的合理

parties that it will discharge those responsibilities (IAS 37).

预期(《国际会计准则第 37 号》)。

contingent asset

或有资产

Possible asset that arises from past events and whose existence will be confirmed only by the occurrence of one or more uncertain future events not wholly within the control of the entity (IAS 37).

由过去的事项形成的潜在资产，其存在须通过未来一个或多个不确定的、不完全由实体控制的事项的发生予以证实(《国际会计准则第 37 号》)。

contingent liability

或有负债

A possible obligation that arises from past events and whose existence will be confirmed only by the occurrence or non-occurrence of one or more uncertain future events not wholly within the entity's control; or

A present obligation that arises from past events but is not recognised because it is not probable that a transfer of economic benefits will be required to settle the obligation; or the amount of the obligation cannot be measured with sufficient reliability (IAS 37).

因过去的事项形成的潜在义务，其存在须通过未来一个或数个不确定的、不完全由实体控制的事项的发生或不发生予以证实；

因过去的事项而承担的现时义务，但履行该义务不一定导致经济利益流出实体；或该义务的金额不能充分可靠地计量(《国际会计准则第 37 号》)。

continuing operation

持续经营

See "discontinued operation".

参见"终止经营"。

contractual inadequacy risk

合同不足风险

Risk that terms of a contract do not fully cover a business against all potential outcomes.

合同的条款不能完全覆盖企业所有可能结果的风险。

control (of an entity)

(实体)控制权

Power to govern the financial and

管理一个实体的财务和经营政

operating policies of an entity so as to obtain benefits from its activities (IFRS 10).

策,以便从其活动中获取利益的权力(《国际会计准则第 10 号》)。

convertibles

可转换证券

convertible share: Convertible preference shares, which can be exchanged for a specified number of ordinary shares on some given future date.

可转换股票:可转换优先股,可在未来某一特定的日期转换为确定数额的股票。

convertible debt: Liability that gives the holder the right to convert into another instrument, normally ordinary shares at a predetermined price /rate and time.

可转换债券:赋予持有人一种权利,可以将可转换债券转换成另外一种工具,通常是按预定价格/比率和时间转换成普通股。

corporate social accounting

企业社会会计

Reporting of the social and environmental impact of an entity's activities   upon those who are directly associated with the entity (for instance, employees, customers, suppliers) or those who are in any way affected by the activities of the entity, as well as an assessment of the cost of compliance with relevant regulations in this area.

就实体的活动对与实体直接相关的各方(例如员工、客户、供应商)或者以各种形式受到实体活动影响的各方所产生的社会和环境影响进行报告,以及对该领域相关规定的合规成本进行评估。

corporation tax

企业所得税

Tax chargeable on companies resident in the UK or trading in the UK. Referred to internationally as income tax.

对注册在英国或在英国经营的企业征收的税,国际上称为所得税。

cost of capital

资本成本

Minimum acceptable return on an investment, generally computed as a discount rate for use in investment appraisal exercises. The computation of the optimal cost of capital can be complex, and many ways of determi-

一项投资可接受的最低回报,通常作为投资评估计算的折现率。最佳资本成本的计算较为复杂,业界已提出多种方法来确定该机会成本。参见"加权平均资本成本"。

ning this opportunity cost have been suggested. See "weighted average cost of capital".

creative accounting

Form of accounting which，while complying with all regulations and practices，nevertheless gives a biased impression（generally favourable）of an entity's financial performance and position. See "window-dressing".

creditor

See "payables".

current account

Record of transactions between two parties. For example，between a bank and its customer or a branch and its head office.

current asset

Asset which satisfies any of the following criteria：

（a）is expected to be realised in，or is intended for sale or consumption in， the entity's normal operating cycle；

（b）is held primarily for the purpose of being traded；

（c）is expected to be realised within twelve months of the balance sheet date；or

（d）is cash or cash equivalent（IAS 1）.

current cost accounting（CCA）

Method of accounting in which profit is

创造性会计

会计处理的一种形式，其操作虽然符合所有规定和实务，但会让人们对实体的财务表现及状况产生有所偏颇的印象（一般是良好的印象）。参见"窗口粉饰"。

债权人

参见"应付款项"。

往来账户

交易双方的交易记录。比如，银行和客户之间的交易记录或者分支机构和母公司之间的交易记录。

流动资产

满足以下任一标准的资产被称为流动资产：

（a）在实体正常运营周期内，有望变现或用于销售或消耗的资产；

（b）以交易目的为主而持有的资产；

（c）有望在资产负债表日的12个月内变现的资产；

（d）现金或现金等价物（《国际会计准则第1号》）。

现行成本会计

一种会计处理方法，该方法将利

defined as the surplus after allowing for price changes on the funds needed to continue the existing business and to maintain its operating capability, whether financed by shares or borrowing.

润定义为在考虑企业持续经营和维持其经营能力所需的资金(不管是发行股票还是借款筹集的资金)的价格变动之后所剩余的部分。

current liability

Liability which satisfies any of the following criteria:

(a) is expected to be settled in the entity's normal operating cycle;

(b) is held primarily for the purpose of being traded;or

(c) is due to be settled within twelve months of the balance sheet date.

All other liabilities are classified as non-current(IAS 1).

流动负债

满足以下任一标准的负债被称为流动负债:

(a)有望在实体正常营运周期内偿还的负债;

(b)以交易目的为主而持有的负债;

(c)应在资产负债表日的12个月内偿还的负债。

其他负债都被分类为非流动负债(《国际会计准则第1号》)。

current purchasing power accounting (CPP)

Method of accounting in which the values of non-monetary items in the historical cost financial statements are adjusted, using a general price index, so that the resulting profit allows for the maintenance of the purchasing power of the shareholders' interest in the entity. A CPP balance sheet shows the effect of financial capital maintenance.

现行购买力会计

一种会计处理方法,利用一般物价指数对财务报表中以历史成本计量的非货币项目进行调整,如此计算得出的利润考虑了股东所拥有的实体权益的购买力的保全。按现行购买力会计法编制的资产负债表显示了财务资本保全的效果。

current tax

Amount of income taxes payable (or recoverable) in respect of the taxable profit (or loss)for a period(IAS 12).

当期所得税

指根据一个期间的应税利润(或可抵扣亏损)计算的应付(或可收回)所得税金额(《国际会计准则》第12号)。

date of transition（to IFRSs）

Beginning of the earliest period for which an entity presents full comparative information under IFRSs in its first IFRS-compliant financial statement（IFRS 1）.

debtor

See "receivables".

deductible temporary difference

Temporary difference that will result in amounts that are deductible in determining taxable profit（or tax loss）of future periods when the carrying amount of the asset or liability is recovered or settled（IAS 12）.

deferred expenditure

Expenditure not charged against income in an accounting period but carried forward as a non-current or current asset to be charged in one or more subsequent periods, for example development expenditure（refer to IAS 38）.

deferred tax

Difference between the tax ultimately payable on the profits recognised in an accounting period and the actual amount of tax payable for the same accounting period. The former figure will be based on the tax implications of accounting profit and the carrying

过渡日（过渡为国际财务报告准则）

实体根据国际财务报告准则编制其第一份国际财务报告准则财务报表并全面列报可比较信息的最早期间的期初（《国际财务报告准则第1号》）。

债务人

参见"应收款项"。

可抵扣暂时性差异

在确定未来按账面金额收回资产或清偿负债期间的应纳税所得额（或可抵扣亏损）时，出现的可抵扣金额的暂时性差异（《国际会计准则第12号》）。

递延支出

未能全部抵减当期收益，而是以流动或者非流动资产的形式抵减一个或多个后续期间收益的支出。例如开发支出（《国际会计准则第38号》）。

递延税项

在一个会计期间内企业基于其会计利润所确认的最终应缴纳税费与其实际缴纳税款之间的差异。前者是基于企业的会计利润和资产负债的账面价值所计算得出的税费。后者是基于税务机关所确认的企业利润而计算得

amounts of assets and liabilities. The latter figure will be based on a calculation of profits as recognised by the tax authorities.

出的税款。

deferred tax asset

Amount of income taxes recoverable in future periods in respect of deductible temporary differences, carried forward unused tax losses and unused tax credits(IAS 12).

递延所得税资产

就可抵扣暂时性差异、未使用的可抵扣损失及未使用的税收抵免而言,公司未来期间可收回的所得税金额(《国际会计准则第 12 号》)。

deferred tax liability

Amount of income taxes payable in future periods in respect of taxable temporary differences(IAS 12).

递延所得税负债

未来期间与应纳税暂时性差异相关的应付所得税金额(《国际会计准则第 12 号》)。

defined benefit plan

Any post-employment scheme other than a defined contribution plan (IAS 19). In such a scheme the employer takes the risk-also known as a final salary scheme.

设定受益计划

除设定提存计划(《国际会计准则第 19 号》)以外的任一离职后计划都称为设定受益计划。在这种方案中,由雇主承担风险(也称为最终薪金计划)。

defined contribution plan

Post-employment benefit plan under which an entity pays fixed contributions into a separate entity(the fund) and will have no legal or constructive obligation to pay further contributions, if the fund does not hold sufficient assets to pay all employee benefits relating to their service in the current and prior periods (IAS 19). In such a scheme the employee takes the risk-also known as a money purchase scheme.

设定提存计划

一项离职后福利计划,实体将固定的款项缴付给独立的机构(基金),如果未来该机构(基金)无法向员工足额支付与他们当前和之前所提供的劳动相关的所有福利(《国际会计准则第 19 号》),那么企业无需承担继续缴付的法定或推定责任。在这种方案中,由员工承担风险(也称为现金购买计划)。

depreciable amount

Cost of an asset，or other amount substituted for cost，less the residual value（IAS 16）.

depreciation

Systematic allocation of the depreciable amount of an asset over its useful life（IAS 16）. Normally applied to tangible assets. See "amortisation".

deprival value

Basis for valuing assets base on the maximum amount which an entity would be willing to pay rather than forgo the asset. Deprival value is the lower of replacement cost and recoverable amount（itself the higher of fair value less costs to sell and value in use）. See "impairment". see Figure 3.6.

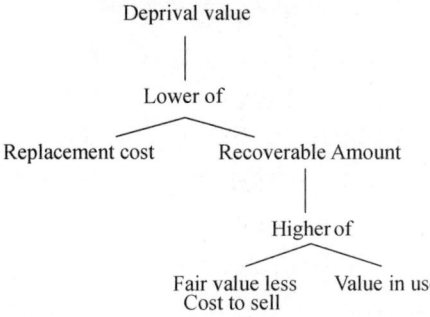

FIGURE 3.6   DEPRIVAL VALUE

de-recognition

Removal of a previously recognised asset （or liability） from an entity's balance sheet.

可折旧金额

一项资产的成本或可替代成本的其他金额减去其残值后的余额（《国际会计准则第16号》）。

折旧

将资产的可折旧金额在其使用寿命内进行系统性分摊（《国际会计准则第16号》），通常适用于有形资产。参见"摊销"。

剥夺价值

是资产的估值基准，基于企业为了不放弃一项资产而愿意支付的最高金额。剥夺价值等于重置成本与可回收金额两者之间的较低者，而可回收金额等于出售资产的公允价值减去销售成本后的净值与资产使用价值两者之间的较高者。参见"减值"。参见图表3.6。

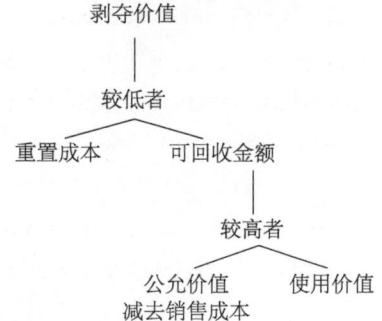

图表3.6　剥夺价值

终止确认

从实体的资产负债表中将先前确认的资产（或负债）移除。

development costs

Costs incurred in applying research findings or other knowledge to a plan or design for the production of new or substantially improved materials，devices，products，processes，systems or services prior to the commencement of commercial production or use (IAS 38).

开发成本

在投入商业性生产或使用之前，将研究发现或其他知识应用于新产品的生产或现有材料、装置、产品、流程、系统或服务的实质性改进而产生的成本(《国际会计准则第 38 号》)。

dilution

Reduction in the earnings and voting power per share caused by an increase or potential increase in the number of shares in issue. For the purpose of calculating diluted earnings per share，the profit attributable to ordinary shareholders and the weighted average number of shares outstanding should be adjusted for the effects of all diluctive potential ordinary shares. Also see "anti-dilution".

稀释

因发行股份数的增加或潜在增加而导致每股收益和每股投票权的减少。在计算稀释后的每股收益时，需考虑所有稀释性潜在普通股的影响，相应调整归属于普通股股东的利润和发行在外的普通股的加权平均数。参见"反稀释"。

directors，role of

The role and responsibilities of directors：directors have a fiduciary duty to shareholders. This means they have been placed in a position of trust and must act in good faith to further the interests of their company，rather than their own interests. They also have a duty to exercise care and skill.

董事角色

董事的角色和职责：董事向股东承担受托责任。这意味着他们身处受信任的位置，行动必须忠于公司未来的利益，而不是自身的利益。他们也有责任关怀公司以及强化自身技能。

discontinued operation

Component of an entity that has either been disposed of or is classified as held for sale and：

终止经营

已被处置或划归为持有以备出售的实体组成部分，并且该组成部分：

(a) represents, or is part of a single plan to dispose of, a separate major line of business or geographical area of operation; or

(b) Is a subsidiary acquired exclusively with a view to resale (IFRS 5). See Figure 3.7.

（a）代表一个单一处置计划或是处置计划的一部分，涉及处置一个独立的主要业务线或经营地区；

（b）或是仅仅为了再次出售而收购的子公司（《国际财务报告准则第5号》）。参见图表3.7。

FIGURE 3.7　RPESENTAITON OF DISCONTNUED OPERATIONS (REER TO IFRS 5)

GROUP INCOME STATEMENT FOR THE YEAR ENDED 31 DECEMBER 2005	Continuing operations $ million	Discontinued operations $ million	Totals $ million
Revenue	3,561	786	4,347
Cost of sales	(2,883)	(766)	(3,649)
Gross profit	678	20	698
Other operating income	73		73
Distribution costs	(241)	(11)	(252)
Administrative expenses	(142)	(31)	(173)
Other operating expenses	(61)	—	(61)
Profit (loss) from operations	307	(22)	285
Finance costs	(72)	(13)	(85)
Finance income	56		56
Share of profits of associates and joint ventures	147	—	47
Profit(loss)before tax	438	(35)	403
Income tax expense	(180)	11	(169)
Profit(loss)for the year	258	(24)	234

Alternative presentation

	$ million
Continuing operations	
Revenue	3,561
Cost of sales	(2,883)
Gross profit	678
Other operating income	73
Distribution costs	(241)
Administrative expenses	(142)
Other operating expenses	(61)
Profit(loss)from operations	307
Finance costs	(72)
Finance income	56
Share of profits of associates and joint ventures	147
Profit before tax	438
Income tax expense	(180)
Profit for the year from continuing operations	258
Discontinued operations	
Loss for the year from discontinued operations	(24)
Profit for the year	234

图表 3.7 终止经营的呈报(参照《国际财务报告准则第 5 号》)

截止 2005 年 12 月 31 日持续经营终止经营总额 集团年度收益表业务	持续经营	终止经营	总额
	$ 百万	$ 百万	$ 百万
收入	3,561	786	4,347
销售成本	(2,883)	(766)	(3,649)
毛利	678	20	698
其他营业收入	73		73
分销成本	(241)	(11)	(252)
管理费用	(142)	(31)	(173)
其他营业费用	(61)		(61)
盈利(亏损)	307	(22)	285
财务费用	(72)	(13)	(85)
财务收入	56		56
应占联营公司和合营公司利润	147		147
税前利润(亏损)	438	(35)	403
所得税费用	(180)	11	(169)
盈利(亏损)总额	258	(24)	234
其他形式的呈报			
			$: 百万
持续经营业务			
收入			3,561
销售成本			(2,883)
毛利			678
其他营业收入			73
分销成本			(241)
管理费用			(142)
其他营业费用			(61)
盈利(亏损)			307
财务费用			(72)
财务收入			56
应占联营公司和合营公司利润			147
税前利润			438
所得税费用			(180)
持续经营业务利润总额			258
终止经营业务			
终止经营业务损失总额			(24)
利润总额			234

disposal group

Group of assets to be disposed of, by sale or otherwise, together as a group in a single transaction, and liabilies directly associated with those assets that will be transferred in transaction(IFRS 5).

处置组

将采用销售或其他方式,以单项交易形式处置的一组资产,以及与这组资产直接相关的、将通过交易一并转移的负债(《国际财务报告准则第 5 号》)。

distributable reserves

Profit for a period, plus retained earnings from previous periods, that are available for payment as dividends(or other distributions to owners). The split between distributable and non-distributable reserves is a UK legal requirement to ensure that creditors have some protection from the effects of losses.

distribution costs

Cost of warehousing saleable products and delivering them to customers. These costs are reported in the income statement.

dividend

Distribution of profits to the holders of equity investments in proportion to their holdings of a particular class of capital.

dominant influence

Influence that can be exercised over an entity to achieve the operating and financial policies designed by the holder of the influence, notwithstanding the rights or influence of any other party.

double-entry bookkeeping/accounting

Most commonly used system of bookkeeping based on the principle that every financial transaction involves the simultaneous

可分配储备

本期利润加上前期的留存收益，可用于支付股息（或以其他方式分配给所有者）。英国法律规定企业需将可分配储备与不可分配储备分开，以保护债权人免受企业亏损的影响。

配送成本

可销售产品的仓储成本和将产品送达客户的运输成本，这些成本体现在利润表中。

股息

按权益投资持有者持有某一特定类别的资产的比例，向其分配的利润。

支配性影响

可实施的、能左右一个实体运营和财务政策选择的影响力，即便还存在其他权利或实体还受到他方的影响。

复式记账/会计处理

最为常用的一种记账体系，其立足于每笔财务交易同时涉及价值收取和价值支付这一原则，因此每笔财务

receiving and giving of value，and is there-fore recorded twice.

交易都需要记录两次。

doubtful debts provision

坏账准备

Amount charged against profit and de-ducted from trade receivables to allow for the estimated non-recovery of a proportion of the trade receivables. See "bad debt".

预估应收账款中可能无法收回的金额，并将其从利润和应收账款中扣除。参见"坏账"。

earnings per share(EPS)，Basic

基本每股收益

Profit for the period that is attributable to ordinary shares（the numerator）divided by the weighted average number of ordinary shares out-standing during the period.（IAS 33）.

企业按照可向普通股股东分配的当期利润（扣除利息、税费和优先股股息后，分子），除以发行在外的普通股的加权平均数（分母），从而计算得出每股收益（《国际会计准则第 33 号》）。

embedded audit facilities

嵌入式审计功能

Embedded audit facilities might be writ-ten into a program，particularly in online/re-al-time systems. These facilities can carry out automatic checks or provide information for subsequent audit.

嵌入式审计功能可能写入网上或者实时系统的程序中。这些功能能够执行自动核查或者为后续审计提供信息。

employee benefits

雇员福利

All forms of consideration given by an entity in exchange for service rendered by employees（IAS 19）.

实体为换取雇员提供的服务而给予的各种形式的报酬（《国际会计准则第 19 号》）。

entity

实体

Economic unit that has a separate，distinct identity，for example an industrial or commer-cial company（or enterprise），charity，local au-thority，government agency or fund.

一个拥有独立的、独特身份的经济单位，例如工业或商业公司（或企业）、慈善机构、地方当局、政府机构或基金。

environmental reporting

Report or disclosure by an entity that discusses and/or quantifies the benefits and costs of the entity's interaction with its operating environment.

equity

Residual interest in the assets of the entity after deducting all its liabilities (IASB Framework). It is comprised of share capital, retained earnings and other reserves of a single entity, plus minority interests in a group, representing the investment made in the entity by its owners.

equity instrument

Contract that evidences a residual interest in the assets of an entity after deducting all of its liabilities (IAS 32).

equity method of accounting

Method of accounting whereby the investment is initially recognised at cost and adjusted thereafter for the post-acquisition change in the investor's share of the net assets of the investee. The profit or loss of the investor includes the investor's share of the profit or loss of the investee. A method used to account for associates and (optionally) joint ventures (refer to IAS 28 and IAS 32).

equity shares

See "ordinary shares".

环境报告

实体提供的报告或披露的信息，其讨论和（或）量化了实体与其经营环境相互作用所产生的收益和成本。

权益

实体资产在扣除所有负债后剩余的部分（《国际会计准则理事会框架》）。它包括：股本、留存收益和单个实体的其他准备，再加上集团中的少数股东权益，代表所有者对实体所作的投资。

权益工具

能证明在扣除所有负债后，对实体剩余资产拥有权益的合同（《国际会计准则第 32 号》）。

会计处理的权益法

一种会计处理方法，投资按照成本进行初始计量，而后根据收购后投资者在被投资企业净资产中拥有的权益比例的变化进行相应调整。投资者的损益包括按照权益比例应分摊的被投资公司的损益。这种方法适用于联营和合营企业（选择性使用）（参考《国际会计准则第 28 号和第 32 号》）。

股票

参见"普通股"。

ethics, CIMA code of ethics

道德,CIMA 道德守则

CIMA' code of ethics is an 81-page document that offers guidance on how to recognise and respond to tricky ethical situations.

CIMA 的道德守则是一个 81 页的文件,它为如何识别和处理棘手的道德处境提供了指导。

ethics, conflict resolution

道德,冲突解决

The code is clear that the professional accountant should respond to an ethical conflict. Inaction or silence may well be a further breach of the code.

该守则明确指出,专业会计师应当对道德冲突做出回应。不作为或保持沉默可能进一步违反守则。

ethics, dilemmas

道德困境

A dilemma will only occur if there are two or more interests at stake, even if it is only an ethical duty to oneself.

An ethical dilemma exists when one or more principles of the code are threatened.

当两个或两个以上的利益受到威胁时(即便对于某人而言只是一项道德义务),困境才会发生。

当一个或多个守则原则面临威胁时,道德困境就会发生。

ethics, fundamental principles

道德的基本原则

Integrity.

Objectivity.

Professional. competence and due care.

Confidentiality.

Professional behavior.

诚实。

客观。

专业胜任能力和保持应有的关注。

保密。

专业行为。

ethics, stances

道德的态度

The extent to which an organisation will exceed its minimum obligations to stakeholders.

对一个组织来讲,道德态度可以用其超越利益相关者最低义务的程度来衡量。

ethics, threats

The self-interest threat.

The self-review threat.

The advocacy threat.

The familiarity or trust threat.

The intimidation threat.

ethics, threats and safeguards

The conflict between requirements of the employer and the fundamental principles and its corresponding safeguards.

events after the balance sheet date

Events，favourable and unfavourable，that occur between the balance sheet date and the date the financial statements are authorized for issue.

adjusting events：Those that provide evidence of conditions that existed at the balance sheet date.

non-adjusting events：Those that are indicative of conditions that arose after the balance sheet date. (Refer to IAS 10).

exceptional items

Material items which derive from events or transactions that should be disclosed in the notes to the financial statements by virtue of their size or incidence in relation to the income statement.

fair value

Amount for which an asset could be

道德威胁

自身利益威胁。

自我审查威胁。

吹捧威胁。

熟悉或信任威胁。

恐吓威胁。

道德威胁和防护措施

雇主的要求和基本原则之间的冲突及对应的防护措施。

资产负债表日后事项

资产负债表日至财务报表批准发布日之间发生的有利或不利事项。

调整事项：对资产负债表日已经存在的情况提供证据的事项。

非调整事项：表明资产负债表日后发生情况的事项(参照《国际会计准则第10号》)。

例外事项

由事项或交易引发的，因其规模或发生与利润表相关，而应该在财务报表附注中披露的重要事项。

公允价值

熟悉市场情况的买卖双方，在正

exchanged，or a liability settled，between knowledgeable and willing parties in an arm's length transaction（IAS 2）

常交易条件下,自愿交换资产或者清偿负债所涉及的金额(《国际会计准则第2号》)。

fair value less costs to sell

公允价值减去销售费用

Amount obtainable from the sale of an asset（or cash generating unit）in an arm's length transaction between knowledgeable and willing parties，less the direct costs of disposal（IAS 36）.

熟悉市场情况的买卖双方,在正常交易条件下,自愿出售资产(或现金产出单元)收到的款项减去处置产生的直接费用(《国际会计准则第36号》)。

financial accounting

财务会计

Classification and recording of the monetary transactions of an entity in accordance with established concepts，principle，accounting standards and legal requirements and their presentation，by means of income statements，balance sheet and cash flow statements，during sheets and cash flow statements，during and at the end of an accounting period.

实体按照既定的概念、原则、会计准则及法律规定,对其货币交易进行分类和记录,并在会计期间结束时通过资产负债表、利润表、现金流量表形式进行列报。

financial position

财务状况

Relationship of the asset，liability and equity of an entity as reported in its balance sheet（IASB Framework）.

某实体资产负债表所报告的资产、负债和所有者权益的关系(IASB框架)。

Financial Reporting Council（FRC）

财务报告委员会

UK's single independent regulator of financial reporting and corporate governance with delegated statutory powers. The FRC oversees the work of the Accounting Standards Board（ASB），the Financial Reporting Review Panel（FRRP），the Professional

英国在财务报告和公司治理上拥有法定授权的单一且独立的监管机构。财务报告委员会监督会计准则理事会(ASB)、财务报告审查小组(FR-RP)、会计专业监督委员会、审计实务委员会(APB)和会计调查与纪律委员

Oversight Board for Accountancy, the Auditing Practices Board(APB) and the Accountancy Investigation and Discipline Board.

会的工作。

Financial Reporting Review Panel

Uk review panel established to examine contentious departures, by large companies, from accounting standards.

财务报告审查小组

英国成立的审查小组,负责研究大公司有争议的、背离会计准则的行为。

Financial Reporting Standard(FRS)

A UK accounting standard issued since 1 August 1990, when the Accounting Standards Board (ASB) succeeded the Accounting Standards Committee(ASC).

财务报告准则

英国于 1990 年 8 月 1 日发布的会计准则。当时,会计准则理事会(ASB)接替了会计准则委员会(ASC)。

financial statements

Complete set of financial statements comprises: balance sheet, income statement, statement of changes in equity or statement of changes in equity or statement of recognised income and expense, cash flow statement, notes comprising a summary of significant accounting policies and other explanatory notes.

财务报表

一套完整的财务报表包括:资产负债表、利润表、所有者权益变动表或已确认的收入和费用表、现金流量表以及包含重要会计政策和其他解释性说明的附注。

financing activities

Activities that result in changes in the size and composition of the contributed equity and borrowings of an entity as reported in its cash flow statement(IAS 7).

筹资活动

企业在现金流量表中报告的,导致企业权益资本和借款的规模和构成发生改变的活动。(《国际会计准则第7 号》)。

financial reporting

According to the International Accounting

财务报告

根据国际会计准则理事会

Standards Board's (IASB's) conceptual framework, the objective of financial reporting is to provide information about the reporting entity that is useful to existing and potential investors, lenders and other creditors in making decisions about providing resources to the entity.

(IASB)的概念框架,财务报告的目标是为现有以及潜在投资者、债权人及其他权利人提供有关报告主体的有用信息,以便于他们进行投资决策。

fixed charge

固定担保

Protection given to creditors whereby they can enforce the sale of specified (non-current) asset(s) if there is a default.

是对债权人的一种保护,即一旦债务人出现违约,那么债权人可以强制出售债务人的指定(非流动)资产。

floating charge

浮动担保

Protection given to creditors whereby they can enforce the sale of any(non-current) asset(s) if there is a default.

是对债权人的一种保护,即一旦债务人出现违约,那么债权人可以强制出售债务人的任何(非流动)资产。

foreign currency transaction

外币业务

Transaction that is denominated in, or requires settlement in, a foreign currency (IAS 21).

以外币标价或者要求以外币来结算的交易(《国际会计准则第 21 号》)。

foreign currency translation

外币折算

Restatement of the transactions or financial statements of a foreign operation into the reporting currency of the parent (or investor) for the purpose of preparing consolidated financial statements.

为了编制合并财务报表,实体将其海外交易或者是海外业务财务报表的金额都折算成以母公司(或投资者)的记账本位币表示的金额。

foreign operation

国外业务

An entity that is a subsidiary, associate, joint venture or branch of the reporting entity, the activities of which are based or

是指报告实体拥有的子公司、联营企业、合营企业或分支机构,其在报告实体所在国以外的国家开展活动

conducted in a country other than the country of the reporting entity(IAS 21).

（《国际会计准则第21号》）。

forensic accounting

Use of accounting records and documents in order to determine the legality or otherwise of past activities.

法务会计

利用会计记录和文件来确定过去活动的合法性等。

fraud investigation

Fraud investigation can be carried out by an auditor. It is not their primary objective when carrying out an audit，but they are duty bound to report a fraud if during the course of their work they identify fraudulent activities.

欺诈调查

欺诈调查可以由审计人员开展，这不是他们审计工作的主要目的。但如果在工作过程中，他们发现了欺诈活动，则有义务进行报告。

fraud prerequisites

There are three prerequisites for fraud to occur：
Dishonesty on the part of the perpetrator.
Opportunity for fraud to occur.
Motive for fraud.

欺诈的前提条件

欺诈发生有三个前提条件：

欺诈者有不诚实行为。
出现欺诈机会。
有欺诈动机。

fraud prevention

The aim of preventative controls is to reduce opportunity and remove temptation from potential offenders. Prevention techniques include the introduction of policies，procedures and controls，and controls，and activities such as training and fraud awareness to stop fraud from occurring.

欺诈预防

预防性控制的目的是减少潜在欺诈机会和消除潜在欺诈诱惑。预防技术包括引入政策、程序和控制、活动，比如培训和提高意识以防止欺诈的发生。

fraud response plans

The fraud response plan sets out the ar-

欺诈应对计划

欺诈应对计划规定了涉嫌欺诈、

rangements for dealing with suspected cases of fraud，theft or corruption.

盗窃或腐败案件的处理安排。

fraud risk

欺诈风险

Fraud risk is the vulnerability of an organisation to fraud. The size of fraud risk for any organisation is a factor of：

The probability of fraud occurring，and

The size of the losses if fraud does occur.

欺诈风险是组织面对欺诈所暴露出的脆弱性。任何组织欺诈风险的大小应考虑：

欺诈的发生概率；

如果欺诈发生，损失的大小。

fraud risk management strategy

欺诈风险管理策略

In common with any other type of risk，a risk management strategy needs to be developed for fraud. This strategy should include：fraud prevention，fraud detection，fraud response.

与其他类型的风险相同，实体也应针对欺诈开发出一种风险管理策略。这一策略应包括：欺诈预防、欺诈检查和欺诈应对。

FRSSE

小企业财务报告准则

Financial Reporting Standard for Smaller Entities. This is a single standard for an optional simplified reporting regime for smaller entities in the UK.

这是为英国境内较小企业提供的以简化报告机制的单独准则，小企业可自行选择是否使用。

fungible assets

可互换资产

Assets which are substantially indistinguishable one from another，for example a holding of shares in an entity.

无法与另一项资产实质性区分开来的资产，如在某实体中持有的股份。

generally accepted accounting practice(GAAP)

公认会计原则

Components of UK GAAP include：the provisions of company law；the accounting

英国公认会计原则的组成包括：公司法的规定、由会计准则理事会颁

standards issued by the ASB；UITF Abstracts；Statements of Recommended Practice；stock exchange listing roles；professional recommendations and pronouncements of the Financial Reporting Review Panel. For matters not covered by these，the practices of leading companies and audit firms are widely accepted as possessing authority.

布的会计准则、紧急问题工作小组摘要、推荐实务公告、股票上市规则、财务报告审查小组的专业建议和声明。对于以上原则未涵盖的事项，可参见会计师事务所和行业领头企业被普遍接受的做法，这些做法具有权威性。

geographic segment

地区分部

Distinguishiable component of an entity that is engaged in providing products or services within a particular economic environment and that is subject to risks and returns that are different from those of components operating in other economnic environments (IAS 14). See "business segment".

一个实体可区分的组成部分，该组成部分在一个特定的经济环境内提供产品或劳务，其承担的风险和收益不同于在其他经济环境中经营的组成部分（《国际会计准则第 14 号》）。参见"业务分部"。

Global Reporting Initiative(GRI)

全球报告倡议组织

The GRI suggests that entities report performance indicators so that users can monitor their performance from economic，environmental and social perspectives.

为实体报告提供规范性框架，建议实体报告其业绩指标以便信息使用者可以从经济、环境、社会角度对实体业绩进行监督。

examples of disclosures

披露示例

Based on the above guidance，the sort of disclosures entities might make to comply with the G4 guidelines are：Economic，Environmental，Social.

基于以上指引，实体应根据 G4 指南进行经济、环境、社会方面的信息披露。

goodwill

商誉

acquired：Future economic benefits arising from assets that are not capable of being individually identified and separately recog-

取得：源自那些不能够被单独识别及单独确认的资产的未来经济利益（参照《国际财务报告准则第 3 号》）。

nised（refer to IFRS 3）.

positive goodwill：Excess of the purchase consideration over the fair value of the identifiable net assets acquired.

negative goodwill：Excess of the fair value of the identifiable net assets acquired over the purchase consideration.

internally generated：An entity's own view of its value above its recorded value which cannot be recognised in financial statements prepared in accordance with accounting standards.

正商誉：购买对价超过被收购的可辨认净资产的公允价值。

负商誉：购买对价低于被收购的可辨认净资产的公允价值。

自有商誉：实体认为其自身价值超过了报表记录的价值。根据会计准则，这部分价值无法在财务报表中确认。

Governance, Combined Code on Corporate

公司治理联合守则

Guidance on good governance for UK listed companies，published in July 2003 and consolidating earlier voluntary corporate governance codes（Cadbury，Greenbury，Hampel，Higgs and Smith）. The Combined Code is annexed to the Listing Rules of the UK Listing Authority，the FSA（Financial Services Authority）. Listed companies are required to state whether they comply with the Code，and justify any departures.

2003 年 7 月发布的英国上市公司良好治理指引，吸纳了早期的企业自愿治理守则。联合守则附属于英国上市管理机构——金融服务管理局的上市规则。上市公司需按要求声明其是否遵守该守则，并证明任何偏离于该守则的活动都具有合理性。

governance, corporate

公司治理

The system by which companies and other entities are directed and controlled. The boards of directors are responsible for the governance of their companies and other entities. The shareholders' role in governance is to appoint the directors and the auditors，and to satisfy themselves that an appropriate governance structure is in place. The responsibilities of the board include setting

用于指导和控制公司或其他实体的体系。董事会对公司和其他实体的治理负责。股东在治理工作中的角色是任命董事及审计师，设置合适的、令自己满意的治理结构。董事会的职责包括：制定本公司（或实体）的战略目标、领导公司（或实体）以实现战略目标、监督公司（或企业）的管理以及向股东报告其受托责任。董事会的行动

the company's（or entity's） strategic aims，providing the leadership to put them into effect，supervising the management of the company（or entity） and reporting to shareholders on their stewardship. The board's actions are subject to laws，regulations and the shareholders in general meeting.

受到法律、法规和股东大会的制约。

governance, enterprise

企业治理

Set of responsibilities and practices exercised by the board and executive management with the goal of providing strategic direction，ensuring that objectives are achieved，ascertaining that risks are managed appropriately and verifying that the organisation's resources are used responsibly（Information Systems Audit and Control Foundation.

董事会和管理层应遵照实施的一套责任体系和实践操作,其目标是提供战略方向,确保企业目标得到实现,确定风险得到妥善管控,验证组织资源得到负责任的使用(信息系统审计与控制基金会)。

Governance, OECD Principles of corporate

经合组织的公司治理原则

Framework for good practice which has been agreed by the governments of all OECD member countries. They have been designed to assist governments and regulatory bodies in both OECD countries and elsewhere in drawing up and enforcing effective rules，regulations and codes of corporate governance. In parallel，they provide guidance for stock exchanges，investors，companies（and other entities） and others that have a role in the process of developing good corporate governance.

已获得经合组织所有成员国政府认可的良好实践框架。设计这些原则旨在帮助经合组织成员国以及其他国家的政府和监管机构制定和执行有效的规则、法规及公司治理守则。与此同时,这些原则为证券交易所、投资者、公司(和其他实体)以及其他组织提供了指导,帮助它们在良好公司治理的发展过程中发挥自身作用。

government grants

政府补助

Assistance by the government （including

政府(包括地方政府、国家政府和

local，national and international agencies) in the form of transfer of resources to an entity in return for past or future compliance with certain conditions relating to the operating activities of the entity (IAS 20). They are of particular importance to small and medium-sized businesses. Their key advantage is that they do not need to be paid back. Grants can be provided by local governments，national governments，and other larger bodies.

国际组织)以转移资源的方式向实体提供援助，以奖励其过去或鼓励其将来按照某些条件开展经营活动(《国际会计准则第 20 号》)。这些援助对中小企业尤为重要，它们的主要优势在于不需要偿还，可由地方政府、国家政府和其他大型组织提供。

group

A parent and all its subsidiaries (IAS 27).

集团

母公司及其所有附属子公司(《国际会计准则第 27 号》)。

group loss relief

Group relief is only available for losses and profits generated after a company joins a group.

Group relief ceases to be available once arrangements are in place to sell the shares of a company. This will usually occur sometime before the actual legal sale of the shares.

对集团的亏损给予税项减免

集团的税项减免只适用于企业加入集团之后产生的损益。一旦集团做出出售企业股份的安排，集团的税项减免将终止，这通常发生在股票法定意义上的实际出售之前。

group accounts

See "consolidated financial statements".

集团账目

参见"合并财务报表"。

hedge effectiveness

Degree to which changes in the fair value or cash flows of the hedged item that are attributable to a hedged risk are offset by changes in the fair value or cash flows of the hedging instrument (IAS 39).

套期保值有效性

通过套期保值工具公允价值或现金流量的变动能够抵销目标风险所引发的套期保值对象公允价值或现金流量变动的程度(《国际会计准则第 39 号》)。

hedged instrument

Designated derivative whose fair value or cash flows are expected to offset changes in the fair value or cash flows of a designated hedged item (IAS 39).

hedged item

Asset, liability, firm commitment, highly probable forecast transaction or net investment in a foreign operation that exposes the entity to risks of changes in fair value or future cash flows and is designated as being hedged (IAS 39).

historical cost

For assets – recorded at the amount of cash (or cash equivalents) paid or the fair value of the consideration given to acquire them at the time of their acquisition.

For liabilities – recorded at the amount of proceeds received in exchange for the obligation (for example, income taxes) or at the amounts of cash (or cash equivalents) expected to be paid to satisfy the liability in the normal course of business.

(Refer to IFRS Framework)

historical cost accounting

System of accounting in which all values are based on the historical costs incurred.

套期保值工具

指定的衍生工具,其公允价值或现金流量变动有望抵销指定的套期保值对象的公允价值或现金流量变动(《国际会计准则》第39号)。

套期保值对象

具有以下特征的资产、负债,确定承诺,极可能发生的未来交易或对国外经营的净投资:使企业面临公允价值或未来现金流量变动风险;被指定为套期保值对象(《国际会计准则第39号》)。

历史成本

对资产而言,历史成本是指按照购买时支付的现金或现金等价物的金额或者所付出的对价的公允价值进行计量。

对负债而言,历史成本是指按照承担现时义务而实际收到的款项(如所得税),或者按照日常经营活动中偿还负债预期需要支付的现金或现金等价物的金额进行计量。

(参考《国际财务报告准则概念框架》)

历史成本会计

所有价值均基于所发生的历史成本的会计系统。

horizontal group

Position where two or more undertakings are controlled by a common parent，such as a private individual，who is not subject to the requirements of regulations or corpoate laws. There is therefore no legal or professional mechanism which can be used to require the preparation of consolidated financial statements. See ＂consolidated financial statements＂.

横向集团

由共同的母公司控制两个或两个以上企业的情形，实施控制的母公司可以是一个不受法规或公司法约束的私人个体。因此，要求其编制合并财务报表没有可依据的法律或者专业机制。参见"合并财务报表"。

human resource accounting

Identification，recording and reporting of the investment in，and return from the employment of，the personnel of an entity.

人力资源会计

识别、记录和报告实体在就业和员工方面的投资及回报。

hyperinflation

Loss of purchasing power of money at such a rate that comparison of amounts from transactions and other events that have occurred at different times, even within the same accounting period, is misleading (IAS 29). As an indication, hyperinflation could exist where the cumulative inflation rate over three years is 100%.

恶性通货膨胀

货币购买力迅速丧失，以至于对不同会计期间(甚至同一会计期间)发生的交易和其他事项进行金额上的比较会令人产生误解(《国际会计准则第29号》)。当3年的累积通胀率达到100%时，就表明存在恶性通货膨胀。

identifiable assets and liabilities

Assets and liabilities of an entity that are capable of being disposed of or settled separately，without disposing of a business of the entity (IFRS 10).

可辨认资产和负债

在不处置实体某个分部的前提下，能够独立处置或清偿的资产和负债(《国际财务报告准则第10号》)。

impairment

Reduction in the carrying value of non-current asset where its recoverable amount (the higher of fair value less costs to sell and value in use) is less than its existing carrying amount.

imprest system

Method of controlling cash or inventory. When the cash or inventory has been reduced by disbursements or issues it is restored to its original level.

inception of a lease

Earlier of the date of the lease agreement and the date of commitment by the parties to the principal provisions of the lease (IAS 17).

income

Increase in economic benefits during an accounting period in the form of inflows or enhancements of assets，or decreases of liabilities that result in inceases in equity，other than those relating to contributions from equity holders(IASB Framework).

income and expenditure account

Financial statement for not-for-profit entities such as clubs，associations and charities. It shows the surplus or deficit，being the excess of income over expenditure or vice

减值

非流动资产账面价值的减少,此时,其可回收金额(公允价值减销售成本与使用价值两者中的较高者)低于现有账面价值。

定额备用金制度

控制现金或库存的方法。当现金或库存因支付或发出而减少时,将其回补到初始水平。

租赁开始日

租赁协议日与租赁各方就主要租赁条款做出承诺日两者中的较早日期(《国际会计准则第 17 号》)。

收入

在一个会计期间内与所有者投入资本无关的经济利益的增加,主要表现为资产流入或增加、负债减少、并最终导致股东权益的增加(《国际会计准则理事会框架》)。

收支结算表

俱乐部、协会和慈善机构等非营利实体的财务报表。它显示这些组织一段时期内的盈余或赤字,盈余即收入超过支出;反之,即为赤字,并像利

versa, for a period and is drawn up on the same accruals basis as an income statement.

润表一样采用权责发生制。

income statement

Financial statement including all the profits and losses recognised in a period, unless an accounting standard requires inclusion elsewhere (refer to IAS 1). See Figure 3.8.

利润表

一种财务报表,其包括了实体一段期间内经确认的所有盈利和亏损,会计准则规定列示在其他地方的盈利和亏损除外(参照《国际会计准则第 1 号》)。参见图表 3.8。

FIGURE 3.8 GROUP INCOME STATEMENT FOR THE YEAR ENDED 31 DECEMBER 2005(REFER TO IAS 1)

	$ million	$ million
Classifies expenses by function		
Revenue		4,347
Cost of sales		(3,649)
Gross profit		698
Other operating income	73	
Distribution costs	(252)	
Administrative expenses	(173)	
Other operating expenses	(61)	(413)
Profit from operations		285
Finance costs	(85)	
Finance income	56	
Share of profits of associates and joint ventures	147	118
Profit before tax		403
Income tax expense		(169)
Profit for the year		234
Attributable to		
Equity holders of the parent		199
Minority interests		35
Profit for the year		234
Alternative presentation		
Classifies expenses by nature		$ million
Revenue		4,347
Other operating income		73
Changes in inventories of finished goods and work-in-progress		(42)
Work performed by the enterprise and capitalised		NIL
Raw materials and consumables used		(2,220)
Employee benefit costs		(1,539)
Depreciation and amortisation expense		(273)
Other operating expenses		(61)
Profit from operations		285

Thereafter the income statement is the same as above.

图表 3.8　截至 2005 年 12 月 31 日的集团年度利润表（参照《国际会计准则》第 1 号）

	$：百万	$：百万
支出按功能分类		
收入		4 347
销售成本		(3 649)
毛利		698
其他营业收入	73	
分销成本	(252)	
管理费用	(173)	
其他营业费用	(61)	(413)
营业利润		285
财务费用	(85)	
财务收入	56	
应占联营公司和合营公司利润	147	118
税前利润		403
所得税费用		(169)
利润总额		234
归属于		
母公司股东权益		199
少数股东权益		35
本年利润		234

	$：百万
另一种表述	
支出按性质分类	
收入	4 347
其他营业收入	73
产成品和在产品存货的变动	(42)
企业已完成的且已资本化的工作	0
使用的原材料及消耗品	(2 220)
员工福利成本	(1 539)
折旧及摊销费用	(273)
其他营业费用	(61)
营业利润	285

之后的利润表项目与前面表述相同。

incomplete records

Accounting system which is not double entry bookkeeping. Various degrees of incompleteness can occur，for example single-entry bookkeeping，in which usually only a cash book is maintained.

intangible assets

Identifiable non-monetary asset without physical substance which must be controlled

不完整记录

非复式记账法的会计系统，会产生不同程度的会计记录不完整情况，例如单式记账法，其通常只保留现金账簿。

无形资产

可辨认的、不具实物形态的非货币性资产，这些资产是由实体过去事

by the entity as the result of past events and from which the entity expects a flow of future economic benefits (refer to IAS 38).

项所形成、由实体控制的、有望给实体带来未来经济利益的流入(《国际会计准则第38号》)。

integrity

Integrity implies fair dealing and truthfulness.

诚信

诚信意味着公平和真实。

interim financial report

Financial report containing either a complete set of financial statements or a set of condensed financial stamements for an interim period (one shorter than a full financial year)(refer to IAS 34).

中期财务报告

以中期为基础所编制的包含一套完整的财务报表或一套财务报表摘要的财务报告,中期是指短于一个完整会计年度的报告期间(参照《国际会计准则第34号》)。

internal audit scope

Review economy efficiency and effectiveness of operations;

Examine financial and operating information;

Review accounting and internal control systems;

Assist in carrying out external audit procedures;

Assist with identification of significant risks;

Special investigations;

Review compliance with laws, regulations or internal policies.

内部审计范围

审查经营的经济效率和效果;

审查财务和经营信息;

检查会计和内部控制系统;

协助开展外部审计程序;

协助识别重大风险;

特别调查;

审查法律、法规或内部政策的合规情况。

internal check

Procedures designed to provide assurance that:

(a) everything which should be recorded

内部检查

旨在为以下项目提供保证的程序:

(a) 一切应记录的事项均已得到

has been recorded ;

(b) errors or irregularities are identified;and

(c) assets and liabilities exist and are correctly recorded.

记录；

(b) 错误或违规行为得以发现；

(c) 资产及负债确实存在并已得到正确记录。

internal control

Management system of controls，financial and otherwise，established in order to provide reasonable assurance of：
(a) effective and efficient operation；
(b) internal financial control；and
(c) compliance with laws and regulations.

Good internal control systems should make accounting records more reliable and the occurrence of fraud and error more difficult.

内部控制

针对控制、财务和其他方面的管理系统,旨在提供以下合理保证:

(a) 有效和高效的经营；
(b) 内部财务控制；
(c) 遵守法律法规。

良好的内部控制系统应使会计记录更可靠,欺诈和错误更不可能发生。

internal control environment

See"control environment".

内部控制环境

参见"控制环境"。

internal financial control

Internal controls established in order to provide reasonable assurance of：
(a) the safeguarding of the entity's assets against unauthorised use or disposal；and
(b) the maintenance of proper accounting records and the reliability of financial information used within the entity or for publication.

内部财务控制

旨在为以下项目提供保证而建立的内部控制:
(a) 保护实体资产,避免未经授权就使用或处置；
(b) 维持恰当的会计记录,确保实体自用或公开的财务信息具有可靠性。

International Accounting Standards Board(IASB)

Has sole responsibility for the development

国际会计准则理事会

全权负责《国际财务报告准则》的

and publication of IFRSs. Seeks to develop a single set of high quality global Accounting Standards requiring transparent and comparable information in general purpose financial statements. Over 90 countries will either require or permit the use of the IASB's Standards and Interpretations for domestically listed entities by 2007.

Also see "Standards Advisory Council (SAC)" and "International Financial Reporting Interpretations Committee(IFRIC)".

制定和发布,旨在建立一套高质量的全球会计准则,提升通用财务报表信息的透明度和可比性。90 多个国家要求或允许境内上市实体从 2007 年开始使用国际会计准则理事会的准则及解释。

参见"准则咨询委员会(SAC)"和"国际财务报告解释委员会(IFRIC)"。

International Auditing and Assurance Standards Boards(IAASB)

Independent standard setting body under the auspices of the International Federation of Accountants(IFAC). The IAASB issues:

- International Standards on Auditing (ISAs);

- International Standards on Assurance Engagements(ISAEs);

- International Standards on Related Services (ISRSs); and

- International Standards on Quality Control(ISQCs).

国际审计与鉴证准则理事会

由国际会计师联合会(IFAC)主办的独立准则制定机构,负责发布:

-国际审计准则(ISAs);

-国际鉴证业务准则(ISAEs);

-国际相关服务准则(ISRSs);

-国际质量控制准则(ISQCs)。

International Financial Reporting Interpretations Committee(IFRIC)

Assists the IASB in improving standards of financial accounting and reporting. This is achieved by providing timely guidance on newly identified financial reporting issues not specifically addressed by IFRSs or where unsatisfactory or conflicting interpretations have developed or seem likely to develop.

国际财务报告解释委员会

协助国际会计准则理事会提高财务会计和报告准则,针对《国际财务报告准则》未解决的财务报告新问题,或是存在或可能形成不尽如人意或相互矛盾的解释时,提供及时的指导。

International Financial Reporting Standards(IFRSs)

Standards and Interpretations published or adopted by the International Accounting Standards Board (IASB). They comprise:

International Financial Reporting Standards (IFRSs);

International Accounting Standards (IASs);
Interpretations originated by the International Financial Reporting Interpretations Committee(IFRIC) or the former Standing Interpretations Committee (SIC).

See Appendix 1 for a full list of current IASs and IFRSs.

International Integrated Reporting Council(IIRC)

The IIRC was formed in August 2010 and aims to create a globally accepted framework for a process that results in communications by an organisation about value creation over time. The IIRC brings together a cross section of representatives from corporate, investment, accounting, securities, regulatory, academic and standard-setting sectors as well as civil society.

inventories

Assets held for sale in the ordinary course of business in the process of production for such a sale or in the form of materials or supplies to be consumed in the

国际财务报告准则

国际会计准则理事会(IASB)发布或采纳的准则和解释。它们包括:

国际财务报告准则(IFRSs);

国际会计准则(IASs);

来自国际财务报告解释委员会(IFRIC)或前常设解释委员会(SIC)的解释。

参见附录1现有《国际会计准则》和《国际财务报告准则》的完整列表。

国际综合报告委员会

成立于2010年8月,汇集了来自企业界、投资界、会计界、证券界、监管界、学术界、准则制定部门以及民间社团的代表,旨在建立一个全球通用的综合报告框架,组织可借助这个框架来介绍自身随着时间推移创造价值的情况。

存货

是指企业在正常经营过程中持有以备出售的产成品或商品、处在生产过程中的在产品、在生产或提供劳务过程中耗用的材料和物料等资产(《国

production process or in the rendering of services(IAS 2). Synonym for stock.

际会计准则第 2 号》)。与库存同义。

investing activities

投资活动

Acquisition and disposal of long-term (non-current) assets and other investments not included in cash equivalents as reported in the entity's cash flow statement(IAS 7).

在实体现金流量表中报告的,收购及处置长期(非流动)资产和其他未包括在现金等价物中的投资(《国际会计准则第 7 号》)。

investment

投资

Any application of funds which is intended to provide a return by way of interest, dividend or capital appreciation.

任何形式的资金应用,其目的是通过利息、股息或资本增值的方式来得到回报。

investment property

投资性房地产

Property(land or building or part of a building) held by the owner(or by the lessee under a finance lease) to earn rentals and/or for capital appreciation(IAS 40).

为赚取租金或资本增值,或两者兼而有之,由业主(或融资租赁的承租人)持有的不动产(土地、建筑物或建筑物的一部分)(《国际会计准则第 40号》)。

joint control-joint venture

共同控制-合营企业

Contractually agreed sharing of control over an economic activity which exists only when the strategic and operating decisions relating to the activity require the unanimous consent of the parties sharing control (the ventures) (IFRS 11).

控制各方通过签订合同分享某项经济活动(企业)的控制权,与此项经济活动相关的战略和经营决策必须得到控制各方的一致同意(《国际财务报告准则第 11 号》)。

joint control-related parties

共同控制-关联方

Contractually agreed sharing of control over an economic activity(IAS 24).

就某项经济活动分享控制权的合同各方(《国际会计准则第 24 号》)。

joint venture

Contractual arrangement whereby two or more parties undertake an economic activity which is subject to joint control (IFRS 11).

key management personnel

Those persons having authority and responsibility for planning, directing and controlling the activities of the entity, directly or indirectly, including any director (whether executive or otherwise) of that entity (IAS 24).

lease

Agreement whereby the lessor conveys to the lessee, in return for a payment or series of payments, the right to use an asset for an agreed period of time. (IAS 17).

lease, finance: Lease agreement that transfers substantially all the risks and rewards incidental to ownership of an asset from the lessor to the lessee. Title in the asset may or may not eventually be transferred(IAS 17).

lease, operating: Lease agreement other than a finance lease (IAS 17).

lease term

Non-cancellable period for which the lessee has contracted to lease the asset together with any further term for which the lessee has the option to continue to lease the asset, with or without further payment, which at the inception of the lease it is reasonably

合营企业

双方或多方为共同控制某项经济活动而做出的合同约定(《国际财务报告准则第 11 号》)。

关键管理人员

实体中有权力和责任直接或间接规划、指挥和控制实体活动的那些人员,包括董事(无论是执行董事还是非执行董事)(《国际会计准则第 24 号》)。

租赁

在一个约定的期间内,出租人将某项资产的使用权让与承租人,以获取一项或一系列租金的协议(《国际会计准则第 17 号》)。

融资租赁:实质上转移了与一项资产所有权有关的全部风险和报酬的租赁协议。所有权最终可能转移,也可能不转移(《国际会计准则第 17 号》)。

经营租赁:除融资租赁以外的租赁协议(《国际会计准则第 17 号》)。

租赁期限

指承租人签约租赁资产的不可撤销的租赁期间。如承租人有权选择继续租赁该资产,而且在租赁开始时就可以合理确定承租人将会行使这项选择权,那么,不论是否需要再支付租金,续租期也算在租赁期内(《国际会

certain that the lessee will exercise(IAS 17).

计准则第 17 号》)。

lease, finance

Lease agreement that transfers substantially all the risks and rewards incidental to ownership of an asset from the lessor to the lessee. Title in the asset may or may not eventually be transferred(IAS 17).

融资租赁

实质上转移了与一项资产所有权有关的全部风险和报酬的租赁协议。所有权最终可能转移，也可能不转移（《国际会计准则第 17 号》）。

lease, operating

Lease agreement other than a finance lease(IAS 17).

经营租赁

除融资租赁以外的租赁协议（《国际会计准则第 17 号》）。

legal obligation

Obiligation that derives from：
（a）contract（through its explicit or implicit terms）；
（b）legislation；
（c）or other operation of law(IAS 37).

法律责任

源于以下项目的责任：
（a）合同（通过其明确或隐含的条款）；
（b）立法；
（c）法律的其他实施（《国际会计准则第 37 号》）。

liability

Present obligation of the entity arising from past events，the settlement of which is expected to result in an outflow from the entity of resources embodying economic benefits(IAS 37).

负债

由过去事项所形成的、预计清偿会导致经济利益流出实体的现时义务（《国际会计准则第 37 号》）。

liability method

Method of computing deferred tax by calculating it at the rate of income tax that it is estimated will be applied in the period when the temporary difference reverses. This

债务法

以所得税暂时性差异转回期间所适用的所得税税率为基础，计算递延税项的方法。这就意味着根据估计将支付或收回的所得税额来计量负债。

means the liability is measured at the amount of income tax that it is estimated will be paid or recovered.

liquid assets

Cash，cash equivalents and other assets readily convertible into cash，for example short-term investments.

loans and receivables

Non-derivative financial assets with fixed or determinable payments that are not quoted in an active market(IAS 39).

Management's Discussion and Analysis(MD&A)

Narrative element of the statutory reporting package required in the US. It is intended to allow users to understand an entity's financial condition, changes in financial condition and results of operations, and is a discussion and analysis of the entity's operations and prospects, by management.

It should fulfil the following objectives：

(a) to provided a narrative explanation of an entity's financial statements that enables investors to see the company through the eyes of its management；

(b) to enhance the overall financial disclosure and provide the context within which financial information should be analysed;and

(c) to provide information about the quality of, and potential variability of, an entity's earnings and cash flow, so that

速动资产

现金、现金等价物及其他可随时转换成现金的资产,如短期投资。

贷款及应收款项

回收金额固定或确定的,在活跃市场上没有报价的非衍生金融资产(《国际会计准则第 39 号》)。

管理层讨论与分析

美国法定报告所必须具备的描述性要素,旨在让用户了解实体的财务状况、财务状况的变化以及经营成果,它也是管理层对实体经营与前景的讨论和分析。

管理层讨论与分析应该实现下列目标:

(a) 对实体的财务报表加以描述性解释,让投资者能够从管理层角度看待公司;

(b) 加强整体财务披露,为财务信息分析提供背景;

(c) 提供实体收入和现金流质量及潜在变化方面的信息,以便投资者能够确定根据过去业绩预测未来业绩

investors can ascertain the likelihood that past performance is indicative of future performance.

(SEC Statement About Management's Discussion &Analysis of Financial Condition and Results of Operations，Release No. 33 - 8056，2002).

的可能性。

(《美国证券交易委员会关于管理层对财务状况和经营成果的讨论与分析的声明》，发布号 33 - 8056，2002年)。

maximization shareholder wealth

It is generally accepted that the primary strategic objective of a commercial company is the long-term goal of the maximization of the wealth of the shareholders.

股东财富最大化

业界普遍认为,商业公司的主要战略目标是实现股东财富最大化这一长期目标。

minority interest

Portion of the profit or loss（income statement) and net assets（balance sheet)of a subsidiary attributable to equity interests that are not owned，directly or indirectly，by the parent(IFRS 3).

少数股东权益

不属于母公司直接或间接拥有的,归属于股东权益的附属子公司的利润或亏损(利润表)及净资产(资产负债表)(《国际财务报告准则第 3 号》)。

monetary items

Units of currency held and assets and liabilities to be received or paid in a fixed or determinable number of units of currency（IAS 21).

货币性科目

实体持有的货币资金以及将以固定或可确定的货币金额来收取的资产或支付的负债(《国际会计准则第 21 号》)。

money laundering

Funnelling of cash or other funds generated from illegal activities through legitimate financial institutions and businesses to conceal the source of the funds（Anti-Money Laundering，2nd，IFAC，2004).

洗钱

将非法活动产生的现金或者其他资金,通过合法的金融机构和企业转移出去,以隐瞒资金来源(《反洗钱》第二版,国际会计师联合会,2004 年)。

M's model

This model suggests that the items in a position audit can be categorized into factors beginning with ＂M＂—manpower, money, management，machinery，markets，materials，methods，management information，make-up.

net assets

Excess of the carrying amount of assets over liabilities. Equivalent to net worth or equity.

net realizable value

Estimated selling prices less costs to completion less costs to sell.

non-current asset

Any asset that does not meet the definition of a current asset（IFRS 5）. Tangible or intangible asset，acquired for retention by an entity for the purpose of providing a service to the entity and not held for resale in the normal course of trading. Previously known as a fixed asset.

non-executive director

Director of a company（or other entity）who is not involved in the day-to-day running of operation and is therefore expected to provide an independent view on board issues.

M 模型

该模型提出了地位审计所涉及的、可以分类为以"M"开头的项目——人力资源、资金、管理、机械设备、市场、材料、方法、管理信息、构成框架。

净资产

资产大于负债的账面金额，相当于净资产或权益。

可变现净值

估计售价减去完工成本和销售成本。

非流动资产

所有不符合流动资产定义的资产（《国际财务报告准则第 5 号》）。实体购入并持有，旨在为实体提供服务而非通过正常交易进行转售的有形或者无形资产，以前称为固定资产。

非执行董事

不参与公司（或其他实体）日常运营的董事，因此，他们有望对董事会事宜发表独立意见。

not for profit entity

Entities such as charities, trade unions and associations(such as accountancy bodies) are not run to make profits but to benefit prescribed groups of people.

非营利实体

包括慈善机构、工会、协会(如会计组织)等在内的不以营利为目的,而为特定人群谋取福利的组织。

notes to financial statements

Contain information in addition to that presented in the balance sheet, income statement, statement of changes in equity and cash flow statement. Notes provide narrative descriptions or disaggregations of items disclosed in those statements and information about items that do not qualify for recognition in those statements (IAS 1).

财务报表附注

对资产负债表、利润表、股东权益变动表和现金流量表所列报的信息加以补充说明。附注针对报表所披露项目提供叙述性描述或加以分拆说明,或针对无法在报表中加以确认的项目补充相关信息(《国际会计准则第1号》)。

obligating event

Event that creates a legal or constructive obligation that results in an entity having no realistic alternative to settling that obligation (IAS 37).

义务事项

形成法定或者推定义务的事项,且实体没有切实可行的替代方法来履行这一义务《国际会计准则第37号》。

objectivity

Accountants need to ensure that their business/professional judgement is not compromised because of bias or conflict of interest.

客观性

会计人员需要保证他们的业务/职业判断不会因为偏见或利益冲突而受到影响。

obsolescence

Loss of value of a non-current asset due to advances in technology or changes in market conditions for its product.

无形损耗

非流动资产价值因技术进步或产品市场环境发生变化而遭受损失。

off balance sheet finance

Funding or refinancing of an entity's operations in such a way that, under existing legal requirements and accounting practices, some or all of the financing may not be shown on the entity's balance sheet.

onerous contract

Contract in which the unavoidable costs of meeting the obligations under the contract exceed the economic benefits expected to be received under it(IAS 37).

operating activities

The principal revenue-producing activities of an entity and other activities not reported elsewhere in the entity's cash flow statement(IAS 7).

Operating and Financial Review(OFR)

Narrative element of the statutory reporting package, from April 2005 required by law for listed companies in the UK.

It is a balanced and comprehensive analysis of：

(a) the development and performance of the business of the entity during the financial year；

(b) the position of the entity at the end of the year；

(c) the main trends and factors underlying the development, performance and position of the business of the entity during the financial year；and

（资产负债表）表外融资

企业为业务发展进行的筹资或再融资,但根据现有的法律规定和会计惯例,部分或全部融资可能没有反映在实体的资产负债表上。

亏损合同

履行合约义务将造成成本不可避免地超过预期经济收益的合同(《国际会计准则第 37 号》)。

经营活动

能为实体带来收入的主要活动以及其他未在现金流量表中报告的活动(《国际会计准则第 37 号》)。

经营和财务回顾

从 2005 年 4 月开始,根据法律规定,英国上市公司必须披露的法定财务报告的叙述性元素。

它对以下方面进行平衡和全面的分析：

(a) 实体在本会计年度内的业务发展和业绩；

(b) 实体在年底的整体状况；

(c) 在财务年度,实体的业务发展、业绩和状况的主要趋势和要素；

(d) the main trends and factors which are likely to affect their future development, performance and position, prepared so as to assist investors to assess the strategies adopted by the entity and the potential for those strategies to succeed(ABS Reporting Standard 1:Operating and Financial Review).

(d) 可能影响到实体未来发展、绩效和状况的主要发展趋势及因素，旨在帮助投资者评估实体所采用的战略以及这些战略的成功可能性(《ABS报告准则第1号:经营及财务回顾》)。

ordinary shares

Equity instrument that is subordinate to all other classes of equity instrument (refer to IAS 33).

普通股

索取权是排在所有其他类别的权益工具之后的权益工具(参阅《国际会计准则第33号》)。

parent

Entity that has one or more subsidiaries (IFRS 3).

母公司

拥有一个或多个附属公司的实体(《国际财务报告准则第3号》)。

payables

Person, or an entity, to whom money is owed as a consequence of the receipt of goods or services in advance of payment, known as trade payables in IASs.

应付款项

实体因在支付款项前收到货物或者接受服务而欠个人或其他实体的款项,在《国际会计准则》中称为应付账款。

percentage of completion method

Method by which construction contract revenue is matched with the contract costs incurred in reaching the stage of completion, resulting in the reporting of revenue, expenses and profit which can be attributed to the proportion of work completed(IFRS 15).

完工百分比法

将建造合同的收入与达到目前完工水平已发生的合同成本进行匹配的方法,从而能够根据完工比例确认收入、费用和利润(《国际财务报告准则第5号》)。

post-employment benefit plans

Formal or informal arrangements under

离职后福利计划

实体为员工提供离职后福利的正

which an entity provides post-employment benefits for its employees (refer to IAS 19).

式或非正式安排(《国际会计准则第 19 号》)。

post-employment benefits

Employee benefits(other than termination benefits) which are payable after the completion of employment(IAS 19).

离职后福利

实体在员工离职后提供给员工的福利(辞退福利除外)(《国际会计准则第 19 号》)。

potential ordinary share

Financial instrument or other contract that may entitle its holder to ordinary share (IAS 33).

潜在普通股

可能赋予持有人普通股权益的金融工具或者其他合同(《国际会计准则第 33 号》)。

pre-acquisition profits/losses

Profits or losses of a subsidiary attributable to a period prior to acquisition of control by the parent.

收购前盈亏

在母公司获取控制权之前,子公司产生的利润或损失。

preference shares

Shares carrying a fixed rate of dividend, the holders of which, subject to the conditions of issue, have a prior claim to any profits available for distribution. Preference shareholder may also have a prior claim to the repayment of capital in the event of winding up.

优先股

优先股享有固定的股利支付率,根据发行条件,持有人对所有可供分配的利润享有优先分配权利。此外,优先股股东在资产清算时可能享有资本优先受偿的权利。

preferred creditors

Creditors entitled to full satisfaction of their claims in insolvency before other claims are met.

优先级债权人

当实体破产时,在其他债权人得到偿还之前,有权优先获得全额偿还的债权人。

presentation currency

Currency in which the reporting entity's

列报货币

实体财务报表列报所使用的货币

financial statements are presented(IAS 21).

《国际会计准则第 21 号》)。

previous GAAP

Generally accepted accounting practice that a first-time adopter used immediately before adopting IFRSs(IFRS 1).

以前的公认会计原则

在首次采用《国际财务报告准则》之前,实体所使用的公认会计原则(《国际财务报告准则第 1 号》)。

primary financial instruments

Financial instruments such as receivables, payables and equity securities that are not derivative financial instruments(IAS 32).

主要金融工具

包括应收账款、应付账款及权益性证券等非衍生金融工具(《国际会计准则第 32 号》)。

prior period errors

Omission from, and misstatements in, the entity's financial statements for one or more periods arising from a failure to use, or misuse of, reliable information that was available when the financial statements for those periods were authorised for issue. Such errors include the effects of mathematical mistakes in applying accounting policies, oversights or misinterpretation of facts and fraud(IAS 8).

前期差错

由于没能利用或错误利用财务报表批准报出时能够取得的可靠信息,从而造成一个期间或多个期间的财务报表发生遗漏和错报。前期差错包括应用会计政策时所犯的计算错误、对事实和欺诈的疏忽或曲解所产生的影响(《国际会计准则第 8 号》)。

profit

Residual amount that remains after expenses(including capital maintenance adjustments where appropriate)have been deducted from income (IASB Framework).

利润

收入减去费用(适当的时候,还应包括资本保全调整)后的余额(《国际会计准则理事会框架》)。

profit and loss account

See "income statement".

损益账户

参见"利润表"。

property, plant and equipment

Tangible items(non-current assets)held for use in the production or supply of goods or services for rental to others or other administrative purposes and expected to be used during more than one period(IAS 16).

proportionate consolidation - joint ventures

Method of accounting whereby a venturer's share of each of the asset, liabilities, income and expenses of a jointly controlled entity is combined with similar items, or reported as a separate line, in the venturer's financial statements(IFRS 11).

prospective application

Applying a new accounting policy to transactions, other events and conditions occurring after the date at which the policy is changed and recognising the effect of the change in accounting estimates in the current and any future periods affected by the change (IAS 8).

provision

Liability of uncertain timing or amount (IAS 37).

purchase method

Method of consolidation that views a business combination from the perspective of

不动产、厂房和设备

企业持有的,用于生产、出租或其他管理目的,且使用期限预计超过一个会计期间的有形资产(非流动资产)(《国际会计准则第 16 号》)。

比例合并-合营企业

按投资企业在共同控制实体中拥有的权益比例将共同控制实体的资产、负债、收入和费用并入投资企业财务报表的相似项目或单独予以报告的会计处理方法(《国际财务报告准则第 11 号》)。

未来适用法

未来适用法是指将变更后的会计政策应用于变更日及以后发生的交易、事项及情况,同时在受变更影响的当前和未来会计期间确认变更对会计估计的影响(《国际会计准则第 8 号》)。

预计负债

在时间或金额上具有不确定性的负债(《国际会计准则第 37 号》)。

购买法

一种企业合并的会计处理方法,它从收购方的角度看待企业合并,收

the acquirer who purchases a controlling interest in the net asset of the acquiree. According to IFRS 3, all business combinations should be accounted for by applying the purchase method.

购方通过购买获取了被收购方净资产的控制性权益。根据《国际财务报告准则第3号》,所有企业合并都应采用购买法进行会计处理。

receipts and payments account

Report of cash transactions during a period. It is used in place of an income and expenditure account when it is not considered appropriate to distinguish between capital and revenue transactions or to include accruals.

现金收支账户

报告一定期间内的现金交易。在不适合区分资本与收入交易时或是包涵权责发生额时,现金收支账户被用来替代收入和支出账户。

receivables

Monetary amount owed by a person or organisation to the entity as a consequence of the sale of goods or services, known as trade receivables in IASs.

应收款项

实体向个人或者组织销售商品或提供服务而应收取的货币金额,在《国际会计准则》中称为应收账款。

recoverable amount

Higher of an asset's (or a cash generating unit's) fair value less costs to sell and its value in use (IAS 36).

可回收金额

一项资产(或现金产出单元)的公允价值减去销售成本后的余额与其使用价值两者之间的较高者(《国际会计准则第36号》)。

related parties

A party is a related party of an entity if it complies with one or more of the following conditions:

(a) directly or indirectly through intermediaries, it controls or is controlled by or is under common control with the entity (this includes parent, subsidiaries and fellow sub-

关联方

满足以下一项或多项条件时,一方则为另一方的关联方:

(a) 直接或通过中间机构间接控制其他实体或被其他实体直接或间接控制,或者受同一实体的共同控制(这包括母公司、子公司及附属公司);

sidiaries)；

　　(b) It has an interest in the entity that gives it significant influence or joint control over the entity (this includes associates and joint ventures)；

　　(c) It is a member of the key management personnel of the entity or its parent；

　　(d) It is a close member of the family of any individual noted above；and

　　(e) It is a post-employment benefit plan for the benefit of the employees of the entity or of any entity that is itself a related party (summarised from IAS 24).

related party transaction

　　Transfer of resources，services or obligations between related parties，regardless of whether a price is charged (IAS 24).

reporting entity

　　Entity for which there are users who rely on the financial statements for Information about the entity that will be useful to them for making decisions about resource allocation. A reporting entity can be a single entity or a group comprising a parent and all of its subsidiaries (refer to IASB Framework and IFRS 3).

research

　　Original and planned investigation undertaken with the prospect of gaining new scientific or technical knowledge and understanding (IAS 38).

　　(b) 在实体中拥有权益，能对实体施加重大影响或实施共同控制(包括联营企业和合营企业)；

　　(c) 属于实体或其母公司的关键管理人员；

　　(d) 与上述人员关系密切的家庭成员；

　　(e) 为实体或实体关联方员工设立的离职后福利计划(摘自《国际会计准则》第 24 号)。

关联方交易

　　不论是否收取费用，关联方之间的资源、服务或责任的转移都视为关联方交易(《国际会计准则第 24 号》)。

报告主体

　　报告主体为使用者提供赖以依靠的财务报表，帮助他们获取实体相关信息并做出资源分配决策。报告主体可以是单个实体或由母公司及其所有附属公司组成的集团(《国际会计准则理事会框架》和《国际财务报告准则第 3 号》)。

研究

　　为获取并理解新的科学或技术知识，而进行的有计划的初始调查。《国际会计准则第 38 号》。

reserves

Retained profits or surpluses. In a not-for-profit entity they are described as accumulated funds.

准备金

未分配的利润或盈余。在非营利实体中,称为累计基金。

residual value – intangible asset

Estimated amount which an entity would currently obtain from disposal of the asset，after deducting the expected costs of disposal，if the asset were already of the age and condition expected at the end of its useful life (IAS 38).

残值-无形资产

如果资产已到服务年限或已处于使用寿命完结之时的状态,实体当前处置该资产能够收到的预计款项减去预计处置成本后的余额(《国际会计准则第 38 号》)。

residual value – tangible asset

Net amount which an entity expects to obtain for an asset at the end of its useful life after deducting the expected costs of disposal (IAS 16).

残值-有形资产

资产在使用寿命终了时,实体处置该资产有望收取的款项减去预计处置成本后的净额(《国际会计准则第 16 号》)。

restructuring

Programme that is planned and controlled by management，and materially changes either the scope of a business undertaken by an entity or the manner in which that business is conducted (IAS 37).

重组

管理层制定和控制的,将显著改变实体经营范围或经营方式的计划(《国际会计准则第 37 号》)。

retention money or payments withheld

Agreed proportion of a contract price withheld for a specified period after contract completion as security for fulfilment of obiligations.

保留款或扣留款项

在合同完成后的一定期间内,按合同各方约定的比例扣留一部分合同金额,作为履行义务的担保。

retirement benefit plans

Arrangements whereby an entity provides benefits for its employees on or after termination of service(either in the form of annual income or as a lump sum or both) when such benefits, or the employer's contribution towards them, can be determined or estimated in advance of retirement (IAS 26).

retrospective application

Applying a new accounting policy to transactions, other events and conditions as if that policy had always been applied(IAS 8).

revalued amount of an asset

Fair value of an asset at the date of a revaluation, less any subsequent accumulated depreciation and accumulated impairment losses(IAS 16).

revenue

Gross inflow of economic benefits during the period arising in the course of the ordinary activities of an entity when those inflows result in increases in equity, other than increases relating to contributions, from equity holders (IFRS conceptual Framework).

revenue expenditure

Expenditure on the manufacture of goods, the provision of services or on the

退休福利计划

退休福利计划是指实体在员工退休之际或退休之后所提供的福利(以年收入或一次性支付形式,或者两者结合的形式予以发放),并且在员工实际退休之前就能确定或预估此类福利或雇主为此需承担的金额(《国际会计准则第 26 号》)。

追溯性应用

追溯性应用是指将新的会计政策应用于以前发生的交易、事项及情况,如同实体一直在采用新会计政策一样(《国际会计准则第 8 号》)。

资产重估价值

资产在重估日的公允价值减去后续累计折旧和累计减值损失(《国际会计准则第 16 号》)。

收入

收入是指实体在日常活动中形成的、会导致所有者权益增加的、但与所有者投入资本无关的经济利益的总流入(《国际财务报告准则概念框架》)。

收益性支出

收益性支出是指实体制造产品、提供服务或开展一般活动所发生的费

general conduct of the entity which is charged to the income statement in the period the expenditure is incurred. This will include charges for depreciation and impairment of non-current assets as distinct from the cost of the assets. See "capital expenditure".

用,这些费用都应记入发生当期的利润表。这类支出包括非流动资产的折旧及减值,但不包括资产的成本。参见"资本性支出"。

reverse acquisition

反向收购

Acquisition where the acquirer is the entity whose equity interests have been acquired and the issuing entity is the acquiree. For example, a private entity arranges to have itself acquired by a smaller public entity as a means of obtaining a stock exchange listing (IFRS 3).

在反向收购中,收购方是权益被收购的实体,而被收购方是发行实体。例如,一个私营实体安排自己被一个小型上市实体收购,从而借助这种方式实现上市(《国际财务报告准则第3号》)。

round the computer

计算机测试

Under this approach the auditor does not attempt to understand the operation of the computer system, but rather treats it as a 'black box'. To audit the system, the auditor matches up inputs to predicted outputs to ensure that the outputs are being processed correctly.

采用这种方法时,审计人员并不试图了解计算机系统的运行,而是将其视为"黑匣子"。在对系统进行审计时,审计人员将输入值与输出值进行预测并匹配,以检验是否计算机输出结果得到了正确的处理。

sampling

抽样

Sampling is testing a proportion of a population to gain assurance about the population as a whole.

抽样是对全部样本的一部分进行测试,从而针对整个样本做出推断。

sale and leaseback transaction

售后回租交易

Sale of an asset to the lessor and the subsequent leasing back of the asset under an

将资产出售给出租方,而后通过经营租赁或者融资租赁的方式租回资

operating lease or a financial lease. The lease payments and the sale price are usually inter-dependent because they are negotiated as a package (IAS 17).

产。由于资产的出售和回租是一并协商的,因此,租赁付款和售价通常是相互关联的(《国际会计准则第 17 号》)。

Sarbanes – Oxley(SOX)

萨班斯-奥克斯利法案

Act passed by US Congress in response to corporate accounting scandals" to protect investors by improving the accuracy and reliability of corporate disclosures made pursuant to the securities laws and for other purpose".

美国国会为应对公司会计丑闻而通过的一项法案,"出于保护投资者及其他目的,要求公司遵守证券法,提高公司信息披露的准确性和可靠性"。

Section 404 of SOX

萨班斯-奥克斯利法案的第404 条

Section 404 of the Sarbanes-Oxley Act: Management Assessment of Internal Controls requires each annual report of an issuer to contain an internal control report,which should:

(a) state the responsibility of management for establishing and maintaining an adequate internal control structure and procedures for financial reporting; and

(b) contain an assessment, as of the end of the issuer's fiscal year, of the effectiveness of the internal control structure and procedures of the issuer for financial reporting.

These internal control reports are subjects to audit.

Each registered public accounting firm that prepares or issues the Audit report for the issuer shall attest to, and report on, the assessment made by the management of the issuer. An attestation made under this section shall be in accordance with standards for attestation engagements issued or adopted by

萨班斯-奥克斯利法案第 404 条:"管理层对内部控制的评估"要求发行人在年度报告中包括内部控制报告,此报告应:

(a) 申明管理层在针对财务报告建立和维护充分的内部控制结构和程序时所承担的责任;

(b) 包含发行人在财务年度末尾对财务报告内部控制结构和程序有效性的评估。

这些内部控制报告必须经过审计。

负责编制或发布发行人审计报告的每个注册公共会计师事务所,都应对管理层所做评估予以鉴证和报告。本条例规定的鉴证必须依照委员会颁布或采用的鉴证业务准则。鉴证业务不能作为一项单独业务。

the Board. An attestation engagement shall not be the subject of a separate engagement.

secured creditors

Creditors whose claims are wholly or partly secured on the assets of a business.

security

In the event of default, the lender will be able to take assets in exchange of the amounts owing. There are two types of 'charge' or security that may be offered/required: fixed charge and floating charge.

Securities and Exchange Commission (SEC)

US Committee whose purpose is to protect investors and maintain the integrity of the securities markets. It does this by requiring public companies to disclose meaningful financial and other information to the public. The SEC also oversees other participants in the securities markets such as stock exchanges, broker-dealers, investment advisors, mutual funds, and public utility holding companies. The SEC is also an enforcement authority bringing four to five hundred civil actions each year against individuals and organisations which break securities laws, through insider trading, accounting fraud, or providing false or misleading information about securities or issuers.

segment reports

Reports within the financial statements

取得担保的债权人

债权全部或部分得到企业资产担保的债权人。

担保

当债务人违约时,债权人能用债务人资产来顶替欠款。担保可分为两类:固定担保和浮动担保。

美国证券交易委员会

美国证券交易委员会的宗旨是保护投资者和维护证券市场的完整性。为此,它要求上市公司向公众披露有意义的财务信息及其他资料。此外,美国证券交易委员会还负责监督证券市场的其他参与者,如证券交易所、证券经纪商和自营商、投资顾问、共同基金和公用事业控股公司。美国证券交易委员会也是一个执行机关,它每年针对违反证券法的个人和组织提起四五百件民事诉讼,这些案件的主要犯罪方式包括内幕交易、会计欺诈、提供证券或发行人的虚假或误导性信息。

分部报告

分部报告是分析分部收入、经营

that analyse revenue，profit from operations，total assets and total liabilities by reportable segments. The segments may be by business activity or geographic area(refer to IAS 14). See Figure 3.9.

利润、总资产、总负债等信息的财务报告。分部可按业务活动或地区加以划分(参照《国际会计准则第 14 号》)。参见图表 3.9。

FIGURE 3.9　SEGMENT REPORT FOR THE YEAR ENDED 31 DECEMBER 2005 (REFER TO IAS 14)

	Segment A $ million	Segment B $ million	Other operations $ million	Eliminations $ million	Consolidated totals $ million
Revenue					
External sales	1,943	1,866	538		
Inter-segment sales	211	103	67	(381)	
Total revenue	2,154	1,969	605	(381)	4,347
Result					
Segment result	194	141	33	(31)	337
Unallocated corporate expenses					52
Profit from operations					285
Finance costs					(85)
Finance income					56
Share of profits of associates and joint ventures	127		20		147
Income tax expense					169
Profit for the year					234
Other information					
Segment assets	1,743	1,828	366		3,937
Investment in associates and joint ventures	652		158		810
Unallocated corporate assets					320
Consolidated total assets					5,067
Segment liabilties	(814)	(689)	(139)		(1,642)
Unallocated corporate liabilities					(1,155)
Consolidated total liabilities					(2,797)
Capital expenditure	89	99	85		273
Depreciation	40	25	15		80

图表 3.9　截至 2005 年 12 月 31 日分部报告(参照《国际会计准则第 14 号》)

	A 分部	B 分部	其他业务	冲销	总额
单位:百万美元					
收入					
外部销售	1 943	1 866	538		
分部间内部销售	211	103	67	(381)	
总收入	2 154	1 969	605	(381)	4 347
成果					
分部成果	194	141	33	(31)	337
未分配公司费用					(52)
营业利润					285
财务费用					(85)
财务收入					56
联营合营企业分配的利润	127		20		147
所得税					(169)
本年利润					234
其他信息					
分部资产	1 743	1 828	366		3 937
联营合营企业的投资	652		158		810
未分配企业资产					320
合并总资产					5 067
分部负债	(814)	(689)	(139)		(1 642)
未分配企业负债					(1 155)
合并总负债					(2 797)
资本支出	89	99	85		273
折旧	40	25	15		80

share

Fixed identifiable unit of capital in a company (or other entity) which normally has a fixed nominal or face value, which may be quite different from its market value.

convertible share: Non-equity share such as a preference share, carrying rights to convert into equity shares on predetermined terms.

cumulative preference shares: Shares which entitle the holder to a fixed rate of dividend, and the right to have any arrears of dividend paid out of future profits with priority over any distribution of profits to the

股份

一个公司(或其他实体)可辨认的固定单位资本,其票面价值可能不同于它的市场价值。

可转换股票:非权益股票,如优先股,其有权按事先确定的条款转换为权益股票。

累积优先股:持有人享有固定的股息率,亏损年度拖欠的股息可累积到未来盈利年度,在普通股的红利发放之前,连同本年的优先股股息一并发放。

holder of ordinary share capital.

deferred/founders' shares: Special class of shares ranking for dividend after preference and ordinary shares.

non-voting shares: Shares which carry no voting rights.

ordinary shares: Equity instrument that is subordinate to all other classes of equity instrument (refer to IAS 33).

participating preference shares: Shares which entitle the holder to a fixed dividend and, in addition, to the right to participate in any surplus profits after payment of agreed levels of dividends to ordinary shareholders have been made.

preference shares: Shares carrying a fixed rate of dividend, the holders of which, subject to the conditions of issue, have a prior claim to any profits available for distribution. Preference shareholders may also have a prior claim to the repayment of capital in the event of winding up.

redeemable shares: Shares which are issued on terms which may require them to be bought back by the issuer at some future date either at the discretion of the issuer or of the holder.

share capital

authorised/nominal/registered share capital: Type, class, number and amount of the shares which a company (or other entity) may issue, as empowered by its memorandum of association.

called-up share capital: Amount which the entity has required shareholers to pay on the shares issued.

递延/发起人股份：特殊类别的股份，在优先股和普通股之后派发股息。

无投票权股份：指不享有投票权的股份。

普通股：索取权排在所有其他类别的权益工具之后（参照《国际会计准则第33号》）。

参与优先股：持有人享有固定的股息，除此之外，在实体向普通股股东支付一定水平的股利之后，还有权参与剩余利润的分配。

优先股：股东享有固定的股息率，根据发行条件，持有人对所有可供分配的利润享有优先分配权利。此外，优先股股东在资产清算时可能享有资本优先受偿的权利。

可赎回股份：发行条款规定，在未来某个时日，发行人或持有人可按自身意愿，要求发行人购回已发行的股份。

股本

授权的/名义的/注册的股本：根据公司章程规定，公司（或者其他实体）发行的股份的类型、等级、数量和金额。

催缴股本：实体已要求股东就已发行股份支付的数额。

issued/subscribed share capital：The type，class，number and amount of the shares held by shareholders.

paid-up share capital：Amount which shareholders are deemed to have on the shares issued and called up.

uncalled share capital：Amount of the nominal value of a share which is unpaid and has not been called up by the entity.

unissued share capital：Amount of the share capital authorised but not yet issued.

发布/认购股本：股东所持有的股份的种类、等级、数量和金额。

实收股本：股东就已发行并经催缴的股份支付的数额。

未催缴股本：未支付且公司尚未催缴的股份的账面额。

未发行股本：已授权但尚未发行的股本数额。

share exchange

股票置换

In a share exchange，the bidding company issues some new shares and then exchanges them with the target company shareholders. The target company shareholders therefore end up with shares in the bidding company，and the bidding company's shares all end up in the possession of the targeting company.

在股票交换中，招标公司发行新股，并与目标公司股东进行交换。最终，目标公司股东拥有招标公司的股份，而招标公司发行的新股全部用于换取目标公司的股份。

share option

股票期权

Contract that gives the holder the right，but not the obligation，to subscribe to entity's shares at a fixed or determinable price for a specific period of time(IAS 39).

赋予持有人一项权利（而非义务），在特定的时间段内可以固定或可确定的价格认购实体股份的合同（《国际会计准则第 39 号》）。

share premium

股本溢价

Excess received，either in cash or other consideration，over the nominal or face value of the shares issued.

实际收到的款项或者其他形式的对价超过了已发行股票名义价值或面值的部分。

share repurchase

股份回购

A share repurchase can be used to return

公司可通过股份回购将多余现金

surplus cash to shareholders. It tends to be used when the company has no positive NPV projects to invest the cash in, so it returns the cash to shareholders so that they can make better use of it rather than it sitting idle (in cash investment) in the company.

返还给股东。在没有可供投资的、拥有正的净现值的项目时,公司倾向于如此操作,将现金返还给股东,以便让这些现金能够得到更好的利用,而不是闲置在公司(无法进行现金投资)。

share-based payment arrangement

An agreement between the entity and another party (including an employee) to enter into a share-based payment transaction which thereby entitles the other party to receive cash or other assets of the entity for amounts that are based on the price of the entity's shares (or other equity instruments) or to receive equity instruments in the entity (IFRS 2).

股份支付协议

实体与另一方(包括雇员)签订的以股份为基础的支付协议,赋予对方一项权利,可按实体股票(或其他权益工具)的价格从实体获取相应数额的现金或其他资产,抑或获取权益工具。(《国际财务报告准则第 2 号》)。

share-based payment transaction

Transaction in which the entity receives goods or services as consideration for equity instruments of the entity (including shares or share options) or acquires goods or services for amounts that are based on the price of the entity's shares (or other equity instruments)(IFRS 2).

股份支付交易

在此类交易中,实体接收货物或者服务,并将其作为换取自身权益工具(包括股份或股票认购权)的对价,或者实体按自身股票(或其他权益工具)价格所确定的金额来获取商品或服务(《国际财务报告准则第 2 号》)。

significant influence

Power to participate in the financial and operating policy decisions of an entity, but not have control over those policies. This may be gained by share ownership, statute or agreement (IAS 28).

显著影响

对实体的财务和经营政策享有参与决策权,但不享有控制权。显著影响可以通过股份所有权、法规或者协议来获得(《国际会计准则第 28 号》)。

sinking fund

Money put aside periodically to settle a

偿债基金

为偿还债务或更换资产而定期提

liability or replace an asset. The money is invested to produce a required sum at an appropriate time.

存的资金。这笔资金可在适当的时候用于投资以获取所需金额。

social cost

Tangible and intangible costs and losses sustained by third parties or the general public as a result of economic activity, for example pollution by industrial effluent.

社会成本

经济活动所导致的,由第三方或者公众承担的有形和无形成本和损失,例如工业废水污染。

social responsibility accounting

Identification, measurement and reporting of the social costs and benefits resulting from economic activities.

社会责任会计

识别、计量和报告经济活动所带来的社会成本和利益。

Statement of Recommended Practice(SORP)

Supplement UK accounting stand-ards, approved by the ASB, which recommend accounting practices for specialised industries or sectors, to allow for features or transactions undertaken in that particular industry or sector.

推荐实务公告

由会计准则理事会批准的英国会计准则补充,其鉴于特殊行业或部门的特点或特殊交易,向这些行业或部门推荐的会计实务操作。

statement of affairs

Statement, usually prepared by a receiver, in a prescribed form, showing the estimated financial position of a debtor or of a company (or other entity) which may be unable to meet its debts. It contains a summary of the debtor's asset and liabilities. The assets are shown at their estimated realisable values. The various classes of creditors, such as preferential, secured, partly secured and

财务状况说明书

财务状况说明书,通常是由债权人按规范格式编写的,以说明债务人或公司(或其他实体)的财务状况可能无法偿还其债务。说明书包括债务人的资产和负债摘要,其中资产以预计的可变现价值进行列报。不同类别的债权人需要分开说明,比如有优先权的、有抵押的、部分有抵押和部分无抵押的。

unsecured, are shown separately.

Statement of Auditing Standards (SAS)

A standard issued by the Auditing Practices Board (APB), containing prescriptions as to the basic principles and practices which members of the UK accountancy bodies are expected to follow in the course of an audit. Superseded from 2005 by International Standards on Auditing (UK and Ireland)(ISAs(UK and Ireland)), and International Standard on Quality Control (ISQC)issued by the IAASB. See "IAASB".

审计准则声明

审计实务委员会（APB）颁布的一项准则,其中规定了英国会计团体成员在执行审计过程中应该遵循的基本原则和惯例。从 2005 年起,这项准则已被《国际审计准则》(英国和爱尔兰)和国际审计与鉴证准则理事会发布的《国际质量控制准则》(ISQC)取代。参见"国际审计与鉴证准则理事会"。

statement of changes in equity

Summary of all the component changes in equity for a period(see Figure 3. 10)or a summary of changes in equity other than those arising from transactions with equity holders in their capacity as equity holders(see Figure 3. 11). Refer to IAS 1.

所有者权益变动表

全面反映某个期间内所有者权益各个组成部分的变动情况(参见图表 3.10)或反映权益的变动,但不包括权益持有人进行交易而导致的权益变动(参见图表 3.11)。(参照《国际会计准则》第 1 号)。

FIGURE 3. 10　STATEMENT OF CHANGES IN EQUITY FOR THE YEAR ENDED 31 DECEMBER 2005(REFER TO IAS 1)

	Attributable to equity holders of the parent					Minority interest	Total equity
	Share capital $ million	Other reserves (see note) $ million	Translation reserve $ million	Retained earnings $ million	Total $ million	$ million	$ million
Balances at 1 January 2005	1,000	288	56	372	1,716	227	1,943
Change in accounting policy				(44)	(44)	(8)	(52)
Restated balances	1,000	288	56	328	1,672	219	1,891
Changes in equity for 2005							

CONTINUED

	Attributable to equity holders of the parent					Minority interest	Total equity
	Share capital $ million	Other reserves (see note) $ million	Translation reserve $ million	Retained earnings $ million	Total $ million	$ million	$ million
Gain on property revaluation		110			110	20	130
Available-for-sale investments							
Valuation losses taken to equity		(48)			(48)	(11)	(59)
Cash flow hedges							
Gains taken to equity		72			72	14	86
Exchange differences on translation of foreign operations			(83)		(83)	(12)	(95)
Tax on items taken directly to or transferred from equity		(20)	15		(5)	(1)	(6)
Net income recognised directly in equity		114	(68)		46	10	56
Profit for the year		—	—	199	199	35	234
Total recognised income and expense for the year		114	(68)	199	245	45	290
Dividends				(93)	(93)	(18)	(111)
Issue of share capital	150	50	—	—	200	—	200
	150	164	(68)	106	352	27	379
Balances at 31 December 2005	1,150	452	(12)	434	2,024	246	2,270

Note-"other reserves" would include the share premium and revaluation reserves which would need to be analysed separately.

图表 3.10 截至 2005 年 12 月 31 日所有者权益变动表(参照《国际会计准则第 1 号》)

	归属于母公司的权益					少数股东权益	所有者权益合计
	股本 单位：百万美元	盈余公积 单位：百万美元	报表外币折算差额 单位：百万美元	留存收益 单位：百万美元	合计 单位：百万美元	单位：百万美元	单位：百万美元
期初余额	1,000	288	56	372	1,716	227	1,943
会计政策变更影响数				(44)	(44)	(8)	(52)
本年期初数	1,000	228	56	328	1,672	219	1,891

（续表）

	归属于母公司的权益					少数股东权益	所有者权益合计
	股本	盈余公积	报表外币折算差额	留存收益	合计		
	单位：百万美元	单位：百万美元	单位：百万美元	单位：百万美元	单位：百万美元	单位：百万美元	单位：百万美元
本年变动数							
资产重估利得		110			110	20	130
计入所有者权益的可供出售金融资产价值变动损失		(48)			(48)	(11)	(59)
计入所有者权益的现金流套期保值收益		72			72	14	86
境外业务产生的汇兑差额			(83)		(83)	(12)	(95)
直接计入或从所有者权益转出的纳税项目		(20)	15		(5)	(1)	(6)
直接在权益中确认的净收益		114	(68)		46	10	56
本年利润				199	199	35	234
本年确认的收入和支出总额		114	(68)	199	245	45	290
股利				(93)	(93)	(18)	(111)
发行股本	150	50			200		200
	150	164	(68)	106	352	27	379
资产负债表年末余额	1,150	452	(12)	434	2,024	246	2,270

注："盈余公积"包括股本溢价及需要单独重估的重估准备。

FIGURE 3.11 STATEMENT OF RECOGNISED INCOME AND EXPENSE FOR THE YEAR ENDED 31 DECEMBER 2005 (REFER TO IAS 1)

	$ million
Gain on property revaluation	130
Available-for-sale investments	(59)
Valuation losses taken to equity	
Cash flow hedges	86
Gains taken to equity	
Exchange differences on translation of foreign operations	(95)
Tax on items taken directly to or transferred from equity	(6)
Net income recognised directly in equity	56
Profit for the year	234

CONTINUED

	$ million
Total recognised income and expense for the period	290
Attributable to:	245
Equity holders of the parent	245
Minority interests	45
	290
Effects of changes in accounting policy	
Equity holders of the parent	(44)
Minority interests	(8)
	(52)

图表 3.11　截至 2005 年 12 月 31 日已确认收入及支出表(参照《国际会计准则第 1 号》)

单位:百万美元

资产重估利得	130
计入所有者权益的可供出售金融资产公允价值损失	(59)
计入所有者权益的现金流套期保值收益	86
境外业务产生的汇兑差额	(95)
直接计入或从所有者权益转出的纳税项目	(6)
直接在权益中确认的净收益	56
本年利润	234
本年确认的收入和支出总额	290
分配	
归属于母公司权益	245
少数股东权益	45
	290
会计政策变更影响	
母公司权益	(44)
少数股东权益	(8)
	(52)

Statement of Standard Accounting Practice(SSAP)

标准会计实务公告

Standard issued by the Councils of CCAB member bodies following proposals developed by the Accounting Standard Committee. The ASC has been replaced by the ASB who a-dopted all the existing SSAP; those still extant

由会计团体咨询委员会(CCAB)的成员机构根据会计准则委员会的提案所发布的准则。会计准则委员会已经被会计准则理事会取代,而会计准则理事会已经采用了现行的所有标准会计

in the UK are listed in Appendix 2. See "Financial Reporting Standard".

实务公告；英国仍在采用的实务公告列示于附录 2 中。参见"财务报告准则"。

statutory body

Entity formed by a UK Act of the parliament.

法定组织

根据《英国议会法》成立的实体。

stewardship

Responsibilities of agents to act in the best interests of their principals，by keeping adequate records of transactions and by acting so as to maintain or increase both the capital and income of the principal.

管理层职责

代理人有责任以符合委托人最佳利益为原则，保存充分的交易记录，实现委托人收入和资本的保值增值。

stock（goods）

See "inventories".

库存

参见"存货"。

subordinated debt

Ranked below other debt under the terms of the agreement between the borrower and the lender.

次级债

根据借款人与贷款人达成的协议条款，等级低于其他债务的债务。

subsidiary

Entity，including an unincorporated entity such as a partnership，that is controlled by another entity（known as the parent）（IFRS 3）.

子公司

由一个实体（称为母公司）控制的另一个实体，这个实体可以是非法人实体，如合伙企业（《国际财务报告准则第 3 号》）。

tax base（of an asset/liability）

Amount attributable to that asset or liability for tax purposes（IAS 12）.

（资产/负债）税基

从税务角度界定的属于资产或负债的金额（《国际会计准则第 12 号》）。

taxable profit or loss

Profit or loss for a period, determined in accordance with the rules established by the taxation authortities, upon which income (corporation)taxes are payable (or recoverable)(IAS 12).

应税收入或损失

按照税务机关制定的规则确定的,(公司)某个期间内应缴纳所得税的收入或者损失(《国际会计准则第12号》)。

taxation

impact on financial strategy：

The financial manager will have to consider the taxation implications of all his decisions when setting the entity's financial strategy. For companies with operations in several countries, there will be both domestic and international tax implications.

in mergers/acquisitions：

There are several tax implications of mergers and acquisitions：differences in tax rates and double tax treaties；group loss relief；withholding tax.

in Modigliani and Miller's gearing theory：

In 1963, M & M amended their model to include the impact of corporation tax. This alteration changes the results of their analysis significantly.

M & M, therefore, conclude that geared companies have an advantage over ungeared companies, i. e. they pay less tax and will, therefore, have a greater market value and a lower weighted average cost of capital.

tax exhaustion：

M & M's with tax theory suggests that the benefits of tax relief on debt interest will help to reduce the company's cost of capital at all levels

税收

对财务战略的影响:

财务经理在制定财务战略时必须考虑税收对其所有决策的影响。跨国经营的企业会面临来自国内和国外的税收影响。

对并购的影响:

并购时需要考虑的税务问题有:税率差异以及双重征税协定;对集团亏损给予税项减免;预提税。

M & M 杠杆理论中的征税问题:

1963 年,莫迪利安尼和米勒修订了他们的 M & M 模型,将公司税的影响纳入其中。这一修正明显改变了他们的分析结果。因而,M & M 模型得出结论,有杠杆的公司比没有杠杆的公司更具优势,比如,前者支付的税金更少,因此可以获得更大的市场价值并降低加权平均资本成本。

税收损耗:

结合了税收理论的 M & M 模型认为,债务利息所具备的减税效果可以降低公司所有财务杠杆水平上的资

of gearing. This is not the case in practice.

At some level of gearing in the interest payable will be so high that taxable profit will be reduced to zero. Beyond this point, there will be no future benefit of raising debt finance.

本成本。但在实践中,情况并非如此。

当财务杠杆达到一定的水平,应付利息的数额非常高,在抵减之后,公司的应税利润下降为零。然而,超过这一临界点,提高债务融资不会给公司带来任何未来收益。

teeming and lading

Fraud based on a continuous cycle of stealing and later replacing assets(generally cash), each theft being used in part, or in full, to repay a previous theft in order to avoid detection.

挪用资金

一种舞弊,周而复始地偷盗资产而后再予以归还(通常是现金),每次偷窃所得的一部分或全部用于填补上一次偷窃的漏洞,以避免被发现。

temporary difference

Difference between the carrying amount of an asset or liability in the balance sheet and its tax base. It may be either a taxable temporary difference(IAS 12).

暂时性差异

资产或负债在资产负债表上的账面金额与其计税基础之间的差额。它可以是应纳税暂时性差异或可抵扣暂时性差异(《国际会计准则第 12 号》)。

temporary difference, taxable

Temporary difference that will result in taxable amounts in determining taxable profit (or loss) of future periods when the carrying amount of the asset or liability is recovered or settled(IAS 12).

应纳税暂时性差异

未来期间,资产或负债的账面金额得以恢复,在确定恢复当期的应税利润(或损失)时,它将导致应税金额出现暂时性差异(《国际会计准则第 12 号》)。

termination benefits

Employee benefits payable either as a result of an entity's decision to terminate an employee's employment before the normal retirement date or an employee's decision to accept voluntary redundancy in exchange for these benefits(IAS 19).

辞退福利

指在职工正常退休之前,企业提前终止劳动合同而支付给员工的福利,或者员工决定接受自愿裁员以换取这项福利《国际会计准则第 19 号》。

tests of control

Tests performed to obtain audit evidence about the operating effectiveness of controls in preventing, or detecting and correcting, material misstatements at the assertion level (Glossary of terms, Auditing Standards (ISAs (UK and Ireland))).

控制测试

控制测试是为了获取审计证据, 借以了解控制在预防、发现及更正报表认定层次的重大错报方面运行的效果如何(术语表,《国际审计准则》(英国及爱尔兰))。

timing difference

Difference between the balance held on related accounts which are caused by differences in the timing of the input of common transactions, for example a direct debit will appear on the bank statement before it is entered into the bank account. Knowledge of the timing difference allows the balances on the two accounts to be reconciled.

时间差异

同一交易由于确认时间差异而导致相关账户的余额差异,比如,直接付款会在银行对账单上得到显示,但却尚未记入银行账户。基于对时间差异的认识,因而可以对两个账户的余额进行调节。

total assets

Total carrying value of all assets (non-current and current, tangible and intangible).

总资产

所有资产(非流动及流动资产,有形及无形资产)账面价值的总额。

treasury shares

Shares held by an entity when it re-acquires its own equity instruments. These should be deducted from equity in the balance sheet (refer to IAS 32).

库存股

实体通过重新购回自身权益工具而持有的股份。这些股份应从资产负债表的所有者权益中扣除(参照《国际会计准则第 32 号》)。

turnover/sales

See "revenue".

营业额/销售收入

参见"收入"。

Urgent Issues Task Force(UITF)

Committee of the ASB whose aim is to assist the ASB in areas where unsatisfactory or conflicting interpretations of an accounting standard have developed, or seem likely to develop. Abstracts published by the UITF have the same legal status as accounting standards.

useful life(assets)

Estimated period over which an asset is expected to be available for use by an entity or the number of production or similar units expected to be obtained from the asset by the entity (IAS 16).

user groups

Different interest groups who may make use of publicly available financial statements. Lenders, employees, investors and competitors may be classed as separate user groups.

value in use

Present value of the estimated future cash flows expected to arise from the continuing use of an asset(or cash generating unit) and from its disposal at the end of its useful life(IFRS 5).

venturer

Party to a joint venture that has joint control over that joint venture .

紧急问题工作小组

会计准则理事会下属的紧急问题工作小组,其目标是就已经存在或可能形成的不尽如人意或相互矛盾的会计准则解释向会计准则理事会提供协助。紧急问题工作小组发表的摘要与会计准则具有同等的法律地位。

(资产)使用年限

资产使用年限是指实体可以使用该资产的预计期限,或者该资产有望生产的产品数量或类似单位(《国际会计准则第16号》)。

用户组

可能使用公开财务报表的、具有不同利益的群体。贷款人、雇员、投资者和竞争对手可划分为不同的用户组。

使用价值

持续使用资产(或现金产出单元)可产生的预计未来现金流量以及资产在使用寿命结束时处置所得的现值(《国际财务报告准则第5号》)。

合营者

合营企业的各方,他们对合营企业拥有共同控制权。

wasting asset

Non-current asset which is consumed or exhausted in the process of earning income, for example a mine or quarry.

递耗资产

在取得收入的过程中不断消耗或耗尽的非流动资产,例如矿山或采石场。

window-dressing

Creative accounting practice in which changes in short-term funding have the effect of disguising or improving the reported liquidity position of the reporting entity.

粉饰报表

一种创造性会计操作,其对短期筹资加以修改借以掩饰或改善报告实体的流动性状况。

withholding tax

Tax on dividends or other income that is deducted by the payer of the income and paid to the taxation authotities on behalf of the recipient.

代扣所得税(预提税)

股利或其他收入的支付者在向纳税人支付这些款项时,代扣相关税金并上缴税务机关。

working capital

Capital available for conducting the day-to-day operations of an entity, normally the excess of current assets over current liabilities.

营运资金

实体可用于日常经营的资金,通常指流动资产超出流动负债的部分。

CHAPER 4
Corporate Finance and Treasury

第四章
公司金融与司库

ad valorem (duty)

Duty based on the value of a product or service.

从价(税)

按照产品或服务的价值征税。

adjusted present value (APV)

Net present value of an asset that also takes account of any financing side effects.

调整后的净现值

考虑所有财务影响后的某项资产的净现值。

alpha value

The alpha value of a share is simply its average abnormal return. Alpha value can be either positive or negative, and in a perfect world they should be zero.

α 值

股票的 α 值指的是股票的平均超额收益。α 值可正可负,在信息完全对称的市场中为零。

Alternative Investment Market (AIM)

Securities market designed primarily for small companies, regulated by the UK stock exchange but with less demanding rules than apply to the stock exchange official list of companies.

伦敦交易所另类投资市场

主要面向小型公司的证券市场,该市场受英国证券交易所监管,但监管规则不及在证券交易所挂牌上市的公司所需遵守的规则那样严苛。

annual equivalent rate（AER）

Notional annual rate which is equivalent to another set of rates that may be paid other than annually.

年等价利率

与非 1 年一付的利率等价的名义年利率。

annuity

Fixed periodic payment which continues either for a specified time，or until the occurrence of a specified event. See perpetuity.

年金

在某一特定期间内或者直到某一特定事件发生为止持续支付的等额定期款项。参见"永续年金"。

arbitrage

Simultaneous purchase and sale of a security in different markets with the aim of making a risk-free profit through the exploitation of any price difference between the markets.

套利

在不同市场中同时买入和卖出证券，以期利用不同市场的价格差异来获取无风险利润。

arrangement fees

See "issue costs".

手续费

参见"发行成本"。

articles of association

Document which，with the memorandum of association，provides the legal constitution of a company. The articles of association define the rules and regulations governing the management of the affairs of the company，the rights of the members（shareholders），and the duties and powers of the directors. See "memoranduom of association".

组织章程

组织章程是公司的法律性文书，明确了公司事务管理、股东权利以及董事职责和权力等事项。参见"组织章程大纲"。

asset based valuation

A model for business valuation. The

基于资产的评估

一种企业价值评估模型。企业的

business's assets form the basis for the valuation. Asset based valuation methods are difficult to apply to businesses with high levels of intangible assets. In this method the company is viewed as being worth the sum of the value of its assets. An asset based valuation is most useful when a company is being broken up, rather than purchased as a going concern.

资产是估值的依据。无形资产较多的企业很难基于资产对企业价值进行评估。在这种方法下,企业的价值被视作其资产价值的总和。相对于持续经营,资产计价法在企业破产时更为适用。

asset beta

资产的 β 值

The asset beta measures the systematic business risk only.

资产的 β 值只衡量系统风险。

back-to-back loan

背对背贷款

Form of financing whereby money borrowed in one country, or currency is covered by lending an equivalent amount in another.

一种融资形式,某个国家以该国货币借入资金,同时以其他国家的货币提供等额贷款,以此相互抵销。

BACS

银行自动结算业务

(Formerly the Bankers Automated Clearing Services). UK electronic bulk clearing system generally used by banks and building societies for low-value and/or repetitive items such as standing orders, direct debits and automated credits such as salary payments.

(前称 Bankers Automated Clearing Services,是"银行自动结算业务"的英文。)在英国,银行和建筑协会普遍使用的电子化批量结算系统,常见于经常性订单、直接负债和自动贷记(如支付工资)等小额和(或)重复业务。

balancing allowance/charge

结余免税/结余课税

Relief for tax purposes of capital expenditure, or the claw back of relief already given, administered in the year in which a real asset is disposed of or an entity ceases to exist.

在处置实物资产或实体不复存在的年度内,针对资本支出进行税收减免或者追缴已减免的税款进行。

bank charge

Amount charged by a bank to its customers for services provided，for example for servicing customer accounts or arranging foreign currency transactions or letters of credit，but excluding interest.

银行手续费

银行在向客户提供服务账户、安排外币交易或信用证等服务时收取的费用，不包含利息。

bank borrowings

Long-term loans or short-term loans，including bank facilities such as revolving credit facilities（RCFs）and money market lines.

银行借款

长期借款、短期借款以及包含循环信贷额度和货币市场线等在内的银行贷款。

bank overdraft

Borrowings from a bank on current account，normally repayable on demand. The maximum permissible overdraft is normally agreed with the bank prior to the facility being made available，and interest，calculated on a daily basis，is charged on the amount borrowed，and not on the agreed maximum borrowing facility.

银行透支

从银行借款，记入活期存款账户，通常需要立刻偿还。在透支之前，借款人要与银行就最高允许透支额度达成一致，并按天根据借款金额、而不是商定的最高借款额度计算利息。

bank reconciliation

Detailed statement reconciling，at a given date，the cash balance in an entity's cash book with that reported in a bank statement. An example is given below：

Bank Reconciliation Statement

	$	$
Cash book balance		
Cash book balance o/d		(1,205)
Bank charges not in cash book	(110)	
Dividends collected by the bank, not in cash book	(113)	3

银行对账单

在某一特定日期发出、用于核对实体现金日记账与银行资金进入记录的明细表。举例如下：

银行对账单

	$	$
现金日记账余额		
现金透支额		(1 205)
现金日记账未记录的银行手续费	(110)	
现金日记账未记录但银行已收取的股利	3 113	

Updated cash book balance*		(1,202)
Cheques drawn, not presented to bank	4,363	
Cheque recerved, not yet credited by bank	(1,061)	3,302
Bank statement balance		2,100

更新现金日记账余额*		(1 202)
已开具但尚未向银行兑现的支票	4 363	
已收到但银行尚未登记的支票	(1 061)	
银行对账单余额		2 100

* The balance sheet will show a bank overdraft of $1,202, which is the true position at the date of the reconciliation, after corrections by journal entry.

* 在完成对账之后,对账当日的资产负债表显示的银行透支金额为1,202美元。

bankruptcy

Legal status of an individual against whom an adjudication order has been made by the court primarily because of inability to meet financial liabilities.

破产

由于无力偿还财务负债,法院作出判决令之后,某人所处的一种法律状态。

basis risk

Basis risk is the risk that when a hedge is constructed, the size of the basis when the futures position is closed out is different from the expectation, when the hedge was created, of what the basis ought to be.

基差风险

基差风险是指构建套期保值时,期货平仓头等与预期的现货头等存在差异的风险。

bear market

Securities market experiencing a prolonged widespread decline in prices. See "bull market".

熊市

证券市场经历股价持续大范围下跌。参见"牛市"。

bearer bond

Negotiable bond (or security) whose ownership is not registered by the issuer, but is presumed to lie with whoever has physical possession of the bond.

不记名债券

发行人未登记所有人、但可以假定实际持有人拥有所有权的可转让债券(或证券)。

beta factor

Measure of systematic risk of a security relative to the market portfolio. If a security were to rise or fall at double the market rate，it would have a beta factor of 2.0. Conversely，if the security price moved at half the market rate，the beta factor would be 0.5. See "risk，market/systematic".

bid-ask spread/bid-offer spread

Difference between buying and selling prices of a traded commodity or a financial instrument. Also known as bid-offer spread.

bill of lading

Document prepared by a consignor by which a carrier acknowledges the receipt of goods and which serves as a document of title to the goods consigned.

bill payable

Bill of exchange or promissory note payable.

bill receivable

Bill of exchange or promissory note receivable.

Black-Scholes method (share options)

Equation developed by F. Black and M.

贝塔系数

衡量某个证券与相关市场投资组合的系统性风险。如果某一证券的涨跌幅度为市场大盘涨跌幅度的两倍，那么贝塔系数即为2.0。相反，如果某一证券的波动幅度为市场大盘涨跌幅度的一半，那么贝塔系数即为0.5。参见"市场/系统性风险"。

买卖价差

可交易的商品或金融工具买入价与卖出价之间的差异。

提货单

由托运人编制的、承运人据此确认收到商品的文件，该文件可作为所托运商品的所有权文件。

应付票据

应付汇票或期票。

应收票据

应收汇票或期票。

布莱克-斯克尔斯期权定价模型

由费雪・布莱克和迈伦・斯科尔

Scholes to value a European-style call option that uses the share price, the exercise price, the risk-free interest rate, the time to maturity and the standard deviation of the share return. A European option can be exercised only on the expiration date. See "European-style option(option)".

斯创建的方程式,利用股价、行权价、无风险利率、到期时间和股票回报标准偏差对欧式认购期权进行定价。欧式期权仅可在到期日行权。参见"欧式期权(期权)"。

blue chip

Description of an equity or company which is of the highest quality, and in which an investment would be regarded as low risk with regard to both dividend payments and capital values.

蓝筹股

优质公司的股票,在股利分配和资本价值方面,这类公司的投资风险极低。

bond

Debt instrument, normally offering a fixed rate of interest(coupon)over a fixed period of time, and with a fixed redemption value(par).

债券

一种债务工具,通常而言,期限、利率(票息)以及赎回价值(面值)都是固定的。

bonus/scrip issue

Capitalisation of the reserves of an entity by the issue of additional shares to existing shareholders in proportion to their holdings. Such shares are normally fully paid-up with no cash called for from the shareholders. See "right issue".

红利/股利股票发行

按照持股比率向现有股东额外发行的股份,以便将实体的盈余公积资本化。通常,此类股份的款项均已足额缴纳,无需再向股东催缴。参见"配股"。

borrowing costs

Interest and other costs incurred by an entity in connection with the borrowing of funds. They may include:

(a) interest on bank overdrafts and bor-

借款成本

实体发生的、与借入资金有关的利息和其他成本。借款成本包括:

(a)银行透支和借款利息;

rowings；

（b）amortisation of discounts or premiums related to borrowings；

（c）amortisation of ancillary costs incurred in connection with the arrangement of borrowings ；

（d）finance charges in respect to finance leases；and

（e）exchange differences arising from foreign currency borrowings to the extent they are regarded as an adjustment to interest costs（IAS 23）.

（b）与借款有关的折价或溢价的摊销；

（c）与安排借款有关的辅助费用摊销；

（d）与融资租赁有关的财务费用；

（e）作为利息费用调整的外币借款汇兑差额（《国际会计准则第 23 号》）。

bull market

Securities market experiencing prolonged widespread price increase. See "bear market".

牛市

证券市场经历股价持续大范围上涨。参见"熊市"。

business angels

Wealthy individuals prepared to invest in a start-up，early stage or developing firm. Often，they have managerial and/or technical experience to offer to the management team as well as debt and equity finance.

天使投资人

具有一定财富的个人准备对处于起步阶段、早期阶段或发展阶段的公司进行投资。通常，这类投资人都拥有丰富的管理和（或）技术经验，能提供管理团队以及债权和股权融资方面的帮助。

calculated intangible value（CIV）.

The calculated Intangible Value（CIV） method of company valuation has been developed to estimate the value of a company's intellectual capital. Therefore it is an advance on the basic asset valuation. The CIV method is based on a comparison of the total return that the company is producing against the return that would be expected based on industry

无形资产价值计算法

公司的无形资产价值计算（CIV）方法可用于估计公司智力资本的价值。因此，这是在基础资本估值上的进一步发展。CIV 方法是通过比较公司的总收益和行业基于有形资产计算出的预期收益，即两者之间的差额来得出公司的无形资产价值。即，实体的总价值＝有形资产价值＋CIV。

average returns on tangible assets. Any additional return is assumed to be the return on intangible assets. The value of intangible assets thus calculated is then added to the value of the tangible assets of the business to generate a total value. i. e. Total value of the entity = Value of tangible assets + CIV.

call

Request made to the holders of partly paid-up share capital for the payment of a predetermined sum due on the share capital, under the terms of the original subscription agreement. Failure on the part of the shareholder to pay a call may result in the forfeiture of the relevant holding of partly paid shares.

催缴

要求已缴部分股本的股份持有人按照原始认购协议的条款,支付应付的预定股本。若股东未能支付剩余股本,则可能丧失已缴股本的相关持有权。

call option

Option to buy a specified underlying asset at aspecified exercise price on, or before, a specified exercise date. See "exercise price" "option" "put option".

认购期权

在规定的行权日或之前,以约定的行权价买入约定标的资产的权利。参见"行权价""期权""认沽期权"。

capital allowance

Relief from income tax or corporation tax on capital expenditure on eligible assets.

资本减免

对符合条件的资产资本支出给予所得税或公司税减免。

capital asset pricing model, (CAPM)

Theory which predicts that the expected risk premium for an individual stock will be proportional to its beta, such that:

（Expected risk premium on a stock = beta ×

资本资产定价模型

预测某只股票的预期风险溢价与其贝塔值线性比例关系的理论,即:

（股票的预期风险溢价 ＝ 贝塔值 × 市

expected risk premium in the market)

Risk premium is defined as the expected incremental return for making a risky invrestment rather than a safe one.

场预期风险溢价)

风险溢价是指进行风险性投资的预期增值回报。

capital budgeting

资本预算

Process concerned with decision-making in respect of the choice of specific investment projects and the total amount of capital expenditure to commit.

与特定投资项目选择及资本支出总额有关的决策过程。

capital instrument

资本工具

All instruments that are issued by reporting entities as a means of raising finance, including shares, debentures, loans and debt instruments, options and warrants that give the holder the right to subscribe for or obtain capital instruments. In the case of consolidated financial statements the term includes capital instruments issued by sudsidiaries except those that are held by another member of the group included in the consolidation (FRS 4).

报告实体发行的、作为融资手段的所有工具,包括股份、信用债券、贷款、债务工具以及持有人有权认购或获取资本工具的期权和权证。在合并财务报表中包括了子公司发行的资本工具,但其他集团成员公司持有的资本工具除外(《财务报告准则第4号》)。

capital investment appraisal

资本投资评估

Application of a set of methodologies (generally based on the discounting of projected cash flows) whose purpose is to give guidance to managers with respect to decisions as to how best to commit long-term investment funds. See "discounted cash flows".

利用一套方法进行评价(通常基于预计现金流量折现),为管理层决策如何以最佳方式投入长期投资资金提供指引。参见"现金流折现"。

capital rationing

资本限制

Restriction on an entity's ability to invest capital funds, caused by an internal

因管理层对资本支出规定了内部预算上限,或者公司受到外部限制,无

budget ceiling being imposed on such expenditure by management（soft capital rationing）, or by external limitations being applied to the company, as when additional borrowed funds cannot be obtained（hard capital rationing）.

法获取更多借入资金,从而使得实体投入资本资金的能力受到限制,前者称为软性资本限制,后者称为硬性资本限制。

capital structure

Relative proportions of equity capital and debt capital within an entity's balance sheet.

资本结构

实体的资产负债表中权益资本与债务资本的相对比例。

capitals

For the purpose of the〈IR〉（integrated reporting）Framework, the capitals are categorized and described as follows: Financial capital, manufactured capital, intellectual capital, human capital, social and relationship capital, natural capital.

资本

在综合报告框架下,资本包括:金融资本、生产资本、知识资本、人力资本、社会关系资本和自然资本。

caps

An interest rate guarantees（IRG）is a contract with a bank fixing a maximum/（minimum）borrowing/（lending）rate on a notional loan for a stated period from a stated future date, in exchange for an up front fee. IRGs are sometimes referred to as interest rate options or interest rate caps/floors.

利率上限

利率保证(IRG)是一种与银行签订的、在未来某一段时间内确定最大(或最小)借款(或贷款)利率、以预付费作为交换的合同。有时也被称为利率期权、利率上限或下限。

cash management models

Sophisticated cash flow forecasting models which assist management in determining how to balance the cash needs of an entity. Cash management models can help: to

现金管理模型

成熟的现金流量预测模型,有助于管理层确定如何平衡实体的现金需求。现金管理模型有助于:优化现金结余;管理客户、供应商、投资者和公

optimise cash balances；to manage customer，supplier，investor and company needs；to determine whether to invest or buy back shares；and to decide what is the optimum of financing working capital.

司需求；确定是否投资或回购股份；确定最适宜的营运资金融资方式。

certainty equivalent method

确定等值法

Approach to dealing with risk in a capital budgeting context. It involves expressing risky future cash flows in terms of the certain cash flow which would be considered，by the decision maker，as their equivalent，that is the decision maker would be indifferent between the risky amount and the（lower）riskless amount considered to be its equivalent.

在进行资本预算时处理风险的方法，决策者通过此方法将具有风险的未来现金流量转化为相同价值的确定现金流量，也就是说，决策者认为风险性现金与视为等值的无风险（或低风险）现金无差别。

certificate of deposit

存款单

Negotiable instrument which provides evidence of a fixed-term deposit with a bank. Maturity is normally within 90 days，but can be longer.

证明在银行存有定期存款的可转让票据，通常在 90 天内到期，但期限也可以更长。

chartered entity

特许经济实体

Organiation formed by the grant of a Royal Charter(in the UK). The charter authorises the entity to operate and states the powers specifically granted.

在被授予皇家特许证后成立的组织(英国)。特许证授权实体开展业务，明确特别授予的权力。

Clearing House Automated Payment System (CHAPS)

交换银行自动收付系统

Clearing House Automated Payment System. UK method for the rapid eletronic transfer of funds between participating banks on behalf of large commercial customers，where transfers

交换银行自动收付系统是英国一种代表大型商业客户的银行之间进行大额资金快速电子转账的常用方法。

tend to be of significant value.

collar

Simultaneously buying a put and selling a call option creates a collar.

领子期权

买入一个看跌期权的同时卖出一个看涨期权,这类期权买卖被称作领子期权。

collateral

Security，in the form of a claim over assets，generally given for borrowed funds over the period of a loan.

抵押品

为了在贷款期内获得资金,以具有申索权的形式抵押的资产。

commercial paper

Unsecured short-term loan notes issued by companies，and generally maturing within a period of up to one year.

商业票据

公司签发的无担保短期贷款票据,通常在 1 年内到期。

commodity price risk

Risk of a rise in commodity prices.

大宗商品价格风险

大宗商品价格上涨的风险。

commodity pricing

Pricing a product or service on the basis that it is undifferentiated from all competitive offerings，and cannot therefore command any price premium above the base market price.

商品定价

提供的商品和服务与所有竞争对手没有差别,因此无法以高于基础市场价格的溢价对商品或服务进行定价。

company limited by guarantee

Company in which each member undertakes to contribute（to the limit of the guarantee），on a winding up，towards payment of the liabilities of the company.

担保责任有限公司

每位股东在清算时以担保额为限偿还债务的公司。

company limited by shares/joint stock company/limited liability company

股份有限公司/股份制公司/有限责任公司

Company in which the liability of members for the company's debts is limited to the value of the shares taken up by them. See "private company" and "public company".

股东对公司债务责任仅限于自身所持股份价值的公司。参见"私营公司"和"上市公司"。

company/corporation

公司

Legal entity, whose life is independent of that of its members. In the UK, companied or corporations are predominantly formed through registration under the Uk Companies Act 1985.

存续期独立于股东的法律实体。在英国,公司或企业主要根据 1985 年《英国公司法》进行注册登记后才能成立。

compound interest

复利

Interest which is calculated over successive periods based on the principal plus accrued interest. See "simple interest". The future value of an investment, over whose period interest is compounded, can be found by using the following formula:

$$S = X(1 + r)^n$$

where:

S = Future value in year n

X = Initial investment, principal or value at year 0

r = Annual rate of return expressed as a decimal fraction

N = Number of years

在连续期间内根据本金加累计利息计算的利息。参见"单利"。若某项投资在投资期内以复利计息,其终值可使用以下公式计算获得:

$$S = X(1 + r)^n$$

其中:

S = 第 n 年的终值

X = 初始投资、初始本金或初始价值

r = 以十进制小数表示的年收益率

n = 年限

consol

统一公债

Certain irredeemable UK government stocks carrying fixed coupons. Sometimes

利息固定且不可赎回的英国政府债券。有时也作为无到期日或不可赎

used as a general term for an undated or irre-deemable bond.

回债券的统称。

consortium

Association of several entities with a view to carrying out a joint venture. See "joint venture".

财团

多个实体为经营合营企业而组成的联合体。参见"合营企业"。

countertrade

Form of trading activity based on other than an arm's-length goods for cash ex-change. Types of countertrade include：

barter：Direct exchange of goods and services between two parties without the use of money.

counterpurchase：Trading agreement in which the primary contract vendor agrees to make purchases of an agreed percentage of the primary contract value，from the primary contract purchaser，through a linked counter-purchase contract.

offsets：Trading agreement in which the purchaser becomes involved in the production process，often acquiring technology supplied by the vendor.

对销贸易

现金公平交易之外的其他贸易活动形式，包括：

以货易货：交易双方在不使用金钱的情况下直接交换商品和服务。

回购：主合同卖方同意通过一份挂钩的回购合同，向主合同买方购买一定比例主合同价值的贸易协议。

抵销：买方参与生产过程，获得卖方技术的贸易协定。

coupon

Interest payable on a bond expressed as a percentage of the nominal value.

票息

以票面价值的百分比表示的债券应付利息。

credit rating

Credit ratings are issued by an independ-ent credit rating agencieswhich monitor the performance of major businesses and rate

信用评级

信用评级由独立的信用评价机构发布，其对主要机构的业绩进行监控，并根据它们偿还债务的可能性进行

them according to how likely it is that they will be able to afford to repay any debts.

评分。

credit scoring

信用评分

Assessment of the creditworthiness of an individual or company by rating numerically a number of both financial and non-financial aspects of the target's present position and previous performance.

对个人或公司的财务和非财务方面的现状和过往业绩给出分数,评估个人或公司的信誉。

cum

含

"with", as in cum dividend, where security purchases include rights to the next dividend payment. and cum rights, where shares are traded with rights, such as to a scrip issue，attached.

"附有"之意。"含息"是指购买证券时,就拥有了获得下期股息的权利;"含权"是指交易股份时,附带了发行红股等的权利。

currency futures

货币期货

Currency futures are standardized contracts for fixed amounts of money for a limited range of future dates.

货币期货是指在未来某一固定期限内,货币金额固定的标准合约。

currency options

货币期权

A currency option is a right，but not an obligation，to buy or sell a currency at an exercise price on a future date.

货币期权是一项权利,而不是义务,是在未来某一日期按行权价买入或卖出一种货币。

debt beta

债务 β 值

The debt beta measures the risk associated with the debt finance.

债务 β 值用于衡量与债务融资相关的风险。

debt capacity

借债能力

Extent to which an entity can support and/or

实体能够支持和(或)获取贷款的

obtain loan finance. A project's debt capacity denotes its ability to act as security for a loan.

程度。一个项目的借债能力说明了其作为担保品获得贷款的能力。

deep discount bond

Bond offered at a large discount on the face value of the debt so that s significant proportion of the return to the investor comes by way of a capital gain on redemption, rather than through interest payments.

高折价债券

以大幅度低于面值折价发行的债券,投资者主要通过以面值赎回而不是利息收入来获得绝大部分投资收益。

demerger

In a spin-off (or demerger)a new entity is created, where the shares of that new entity are owned by the shareholders of the entity that made the transfer of assets into the new entity. There are now two entities, each owning some of the assets of the original single entity. The ownership has not changed, and in theory the value of the two individual entities should be the same as the value of the original single entity.

拆分

拆分会产生新的实体,新实体的股份由将转移资产至新实体的股东所持有。现在有两个实体,每个实体都拥有原有单一实体的某些资产。所有权没有发生变化,且理论上两个新实体的价值之和与原有单一实体的价值相同。

discount rate（capital investment appraisal）

Percentage rate used to discount future cash flows generated by a capital project.

折现率(资本投资评估)

用于将某个资本项目未来现金流折现的百分比。

discounted cash flow（DCF）

Discounting of the projected net cash flows of a capital project to ascertain its return or present value. The methods commonly used are:

discount payback: The discount rate is used to calculate the present values of

折现现金流量

对某个资本项目的预计现金净流量进行折现,以确定其收益或现值。常用方法有:

折现回收期:利用折现率计算某一期间的现金流量现值,然后在此基

periodic cash flows with a payback period then being calculated.

net present value（NPV）：The discount rate is chosen and the present value is expressed as a sum of money.

yield or internal rate of return（IRR）：The calculation determines the return in the form of a percentage.

See "capital investment appraisal" "net present value" "internal rate of return" and "discounted payback".

础上计算出回收期。

净现值：选定折现率，列示总现值。

收益率或内部收益率：通过计算，确定收益百分比。

参见"资本投资评估""净现值""内部收益率"和"折现回收期"。

discounted payback

Capital investment method with the aim of determining the period of time required to recover initial cash outflow when net cash inflows are discounted at the opportunity cost of capital. Also see "payback" and "discounted cash flow".

折现回收期

一种资本投资评估方法，旨在确定当以资本的机会成本对净现金流入进行折现后，从中收回初始现金流出的年限。亦请参见"回收期"和"折现现金流量"。

divestment

Disposal of part of its activities by an entity.

撤资

实体处置其部分活动。

dividend growth model

Way of assessing the value of shares by capitalising future dividends that grow at a constant rate.

股利增长模型

通过按恒定的速率增长对未来股利予以资本化来评估股票价值的一种方法。

Dividend irrelevancy theory

See"Modigliani and Miller".

股息无关论

参见"M & M理论"。

dividend yield

Post-tax dividend return on market

股息率

税后股息收益与股票市场价值的百

value offered by the shares shown as a percentage.

$$\frac{\text{Dividend per share net of any taxes deducted at source}}{\text{Market price per share}} \times 100\%$$

分比。

$$\frac{每股税后净股利}{每股市价} \times 100\%$$

dividend growth

An analysis of growth rates of earnings and dividends can enable investors to make an assessment of the performance of an entity. High growth rates in earnings and dividends are usually viewed positively.

The growth rate for a single year is：

$$[(\text{current figure/last year's figure}) - 1] \times 100\%$$

股利增长率

对股利增长率进行分析可以使投资者对实体业绩做出评估。股利增长率高通常被视为积极的信号。

单一年度的股利增长率为：

$$[(本年数字 \div 上一年度的数字) - 1] \times 100\%$$

documentary credit

Arrangement，used in the finance of international transactions，whereby a bank undertakes to make a payment to a third party on bahalf of a customer.

跟单信用证

国际贸易财务中所使用的一种付款安排，银行代表客户向第三方付款。

double taxation agreement

Agreement between two countries intended to avoid the double taxation of income which would otherwise be subject to taxation in both.

双重征税协议

两国共同签订的、避免两个国家重复征收所得税的协定。

downside risk

The term "risk" is often associated with the chance of something "bad" happening, and that a future outcome will be adverse. This type of risk is called downside risk，which is a risk involving the possibility of loss，with no chance of gain.

下行风险

"风险"一词往往与"坏"事发生的几率有关，而且未来的结果也是不利的。下行风险是一种可能发生损失而不可能有收益的风险。

earnings based valuation

The projected earnings for a business will give an indication of the value of that business. For example, a business with high forecasted earnings will be attractive to a potential purchaser, and hence will be valued highly.

基于收益的价值评估

企业的预计收益是判断企业价值的一个指标。例如,预计收益越高的企业对于潜在的买主更有吸引力,因此企业的估价更高。

earnings yield

$$\frac{\text{Earnings per share}}{\text{Market price of a share}} \times 100\%$$

As a percentage, indicates the total amount earned in respect of each equity share in issue, in relation to the market price of the share. The earnings yield computation can also be based on the aggregate earnings and the market value of the equity capital.

收益率

$$\frac{每股收益}{每股市价} \times 100\%$$

该比率能够反映已发行的每股普通股在当前市价下获得的收益情况。此外,收益率还可以根据收益总额和股本市值计算得出。

earn-outarrangement

A procedure whereby owners/managers selling an entity receive a portion of their consideration linked to the financial performance of the business during a specified period after the sale. The arrangement gives a measure of security to the new owners, who pass some of the financial risk associated with the purchase of a new entity to the sellers.

盈利能力支付计划

出售实体的所有人/管理人在完成出售后的一段特定期间内,收到与已出售公司财务业绩挂钩的部分对价的过程。这种安排能够给予实体新所有人一定的保证,将与购买新实体有关的部分财务风险转移给卖方。

economic exposure

Risk that a company's future cash flows will vary as a result of changes in exchange rates.

经济风险敞口

由于汇率波动而导致公司未来现金流量发生变化的风险。

economic value added (EVA)™

Profit less a charge for capital employed in the period. Accounting profit may be adjusted, for example, for the treatment of goodwill and research and development expenditure, before economic value added is calculated(Stern Stewart & Co.).

economies of scale

Reductions in unit average costs caused by increasing the scale of production.

economies of scope

Reduction in unit average costs caused by the simultaneous production of a number of related products, permitting benefits. such as the sharing of joint costs cover a larger volume than would otherwise be possible.

efficient markets hypothesis (EMH)

Hypothesis that the stock market responds immediately to all available information with the effect that an individual investor cannot, in the long run, expect to obtain greater than average returns from a diversified portfolio of shares. There are three forms:

weak form: Market in which security prices instantaneously reflect all information on past price and volume changes in the market.

semi-strong form: Market in which security prices reflect all publicly available information.

经济增加值

一定时期内的利润减去投入资本后的剩余价值。在计算经济增加值之前,可能要对会计利润进行调整,例如,调整商誉和研发费用(斯特恩·斯图尔特公司)。

规模经济

因生产规模扩大引起单位平均成本下降。

范围经济

因同时生产多种相关产品引起单位平均成本下降,从而创造利润。

有效市场假说

假设股票市场能够对所有可获得信息迅速做出响应,从而从长远来看,个人投资者将无法从多元化证券组合中获得超出平均水平的回报。有效市场假说的三种形态:

弱式有效市场假说:在该市场内,证券价格能够对以往所有的市场价格和成交量变动信息即刻做出响应。

半强式有效市场假说:在该市场内,证券价格反映了所有已公开的信息。

strong form：Market in which security prices reflect instantaneously all information available to investors whether publicly available or otherwise.

强式有效市场假说：在该市场内，证券价格能够对投资者可获得的所有信息即刻做出响应，不管这些信息是否公开。

electronic funds transfer

电子资金转账

System used by the banking sector for the movement of funds between accounts and for the provision of services to the customer.

银行业用于直接在账户之间划拨资金和向客户提供服务的系统。

equity beta

权益 β 值

See "geared beta".

参见"杠杆 β 值"。

eurobond

欧洲债券

Bond sold outside the jurisdiction of the country in whose currency the bond is denominated.

票面金额货币并非发行国家当地货币的债券。

eurodollars

欧洲美元

US dollars deposited with，or borrowed from，a bank outside the US.

存放在美国以外银行的美元存款或是从这些银行借到的美元贷款。

ex

除

"without"，as in ex dividend，where security purchases do not include rights to the next divided payment，and ex rights，where rights attaching to share ownership, such as a scrip issue，are not transferred to a new purchaser.

"不附有"之意，"除息"是指购买证券时，不附带接收下一次股息派付的权利，"除权"是指不向新购买人转让股份所有权随附的如发行红股之类的权利。

ex rights price

除权价

See "TERP".

参见"理论除权价(TERP)"。

exchange controls

Restrictions in the convertibility of a currency, generally enforced by central banks on the instruction of national governments.

外汇管制

限制货币自由兑换，通常由中央银行按照国家政府的指示执行。

exchange difference

Difference(profit or loss)resulting from translating a given number of units of one currency into another currency at different exchange rates(IAS 21).

汇率差异

在不同汇率下将一定数量的某一货币转换为另一种货币所产生的损益（《国际会计准则第 21 号》）。

exchange rate

Rate at which a national currency exchanges for other national currencies, being set by the interaction of demand and supply of the various currencies in the foreign exchange market (floating exchange rate), or by government intervention in order to maintain a constant rate of exchange (fixed exchange rate).

closing rate：Spot transactions ruling at the balance sheet date, being the mean of the buying and selling rates at the close of business on the day for which the rate is to be ascertained.

forward exchange rate：Set for the exchange of currencies at some future date.

spot exchange rate：Set for the immediate delivery of a currency.

汇率

一国货币兑换为另一国货币的比率，由外汇市场内不同货币的供需情况来确定（浮动汇率）或者政府干预设定恒定的汇率（固定汇率）。

收盘汇率：就资产负债表日的现货交易而言，当天营业结束时买入汇率与卖出汇率的平均值。

远期汇率：未来某天的外汇汇率。

即期汇率：立即兑换外币的汇率。

executive share options（ESOPS）

An ESOP is part of a manager's remuneration package. The options can

管理层股票期权

管理层股票期权是管理层薪酬的组成部分。管理层可在等待期结束后

normally be exercised on a specific date at the end of the vesting period. If the manager resigns or leaves the company during that period then the options will lapse.

exercise price

The price at which an option to purchase or to sell shares or other items(call option or put option) may be exercised. See "call option", "put option".

expected value/payoff

Financial forecast of the outcome of a course of action multiplied by the probability of achieving that outcome. The probability is expressed as a value ranging from 0 to 1.

expectations theory

$$S_1 = S_0 \times \frac{1 + r_{var}}{1 + r_{base}}$$

S_0 = spot rate of exchange

S_1 = expected rate of exchange in one year

r_{var} and r_{base} are the interest rates associated with the variable and base currencies respectively.

The expectations theory shows that the spot rate in the future can be forecast by adjuting the spot rate of exchange to reflect the differential in interest rates between the two countries.

externalities

Benefits or costs arising from an activity

行权价

行使购买或出售股份及其他工具权利("认购期权"或"认沽期权")时的价格。参见"认购期权"和"认沽期权"。

期望值/收益

某项措施期望实现的成果可能性乘以预计的财务收益。可能性介于0~1之间。

期望理论

$$S_1 = S_0 \times \frac{1 + r_{var}}{1 + r_{base}}$$

S_0 = 即期外汇汇率

S_1 = 1年后的预期汇率

r_{var} 和 r_{base} 表示与可变货币和基础货币相对应的利率。

期望理论表明,通过调整即期汇率来反映两国的利率差就可以预测未来即期汇率。

外部性

实体或个人进行某项活动,而该

which does not accrue to the entity or person carrying on the activity.

factoring

Sale of debts to a third party(the factor) at a discount in return for prompt cash. A factoring service may be with recourse，in which case the supplier takes the risk of the debt not being paid，or without recourse when the factor takes the risk. See "invoice discounting".

fair value hedge

The risk being hedged is the change in the fair value of an asset or liability，which is already recognised in the financial statement. Hedged accounting requires both the hedged item and the hedging instrument to be measured at fair value at each year end.

financial asset

Any asset that is：

(a) cash；

(b) an equity instrument of another entity；

(c) a contractual right：(ⅰ) to receive cash or another financial asset from another entity，or(ⅱ) to exchange financial asset or financial liabilities with another entity under conditions that are potentially favourably to the entity；or

(d) a contract that will or may be settled in the entity's own equity instruments and is：(ⅰ) a non-derivative for which the entity is or may be obliged to receive a variable number of the entity's own equity instruments，or

活动所产生的收益或成本并不归属于实体或个人。

保理

为了立即获得现金，以一定折扣向第三方(保理商)出售债务。保理服务可分为有追索权保理和无追索权保理，前者由供应商承担未偿还债务的风险，后者由保理商承担风险。参见"发票贴现"。

公允价值套期

被套期的风险指的是资产或负债公允价值的变动，并且已经在财务报表中得以确认。套期会计要求被套期项目和套期工具都要在每年年末以公允价值计量。

金融资产

包括：

(a) 现金；

(b) 其他实体的权益工具；

(c)以下合同权利：(ⅰ)从其他实体获取现金或其他金融资产的权利，或(ⅱ)在对自身潜在有利的条件下，与其他实体交换金融资产或金融负债的权利；

(d) 将有可能以实体自身的权益工具结算的合同，且为(ⅰ)实体将会或有义务接收数量可变的自身权益工具的非衍生合同，或(ⅱ)以固定现金金额或其他金融资产交换固定数量的

（ⅱ）a derivative that will or may be settle other than by the exchange of a fixed amount of cash or other financial asset for a fixed number of the entity's own equity instruments(IAS 32).

实体自身权益工具以外的方式结算的衍生合同(《国际会计准则第 32 号——金融工具》)。

financial control

Control of the performance of an entity by setting a range of financial targets and the monitoring of actual performance towards these targets.

财务控制

通过设定一系列财务目标并对比这些目标的实际业绩进行监控来对实体业绩进行控制。

financial instrument

Any contract that gives rise to a financial asset of one entity and a financial liability of another entity(IAS 32).

金融工具

在两个实体间形成金融资产和金融负债的合同(《国际会计准则第 32 号——金融工具》)。

financial instrument, derivative

Financial instrument or other contract with all three of the following characteristics:

（a）its value changes in response to the change in specified interest rate, financial instrument price, commodity price, foreign exchange rate, index of prices or rates, credit rating or credit index, or other variable, provided in the case of a non-financial variable that the variable is not specific to a party to the contract(sometimes called the underlying);

（b）it requires no initial net investment or an initial net investment that is smaller than would be required for other types of contracts that would be expected to have a similar response to changes in market forces; and

金融衍生工具

同时具有以下三大特征的金融工具或其他合同:

（a）价值随特定利率、金融工具价格、商品价格、外汇汇率、价格指数、信用等级、信用指数或其他变量的变动而变动,且提供的非财务变量与合同的任何一方不存在特定关系(有时也称作"基础金融工具");

（b）不要求初始净投资,或初始投资小于对市场情况变化有类似反应的其他类型的合同;及

(c) it is settled at a future date(IAS 39).

financial leverage/gearing

Amount of debt, in relation to equity, in the capital structure of an entity or debt interest in relation to profit. An entity with no gearing has no debt.

financial liability

Any liability that is:

(a) a contractual obiligation:（ⅰ）to deliver cash or another financial asset to another entity;or（ⅱ）to exchange financial assets or financial liabilities with another entity under conditions that are potentially unfavourable to the entity;or

(b) a contract that will or may be settled in the entity's own equity instruments and is:（ⅰ）a nonderivative for which the entity is or may be obliged to deliver a variable number of the entity's own equity instruments ;or（ⅱ）a derivative that may or will be settled other than by the exchange of a fixed amount of cash or another financial asset for a fixed amount of the entity's own equity instruments(IAS 32).

financial management

Management of all the processes associated with the efficient acquisition and deployment of both short-and long-term financial resources.

（c）在未来某个日期结算(《国际会计准则第 39 号》)。

财务杠杆/举债经营

在实体的资本结构中,与股本有关的债务金额或者与利润有关的债务利息。不举债经营的实体不存在债务。

金融负债

包括:

（a）合同义务:（ⅰ）向其他实体支付现金或其他金融资产,或（ⅱ）在对自身潜在不利的条件下,与其他实体交换金融资产或金融负债;

（b）将会或有可能以实体自身的权益工具结算的合同,且为:（ⅰ）实体将会或有可能必须支付可变数量的自身权益工具的非衍生合同,或（ⅱ）以固定现金金额或其他金融资产交换固定数量的实体自身权益工具以外的方式结算的衍生合同(《国际会计准则第32 号——金融工具》)。

财务管理

与高效收购、长短期财务资源配置有关的所有流程管理。

financing decision

For both non-current asset and working capital investment，the financial manager must decide on most appropriate type and source of funding. Financial decisions relate to acquiring the optimumfinance to meet financial objectives and seeing that non-current assets and working capital are effectively managed.

融资决策

对于非流动资产和营运资本的投资,财务经理必须决定最恰当的资金类型及来源。融资决策涉及获取最优的融资资金以实现财务目标,并且非流动资产和营运资本都得到有效的管理。

Fisher effect

The Fisher effect looks at the relationship between interest rates and inflation. The relationship between the nominal rate of interest，the real rate of interest and inflation can be expressed by the formula：

$$1 + \frac{\text{nominal}}{\text{rate}} = \left(1 + \frac{\text{real}}{\text{rate}}\right) \times \left(1 + \frac{\text{inflation}}{\text{rate}}\right)$$

费雪效应

费雪效应揭示了利率与通货膨胀之间的关系。名义利率、实际利率和通货膨胀中间的关系可用以下公式表达：

$$1 + \frac{名义}{利率} = \left(1 + \frac{实际}{利率}\right) \times \left(1 + \frac{通货}{膨胀率}\right)$$

floating rate financial assets and financial liabilities

Financial assets and financial liabilities that attract an interest charge and have their interest rate reset at least once a year. For the purpose of the FRS，financial assets and financial liabilities that have their interest rate reset less frequently than once a year are to be treated as fixed rate financial assets and financial liabilities(FRS 13).

浮动利率金融资产和金融负债

具有利息费用且利率至少每年重新设定一次的金融资产和金融负债。根据财务报告准则的规定,利率设定频率少于1年一次的金融资产和金融负债被视作固定利率金融资产和金融负债(《财务报告准则第13号——衍生和其他金融工具:披露》)。

flotation

Shares are offered for sale to investors，through an issuing house. The offer could be

浮动

股份通过证券发行公司出售给投资者。公司可以设定一个固定价格,

made at a fixed price set by the company, or in a tender offer investors are invited to tender for new shares issued at their own suggested price.

也可以通过招标竞价，由投资者们提出建议股价。

floors

See "caps".

利率下限

参见"利率上限"。

forecasting cash flows

See "free cash flows".

预测现金流

参见"自由现金流"。

foreign direct investment (FDI)

Establishment of new overseas facilities or the expansion of existing overseas facilities by an investor. FDI may be inward (domestic investment by overseas companies) or outward (overseas investment by domestic companies)

外国直接投资

投资者新成立境外公司或扩充现有境外公司。外国直接投资可以是对内投资(境外公司对内投资)或对外投资(内资公司对外投资)。

Forfoiting

Purchase of financial instruments such as bills of exchange or letters of credit on a non-recourse basis by a forfoiting, who deducts interest (in the form of a discount) at an agreed rate for the period covered by the notes. The forfoiter assumes the responsibility for claiming the debt from the importer(buyer) who initially accepted the financial instrument drawn by the seller of the goods. Traditionally, forfoiting is fixed-rate, medium-term (one-to five-year) finance. See "invoice discounting".

福费廷

买断行购买无追索权的汇票或信用证等金融工具，并在票据涵盖期内按商定的比率扣除利息（以折扣形式）。买断行承担向最初已接受卖方所提取金融工具的进口方（买方）申索债务的职责。传统的无追索权融资为固定利率的中期融资（1～5年）。参见"发票贴现"。

forward contract

Agreement to exchange different currencies

远期合约

在未来某个特定日期按特定汇率

at a specified future date and at a specified rate. The difference between the specified rate and the spot rate ruling on the date the contract was entered into is the discount or premium on the forward contract(SSAP 20).

兑换不同货币的协议。特定汇率与合同当日即期汇率的差异为远期合同的折价或溢价(标准会计实务公告第 20 号)。

forward rate agreement (FRAs)

A FRA is a forward contract on an interest rate for a future short-term loan or deposit. Forward rate agreements can be used to fix the interest charge on a floating rate loan.

远期利率协议

远期利率协议是一个针对未来短期借款或存款的远期合约。远期利率协议被用来固定浮动利率贷款的利息费用。

free cash flow

Cash flow from operations after deducting interest, tax, preference dividends and ongoing capital expenditure, but excluding capital expenditure associated with strategic acquisitions and/or disposal and ordinary share dividends.

自由现金流量

经营活动产生的,扣除利息、税金、优先股股利以及持续资本支出后的现金流量,但上述持续资本支出不包括与战略收购和(或)处置以及普通股股利有关的资本开支。

functional currency

Currency of the primary economic environment in which the entity operates (IAS 21).

功能性货币

实体营运活动所处的主要经济环境使用的货币(《国际会计准则第 21 号——外汇汇率变动的影响》)。

fundamental analysis

Analysis of external and internal influences that directly affect the operations of a company with a view to assisting in investment decisions. Information accessed might include fiscal/monetary policy, financial statements, industry trends and competitor analysis. See "technical analysis".

基本面分析

对直接影响公司营运活动的内外部影响进行分析,以协助制定投资决策。所获取的信息包括财政/货币政策、财务报表、行业趋势和竞争对手分析。参见"技术分析"。

futures contract

Contract relating to currencies, interest rates, commodities or shares that obliges the buyer (seller) to purchase (sell) the specified quantity of the item represented in the contract at a predetermined price at the expiration of the contract. Unlike forward contracts, which are entered into privately, futures contracts are traded on organised exchanges, carry standard terms and conditions have specific maturities and are subject to rules concerning margin requirements.

futures market

Exchange-traded market for the purchase or sale of a standard quantity of an underlying item such as currencies, commodities or shares for settlement at a future date at an agreed price.

futures, interest-rate

IRFs are similar in principle to forward rate agreements in that they give a commitment to an interest rate for a set period.

geared beta

The equity (geared) beta measures the systematic business risk and the systematic financial risk of a company's shares.

gearing

The relationship between an entity's

期货合同

与货币、利率、商品或股票有关的合同,买方(卖方)必须在合同届满时,以事先确定的价格购买(出售)合同约定数量的标的物。与远期合同不同的是,远期合同是交易双方私下签订的,而期货合同是在组织有序的交易所交易,具有标准条款和条件以及明确的到期日,并且需要遵守与保证金要求有关的规定。

期货市场

在未来某个日期,以商定的价格买入或卖出标准数量的标的物(如货币、商品、股票)的交易市场。

利率期货

利率期货与远期利率协议大体相似,均对未来一段时期的利率给出承诺。

杠杆 β 值

权益(杠杆)β 值用于衡量企业的系统经营风险和系统财务风险。

杠杆比率

实体的借入资金(包括优先股和

borrowings, which includes both prior charge capital and long-term debt, and its shareholders' funds.

长期负债）与股东自有资金之间的关系。

gearing risk

Risk in the way a business is financed (debt vs. equity) (sometimes this is considered part of interest rate risk).

杠杆风险

企业融资方式（债务融资 VS 权益融资）所引起的风险（这种风险有时被视为是利率风险的组成部分）。

hedge

Transaction to reduce or eliminate an exposure to risk.

套期保值

减少或消除敞口风险的交易。

hedge accounting rules

Hedge accounting may only be used if certain conditions are met: arrangement must be designated as a hedge at the inception; hedge is expected to be highly effective (80% ~ 125%); effectiveness is capable of reliable measurement; assessment of effectiveness takes place on an ongoing basis.

There are three types of hedging arrangement: fair value hedge; cash-flow hedge; net investment in a foreign operation.

套期会计规则

套期会计只有在满足一定条件时才能使用：相关协议在一开始就必须被指定为一项套期；套期预计将高度有效（80%～125%）；有效性能够可靠计量；在持续的基础上对有效性进行评估。

套期协议有三种类型：公允价值套期、现金流量套期、境外经营净投资套期。

hedge funds

Generally actively managed with greater freedom than conventional mutual funds to borrow heavily and use high-risk investment strategies, such as selling short and using derivatives, to make absolute returns even in falling markets.

对冲基金

相比传统的共同基金，对冲基金的管理自由度更大，可以借入大量资金并使用高风险投资战略（例如卖空和使用衍生工具），即使是在市场下跌行情中也能获取绝对收益。

hedging, derivatives

A derivative is a financial instrument whose value depends on the price of some other financial asset or underlying factor (such as oil, gold, interest rate or currencies).

hedging: Used as a risk management tool to reduce/eliminate financial risk.

hedging, external techniques

If a company wants to remove transaction risk it is also possible to hedge this externally in a number of ways including: forward contracts, money market hedges, futures, options, swaps.

hire purchase

Hire purchase is similar to leasing, except that the legal title to the asset passes to the hire purchase customer on payment of the final installment payment. In a lease agreement ownership of the asset does not transfer to the lease.

hire purchase contract

A contract for the hire of an asst that contains a provision giving the hirer an option to acquire title to the asset upon the fulfilment of agreed conditions (IAS 17).

hurdle rate

Rate of return which a capital

衍生工具, 套期保值

衍生工具是一种财务工具, 它的价值取决于其他金融资产的价格或潜在因素(例如石油、黄金、利率或货币)。

套期保值: 一种减少或消除财务风险的风险管理工具。

套期保值的外部方法

如果一家公司想消除交易风险, 可以采用以下外部套期保值方法: 远期合约、货币市场套期、期货、期权、互换。

分期付款

除了在最后一次分期付款时资产的所有权转移至付款人之外, 分期付款与租赁类似。在租赁协议里, 资产的所有权不转移至承租人。

租购合同

包含了租借人在履行协定条件后有权获得资产所有权条款的资产租赁合同(《国际会计准则第 17 号》)。

门槛回报率

一项资本投资草案获得批准所要

investment proposal must achieve if it is to be accepted. Set by reference to the cost of capital, the hurdle rate may be increased above the basic cost of capital to allow for different levels of risk.

达到的回报率。门槛回报率参考资本成本设定,在基本资本成本的基础上再考虑不同程度的风险。

incremental yield

Measure used in capital investment appraisal where a choice lies between two projects. A rate of return is calculated for the difference between the cash flows of the projects.

增量收益率

在两个项目之间进行抉择时所采用的资本投资评估方法,该收益率由两个项目现金流量之间的差异计算得出。

inflation

General increase in the price level over time measured by a retail price index.

通货膨胀

物价水平随时间整体上升的程度,以零售价格指数来衡量。

initial public offering (IPO)

One of the most commonly used methods of issuing shares. AIPO is more suitable when a company seeks a listing on the stock exchange for the first time.

首次公开募股

发行股份最为常见的一种方法。当一家公司谋求首次在证券交易所上市,IPO 是比较好的一种方式。

IPO, Advisors

Investment banks usually take the lead role in an IPO and will advise on: the appointment of other specialists (e. g. lawyers); stock exchange requirements; forms of an new capital to be issued and issue price; arrangements for underwriting; publishing the offer.

Stockbrokers provide advice on the various methods of obtaining a listing. They may

IPO 财务顾问

首次公开募股的顾问有投资银行、股票经纪人和机构投资者,它们为企业上市提供各方面建议。

投资银行在 IPO 中发挥着主导作用,在以下方面提供建议:其他专业中介机构的选聘(如:律师);证券交易所的要求;新股发行的形式和发行价;承销安排;公布报价等。

股票经纪人在获得投资者方面提供建议,他们一般和投资银行一起确

work with investment banks on identifying institutional investors，but usually they are involved with smaller issues and placings.

认机构投资者。不过，他们一般出现在小规模的发行和承销中。

Institutional investors have little direct involvement other than as investors，agreeing to buy a certain number of shares.

机构投资者和普通投资者类似，基本不参与 IPO，只是决定购买的股票数量。

insolvency

破产

Inability of a debtor to pay debts when they fall due.

债务人无能力偿还到期债务。

interest rates

利率

Changes in interest rates affect the economy in many ways. The following consequences are the main effects of an increase in interest rates：spending falls，asset values fall，foreign funds are attracted into the country，the exchange rate rises，inflation falls.

利率的变化会以多种形式影响经济。利率上升带来的主要后果包括：支出减少、资产价值下降、吸引外资进入本国、外汇汇率上升以及通胀下降。

interest rates caps

利率上限

See "caps".

参见"利率上限"。

interest rates collars

利率上下限

See "collar".

参见"领子期权"。

interest rates floors

利率下限

See "caps".

参见"利率上限"。

interest rates forward-rate agreement

利率远期利率协议

See "forward-rate agreements".

参见"远期利率协议"（FRAs）。

interest rates futures

See "interest-rate".

interest rates guarantees

See "caps".

interest rates swaps

An agreement whereby the parties agree to swap a floating stream of interest payments and vice versa.

interest yield

Annual rate of interest earned on a security，excluding the effect of any increase in price to maturity.

inter-firm comparison

Systematic and detailed comparison of the performance of different entities generally operating in a common industry. Entities participating in such a scheme normally provide standardised，and therefore comparable，information to the scheme administrator，who then distributes to participating members only the information supplied by participants. Normally the information distributed is in the form of ratios，or in a format which prevents the identity of individual scheme members from being identified.

internal rate of return，IRR

Annual percentage return achieved by a

利率期货

参见"利率"。

利率担保

参见"利率上限"。

利率互换

一项双方同意交换浮动利息支付的协议。

利息收益率

证券利息的年利率，不包括价格上涨对到期日的影响。

公司间比较

对同一行业内不同实体的业绩进行深入的系统比较。参与比较的实体通常会向比较管理者提供标准化的可比信息，然后比较管理者再向参与成员分配实体所提供的信息。通常，信息会按一定比率，或者以确保参与比较的成员的身份不被识别出来的形式进行分配。

内含报酬率

某个项目能够实现的年度收益百

project，at which the sum of the discounted cash inflows over the life of the project is equal to the sum of the discounted cash outflows. See "discounted cash flow".

分比,项目生命周期内的折现现金流入总额与折现现金流出总额相等。参见"折现现金流量"。

international debt finance

Large companies can borrow money in foreign currencies as well as their own domestic currency from banks at home or abroad. The main reason for wanting to borrow in a foreign currency is to fund a foreign investment project or foreign subsidiary.

国际债务融资

大型企业能够从本国或国外的银行获得外币借款,以便为国外的投资项目或子公司提供资金。

international Fisher effect

See "Fisher effect".

国际费雪效应

参见"费雪效应"。

intrinsic value

The difference between the current price of the underlying asset and its option strike (exercise)price.

内在价值

内在价值是标的资产现货价格和期权行权价之间的差额。

investment decision

Financial managers have responsibility for the allocation of financial resources to achieve the organisation's objectives. An important part of their job is to understand the short，medium and long-term capital requirements for investment in fixed assets and working capital that fits with the overall strategy.

Whilst financial managers are unlikely to be solely responsible for the final choice of capital investment projects to be undertaken，they will be actively involved in the evalua-

投资决策

财务经理有责任对财务资源进行配置,以期实现组织目标。他们工作的一个重要内容是针对实现总体战略所需的固定资产和营运资金,深入理解短期、中期以及长期资金投资需求。

尽管财务经理不是资本投资项目抉择的唯一决策者,但他们可以积极地参与到投资机会的评估活动中。

tion of possible investment opportunities.

investor ratios

Investors will wish to assess the performance of the shares they have invested in. There are number of ratios which will be of specific interest to investors，EPS，P/E…

投资者比率分析

投资者希望能够对他们所投资的股票业绩进行评估,有大量的比率可供投资者分析所用,包括了 EPS、P/E……

invoice discounting

Sale of debts to a third party at a discount in return for prompt cash. The administration is managed in such a way that the debtor is generally vnaware of the discounter's involvement and continues to pay the supplier. See "factoring" and "foiting".

发票贴现

为了立即获得现金,以一定折扣向第三方出售债务。需对贴现过程进行管理,防止债务方不清楚原债权人已经贴现了发票,继续向原债权人支付款项。参见"保理"和"无追索权融资"。

irrelevancy theory

See "Modigliani and Miller(M & M)".

股利无关论

参见"M & M 理论"。

issue cost

The costs that are incurred directly in connection with the issue of a capital instrument，that is those costs which would have not been incurred if the specific instrument in question had not been issued(FRS 4).

发行成本

因发行某个资本工具而直接产生的成本,即如果不发行该工具,就不会产生的成本(《财务报告准则第 4 号》)。

junk bond

High-yielding bond issued on low-grade security. The issue of junk bonds has most commonly been linked with takeover activity. Bonds may also assume junk status when the issuer is at risk of insolvency.

垃圾债券

以低评级发行的高收益债券。大多数情况下,垃圾债券的发行与收购活动有关。如果发行人具有无力偿债的风险,其发行的债券也被认为是垃圾债券。

junior debt

Junior debt is usually called mezzanine finance，which is an intermediate stage between senior debt and equity finance in relation to both risk and return.

次级债务

次级债务通常也被称为夹层融资，就风险和回报而言，处于优先债务和股权融资之间的中间阶段。

lagging

Delaying a payment for as long as possible.

延后支付

尽可能推迟付款。

leading

Making a payment before it is due.

提前支付

在到期前付款。

lender /gearing ratios

Gearing is the mix of debt to equity with a firm's permanent capital. There are two particularly useful measures：

（a）Capital gearing—a statement of financial position(balance sheet) measure.

（b）Interest cover—a statement of profit or loss measure.

贷款/杠杆比率

杠杆比率是公司债务与永久性权益资本的一种搭配比率，有两种有效的衡量指标：

（a）资本杠杆率——财务状况（资产负债表）衡量法。

（b）利息保障倍数——利润表衡量法。

Leveraged buyout

A leveraged buyout occurs when an investor，typically a private equity firm，acquires a controlling interest in a company's equity and where a significant percentage of the purchase price is financed through leverage（borrowing）.

杠杆收购

当一位投资者（主要是私人股权公司）想要控制某家公司的股权，而大部分收购资金是通过杠杆（借贷）融资方式获得的，那么这就是杠杆收购。

LIBID

LIBID is the rate of interest that a top-

伦敦银行同业拆入利率

伦敦银行同业拆入利率是在伦敦

rated London bank could obtain on short-term wholesale deposits with another bank in the London money markets.

货币市场上，一家银行为获取另一家银行的短期大额存款而支付的利率。

liquidation

Winding up of a company, in which the assets are sold, liabilities settled as far as possible and any remaining cash returned to the members. Liquidation may be voluntary or compulsory.

清算

公司清盘，此时，公司将尽可能地出售资产，偿还债务并将剩余资金返还给股东。清算可分为自愿清算和强制清算。

liquidity

Availability of sufficient funds to meet financial commitments as they fall due (refer to IAS 30).

流动性

拥有履行到期财务承诺的充足资金（参见《国际会计准则第 30 号——银行和类似金融机构财务报表中的披露》）。

liquidity risk

The risk that an entity will encounter difficulty in meeting obligations associated with financial liabilities.

流动性风险

实体在履行财务负债义务时面临困难的风险。

listing

When an entity obtains a listing for its shares on a stock exchange this is referred to as a flotation or an Initial Public Offering.

上市

当一家实体的股票获准在股票交易市场挂牌，就被称作上市或首次公开募股。

loans

See "debt-finance".

贷款

参见"债务融资"。

London interbank offered rate (LIBOR)

伦敦银行同业拆借利率

Rate of interest at which banks borrow

银行在伦敦银行同业拆借市场借

funds in the London interbank market for a given maturity, normally ranging between overnight and one year.

入一定期限（通常在隔夜到 1 年之间）的资金时的利率。

London International Financial Futures and Options Exchange (LIFFE)

伦敦国际金融期货及期权交易所

The combined French, Belgian, Portuguese and Dutch exchange operator. Now known as Euronext. liffe since its takeover in 2002 by Euronext.

融合了法国、比利时、葡萄牙以及荷兰等国的交易机构。2002 年被欧洲交易所（Euronext）收购后，更名为 Euronext. liffe。

management buy-in (MBI)

外部管理团队收购

New team of managers makes an offer to an entity to buy the whole entity, a subsidiary or a section of it, with the intention of taking over the entity.

新的管理团队出于接管实体的目的，向实体发出购买整个实体、子公司或部分业务的要约。

management buy-out (MBO)

管理层收购

Purchase of a business from its existing owners by members of the management team, generally in association with a financing institution. Where a large proportion of the new finance required to purchase the business is raised by external borrowing, the buy-out is described as leveraged.

管理团队向公司现有所有者购买该公司，这种收购通常与融资机构有关。当大部分收购资金是从外部借款筹集而来时，此项收购可被称为"杠杆收购"。

market risk premium

市场风险溢价

Difference between the expected rate of return on a market portfolio and the risk-free rate of return over the same period. See "risk, market/systematic".

某个市场投资组合的预期收益率与同期无风险收益率之间的差额。参见"市场/系统性风险"。

market value added（MVA）

The difference between a company's market value（derived from the share price）and its economic book value（the amount of capital that shareholders and debt holders have committed to the firm throughout its existence，including any retained earnings）.

memorandum of association

Document which，with the articles of association，provides the legal constitution of a company. The memorandum states the name and registered office of the company. It also defines its powers and objects and usually states that the liability of its members is limited. See "articles of association".

merger

Business combination that results in the creation of a new reporting entity formed from the combining parties，in which the shareholders of the combining entities come together in a partnership for the mutual sharing of the risks and benefits of the combined entity，and in which no party to the combination in substance obtains control over any other，or is otherwise seen to be dominant，whether by virtue of the proportion of its shareholders' rights in the combined entity，the influence of its directors or otherwise（FRS 6）.

However，IFRS 3 Business Combinations requires all business combinations to be accounted for by applying the purchase method

市场增加值

公司的市值(按股价计算)与其经济账面值(股东和债权人在公司存续期间向公司投入的资本金额,包括留存收益)之间的差额。

公司章程

公司章程与细则共同构成公司的法律章程文件。章程列明公司的名称和登记注册的办公地点,界定了公司的权力和目标,通常也会说明股东的责任为有限责任。参见"组织章程细则"。

兼并

企业兼并将形成一个由合并各方组成的新的报告实体,在新实体中,合并方的股东将共同承担被合并实体的风险和利益。但是,无论在合并实体中占据多少份额、董事是否具有影响力,合并各方均不获得针对其他合并方的实质控制权,或被认为在合并实体中占据主导地位(《财务报告准则第6号》)。

然而,《国际财务报告准则第3号》要求根据收购法来处理所有的企业合并业务,以便识别购买方和出售

which necessitates the identification of a purchaser and seller and so effectively rules out the possibility of using merger accounting as opposed to acquisition accounting.

A demerger takes place when the merger process is reversed, and separate entities emerge from the merged body.

方,从而有效地消除使用兼并会计而不是收购会计进行处理的可能性。

与并购过程相对应的是企业拆分,被兼并企业为拆分为多个独立的实体。

Modigliani and Miller (M&M)

M&M's dividend irrelevancy theory says that the pattern of dividend payout should be irrelevant. As long as companies continue to invest in positive NPV projects, the wealth of the shareholders should increase whether or not the company makes a dividend payment this year. See Figure 4.1.

M&M 理论

M&M 的股利无关理论认为股利分配不会影响股票价格。只要企业持续对净现值为正的项目进行投资,无论公司本年是否支付股利,股东财富都会增加。参见图表 4.1。

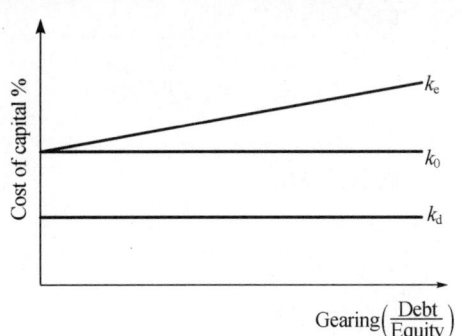

Figure 4.1　Modighani and Miller view (no taxation)

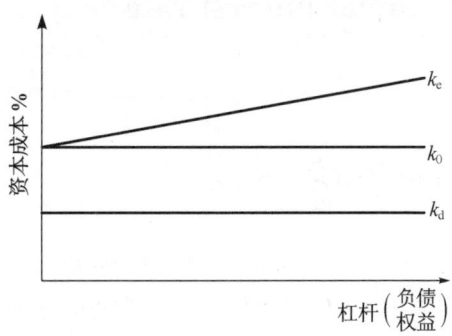

图表 4.1　M & M 理论(无税情况)

money market

Short-term wholesale market for securities usually maturing in less than one year such as certificates of deposit, treasury bills and commercial paper.

货币市场

通常在 1 年内到期的短期证券批发市场,包括存款证明、国债和商业票据。

moral hazard

Risk that the existence of a contract will

道德风险

合同的存在会导致合同一方或双

cause behavioural changes in one or both parties to the contract. For example, insuring an asset causes its owner to take less care of it.

方的行为发生变化的风险。例如,为一项资产投保导致其所有人疏于管理。

negotiable instrument

可转让票据

Document of title which can be freely traded such as a bill of exchange or other certificate of debt.

可以自由交易的凭证,例如汇票或其他债务凭证。

net present value (NPV)

净现值

Difference between the sum of the projected discounted cash inflows and outflows attributable to a capital investment or other long-term project. See "discounted cash flow".

归属于资本投资或其他长期项目的预测折现现金流入额与流出额之间的差额。参见"折现现金流量"。

nominal interest rate

名义利率

Interest rate expressed in money terms.

货币术语中表达的利率。

nominee holding

名义持股

Shareholding in a company registered in the name of an agent, instead of that of the owner.

以代理人而非所有人的名义登记持有公司股份。

offer for sale

公开发售

An invitation to the public to apply for shares in a company based on information contained in a prospectus.

邀请公众根据招股章程内载明的信息申请认购公司股份。

option

期权

Right of an option holder to buy or sell a specific asset on predetermined terms on, or

期权持有人在未来某一日期或之前按照事先确定的条款购买或出售特

before，a future date.

european-style option：Option that can be exercised only at the expiration date.

american-style option：Option that can be exercised at any time prior to expiration. See "call option"，"put option".

定资产的权利。

欧式期权：仅可在到期日执行的期权。

美式期权：可在到期日之前的任何时间执行的期权。参见"认购期权"、"认沽期权"。

over the counter (OTC) market

场外交易(OTC)市场

Securities trading carried on outside regulated exchanges. Allows tailor-made transactions.

在受监管的交易所之外进行证券交易，允许进行度身打造的交易。

over / under capitalisation

过度资本化/资本化不足

Surplus or deficiency of permanent capital in reation to the current level of activity of a business.

相对现有水平的企业活动而言，永久资本盈余或短缺。

overtrading

过量交易

The condition of an entity's which enters into commitments in excess of its available short-term resources. This can arise even if an entity is trading profitably，and is typically caused by a lengthy operating cycle or production cycle. Undercapitalised new business are prone to suffer from overtrading.

实体所作承诺超出其短期可用资源的情形。即便实体进行的交易可以获利，也可能会出现这种情形，这通常是因为营运周期或生产周期过长导致出现融资压力所致。新成立的资本化不足的公司比较容易出现过量交易的情况。

par

面值

Nominal value of a bond，being the price denominated for the purpose of setting the interest rate（coupon）payable.

债券的票面价值，即为设定应付利率（票息）而确定的价格。

partnership

合伙

Relationship which exits between

以共同利益为宗旨开展业务的个

persons carrying on business in common with a view to profit(UK Partnership Act 1890). The liability of the individual partners is unlimited unless the partnership agreement provides for any limitation.

The Uk Limited Partnership Act 1907 allows a partnership to contain one or more partners with limited liability so long as there is at least one partner with unlimited liability.

A partnership consists of not more than twenty persons, except in certain cases, for example practising solicitors, professional accountants and members of the Stock Exchange, where this figure may be exceeded. Other limited partnerships may exist.

人之间存在的一种关系(1890 年《英国合伙法》)。除非合伙协议中做出了限制,否则,各合伙人的责任为无限责任。

1907 年《英国有限合伙法》规定只要合伙企业中至少有 1 位合伙人承担无限责任,则允许该合伙企业包含 1 位或多位承担有限责任的合伙人。

合伙企业的合伙人不得超过 20 人,但少数情况例外,例如,如果合伙人是执业律师、专业顾问和证券交易所成员的话,则可以超过此上限。存在其他有限合伙企业。

partnership, limited liability (LLP)

有限责任合伙

Legal entity that combines the organisational flexibility and tax status of a partnership with limited liability for its members. This limited liability is possible because an LLP is a legal person separate from its members(UK Limited Liability Partnerships Act 2000).

融合了合伙企业的组织灵活性、纳税状况以及成员有限责任的一种法律实体。由于有限责任合伙企业是独立于其成员的法人(2000 年《英国有限责任合伙法》),因此有限责任是可能的。

payback

回收期

Time required for the cash inflows from a capital investment project to equal the cash outflows. See "discounted payback".

使得从资本投资项目中获得的现金流入等于现金流出与所需要的年限。参见"折现回收期"。

perpetuity

永续年金

Periodic payment continuing for a limitless period. See "annuity".

无限期的持续定期付款。参见"年金"。

placing

Method of raising share capital in which there is no public issue of shares, the shares being issued, rather, in a small number of large 'blocks', to persons or institutions who have previously agreed to purchase the shares at a predetermined price. See "private placement".

配售

在不公开发行股份的情况下,向先前同意按照预定价格购买股份的个人或机构发行少量大额股份来筹集股本的一种方式。参见"私人配售"。

present value

Cash equivalent now of a sum receivable or payable at a future date. See Figure 4.2.

现值

未来某个时点应收或应付款项的现金等价物现有价值。参见图表 4.2。

Figure 4. 2　Present Vclue table

Cumulative present value of ＄1
This table shows she present value of ＄1 per annum. Receivable or payable at the end of each year for n years.

Periods (n)	Discount rates(r)									
	1%	2%	3%	4%	5%	6%	7%	8%	9%	10%
1	0.990	0.980	0.971	0.962	0.952	0.943	0.935	0.926	0.917	0.909
2	1.970	1.942	1.913	1.886	1.859	1.833	1.808	1.783	1.759	1.736
3	2.941	2.884	2.829	2.775	2.723	2.673	2.624	2.577	2.531	2.487
4	3.902	3.808	3.717	3.630	3.546	3.465	3.387	3.312	3.240	3.170
5	4.853	4.713	4.580	4.452	4.329	4.212	4.100	3.993	3.890	3.791
6	5.795	5.601	5.417	5.242	5.076	4.917	4.767	4.623	4.486	4.355
7	6.727	6.472	6.230	6.002	5.786	5.582	5.389	5.206	5.033	4.868
8	7.652	7.325	7.020	6.733	6.463	6.210	5.971	5.747	5.535	5.335
9	8.566	8.162	7.786	7.435	7.108	6.802	6.515	6.247	5.995	5.759
10	9.471	8.983	8.530	8.1111	7.722	7.360	7.024	6.710	6.418	6.145
11	10.368	9.787	9.253	8.760	8.306	7.887	7.499	7.139	6.805	6.495
12	11.255	10.575	9.954	9.385	8.863	8.384	7.943	7.536	7.161	6.814
13	12.134	11.348	10.635	9.986	9.394	8.853	8.358	7.904	7.487	7.103
14	13.004	12.106	11.296	10.563	9.899	9.295	8.745	8.244	7.786	7.367
15	13.865	12.849	11.938	11.118	10.38	9.712	9.108	8.559	8.061	7.606

图表 4. 2　现 值 系 数 表

现值表
1元的现值为$(1+r)^{-n}$,其中 r ＝折现率,n ＝付款前的期数。

期数 (n)	折现率(r)									
	1%	2%	3%	4%	5%	6%	7%	8%	9%	10%
1	0.990	0.980	0.971	0.962	0.952	0.943	0.935	0.926	0.917	0.909
2	1.970	1.942	1.913	1.886	1.859	1.833	1.808	1.783	1.759	1.736
3	2.941	2.884	2.829	2.775	2.723	2.673	2.624	2.577	2.531	2.487

（续表）

现值表

1元的现值为$(1+r)^{-n}$,其中 $r=$ 折现率,$n=$ 付款前的期数。

期数	折现率(r)									
4	3.902	3.808	3.717	3.630	3.546	3.465	3.387	3.312	3.240	3.170
5	4.853	4.713	4.580	4.452	4.329	4.212	4.100	3.993	3.890	3.791
6	5.795	5.601	5.417	5.242	5.076	4.917	4.767	4.623	4.486	4.355
7	6.727	6.472	6.230	6.002	5.786	5.582	5.389	5.206	5.033	4.868
8	7.652	7.325	7.020	6.733	6.463	6.210	5.971	5.747	5.535	5.335
9	8.566	8.162	7.786	7.435	7.108	6.802	6.515	6.247	5.995	5.759
10	9.471	8.983	8.530	8.1111	7.722	7.360	7.024	6.710	6.418	6.145
11	10.368	9.787	9.253	8.760	8.306	7.887	7.499	7.139	6.805	6.495
12	11.255	10.575	9.954	9.385	8.863	8.384	7.943	7.536	7.161	6.814
13	12.134	11.348	10.635	9.986	9.394	8.853	8.358	7.904	7.487	7.103
14	13.004	12.106	11.296	10.563	9.899	9.295	8.745	8.244	7.786	7.367
15	13.865	12.849	11.938	11.118	10.38	9.712	9.108	8.559	8.061	7.606

private company

Company which has not been registered as a public company under the UK companies Act 1985. The major practical distinction between a private and public company is that the former may not offer its securities to the public. See "public company".

私营公司

未按照 1985 年《英国公司法》登记为上市公司的公司。私营公司与上市公司的主要实际区别在于前者不可以向公众发售证券。参见"上市公司"。

private equity

Private equity is equity capital that is not quoted on a public exchange. It consists of investors and funds that make investments directly into private companies or conduct buyouts of public companies that result in a delisting of public equity.

私募股权

不通过证券交易所公开发行股票募集的股权资本,包含了直接投资于私营企业的投资者和资金,或是购买上市公司后退市。

private finance initiative (PFI)

UK Policy designed to harness private sector management and expertise in the delivery of public services. Under PFI, the public sector does not buy assets, it buys the asset-based

私人融资计划

一项在提供公共服务时利用私营部门的管理和专业知识的英国政策。在民间主动融资模式下,公营部门在合同基础上向私营部门购买所需要

services it requires, on contract, from the private sector, the latter having the responsibility for deciding how to supply these services, the investment required to support the services and how to achieve the required standards.

的、基于资产的服务,而不是直接购买资产,私营部门将负责确定如何提供这些服务、支持服务所需的投资以及如何达到规定标准。

private placement

Issue of shares sold to one or to a limited number of investors, rather than being offered to the market. See "placing".

私人配售

向1位或有限数量的投资者发行股份,而不是直接向市场发售。参见"配售"。

project management

Integration of all aspects of a project, ensuring that the proper knowledge and resources are available when and where needed, and above all to ensure that the expected outcome is produced in a timely, cost-effective manner. The primary function of a project manager is to manage the trade-offs between performance, timeliness and cost.

项目管理

整合项目所有方面,确保在需要时有恰当的知识和资源可用。上述措施是为了确保以一种及时且具有成本效益的方式产生预期的结果。项目经理的主要职能是在绩效、时效性以及成本之间进行权衡。

prospectus

Description of a company's operations, financial background, prospects and the detailed terms and conditions relating to an offer for sale or placing of its shares by notice, circular, advertisement or any form of invitation which offers securities to the public.

招股说明书

概述公司的经营情况、财务背景、发展前景,以通知、传单、广告或其他形式向公众告知股票发售或配售股份的详细条款和条件。

public company

UK Company Limited by shares or by guarantee, with a share capital, whose memorandum of association states that it is public and that it has complied with the registration

上市公司

具有一定股本的英国股份有限公司或担保有限公司,其组织章程大纲会列明公司为上市公司并已遵守相关登记程序规定。

procedures for such a company.

A public company is distinguished from a private company in the following ways:

(a) aminimum issued share capital of £50,000;

(b) public limited company or plc at the end of the name;

(c) public company clause in the memorandum;and

(d) freedom to offer securities to the public. See "private company".

上市公司与私营公司的区别体现在以下方面:

(a)已发行股本最低为5万英镑;

(b)公司名称结尾必须标注股份有限公司(public limited company 或 plc);

(c)章程大纲中载有上市公司条款;

(d)可自由向公众发售证券。参见"私营公司"。

purchasing power parity

购买力平价

Theory stating that the exchange rate between two currencies is in equilibrium when the purchasing power of currency is the same in each country. If a basket of goods costs £100 in the UK and $150 for an equivalent in the US, for equilibrium to exist, the exchange rate would be expected to be £1 = $1. 50. If this were not the case, arbitrage would be expected to take place until equilibrium was recorded.

该理论认为,当两国的货币购买力相同时,两种货币之间的汇率就达到了平衡状态。例如,如果一篮子商品在英国价值100英镑,在美国价值150美元,为了达到平衡状态,汇率预期为1英镑=1.5美元。如果不是的话,就会发生"套利"行为,直到恢复平衡状态。

put option

认沽期权

Option to sell a specified underlying asset at a specified exercise price on. or before, a specified exercise date. See "call option" and "option".

在特定行权日或之前,以特定的行权价出售相关标的资产的期权。参见"认购期权"和"期权"。

quasi-subsidiary

准子公司

Company, trust, partnership or other vehicle that, though not fulfilling the definition of a subsidiary, is directly or indirectly

虽然不符合子公司的定义,但是由报告实体直接或间接控制的、且为报告实体创造的利益与作为子公司的

controlled by the reporting entity and gives rise to benefits for that entity that are in substance no different from those that would arise were the vehicle a subsidiary. Typically used in the UK(refer to FRS 5).

工具所产生的利益并无本质差别的公司、信托、合伙企业或其他工具。常见于英国(参阅《财务报告准则第 5 号》)。

real interest rate

Interest rate approximately calculated by adjusting the nominal or money interest rate for the rate of inflation. It，therefore，represents the rate of interest in the absence of inflation.

$$r = [(1+n)/(1+i)] - 1\%$$

Where,

r = real rate of interest

n = nominal rate of interest

i = rate of inflation

实际利率

根据通胀率对名义利率或货币利率进行调整之后得出的利率。因此，在不存在通胀的情况下，实际利率即代表利率。

$$r = [(1+n)/(1+i)] - 1\%$$

其中：

r ＝实际利率

n ＝名义利率

i ＝通胀率

real option

Right，but not the obligation，to take different courses of action (for example defer，abandon and expand) with respect to real assets (for example an oil well，a new product or an acquisition) as opposed to an option on financial securities or commodities.

实物期权

有权(但非强制约束)对实物资产(例如油井、新产品或并购标的)采取不同的措施(例如推迟、放弃和扩大)，与金融证券或商品期权完全不同。

receivership

Under the control of a receiver，who is appointed by secured creditors or by the court to take control of company property. The most usual reason for the appointment of receiver is the failure of a company to pay principal sums or interest due to debenture holders whose debt is secured by fixed or floating charges over the as-

接管

由担保债权人或法院指定接管人控制公司财产。指定接管人最常见的原因是公司未能偿还债权人的本金或利息，而该所有人所承担的债务源自其对公司的资产进行固定或浮动担保。

sets of the company.

recourse

Source of redress should a debt be dishonoured at maturity.

追索

寻求获得到期未兑现债务的赔偿。

redemption

Repayment of the principal amount（for example，a bond）at the date of maturity.

赎回

在到期日偿还本金（例如债券）。

redemption yield

Rate of interest at which the total of the discounted values of any future payments of interest and capital is equal to the current price of a security.

赎回收益率

使未来支付的利息和资金的折现总价值等于证券当前价格的利率。

refinancing risk

Refinancing risk is associated with interest rate risk because it looks at the risk that loans will not be refinanced or will not be refinanced at the same rates.

再融资风险

再融资风险是与利率风险有关的风险，因为它同"贷款不能在再融资或者不能按照相同的利率再融资的风险"一起波动。

regulated price

Selling price set within guidelines laid down by a regulatory authority，normally governmental.

管制价格

在监管机构（通常为政府）提出的指引范围内设定的售价。

revolving credit

A credit facility which allows the borrower，within an overall credit limit and for a set period，to borrow or repay debt as required.

循环信贷

允许借款人在信贷额度和规定期间内借入或偿还债务的信贷安排。

Revolving Credit Facility (RCF)

Under a RCF the borrower may use or withdraw funds up to a pre-approved credit limit. RCFs are very flexible debt financing options，and they enable a company to minimize interest payments because the amount of funds borrowed fluctuates over time and is never more than the company needs.

循环信贷额度

根据循环信贷额度，借款人可以在一个预先批准的信用额度之内使用或归还资金，循环信贷额度是非常灵活的债务融资方案，由于贷款额度随时间波动且总不会超出公司所需，所以能够使得企业的利息支出降至最低。

rights issue

Raising of new capital by giving existing shareholders the right to subscribe to new shares in proportion to their current holdings. These shares are usually issued at a discount to market price. A shareholder not wishing to take up a rights issue may sell the rights. See "bonus/scrip issue".

配股

通过授予现有股东按照自身现有持股比例认购新股份的权利进行筹资。这些股份通常在市价的基础上折价发行。无意配股的股东可出售此权利。参见"红利/股利股票发行"。

scrip dividend

Dividend paid by the issue of additional company shares，rather than by cash.

股票红利

以额外发行公司股票而非现金的方式派发股利。

Security Market Line (SML)

The Security Market Line(SML)gives the relationship between systematic risk and return.

证券市场线

衡量系统风险与投资回报之间的关系。

securitisation

Conversion of financial or physical assets into financial instruments that can be traded，often through the use of special purpose vehicles.

资产证券化

将金融资产或实物资产转换为可交易的金融工具，通常通过利用特殊目的机构实现。

seed money

Equity investment into a new business by venture capitalists in order to finance the period of start-up and/or early trading. The provision of the (high-risk) seed money enables the new business to become established, such that it can ultimately raise equity on an established exchange, at which time venture capitalists would expect to realise their holding of shares, in so doing hoping to make a significant capital gain.

service level agreement

Contract between service provider and customer which specifies in detail the level of service to be provided over the contract period(for example quality, frequency, flexibility, charges) as well as the procedures to be implemented in the case of default.

shareholder value

Total return to the shareholders in terms of both dividends and share price growth, calculated as the present value of future free cash flows of the business discounted at the weighted average cost of the capital of the business less the market value of its debt.

shareholder value analysis

A variation along the same theme as EVA. The main aim of the organisation is to add value to shareholder wealth. This can be

种子资金

风险投资家向初创企业进行股权投资,为处于初创和(或)早期交易阶段的企业提供资金。提供(高风险)种子资金有助于初创企业稳健发展,进而最终可在成熟交易所募集股本,届时风险投资家将会变现手中的股份,获得大量资本收益。

服务水平协议

服务提供方与客户订立的合同,当中详细规定了在合同期内提供的服务水平(例如质量、频率、灵活性和费用等)以及发生违约时应采取的程序。

股东价值

股东在股利和股价增长方面的总回报,可用于加权平均资本成本作为折现率计算的未来自由现金流量现值减去公司债务的市场价值计算得出。

股东价值分析

从经济增加值(EVA)分化出来的一个议题。组织的主要目标是增加股东财富价值。股东价值分析可以以多

defined in a variety of ways and usually resultsin a form of balanced scorecard being used.

种方式来定义，通常会使用平衡记分卡来呈现。

signaling

Investors read ＂signals＂ into the company's dividend decision and that these signals say as much about the company's future financial performance as they say about its past financial performance.

Thus management will not necessarily reduce the dividend per share just because last year's performance was poor，if they believe that next year's performance will be good.

If this analysis is correct，and investors do indeed read signals into the dividend decision，then the dividend decision becomes important：it becomes important for the company not to give the wrong signal.

信号

投资者从"信号"中读取企业的股利决策，这些信号表示企业的未来财务绩效与过去一样。

因此，如果管理者相信明年的财务绩效会很好，就不会因为去年业绩不好而减少每股股利。

在分析正确的情况下，投资者确实可以从中读取出股利决策信号，届时股利决策也将变得十分重要：企业不要发出错误信号是非常重要的。

simple interest

Interest which is calculated over successive periods based only on the principal. See ＂compound interest＂.

单利

在连续期间内仅基于本金计算的利息。参见"复利"。

small and medium-sized enterprise (SME)

Classification used by policy-makers to specify which categories of enterprise are affected by regulation （for example the requirement for statutory audit）or are eligible for assistance. See Figure 4.3.

中小型企业

决策者所使用的分类，这种分类会明确不同类别的企业应遵守怎样的规定（例如法定审计规定）以及是否有资格接受援助。参见图表4.3。

FLGURE 4.3   CLASSIFICATION FOR SMALL AND MEDIUM-SIZED ENTERPRISES (SMEs)

SMEs	Department of Trade & Industry(UK)	European Cmmission	World bank Group
Medium			
staff	<250	<250	<300
turnover	<£ 22.8 m	<€ 50 m	total annual reserves <US$15 m
balance sheet	<£ 11.4 m	<€ 43 m	total assets US$15 m
Small			
staff	<50	<50	<50
turnover	<£ 5.6 m	<€ 10 m	total annual reserves<US$3 m
balance sheet	<£ 2.8 m	<€ 10 m	total assets<US$3 m
Micro			
staff	n/a	<10	<10
turnover	n/a	<€ 2 m	total annual reserves <US$100,000
balance sheet	n/a	<€ 2 m	total assets<US$100,000

图表 4.3   中小型企业(SMEs)分类

中小型企业	贸易工业部(英国)	欧洲委员会	世界银行集团
中型			
员工	<250	<250	<300
营业额	<£ 22.8 m	<€ 50 m	总年度储备<US$15 m
资产负债表	<£ 11.4 m	<€ 43 m	总资产 US$15 m
小型			
员工	<50	<50	<50
营业额	<£ 5.6 m	<€ 10 m	总年度储备<US$3 m
资产负债表	<£ 2.8 m	<€ 10 m	总资产<US$3 m
大型			
员工	不适用	<10	<10
营业额	不适用	<€ 2 m	总年度储备<US$100 000
资产负债表	不适用	<€ 2 m	总资产<US$100 000

smoothing

The company tries to maintain a certain balance between its fixed rate and floating rate borrowing.

平滑

公司努力保持其贷款的固定利率和浮动利率之间的某种平衡。

sole trader

Person carrying on business with total legal responsibility for his /her actions neither in partnership nor as a company.

个体经营者

既不是以合伙形式也不是以公司形式开展业务、需为自身行动承担全部法律责任的个人。

spot rate

Current rate（typically of interest or currency exchange）available in the market today.

staging

Some investors apply for new issues in the hope of selling immediately and reaping a quick profit. For this to succeed the number of shares purchased must be sufficiently high to cover selling charges. The strategy of selling immediately is called staging. There have been some notable successes for staging，particularly in some of the privatization issues，but there have also been cases where the initial dealing price has been substantially below the offer price.

stock exchange

Registered market in securities.

strategic financial management

Identification of the possible strategies capable of maximising an entity's net present value，the allocation of scarce capital resources among the competing opportunities and the implementation and monitoring of the chosen strategy so as to achieve stated objectives.

strategic investment appraisal

Method of investment appraisal which

即期利率/汇率

当天市场内的成交价（通常为利率或汇率）。

分期

某些投资者希望立即出售新发行的股票并且快速获得利润。因此，购买的股票数量必须足以抵销销售费用。这种快速销售的策略被称为分期。分期有一些显著的成功案例，尤其是在一些私有化问题上，但也存在初始交易价格比发行价低的情况。

证券交易所

注册的证券交易市场。

战略财务管理

识别能够最大限度地提升实体净现值的可行性战略，在各个竞争机会中分配稀缺的资本资源以及执行并监控所选战略，以实现预期目标。

战略投资评价

一种同时考虑了财务和非财务因

allows the inclusion of both financial and non-financial factors. Project benefits are appraised in terms of their contribution to the strategies of the organisation either by their financial contribution or, for non-financial benefits, by the use of index numbers or other means. See " investment appraisal".

素的投资评价方法。通过使用指数或其他方式,从财务和非财务角度,根据项目对于组织战略的贡献来评价项目收益。参见"投资评价"。

swap

Contract to exchange payments of some sort in the future.

互换

在未来交换某些付款的合同。

takeover

Acquisition by a company of a controlling interest in the voting share capital of another company, usually achieved by the purchase of a majority of the voting shares.

收购

一家公司获得另一家公司具有表决权股本的多数股权,通常是通过购买大部分具有表决权的股份来实现的。

tax avoidance

Organisation of a taxpayer's affairs so that the minimum tax liability is incurred. Tax avoidance involves making the maximum use of all legal means of minimising liability to taxation.

避税

组织纳税人的事项,以期承担最少的纳税责任。避税需要最大限度地利用一切法律手段来尽可能地减轻纳税责任。

tax evasion

Minimisation of tax liability by illegal means, such as by the under-declaration of income.

逃税

通过非法途径最大限度地减轻纳税责任,例如低报收入。

tax shield

Reduction in tax payable due to the use

税盾

应税收入中扣除免税额,使得应

of tax-allowable deductions against taxable income. It is measured by the discounted value of future tax savings generated by the available tax reliefs.

交税款减少。税盾可以通过计算税务减免额所产生的未来税收节减额的折现值来衡量。

technical analysis

Analysis of past movements in the prices of，amongst other things，financial instruments，currencies and commodities，with a view to，by applying analytical techniques，predicting future price movements. See "fundamental analysis".

技术分析

利用分析技术来分析金融工具、货币和商品等价格的过往波动,并预测未来价格的波动。参见"基本面分析"。

tender offer

An alternative to a fixed price offer. Under a tender offer，subscribers tender for the shares at，or above，a minimum fixed price. Once all offers have been received from prospective investors，the company sets a "strike price" and allocates shares to all bidders who have offered the strike price or more.

要约收购

要约收购是固定价格收购的一种替代方式。在要约收购时认购者以等于或高于最低固定价格发出要约。一旦报价被预期投资者接受,企业会设置一个"执行价格",将股份分配给那些提供了执行价格或更高价格的投标人。

term（of a capital instrument）

The period from the date of issue of the capital instrument to the date at which it will expire，be redeemed，or be cancelled(FRS 4).

（资本工具的）期限

从发行资本工具开始至资本工具到期、赎回或取消之日的期间(《财务报告准则第4号》)。

Theoretical Ex Rights Price（TERP）

Theoretical Ex Rights Price is the theoretical price that the class of shares will trade at on the first trading day after issue. It is calculated as follows $= \dfrac{(N * \text{cum right sprice}) + \text{Issue price}}{N + 1}$

理论除权价

理论除权价是指股票股利在发行后第一个交易日的理论价格。

$$理论除权价 = \dfrac{(N \times 含权价) + 发行价}{N + 1}$$

thin capitalisation

When a company pays a dividend, there is no tax relief for the payment. When it pays loan interest, the interest is tax allowable. This means that companies would prefer to be financed through borrowings rather than through shares. The thin capitalisation rules aim to stop companies from getting excessive tax relief on interest.

ticks

The minimum price movement for a futures contract.

total shareholder return

Combined capital gain plus dividend income received by an investor over the investment period.

traditional view of gearing

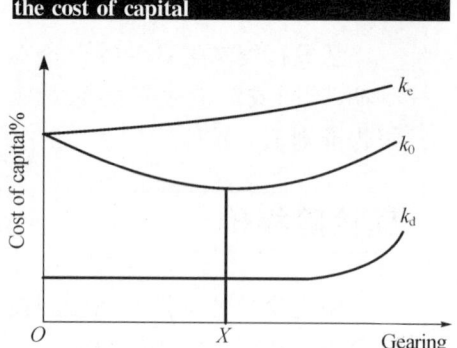

Figure 4.4 Traditional view of gearing and the cost of capital

The traditional view therefore claims that there is an optimal capital structure

资本弱化

当一家企业支付股利时,没有税收减免。当企业支付贷款利息时,利息是可以抵税的。这意味着企业更愿意通过借贷而不是发行股票来融资。资本弱化规则旨在阻止企业在利息上获得过多的税收减免。

跳动点

跳动点是一份期货合约的最小价格变动。

股东总回报

投资者在投资期内所获取的资本收益及股利收入的总和。

杠杆效应的传统观点

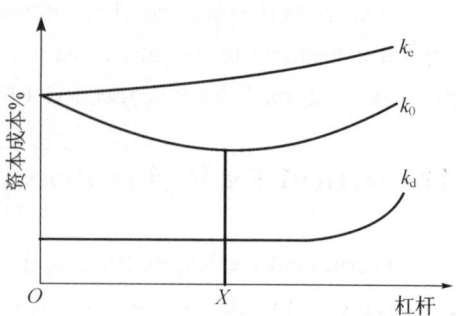

图表4.4 杠杆效应的传统观点及资本成本

传统观点认为存在一个最低加权平均资本成本使得资本结构达到最

where the weighted average cost of capital is at a minimum. This is at point X in the above diagram. X = optimal level of gearing, where k_0 is at a minimum.

优,即上图中的 X 点。X = 最优杠杠,此时的加权平均资本成本 K_0 最低。

transaction exposure

Susceptibility of an entity to the effect of foreign exchange rate changes during the transaction cycle associated with the export/import of goods or services. Transaction exposure is present from the time a price is agreed until the payment has been made/received in the domestic currency.

交易风险

在与进/出口商品或服务有关的交易周期内,实体易受汇率波动的影响。从商定价格起,一直到支付/收到本国货币为止的整个时间段内,交易风险一直存在。

translation exposure

Susceptibility of the balance sheet and income statement to the effect of foreign exchange rate changes. See "foreign currency translation".

折算风险

资产负债表和损益表易受到汇率波动的影响。参见"外汇折算"。

translation risk

The risk is that exchange rate volatility will cause the value of assets to fall or liabilities to increase resulting in losses to the company.

折算风险

折算风险是指汇率的波动引起资产价值下降或负债增加,进而导致公司损失的风险。

treasury bill

Short-term money market instrument issued, used to supply the government's short-term financing needs.

国库券

一国政府发行的、用于满足短期融资需求的短期货币市场工具。

treasury management

Corporate handling of all financial matters, the generation of external and internal funds for business, the management of cur-

司库管理

公司处理所有财务事宜、生成内外部资金和现金流以及复杂的公司财务战略、政策和流程(企业司库协会)。

rencies and cash flows，and the complex strategies，policies and procedures of corporate finance（Association of Corporate Treasurers）. See Figure 4.5.

参见图表 4.5。

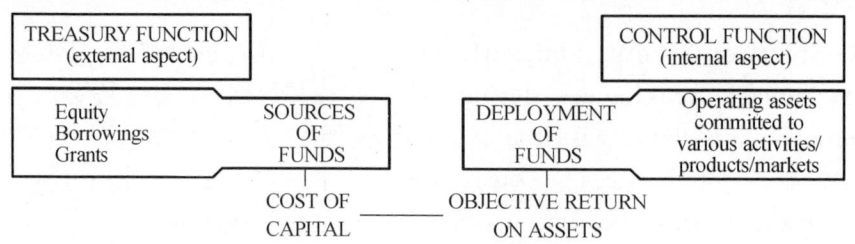

FIGURE 4.5 RELATIONSHIP OF THE TREASURY AND CONTROL FUNCTIONS

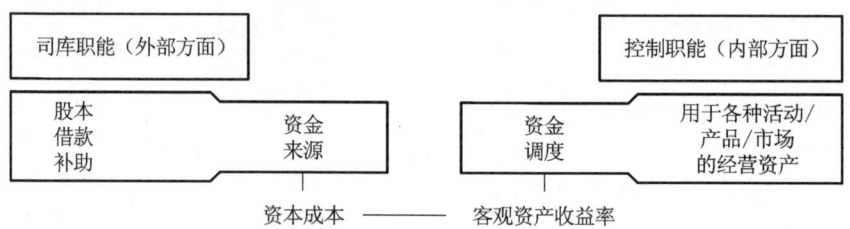

图表 4.5 财政职能与控制职能的关系

uncertainty

Inability to predict the outcome form an activity due to a lack of information about the required input/output relationships or about the environment within which the activity takes place.

不确定性

因缺乏有关必要投入/产出关系或活动发生环境的信息，从而无法预测活动结果。

underwriting

Underwriting avoids the possibility that the entity will not sell all of the shares it is issuing，and so receive less funds than it expects. Underwriters are normally financial institutions such as merchant banks.

承销

承销是为了避免实体无法发售所有股票而获得比预期低的资金。承销商通常是商业银行等金融机构。

value-added tax（VAT）

Tax on consumer expenditure，collection on business transactions and imports. VAT paid by all entities on inputs may be reclaimed or set against output VAT collected.

增值税

针对商业交易和进口业务征收的消费支出税。实体可要求返还已缴纳的进项税额，或者用于抵扣发生的销项税额。

value-based management

Management team preoccupation with searching for and implementing the activities which will contribute most to increases in shareholders value.

基于价值的管理

管理层团队专注于探索和执行为股东创造最大增值的活动。

venture capital

Specialised form of finance provided for new companies，buy-outs and small growth companies which are perceived as carrying above-average risk.

风险投资

向被认为拥有高于平均风险的新创企业、并购基金和小型成长公司提供的特定资金。

warrant

Financial instrument that gives the holder the right to purchase ordinary shares（IAS 33）.

权证

赋予持有人购买普通股权利的一种金融工具（《国际会计准则第 33 号》）。

weighted average cost of capital（WACC）

The average cost of the company's finance（including equity，debentures and bank loans）weighted according to the proportion each element bears to the total pool of catial.

Weighting is usually based on market valuations，current yields and costs after tax.

加权平均资本成本

根据各类资金（包括权益、债券和银行贷款）在资本总额中所占比例计算的加权平均资金成本。

权重通常以市场估值、本期收益率以及税后成本为基础。

Example

Capital	Market Value		Rate
Equity	$ 8M × 10%	=	$ 0.8M
Debt	$ 4M × 8.45%	=	$ 0.338M
Total	$ 12M		$ 1.138M

Weighted average cost 9.483% ($ 1.138 million/ $ 12 million).

The weighted average cost of capital is often used as the measure to used as the hurdle rate for investment decisions or as the measure to be minimised in order to find the optimal capital structure for the company. See "cost of capital".

范例

资本类型	市场价值		价值
权益	$ 8M × 10%	=	$ 0.8M
负债	$ 4M × 8.45%	=	$ 0.338M
总计	$ 12M		$ 1.138M

加权平均成本为 9.483% ($ 1.138 million/ $ 12 million)。

加权平均资本成本通常用于衡量投资决策的最低预期回报率或最小衡量标准,目的是找到公司的最佳资本结构。参见"资本成本"。

working capital cycle

The period of time which elapses between the point at which cash begins to be expended on the production of a product,and the collection of cash from the purchaser.

营运资本周期

从开始投入资金进行产品生产到从买方收回现金的时间段。

write-down

A reduction in the recorded value of an asset to comply with the concept of prudence. The valuation of stock at the lower of cost or net realisable value (SSAP 9) may require the values of some stock to be written down.

减记

出于谨慎性原则,调低某项资产的账面价值。要根据存货成本与可变现净值孰低原则对某些存货进行减记(《标准会计实务公告第 9 号》)。

writing down allowance

A tax allowance,related to a firm's capital expenditure,which reduces profit subject to taxation.

减记备抵

与公司资本性支出有关的税收减免,可减少应税利润。

yield adjusted ex rights price

If an entity expects (and the market

调整收益后的除权价格

如果一个实体预计(并且市场也

agrees) that the new funds will earn a different return than is currently being earned on the existing capital then a yield adjusted ex rights price should be calculated.

Yield adjusted ex rights price = [Cum rights price × N/(N+1)] + [(Issue price/N+1) × (Y_n / Y_0)]

Y_n = Yield on 'old' capital

Y_0 = Yield on 'new' capital

允许），当新筹集的基金的收益率和现有资本不同时，应当计算调整收益后的除权价格。

调整收益后的除权价格 = 含权价 × N/(N+1) + 发行价/(N+1) × (Y_n / Y_0)

Y_n = 原有资本的收益率

Y_0 = 现有资本的收益率

yield curve

A diagrammatical representation of the relationship between interest rates and the maturities of a similar set of securities. An upwardly sloping interest rate curve indicates that interest rates increase as security maturities lengthen. This might indicate that investors are averse to the increased uncertainty associated with future investment，and/or that there is an expectation that interest rates will rise in the future.

收益曲线

一组以图表方式说明的、类似于证券的利率与到期日之间的关系。利率曲线向上倾斜，表示随着证券到期日的延长，利率将上升。这说明，投资者对于未来投资不确定性的增加深感厌恶，或者预期未来利率将会上升。

Z score

A single figure，produced by a financial model，which combines a number of variables（generally financial statement ratios），whose magnitude is intended to aid the prediction of failure，that is a Z score model may predict that a company with a score of 1.8 or less is likely to fail within 12 months. Individual companies are scored against this benchmark.

Z 分值

通过融合多种变量（通常为财务报表比率）的财务模型得出的分值，该分值可用于预测破产可能性。若某公司的 Z 分值在 1.8 及以下，则该公司很可能在 12 个月内破产。各个公司可以以此为基准，进行自我评定。

zero coupon bond

A bond offering no interest payments，all investor return being gained through capital appreciation.

零息债券

一种不支付利息的债券，所有投资者均通过资本增值来获得回报。

APPENDIX 1
International Financial Reporting Standards

附录一
国际财务报告准则

International Financial Reporting Standard 1 —First-time Adoption of International Financial Reporting Standards Objective (IFRS 1)

The objective of this IFRS is to ensure that an entity's first IFRS financial statements, and its interim financial reports for part of the period covered by those financial statements, contain high quality information that:

(a) is transparent for users and comparable over all periods presented;

(b) provides a suitable starting point for accounting in accordance with International Financial Reporting Standards (IFRSs);

(c) can be generated at a cost that does not exceed the benefits.

International Financial Reporting Standard 2—Share-based Payment (IFRS 2)

The objective of this IFRS is to specify

《国际财务报告准则第 1 号——首次采用国际财务报告准则》(IFRS 1)

本准则的目标在于确保实体的首份 IFRS 财务报表,以及这些财务报表所涵盖期间的中期财务报告,包含了符合以下三个目的的高质量信息:

(a) 对使用者透明,所有列报的期间可比;

(b) 为遵循国际财务报告准则(IFRS)进行会计处理提供一个合适的起点;

(c) 生成的成本不超过收益。

《国际财务报告准则第 2 号——以股份为基础的支付》(IFRS 2)

本准则的目标在于规范实体以股

the financial reporting by an entity when it undertakes a share-based payment transaction. In particular, it requires an entity to reflect in its profit or loss and financial position the effects of share-based payment transactions, including expenses associated with transactions in which share options are granted to employees.

份为支付基础的交易的财务报告。本准则要求实体在其损益或财务状况中反映以股份为支付基础的交易影响,包括与向员工授予股份期权的交易有关的费用。

International Financial Reporting Standard 3—Business Combinations(IFRS 3)

The objective of this IFRS is to improve the relevance, reliability and comparability of the information that a reporting entity provides in its financial statements about a business combination and its effects. To accomplish that, this IFRS establishes principles and requirements for how the acquirer:

(a) recognises and measures in its financial statements the identifiable assets acquired, the liabilities assumed and any non-controlling interest in the acquiree;

(b) recognises and measures the goodwill acquired in the business combination or a gain from a bargain purchase;

(c) determines what information to disclose to enable users of the financial statements to evaluate the nature and financial effects of the business combination.

《国际财务报告准则第 3 号——企业合并》(IFRS 3)

本准则的目标在于提高报告实体在其财务报表中关于企业合并及其影响的信息的相关性、可靠性及可比性。为实现这一目标,本准则要求购买方遵守以下原则和要求:

(a) 在财务报表中确认与计量被购买方的可辨认资产、承担的负债及非控制性权益;

(b) 确认与计量企业合并中获得的商誉或廉价收购产生的利得;

(c) 确定应披露哪些信息以便财务报表的使用者对企业合并的性质与财务影响加以评估。

International Financial Reporting Standard 4—Insurance Contracts (IFRS 4)

The objective of this IFRS is to specify the financial reporting for insurance

《国际财务报告准则第 4 号——保险合同》(IFRS 4)

本准则的目标是在国际会计准则理事会(IASB)完成保险合同项目的

contracts by any entity that issues such contracts (described in this IFRS as an insurer) until the Board completes the second phase of its project on insurance contracts. In particular, this IFRS requires:

(a) limited improvements to accounting by insurers for insurance contracts.

(b) disclosure that identifies and explains the amounts in an insurer's financial statements arising from insurance contracts and helps users of those financial statements understand the amount, timing and uncertainty of future cash flows from insurance contracts.

第二阶段之前,详细说明签发保险合同的实体(在本准则中被称为"承保人")针对保险合同发布的财务报告。本准则要求:

(a) 承保人对保险合同会计处理的有限改进。

(b) 承保人在其财务报表中披露用于识别与解释保险合同引起的金额,帮助财务报表使用者理解保险合同未来现金流的金额、时点和不确定性。

International Financial Reporting Standard 5—Non-current Assets Held for Sale and Discontinued Operations(IFRS 5)

《国际财务报告准则第 5 号——持有待售的非流动资产和终止经营》(IFRS 5)

The objective of this IFRS is to specify the accounting for assets held for sale, and the presentation and disclosure of discontinued operations. In particular, the IFRS requires:

(a) assets that meet the criteria to be classified as held for sale to be measured at the lower of carrying amount and fair value less costs to sell, and depreciation on such assets to cease; and

(b) assets that meet the criteria to be classified as held for sale to be presented separately in the statement of financial position and the results of discontinued operations to be presented separately in the statement of comprehensive income.

本准则的目标在于详细说明持有待售资产的会计处理,以及终止经营的列报与披露。本准则要求:

(a) 符合持有待售标准的资产以账面价值与公允价值减去出售成本及资产折旧后的金额孰低计量;

(b) 符合持有待售标准的资产在财务状况表中单独列报,终止经营的结果在综合收益表中单独列报。

International Financial Reporting Standard 6—Exploration for and Evaluation of Mineral Resources (IFRS 6)

The objective of this IFRS is to specify the financial reporting for the exploration for and evaluation of mineral resources.

In particular，the IFRS requires：

（a）limited improvements to existing accounting practices for exploration and evaluation expenditures.

（b）entities that recognise exploration and evaluation assets to assess such assets for impairment in accordance with this IFRS and measure any impairment in accordance with IAS 36 Impairment of Assets.

（c）disclosures that identify and explain the amounts in the entity's financial statements arising from the exploration for and evaluation of mineral resources and help users of those financial statements understand the amount，timing and certainty of future cash flows from any exploration and evaluation assets recognised.

International Financial Reporting Standard 7—Financial Instruments：Disclosures(IFRS 7)

The objective of this IFRS is to require entities to provide disclosures in their financial statements that enable users to evaluate：

（a）the significance of financial instruments for the entity's financial position and performance；and

《国际财务报告准则第 6 号——矿产资源的勘探和评估》(IFRS 6)

本准则的目标在于详细说明矿产资源的勘探和评估的财务报告。

本准则要求：

（a）对勘探和评估支出的现行会计实务的有限改进。

（b）确认勘探和评估资产的实体应遵循本准则对这些资产进行减值评估，并遵循《国际会计准第 36 号——资产减值》(IAS 36)对减值进行计量。

（c）实体在其财务报表中披露用于识别与解释矿产资源的勘探和评估所引起的金额，帮助财务报表使用者理解已确认勘探和评估资产未来现金流的金额、时点和确定性。

《国际财务报告准则第 7 号——金融工具：披露》(IFRS 7)

本准则的目标在于要求实体在其财务报表中提供披露信息以便使用者评估：

（a）金融工具对于实体的财务状况和业绩的重要性；

(b) the nature and extent of risks arising from financial instruments to which the entity is exposed during the period and at the end of the reporting period, and how the entity manages those risks.

The principles in this IFRS complement the principles for recognising, measuring and presenting financial assets and financial liabilities in IAS 32 Financial Instruments: Presentation and IFRS 9 Financial Instruments.

（b）在报告期间与报告期末,由金融工具所引发的、实体面临的风险的性质与程度,以及实体如何管理这些风险。

本准则的原则完善了《国际会计准则第 32 号——金融工具:列报》(IAS 32)与《国际财务报告准则第 9 号——金融工具》(IFRS 9)中涉及金融资产与金融负债的确认、计量与列报的原则。

International Financial Reporting Standard 8 — Operating Segments (IFRS 8)

《国际财务报告准则第 8 号——业务分部》(IFRS 8)

An entity shall disclose information to enable users of its financial statements to evaluate the nature and financial effects of the business activities in which it engages and the economic environments in which it operates.

实体应披露便于财务报表使用者评估实体所从事的业务活动以及所处经济环境的性质和财务影响的有关信息。

International Financial Reporting Standard 9 — Financial Instruments(IFRS 9)

《国际财务报告准则第 9 号——金融工具》(IFRS 9)

The objective of this Standard is to establish principles for the financial reporting of financial assets and financial liabilities that will present relevant and useful information to users of financial statements for their assessment of the amounts, timing and uncertainty of an entity's future cash flows.

本准则的目标在于建立金融资产与金融负债财务报告的原则,向财务报表使用者提供有用的相关信息,以供他们对实体未来现金流的金额、时点与不确定性进行评估。

International Financial Reporting Standard 10 — Consolidated Financial Statements (IFRS 10)

《国际财务报告准则第 10 号——合并财务报表》(IFRS 10)

The objective of this IFRS is to establish

本准则的目标在于建立当控制一

principles for the presentation and preparation of consolidated financial statements when an entity controls one or more other entities.

To meet the objective in paragraph 1, this IFRS:

(a) requires an entity (the parent) that controls one or more other entities (subsidiaries) to present consolidated financial statements;

(b) defines the principle of control, and establishes control as the basis for consolidation;

(c) sets out how to apply the principle of control to identify whether an investor controls an investee and therefore must consolidate the investee;

(d) sets out the accounting requirements for the preparation of consolidated financial statements;

(e) defines an investment entity and sets out an exception to consolidating particular subsidiaries of an investment entity.

This IFRS does not deal with the accounting requirements for business combinations and their effect on consolidation, including goodwill arising on a business combination (see IFRS 3 Business Combinations).

International Financial Reporting Standard 11—Joint Arrangements (IFRS 11)

The objective of this IFRS is to establish principles for financial reporting by entities that have an interest in arrangements that are controlled jointly (ie joint arrangements).

To meet the objective in paragraph 1,

个或多个其他实体的实体合并财务报表时的列报与编制原则。

为了实现第一段中所述的目标，本准则：

（a）要求控制一个或多个实体（子公司）的实体（母公司）列报合并财务报表；

（b）定义控制原则，将控制作为合并的基础；

（c）阐述如何运用控制原则来识别投资方是否控制被投资方，是否必须合并被投资方；

（d）阐述合并财务报表编制的会计处理要求；

（e）定义投资性实体，阐述合并投资性实体特定子公司的例外情况。

本准则未涉及企业合并的会计处理要求，以及这些要求对包括企业合并引起的商誉在内的合并影响（参见IFRS 3）。

《国际财务报告准则第11号——合营安排》（IFRS 11）

本准则的目标在于建立在共同控制安排（即合营安排）中拥有权益的实体的财务报告原则。

为实现第一段中所述目标，本准

this IFRS defines joint control and requires an entity that is a party to a joint arrangement to determine the type of joint arrangement in which it is involved by assessing its rights and obligations and to account for those rights and obligations in accordance with that type of joint arrangement.

International Financial Reporting Standard 12—Disclosure of Interests in Other Entities(IFRS 12)

The objective of this IFRS is to require an entity to disclose information that enables users of its financial statements to evaluate：

（a）the nature of，and risks associated with，its interests in other entities ；

（b）the effects of those interests on its financial position，financial performance and cash flows.

To meet the objective in paragraph 1，an entity shall disclose：

（a）the significant judgements and assumptions it has made in determining：

（ⅰ）the nature of its interest in another entity or arrangement；

（ⅱ）the type of joint arrangement in which it has an interest（paragraphs 7～9）；

（ⅲ）that it meets the definition of an investment entity, if applicable （paragraph 9A）.

（b）information about its interests in：

（ⅰ）subsidiaries（paragraphs 10～19）；

（ⅱ）joint arrangements and associates（paragraphs 20～23）；

（ⅲ）structured entities that are not controlled by the entity（unconsolidated structured entities）（paragraphs 24～31）.

则定义了共同控制,要求作为合营安排一方的实体通过评估其权利与义务确定所涉及合营安排的类型,并根据合营安排的类型对权利与义务进行会计处理。

《国际财务报告准则第 12 号——在其他实体中权益的披露》(IFRS 12)

本准则的目标在于要求实体披露信息以便其财务报表使用者评价：

（a）在其他实体中权益的性质与相关风险；

（b）这些权益对实体财务状况、财务业绩与现金流的影响。

为实现第一段中所述目标,实体应披露：

（a）在确定以下三个方面时做出的重大判断与假设：

（ⅰ）在其他实体或安排中权益的性质；

（ⅱ）拥有权益的合营安排的类型(第7～9 段)；

（ⅲ）如果适用,符合投资性实体的定义(第 9A 段)。

（b）在以下实体中权益的信息：

（ⅰ）子公司(第 10～19 段)；

（ⅱ）合营安排与联营(第 20～23段)；

（ⅲ）不受实体控制的结构化实体(未合并的结构化实体)(第 24～31段)。

If the disclosures required by this IFRS，together with disclosures required by other IFRSs，do not meet the objective in paragraph 1，an entity shall disclose whatever additional information is necessary to meet that objective.

An entity shall consider the level of detail necessary to satisfy the disclosure objective and how much emphasis to place on each of the requirements in this IFRS. It shall aggregate or disaggregate disclosures so that useful information is not obscured by either the inclusion of a large amount of insignificant detail or the aggregation of items that have different characteristics（see paragraphs B2～B6）.

如果本准则所要求披露的信息与其他国际财务报告准则所要求披露的信息不能实现第一段中所述目标，实体应披露为实现该目标所必需的任何额外信息。

实体应考虑为满足披露目标所必需的信息详细程度，以及应在本准则每项要求上所投入的侧重程度。实体应汇总或拆分披露信息，从而使有用信息不因财务报表包含大量无关紧要的细节或将具有不同性质的项目合并而晦涩不明（参见第 B2～B6 段）。

International Financial Reporting Standard 13—Fair Value Measurement（IFRS 13）

《国际财务报告准则第 13 号——公允价值计量》（IFRS 13）

This IFRS：

（a）defines fair value ；

（b）sets out in a single IFRS a framework for measuring fair value；

（c）requires disclosures about fair value measurements.

Fair value is a market-based measurement，not an entity-specific measurement. For someassets and liabilities，observable market transactions or market information might be available. For other assets and liabilities，observable market transactions and market information might not be available. However，the objective of a fair value measurement in both cases is the same—to estimate the price at which an orderly transaction to sell the asset or to transfer the liability

本准则：

（a）定义了公允价值；

（b）在单一一项 IFRS 中阐述了公允价值计量框架；

（c）要求披露关于公允价值计量的信息。

公允价值是以市场为基础、而非实体特有的计量。对于某些资产与负债而言，可以获得可观察到的市场交易或市场信息。对于其他资产与负债而言，无法获得可观察到的市场交易或市场信息。然而，在这两种情况下，公允价值计量的目标是相同的——在当前市场情况下，估计市场参与者之间在计量日发生的有序交易中，出售资产或转移负债的价格（即在计量日，从持有资产或负有负债的市场参与者

would take place between market participants at the measurement date under current market conditions (ie an exit price at the measurement date from the perspective of a market participant that holds the asset or owes the liability).

When a price for an identical asset or liability is not observable, an entity measures fair value using another valuation technique that maximises the use of relevant observable inputs and minimises the use of unobservable inputs. Because fair value is a market-based measurement, it is measured using the assumptions that market participants would use when pricing the asset or liability, including assumptions about risk. As a result, an entity's intention to hold an asset or to settle or otherwise fulfill a liability is not relevant when measuring fair value.

The definition of fair value focuses on assets and liabilities because they are a primary subject of accounting measurement. In addition, this IFRS shall be applied to an entity's own equity instruments measured at fair value.

的角度的出手价格)。

当相同资产或负债的价格无法观察到时,实体运用其他估值技术计量公允价值,应做到相关可观察的输入信息运用的最大化,无法观察的输入信息运用的最小化。由于公允价值是以市场为基础的计量,其计量时运用的假设是市场参与者对资产或负债定价时的假设,包括对风险的假设。因此,在计量公允价值时,实体持有资产、结算或履行债务的意图均是无关信息。

公允价值的定义聚焦于资产和负债,因为它们是会计计量的主要对象。此外,本准则也可应用于实体自身以公允价值计量的权益工具。

International Financial Reporting Standard 14—Regulatory Deferral Accounts(IFRS 14)

《国际财务报告准则第14号——监管递延账户》(IFRS 14)

The objective of this Standard is to specify the financial reporting requirements for regulatory deferral account balances that arise when an entity provides goods or services to customers at a price or rate that is subject to rate regulation.

In meeting this objective, the Standard requires:

本准则的目标在于详细说明当实体以受到费率监管的价格或费率向顾客提供商品或服务时,监管递延账户余额的财务报告要求。

为实现这一目标,本准则要求:

(a) limited changes to the accounting policies that were applied in accordance with previous generally accepted accounting principles (previous GAAP) for regulatory deferral account balances, which are primarily related to the presentation of these accounts; and

(b) disclosures that:

(ⅰ) identify and explain the amounts recognised in the entity's financial statements that arise from rate regulation; and

(ⅱ) help users of the financial statements to understand the amount, timing and uncertainty of future cash flows from any regulatory deferral account balances that are recognised.

The requirements of this Standard permit an entity within its scope to continue to account for regulatory deferral account balances in its financial statements in accordance with its previous GAAP when it adopts IFRS, subject to the limited changes referred to in paragraph 2 above.

In addition, this Standard provides some exceptions to, or exemptions from, the requirements of other Standards. All specified requirements for reporting regulatory deferral account balances, and any exceptions to, or exemptions from, the requirements of other Standards that are related to those balances, are contained within this Standard instead of within those other Standards.

International Financial Reporting Standard 15—Revenue from Contracts with Customers(IFRS 15)

The objective of this Standard is to establish the principles that an entity shall

（a）对遵循以前的公认会计原则（以前的 GAAP）监管递延账户余额的会计政策进行有限的修改,这些会计政策主要与监管递延账户的列报有关;

（b）披露以下信息:

（ⅰ）识别与解释实体财务报表中由费率监管引起的确认金额;

（ⅱ）帮助财务报表使用者理解已确认监管递延账户余额未来现金流的金额、时点与不确定性。

本准则的各项要求允许实体在采用 IFRS 时,在依照上述第 2 段中提及的有限修改的情况下,在其财务报表中遵循以前的 GAAP 对监管递延账户余额进行会计处理。

此外,本准则提供了免于遵守其他准则要求的例外或豁免情况。所有报告监管递延账户余额的特定要求,以及所有对其他准则中有关这些余额的要求的例外或豁免,均包含于本准则,而不在其他准则中。

《国际财务报告准则第 15 号——源自客户合同的收入》（IFRS 15）

本准则的目标在于建立实体向财务报表使用者报告关于源自客户合同

applyto report useful information to users of financial statements about the nature, amount, timing and uncertainty of revenue and cash flows arising from a contract with a customer.

To meet the objective in paragraph 1, the core principle of this Standard is that an entity shall recognise revenue to depict the transfer of promised goods or services to customers in an amount that reflects the consideration to which the entity expects to be entitled in exchange for those goods or services.

An entity shall consider the terms of the contract and all relevant facts and circumstances when applying this Standard. An entity shall apply this Standard, including the use of any practical expedients, consistently to contracts with similar characteristics and in similar circumstances.

This Standard specifies the accounting for an individual contract with a customer. However, as a practical expedient, an entity may apply this Standard to a portfolio of contracts (or performance obligations) with similar characteristics if the entity reasonably expects that the effects on the financial statements of applying this Standard to the portfolio would not differ materially from applying this Standard to the individual contracts (or performance obligations) within that portfolio. When accounting for a portfolio, an entity shall use estimates and assumptions that reflect the size and composition of the portfolio.

的收入与现金流的性质、金额、时点及不确定性时应采用的原则。

为实现第一段中所述目标,本准则的核心原则是实体应当确认的、向顾客转移承诺商品或服务的收入金额应反映实体因交换这些商品或服务而获得的预期对价。

在应用本准则时,实体应考虑合同条款及所有相关事实和情况。实体应将本准则一致地应用于具有类似性质的合同和类似的情况,包括任何实务权宜措施的使用。

本准则规范了与客户之间个别合同的会计处理。然而,作为一项实务权宜措施,如果实体能够合理地预期将本准则应用于具有类似性质的合同组合对财务报表的影响不会与将本准则应用于该组合内个别合同(或业绩义务)对财务报表的影响产生重大差异,实体也可将本准则应用于该合同组合(或业绩义务)。对合同组合进行会计处理时,实体应采用反映组合规模与构成的估计与假设。

APPENDIX 2
International Accounting Standards

附录二
国际会计准则

International Accounting Standard 1—Presentation of Financial Statements(IAS 1)

《国际会计准则第 1 号——财务报表的列报》(IAS 1)

This Standard prescribes the basis for presentation of general purpose financial statements to ensure comparability both with the entity's financial statements of previous periods and with the financial statements of other entities. It sets out overall requirements for the presentation of financial statements，guidelines for their structure and minimum requirements for their content.

本准则规范了通用目的财务报表的列报基础，从而确保与实体的前期财务报表和与其他实体的财务报表具有可比性。本准则阐述了财务报表列报的总体要求、财务报表结构的指引及财务报表内容的最低要求。

International Accounting Standard 2—Inventories (IAS 2)

《国际会计准则第 2 号——存货》(IAS 2)

The objective of this Standard is to prescribe the accounting treatment for inventories. A primary issue in accounting for inventories is the amount of cost to be recognised as an asset and carried forward until the related revenues are recognised. This Standard provides guidance on the determination of cost and its subsequent recognition as an expense，including any write-down to net real-

本准则的目标在于规范存货的会计处理。存货会计处理的一个主要问题是确认为资产，并结转至相关收入得到确认的存货成本金额。本准则提供了确定成本与后期确认为费用的指引，包括按照可变现净值提取减值。本准则还提供了用于分配存货成本的成本公式的指引。

isable value. It also provides guidance on the cost formulas that are used to assign costs to inventories.

International Accounting Standard 7—Statement of Cash Flows1(IAS 7)

Information about the cash flows of an entityis useful in providing users of financial statements with a basis to assess the ability of the entity to generate cash and cash equivalents and the needs of the entity to utilise those cash flows. The economic decisions that are taken by users require an evaluation of the ability of an entity to generate cash and cash equivalents and the timing and certainty of their generation.

The objective of this Standard is to require the provision of information about the historical changes in cash and cash equivalents of an entity by means of a statement of cash flows which classifies cash flows during the period from operating, investing and financing activities.

International Accounting Standard 8—Accounting Policies, Changes in Accounting Estimates and Errors (IAS 8)

The objective of this Standard is to prescribe the criteria for selecting and changing accounting policies, together with the accounting treatment and disclosure of changes in accounting policies, changes in accounting estimates and corrections of errors. The Standard is intended to enhance the relevance and reliability of an entity's financial state-

《国际会计准则第 7 号——现金流量表》(IAS 7)

关于实体现金流的信息有助于财务报表使用者评价实体产生现金与现金等价物的能力的基础以及实体利用这些现金流的需求。使用者所采取的经济决策要求对实体产生现金与现金等价物的能力及产生的时点与确定性做出评价。

本准则的目标在于要求实体通过现金流量表的方式提供关于现金与现金等价物历史变动信息,现金流量表将当期现金流分为经营活动、投资活动及筹资活动产生。

《国际会计准则第 8 号——会计政策、会计估计变更和差错》(IAS 8)

本准则的目标在于规范选择与变更会计政策的标准,以及会计政策变更、会计估计变更和差错更正的会计处理与披露。本准则旨在提高实体财务报表的相关性与可靠性,以及这些报表与实体不同期间的财务报表及与其他实体的财务报表的可比性。

ments, and the comparability of those financial statements over time and with the financial statements of other entities.

Disclosure requirements for accounting policies, except those for changes in accounting policies, are set out in IAS 1 Presentation of Financial Statements.

除会计政策变更披露之外,会计政策的披露要求已在 IAS 1 中明确。

International Accounting Standard 10 — Events after the Reporting Period(IAS 10)

《国际会计准则第 10 号——报告期后事项》(IAS 10)

The objective of this Standard is to prescribe:

(a) when an entity should adjust its financial statements for events after the reporting period; and

(b) the disclosures that an entity should give about the date when the financial statements were authorised for issue and about events after the reporting period.

The Standard also requires that an entity should not prepare its financial statements on a going concern basis if events after the reporting period indicate that the going concern assumption is not appropriate.

本准则的目标在于规范:

(a) 实体何时应当由于报告期后事项而调整财务报表;

(b) 实体应当提供关于授权财务报表发布的日期及报告期后事项的披露信息。

本准则还要求,如果报告期后事项表明持续经营假设已不适用,实体不应在持续经营基础上编制其财务报表。

International Accounting Standard 12—Income Taxes(IAS 12)

《国际会计准则第 12 号——所得税》(IAS 12)

The objective of this Standard is to prescribe the accounting treatment for income taxes. The principal issue in accounting for income taxes is how to account for the current and future tax consequences of:

(a) the future recovery (settlement) of the carrying amount of assets (liabilities) that are recognised in an entity's statement of

本准则的目标在于规范所得税的会计处理。所得税会计处理的主要问题在于如何处理以下事项的当期与未来税务后果:

(a) 实体财务状况表中确认的资产(负债)账面金额的未来收回(清偿);

financial position；

（b）transactions and other events of the current period that are recognised in an entity's financial statements.

It is inherent in the recognition of an asset or liability that the reporting entity expects to recover or settle the carrying amount of that asset or liability. If it is probable that recovery or settlement of that carrying amount will make future tax payments larger (smaller) than they would be if such recovery or settlement were to have no tax consequences，this Standard requires an entity to recognise a deferred tax liability (deferred tax asset), with certain limited exceptions.

This Standard requires an entity to account for the tax consequences of transactions and other events in the same way that it accounts for the transactions and other events themselves. Thus，for transactions and other eventsrecognised in profit or loss, any related tax effects are also recognised in profit or loss. For transactions and other events recognised outside profit or loss (either in other comprehensive income or directly in equity), any related tax effects are also recognised outside profit or loss (either in other comprehensive income or directly in equity, respectively). Similarly, the recognition of deferred tax assets and liabilities in a business combination affects the amount of goodwill arising in that business combination or the amount of the bargain purchase gain recognised

This Standard also deals with the recognition of deferred tax assets arising from unused tax losses or unused tax credits, the presentation of income taxes in the financial statements and the disclosure of information relating to income taxes.

（b）实体财务报表中确认的当期交易与其他事项。

确认资产或负债时的内在假设是报告实体预期可以收回或清偿该项资产或负债的账面金额。如果上述账面金额的收回或清偿可能导致未来支付的税款大于(小于)收回或清偿不具有税务后果情况下未来支付的税款，本准则要求实体确认递延所得税负债(递延所得税资产)，某些限制情况例外。

本准则要求实体采用同样方式对交易与其他事项本身和交易与其他事项的税务后果进行会计处理。所以，对于在损益表中确认的交易与其他事项而言，任何相关税收影响也要在损益表中确认。对于在损益表以外(在其他综合收益中或直接在权益中)确认的交易与其他事项而言，任何相关税收影响也在损益表以外确认(相应地在其他综合收益中或直接在权益中)。同样，企业合并中确认递延所得税资产与递延所得税负债也会影响企业合并中确认的商誉金额或廉价购买利得金额。

本准则还涉及由未使用税收损失或未使用税收抵扣引起的递延所得税资产的确认，所得税在财务报表中的列报及所得税相关信息的披露。

International Accounting Standard 16—Property, Plant and Equipment(IAS 16)

The objective of this Standard is to prescribe the accounting treatment for property, plant and equipment so that users of the financial statements can discern information about an entity's investment in its property, plant and equipment and the changes in such investment. The principal issues in accounting for property, plant and equipment are the recognition of the assets, the determination of their carrying amounts and the depreciation charges and impairment losses to berecognised in relation to them.

International Accounting Standard 17—Leases(IAS 17)

The objective of this Standard is to prescribe, for lessees and lessors, the appropriate accounting policies and disclosure to apply in relation to leases.

International Accounting Standard 19—Employee Benefits(IAS 19)

The objective of this Standard is to prescribe the accounting and disclosure for employeebenefits. The Standard requires an entity to recognise：

（a）a liability when an employee has provided service in exchange for employee benefits to be paid in the future; and

（b）an expense when the entity consumes the economic benefit arising from service

《国际会计准则第 16 号——不动产、厂房和设备》(IAS 16)

本准则的目标在于规范不动产、厂房和设备的会计处理,从而使财务报表使用者可以辨别实体对不动产、厂房和设备的投资及这些投资变动的信息。不动产、厂房和设备的主要会计处理问题在于资产的确认、资产账面金额的确定及与这些资产相关的折旧费用和减值损失确认问题。

《国际会计准则第 17 号——租赁》(IAS 17)

本准则的目标在于规范承租人与出租人开展租赁活动时适用的会计政策与披露。

《国际会计准则第 19 号——雇员福利》(IAS 19)

本准则的目标在于规范雇员福利的会计处理与披露。本准则要求实体确认：

（a）一项负债,以反映雇员提供服务以作为未来支付的雇员福利的交换；

（b）一项费用,以反映实体消耗的经济利益,这种经济利益源自雇员

provided by an employee in exchange for employee benefits.

为交换雇员福利所提供服务产生。

International Accounting Standard 20—Accounting for Government Grants and Disclosure of Government Assistance1 (IAS 20)

《国际会计准则第 20 号——政府补助的会计和政府援助的披露》(IAS 20)

This Standard shall be applied in accounting for, and in the disclosure of, government grants and in the disclosure of other forms of government assistance.

本准则应用于政府补助的会计处理与披露,以及其他形式的政府援助的披露。

International Accounting Standard 21—The Effects of Changes in Foreign Exchange Rates(IAS 21)

《国际会计准则第 21 号——汇率变动的影响》(IAS 21)

An entity may carry on foreign activities in two ways. It may have transactions in foreign currencies or it may have foreign operations. In addition, an entity may present its financial statements in a foreign currency. The objective of this Standard is to prescribe how to include foreign currency transactions and foreign operations in the financial statements of an entity and how to translate financial statements into a presentation currency.

实体可以两种方式开展外币活动:外币交易或境外经营。此外,实体可以一种外币列报其财务报表。本准则的目标在于规范实体如何在其财务报表中纳入外币交易与境外经营,以及如何将财务报表折算为列报货币。

The principal issues are which exchange rate(s) to use and how to report the effects of changes in exchange rates in the financial statements.

主要问题是使用哪种汇率以及如何在财务报表中报告汇率变动的影响。

International Accounting Standard 23—Borrowing Costs(IAS 23)

《国际会计准则第 23 号——借款费用》(IAS 23)

Borrowing costs that are directly attributable to the acquisition, construction or production of a qualifying asset form part of

可直接归属于收购、建造或制造合格资产的借款费用构成该项资产的成本。其他借款成本确认为费用。

the cost of that asset. Other borrowing costs arerecognised as an expense.

International Accounting Standard 24—Related Party Disclosures(IAS 24)

The objective of this Standard is to ensure that an entity's financial statements contain the disclosures necessary to draw attention to the possibility that its financial position and profit or loss may have been affected by the existence of related parties and by transactions and outstanding balances, including commitments, with such parties.

International Accounting Standard 26—Accounting and Reporting by Retirement Benefit Plans(IAS 26)

This Standard shall be applied in the financial statements of retirement benefit plans where such financial statements are prepared.

International Accounting Standard 27—Separate Financial Statements (IAS 27)

The objective of this Standard is to prescribe the accounting and disclosure requirements for investments in subsidiaries, joint ventures and associates when an entity prepares separate financial statements.

International Accounting Standard 28—Investments in Associates and Joint Ventures(IAS 28)

The objective of this Standard is to

《国际会计准则第 24 号——关联方披露》(IAS 24)

本准则的目标在于确保实体的财务报表包含提请使用者注意财务状况与损益可能受到关联方的存在以及与关联方的交易、余额(包括承诺)影响的披露信息。

《国际会计准则第 26 号——退休福利计划的会计处理和报告》(IAS 26)

本准则应用于编制退休福利计划的财务报表。

《国际会计准则第 27 号——单独财务报表》(IAS 27)

本准则的目标在于规范实体编制单独财务报表时对子公司、合营企业及联营企业投资的会计处理与披露要求。

《国际会计准则第 28 号——联营和合营企业的投资》(IAS 28)

本准则的目标在于规范对联营企

prescribe the accounting for investments in associates and to set out the requirements for the application of the equity method when accounting for investments in associates and joint ventures.

业投资的会计处理,阐述了对联营和合营企业的投资采用权益法进行会计处理时的要求。

International Accounting Standard 29—Financial Reporting in Hyperinflationary Economies1(IAS 29)

This Standard shall be applied to the financial statements, including the consolidated financial statements, of any entity whose functional currency is the currency of a hyperinflationary economy.

《国际会计准则第 29 号——恶性通货膨胀经济中的财务报告》(IAS 29)

本准则应用于功能货币是恶性通货膨胀经济中货币的实体的财务报表,包括合并财务报表。

International Accounting Standard 32—Financial Instruments: Presentation(IAS 32)

The objective of this Standard is to establish principles for presenting financial instruments as liabilities or equity and for offsetting financial assets and financial liabilities. It applies to the classification of financial instruments, from the perspective of the issuer, into financial assets, financial liabilities and equity instruments; the classification of related interest, dividends, losses and gains; and the circumstances in which financial assets and financial liabilities should be offset.

The principles in this Standard complement the principles for recognising and measuring financial assets and financial liabilities in IFRS 9 Financial Instruments, and for disclosing information about them in IFRS 7 Financial Instruments: Disclosures.

《国际会计准则第 32 号——金融工具:列报》(IAS 32)

本准则的目标在于建立作为负债或权益的金融工具的列报以及金融资产和金融负债抵销的原则。从金融工具发行者的角度,本准则将金融工具分类为金融资产、金融负债及权益工具;相关利息、股利、损失或利得的分类;金融资产与金融负债应当抵销的情况。

本准则的原则完善了《国际财务报告准则第 9 号——金融工具》(IFRS 9)中金融资产与金融负债的确认、计量原则,以及《国际财务报告准则第 7 号——金融工具:披露》(IFRS 9)中金融资产与金融负债的信息披露原则。

International Accounting Standard 33—Earnings per Share(IAS 33)

The objective of this Standard is to prescribe principles for the determination and presentation of earnings per share, so as to improve performance comparisons between different entities in the same reporting period and between different reporting periods for the same entity. Even though earnings per share data have limitations because of the different accounting policies that may be used for determining 'earnings', a consistently determined denominator enhances financial reporting. The focus of this Standard is on the denominator of the earnings per share calculation.

International Accounting Standard 34—Interim Financial Reporting (IAS 34)

The objective of this Standard is to prescribe the minimum content of an interim financial report and to prescribe the principles for recognition and measurement in complete or condensed financial statements for an interim period. Timely and reliable interim financial reporting improves the ability of investors, creditors, and others to understand an entity's capacity to generate earnings and cash flows and its financial condition and liquidity.

International Accounting Standard 36—Impairment of Assets(IAS 36)

The objective of this Standard is to

《国际会计准则第 33 号——每股收益》(IAS 33)

本准则的目标在于规范每股收益的确定与列报原则,以提高相同报告期不同实体与相同实体不同报告期之间的业绩可比性。即使每股收益数据由于用于确定"收益"的会计政策不同而具有局限性,一个前后一致的确定分母依然有助于改善财务报告。本准则的关注焦点是每股收益公式分母的计算。

《国际会计准则第 34 号——中期财务报告》(IAS 34)

本准则的目标在于规范中期财务报告的最基本内容,以及规范完整或简明中期财务报表的确认与计量原则。及时和可靠的中期财务报告可以提高投资者、债权人和其他相关人员理解实体产生盈利和现金流的能力,了解其财务状况和流动性。

《国际会计准则第 36 号——资产减值》(IAS36)

本准则的目标在于规范实体确保

prescribe the procedures that an entity applies to ensure that its assets are carried at no more than their recoverable amount. An asset is carried at more than its recoverable amount if its carrying amount exceeds the amount to be recovered through use or sale of the asset. If this is the case, the asset is described as impaired and the Standard requires the entity torecognise an impairment loss. The Standard also specifies when an entity should reverse an impairment loss and prescribes disclosures.

其资产账面价值不超过资产可收回金额的程序。如果一项资产的账面金额超过该项资产通过使用或出售可收回的金额,那么该项资产的账面价值就大于其可收回金额。如果出现这种情况,该项资产就被称为减值资产,本准则要求实体确认减值损失。本准则还规范了实体何时应当转回减值损失以及减值的披露。

International Accounting Standard 37—Provisions, Contingent Liabilities and Contingent Assets(IAS 37)

The objective of this Standard is to ensure that appropriate recognition criteria and measurement bases are applied to provisions, contingent liabilities and contingent assets and that sufficient information is disclosed in the notes to enable users to understand their nature, timing and amount.

《国际会计准则第 37 号——准备、或有负债和或有资产》(IAS 37)

本准则的目标在于确保适合的确认标准与计量基础应用于准备、或有负债和或有资产,并确保财务报表附注中有充分信息帮助使用者理解准备、或有负债和或有资产的性质、时点与金额。

International Accounting Standard 38—Intangible Assets(IAS 38)

The objective of this Standard is to prescribe the accounting treatment for intangible assets that are not dealt with specifically in another Standard. This Standard requires an entity torecognise an intangible asset if, and only if, specified criteria are met. The Standard also specifies how to measure the carrying amount of intangible assets and requires specified disclosures about intangible assets.

《国际会计准则第 38 号——无形资产》(IAS 38)

本准则的目标在于规范其他准则中未明确涉及的无形资产的会计处理。本准则要求实体且仅在满足特定标准的情况下确认无形资产。本准则还规范了如何计量无形资产的账面金额,并要求明确披露无形资产。

International Accounting Standard 39—Financial Instruments：Recognition and Measurement(IAS 39)

This Standard shall be applied by all entities to all financial instruments within the scope of IFRS 9 Financial Instruments if，and to the extent that：

（a）IFRS 9 permits the hedge accounting requirements of this Standard to be applied；and

（b）the financial instrument is part of a hedging relationship that qualifies for hedge accounting in accordance with this Standard.

International Accounting Standard 40—Investment Property(IAS 40)

The objective of this Standard is to prescribe the accounting treatment for investment property and related disclosure requirements.

International Accounting Standard 41—Agriculture(IAS 41)

The objective of this Standard is to prescribe the accounting treatment and disclosures related to agricultural activity.

《国际会计准则第 39 号——金融工具:确认和计量》(IAS 39)

本准则应当应用于所有实体 IFRS 9 范围内的所有金融工具。金融工具一定程度上：

（a）IFRS 9 允许应用本准则中的套期保值会计要求；

（b）金融工具是按照本准则符合套期保值会计的套期保值关系的一部分。

《国际会计准则第 40 号——投资性房地产》(IAS 40)

本准则的目标在于规范投资性房地产的会计处理及相关的披露要求。

《国际会计准则第 41 号——农业》(IAS 41)

本准则的目标在于规范农业活动相关的会计处理与披露。